Voices of the Enslaved

Voices *of the* Enslaved

LOVE, LABOR, AND LONGING IN FRENCH LOUISIANA

Sophie White

Published by the
Omohundro Institute of Early American History and Culture,
Williamsburg, Virginia,
and the University of North Carolina Press,
Chapel Hill

*Publication of this book is made possible in part by
support from the Institute for Scholarship in the Liberal Arts,
College of Arts and Letters, University of Notre Dame.*

*The Omohundro Institute of Early American History and Culture (OI) is sponsored
by William & Mary. On November 15, 1996, the OI adopted the present name in
honor of a bequest from Malvern H. Omohundro, Jr., and Elizabeth Omohundro*

Jacket images: Front: Unknown. *Deux Antillaises.* 18th century. Musée
d'Aquitaine, 2003.4.32, Collection Chatillon. Courtesy of the Musée
d'Aquitaine, Bordeaux. Back: Alexandre de Batz. *Sauvages tchaktas
matachez en guerriers qui portent des chevelures* (detail). Courtesy of the
Peabody Museum of Archaeology and Ethnology, Harvard University

Library of Congress Cataloging-in-Publication Data
Names: White, Sophie, author.
Title: Voices of the enslaved : love, labor, and longing
in French Louisiana / Sophie White.
Description: Williamsburg, Virginia : Omohundro Institute of Early
American History and Culture ; Chapel Hill : University of North Carolina
Press, [2019] | Includes bibliographical references and index.
Identifiers: LCCN 2019032062 | ISBN 9781469654041 (cloth) |
ISBN 9781469654058 (ebook)
Subjects: LCSH: Slaves — Louisiana — History — 18th century. |
Slavery — Louisiana — History — 18th century.
Classification: LCC E445.L8 W47 2019 | DDC 306.3/620976309033 — dc23
LC record available at https://lccn.loc.gov/2019032062

The University of North Carolina Press has been a
member of the Green Press Initiative since 2003.

For my incomparable, beloved mother, Margaret,

and with gratitude to Bibi, Sybille, and Bernadette,

for their tenderness

ACKNOWLEDGMENTS

This set of acknowledgments is about my good fortune.

First, my manuscript turned into a book thanks to the Omohundro Institute's visionary Editor of Books, Cathy Kelly, and I wish everyone the bliss of working with someone as brilliant, dynamic, and ever-insightful as she is. It is safe to say that the experience has made us bosom buddies for life. My grateful thanks go also to Chuck Grench, Paul Mapp, Nadine Zimmerli, and to my marvelous and talented copyeditor, Kaylan Stevenson.

This book rests on more than ten years of research. The National Endowment for the Humanities granted me a year-long fellowship in support of this book; they also gave me a fellowship for my first book project, so, truly, I am beyond fortunate. I am not sure how they will feel about my third book project, on red hair. The Gilder Lehrman Center at Yale University offered me a Slavery, Abolition, and Resistance Fellowship at a crucial juncture, and I am enormously privileged to have received every possible kind of support from the University of Notre Dame. I am grateful in particular to the Institute for Scholarship in the Liberal Arts and the Office for Research for the innumerable grants and awards over the years that allowed me to conduct research in the U.S., Canada, France, and the Indian Ocean, to attend conferences, and to acquire forty images for the book.

I have benefited enormously from invitations to present my research over the years and over three continents, yielding precious feedback along the way. At Notre Dame, I am lucky to be a member of a vibrant department where we actively encourage and nurture each other's research and teaching endeavors. I am so grateful for the community offered by those units where I am an affiliate: the Departments of Africana Studies and of History (with special thanks to Patrick Griffin) and the Program in Gender Studies.

And then there is Louisiana. We are a hardy and merry band of scholars who work on Louisiana, French America, and race and slavery in early America. It has been a revelation to learn so much from you, only to find that, more than anything, we have forged bonds of friendship. Thank you Guillaume Aubert, Kristen Block, Trevor Burnard, Céline Carayon, Christian Ayne Crouch, Christine Croxall, Shannon Lee Dawdy, Dominique Deslandres, Kathleen DuVal, Robert Englebert, Lin Fisher, François Furstenberg, Malick Ghachem, Erin Greenwald, M. Scott Heerman, Eric Hinderaker, Jessica M. Johnson, Sara E. Johnson, Hillary Jones, Jacob F. Lee, Ann M. Little, Karen Marrero, Robert Morrissey, Hayley Negrin, Margaret Newell, Jennifer Palmer, Dominique Rogers, Gordon Sayre, Christina Snyder, Jennifer Spear, Miranda Spieler, Yevan Terren, Danielle Terrazas Williams and very many others (including afficionados of The Dinner). Dan H. Usner, your research has never stopped inspiring and galvanizing me, and I hope that you know how much it has meant to me over the years to have you in my corner. Emily Clark, Alexandre Dubé, Jean-Pierre Le Glaunec, Sue Peabody, Brett Rushforth, and Cécile Vidal have a very special place in my world. I want to single out Emily Clark, whose presence permeates this book: she has not only read my manuscript but hosts me in New Orleans, cheers me on at low points, and is unflagging in her mission to make New Orleans real for those of us who have centered our intellectual home there—which has even included announcing that she was taking me to the Rigolets on Lake Pontchartrain so that I could see for myself the topography and grasp how just apprehensive anyone, let alone two runaways, would feel at the thought of crossing that pass. We have shared, professionally and personally, and I treasure having her in my life.

I am from Mauritius, a former French colony in the Indian Ocean. As the project developed, I turned my attention beyond the French Atlantic and so began a decade-long perambulation among the rich archives of Mauritius. It was also a coming to grips with the horrors of slavery in my beloved island, where I grew up living a charmed life while seeing endless examples of how one person's good fortune often comes at the high cost of another's misfortunes. My transition to working on an Indian Ocean colony was considerably eased by friends and colleagues who were generous in sharing their expertise, especially Richard Allen, Marina Carter, Géraldine Loumeau, Nathan Marvin, Sue Peabody, Geoffrey Summers, and Vijaya Teelock. My special appreciation goes to the staff at the National Archives of Mauritius at Coromandel for their care, under ever-precarious conditions, of a precious repository of documents containing the voices of enslaved persons.

I am also grateful to Jean-Pierre Le Glaunec, Dominique Rogers, and Brett Rushforth for helping to acquaint me with the judicial archives of the French Antilles and Nancy Christie, Dominique Deslandres, and Eric Wenzel for doing the same for the judicial archives of New France.

Archival work rests on the shoulders of those who curate, manage, and preserve the archives. I am forever indebted to Greg Lambousy and the staff at the Louisiana Historical Center, Louisiana State Museum. I also want to acknowledge the archivists and staff at the Randolph County Archives, Chester Illinois; the Historic New Orleans Collection, New Orleans; the Parish of Orleans Notarial Archives (now the Notarial Archives Research Center); the Newberry Library, Chicago; the Huntington Library, San Marino, California; the Illinois State Archives, Springfield; the Manuscripts Division at the Library of Congress; the Western Michigan University Regional Archives, Kalamazoo; the Chicago History Museum; the Archives nationales d'outremer, Aix-en-Provence, France; the Bibliothèque nationale de France, Paris; the Archives of the Monastery of the Ursulines in Quebec, Canada; and the National Archives and the National Library at Coromandel, Mauritius. My thanks also to the microfilm division of the Family History Centers of the Church of Jesus Christ of the Latter-Day Saints and to the Interlibrary Loan and Microfilm Divisions of Hesburgh Library at the University of Notre Dame.

This is a book about finding love, labor, and longing where we least expect to find it, yet always hiding in plain sight (or within earshot). Writing it has made me even more attuned to the importance of our connections with others, in good times and in harder ones. This is also a book about intimacy. I'm jolly grateful to live in a time, place, and circumstance that grants me the freedom to love and be loved. Some days, I really do feel that I am the luckiest girl in the world. And I am grateful for so many, many beloved friends. When I was keeling over, three of them propped me up, each in her own stupendous way, and with endless highjinks along the way—here's to you Anna Castellanet, Tama Crisovan, and Margaret Meserve. My family keeps me on my feet in more ways than I could have imagined, though I am still waiting for my parents (Margaret, Peter, and Charlie) to model what it is to be a senior citizen. Staid and dull, they are not; my siblings and I are taking note. My sister Sarah has always shown a special kind of openness that is all the more refreshing in a place like Mauritius, and I am so proud that we have ended up working in parallel ways as she seeks to uncover the lost stories of the enslaved and emancipated people who worked at Anse Jonchée. Charlie Barber was there during much of the research phase for this book, and I would not be here without his love and support of our daughters and of my labor. Cleome and Josephine: you are my most precious loves. I have cherished mothering you even as you have become adults in the time it has taken me to write this book. I don't know what I have done to deserve you, but my love for you is infinite, and I know that your love for me is the same. To have that surety is a feeling beyond compare.

This book is dedicated to my mother, Margaret, the warmest and most nurturing mother anyone could have (I'm quite serious; I frequently get requests from friends in need asking if I would loan her out). The youngest child of eleven, she grew up in Texas during the Depression, knew hardship as a child, yet landed herself a scholarship at the University of Chicago and never learned to stand still. Instead, she stands tall in her spirit, her deep humanity, her amazing sense of fun, and her utter zest for life.

CONTENTS

ILLUSTRATIONS

❧✦❧

TABLES

ABBREVIATIONS

ANOM
Archives nationales d'outre-mer, Aix-en-Provence, France

Code Noir, 1685
Louis Sala-Molin, *Le code noir ou le calvaire de Canaan*
(1987; rpt. Paris, 2001)

Code Noir, 1724
Code Noir, March 1724, III 2852.23, Louisiana Historical Center,
Louisiana State Museum, New Orleans

KM
Kaskaskia Manuscripts, Randolph County Courthouse, Chester, Illinois

NAMC
National Archives of Mauritius, Coromandel

NONA
New Orleans Notarial Archives, Parish of Orleans,
Notarial Archives Research Center, New Orleans

NP
Natchitoches Parish Archives, Natchitoches, Louisiana, microfilm,
Family History Library of the Church of Jesus Christ of Latter-Day Saints,
Salt Lake City, Utah

RSCL
Records of the Superior Council of Louisiana (1717–1769),
Louisiana History Center, Louisiana State Museum, New Orleans

UCANO
Ursuline Convent Archives, microfilm, Historic New Orleans Collection,
New Orleans

NOTE ON TRANSLATION
AND TRANSCRIPTION

Because *Voices of the Enslaved* relies on especially careful attention to two processes, the transcription and modern translation of eighteenth-century texts, a note to the reader is in order.

Eighteenth-century French court testimony was oral; transcriptions were written by scribes. As a whole, these documents are striking in their ability to convey the flavor of the original speech of those who testified, down to the inclusion of dialogue, snatches of Creole, metaphors, and colloquialisms. I have chosen to include the original French alongside an English translation in each case when we hear the voice of an enslaved person. In translating, I have attempted to preserve as much as possible of the sentence structure and, with it, the tone and spontaneity of the original testimony. I have also attempted to convey the original syntax of Creole or other forms of speech. Despite my commitment to preserving the original text, some editorial decisions were required. French court conventions freed scribes from including any punctuation, accent marks included, and spelling was not yet standardized in the eighteenth century. In my transcriptions, I have left both French spellings and punctuation intact, although I have added accent marks to the French when appropriate. In the interests of clarity, however, I have included punctuation in the English translations.

I have also elected to adhere to certain terms that are particularly important to understanding eighteenth-century Louisiana, such as *"negre"* and *"négresse"* (or less commonly, *"negritte"* and *"negrillon,"* for a girl or boy respectively). These terms denoted males and females of African origin, whether born in Africa or not, whether free or enslaved. Because the correct English translation was sometimes elusive, I have determined to use the original French. Likewise, the words for Indian male and female (*"sauvage"* and *"sauvagesse"*) have been left intact in preference to the English translation "savage" in order to retain the original French definition of the word as meaning "wild" or "untamed." Similarly, I have endeavored to preserve the original French meaning with regard to the word *"femme,"* which can sometimes be unclear. In French, "femme" can refer to either a woman or a wife; the word *épouse,* or "spouse," does not appear in the documents where the enslaved are concerned. If I can determine the meaning from the context or the syntax, I will do so; if not, I will translate "femme" as "woman / wife" to maintain the ambiguity of the original rather than interpret it for the reader. The term "Creole" is used in its eighteenth-century meaning as denoting anyone of foreign extraction born in the colony, whether of African or European descent.

Finally, I have retained references to the owners of enslaved individuals, an identification that was required by law when an enslaved person testified. This decision was not undertaken lightly but rather in the interest of making it easier for other scholars to identify and trace individuals who are known only in the archive by their first name.

Unless otherwise specified, all translations are my own.

Voices of the Enslaved

I was afraid that Cudjo might go off on a tangent, so I cut in with,

"But Kossula, I want to hear about you and how you lived in Africa."

He gave me a look full of scornful pity and asked, "Where is de house where de

mouse is de leader? In de Affica soil I cain tellee you 'bout de son before I tellee

you 'bout de father; and derefore, you unnerstand me, I cain talk about de

man who is father (et te) till I tellee you bout de man who he father to him,

(et, te, te, grandfather) now, dass right ain' it?"

ZORA NEALE HURSTON

Barracoon: The Story of the Last "Black Cargo"

"Said, Without Being Asked"

An Introduction

In 1764, Marguerite, a twenty-five-year-old enslaved African, was charged with running away from her master and brought before the Superior Council of Louisiana in New Orleans. She was first made to swear an oath to tell the truth before a crucifix and to identify herself to the court; then her interrogation began. Though she was the defendant in a criminal case, Marguerite placed the blame for her actions on her owners, complaining that she had become a fugitive three weeks earlier because "her master and mistress always beat her, that when she fell sick her mistress came to see her after four days and said 'Mademoiselle is playing at being ill, is she?' and right then beat her with a stick, made her work and clear the courtyard, and threatened that if she did not work she would call the slaves to take her to the public square to give her a hundred lashes of the whip" *(Son Maitre et Sa Maitresse La battaient toujours qu'elle Estoit Malade et que Sa maitresse Etant venu voir au bout de quatre jours Elle luy dit Mademoiselle se fait la malade, que dans l'instant Elle Luy donna des coups de baton et l'envoya travaillé et defriché dans la Cour. et qu'elle La menacée que Si Elle n'aloit pas travailler quelle alloit appeller des negres pour la Conduire sur la place pour luy faire donner cent Coups de fouët)*. Marguerite concluded her narrative by adding to her list of grievances that, "every night, they locked her up like in a convent" *(tous les Soirs ils la faisoient Renfermé comme dans un Couvant)* (Figure 1).[1]

Was Marguerite's testimony tactical? The court did not investigate her claims of abuse or her mistress's threat of a public whipping. Rather, it ruled that she be returned to the home of her master, Mr. Guy Dufossat, a retired captain in the Marine, and his wife, Françoise Claudine Dreux, where she undoubtedly suffered more abuse. Furthermore, although sentences for *marronnage* (running away) were mandatory only for those who had absconded for longer than a month, which was not the case here (perhaps Marguerite knew this and planned to return before the month was out), the Superior

Council nevertheless convicted her of running away and sentenced her to have her ears cut and to be branded with a fleur-de-lis on her right shoulder.[2]

The trial's outcome notwithstanding, Marguerite's words do allow us to glean the dual ways she chose to respond to the abuse. She did so, first, with her feet, by running away, specifically to the cabin of a male slave, Janot (Jeanot), whom she identified as Congo, like her. Janot's owner, Joseph Villars Dubreuil, was the son of the largest slaveholder in the colony, and the plantation where Janot lived was situated a few leagues downriver from New Orleans, requiring Marguerite to leave town to reach him. It was the overseer there who had her seized and taken to prison. Second, she signaled her displeasure verbally, in the particular manner that she conveyed her disapproval of her treatment at the hands of her owners. Her mistress might have thought she was making fun of Marguerite, calling her "Mademoiselle" (Miss) and using the third person to address her slave, in the same way that a servant, following convention, might address the person they were waiting on. But, in court, it was Marguerite who made a mockery of her mistress, making fun of her behind her back by mimicking her words ("'Mademoiselle is playing at being ill, is she?'"). Marguerite also critiqued the behavior of the Dufossat-Dreux couple with a simile referencing New Orleans's Ursuline convent ("they locked her up like in a convent"). Although court procedure required her to identify herself and, as an enslaved woman, to provide the name of her owner, she also volunteered that she was "of the Congo nation," stating that "she was named Margueritte belonging to M. Dufossat former Captain, aged twenty-five years old, of the Congo nation" *(a dit s'appeller Margueritte appartenant à M. dufossat ancient Capne agée de vingt cinq ans de nation Congo).* Her purported origins suggest she might have been familiar with Catholicism as practiced in the kingdom of Kongo. She evidently grasped the fundamental notion of a cloister and of a Catholic model of celibacy, mediated by architecture, that segregated women from men. But this African-born woman, who had herself been captured and enslaved, likely could not fathom that cloistered nuns volunteered to be "locked" up.[3]

This level of detail, this range of experience, touching on labor, abuse, religion, sexuality, and surveillance, is one of the boons of working with eighteenth-century judicial testimony. Seemingly extraneous at first glance, such tidbits are in fact deeply revealing and very often riveting. Certainly, testimony cannot tell us beyond any doubt whether the events described took place. Did Marguerite's owner say those very words to her slave? We cannot know for sure, and perhaps we do not need to know. What we can say is that Marguerite answered the judges' questions and made an assertion about what she considered egregious in the way her mistress and master treated

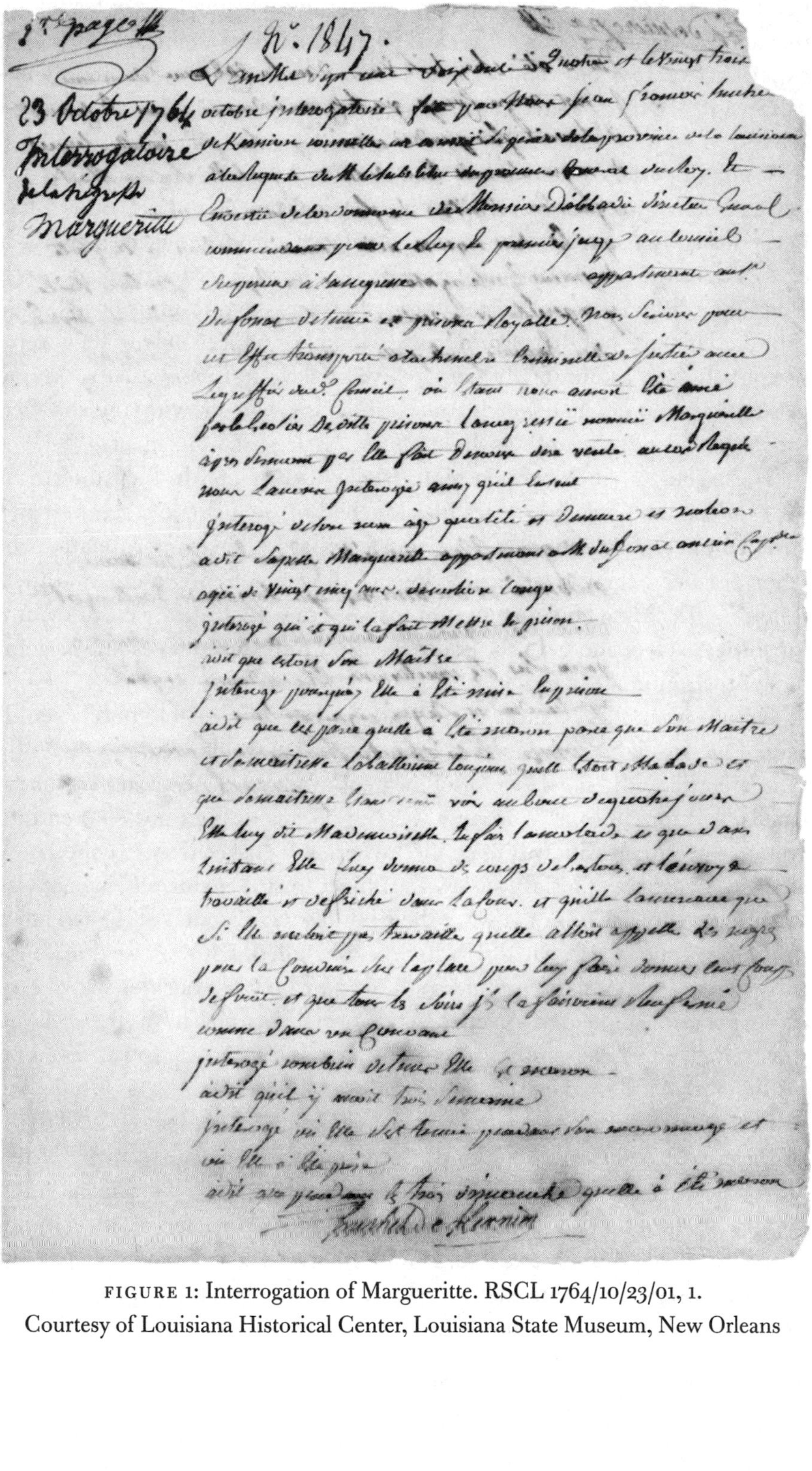

FIGURE 1: Interrogation of Margueritte. RSCL 1764/10/23/01, 1.
Courtesy of Louisiana Historical Center, Louisiana State Museum, New Orleans

her, adding a flourish of sarcasm to her tale. It was the medium of testimony that allowed her to construct this narrative, one that was anchored in her own experience, personality, and ways of knowing, one that was autobiographical because it expressed how she looked at her world, evaluated it, and made sense of it.

If not all enslaved defendants who appeared before New Orleans's Superior Council were as forthright or as expressive as Marguerite, others, like her, constantly redirected the court's focus away from the crimes at hand, crimes that were disproportionately centered on theft or marronnage. And, when they did, in place of straightforward answers to questions posed, they proffered hints about their worldviews and gave glimpses of who they were. The result is an astoundingly rich archive of slave testimony that is unique in scope among colonial North American archives in allowing the enslaved themselves to let us hear their thoughts and their pronouncements.

These court records abound with details of daily life. In their interrogatories, deponents related stories that touched on elements of their oral and aural cultures, their moral and religious compasses, their interpretations of labor practices, their reactions to violence or sexual depredation, and their criteria for deciding how to initiate or respond to sexual, affective, family, and kinship ties. Over and over, the issues that they introduced reveal the particulars of their intimate lives.

On one level, this is hardly surprising. From a physical and bodily standpoint, life in eighteenth-century France and her colonies was inherently intimate, rife with knowledge of other people's bodies, secretions, sounds, smells, and touch. Such closeness was not always desired nor entered into voluntarily. This reality was magnified where the enslaved were concerned, since every aspect of a slave's life was subject to surveillance. Nowhere was this more visible than in the ways their bodies were looked at, lusted after, probed, examined, evaluated, violated, and handled. For these reasons, intimacy offers a particularly useful lens through which to consider the day-to-day experiences of being a slave, a key perspective because it was the enslaved themselves who persistently brought up issues of intimacy and insisted on putting them front and center.[4]

In these narratives, it was the enslaved who chose what they wanted to reply in answer to interrogations, and it is their words that were recorded. After all, it was Marguerite who spoke of running away to the cabin of a man, Janot, and it was she who employed a simile to critique her masters' control of her sexuality — using humor to do so. It was she who seemed genuinely put out that her masters did not treat her as she seemed to expect, for she surely had knowledge of, and had undoubtedly already internalized, what it could mean to be a slave in West Africa, where the concept of slavery allowed for a more flexible range of practices in the treatment of captives. It was also she who described the forced intimacy created when her masters asserted physical and emotional control over her, not only beating her and locking her up but threatening to have her publicly whipped and making fun of her. A slave was supposed to submit to the constraints and violence inherent in such words and actions (and to be contrite if he or she failed to do so in the moment). Marguerite countered both, by running away but also by making a point of explaining her reaction and arguing her point in court.[5]

The trial records of the Louisiana Superior Council brim with details about inner lives as, more often than not, deponents, like Marguerite, signaled that issues centered on intimate matters and their emotional worlds lay at the core of their day-to-day responses to the yoke of slavery. For this reason alone, these documents are invaluable to those who seek to flesh out a richer understanding of the experiences of enslaved Africans. In particular, two linchpins undergird my approach to this extraordinary source material. First, it bears emphasizing that, though this archive can be mined for empirical evidence about slavery, testimony in and of itself does not necessarily enlighten us about the facts of a case: what actually happened, when, where, and to whom. But that is not the purpose of my study. Instead, I seek to understand how and why, in the act of recalling and retelling, those who testified moved past the factual details of the court cases in which they appear. Second, we need to reorient and expand our notion of what a slave's autobiographical narrative can look like. The rewards in doing so are many, for when the enslaved digressed from lines of questioning to introduce other topics that foregrounded their own viewpoints rather than the concerns of their interrogators, they produced a substantial corpus of narratives overflowing with personality, character, subjectivity, and humanity in which they seem to quite literally spring to life.[6]

NARRATIVES

In an article about the release of the film *Twelve Years a Slave*, Annette Gordon-Reed succinctly posed the familiar question: "Which historical voices should be deemed legitimate?" As she observed, "These questions are particularly fraught when one is dealing with past atrocities, like America's racially based system of chattel slavery." "Then there is history's cruel irony," she continued, that "the individuals who bore the brunt of the system—the enslaved—lived under a shroud of enforced anonymity. The vast majority could neither read nor write, and they therefore left behind no documents, which are the lifeblood of the historian's craft." In French colonies, no formal prohibitions existed barring slaves from reading or writing, but not many possessed these skills, meaning that few written sources were produced by the enslaved. The problem of source material is seen as especially acute in the period before the rise of autobiographical slave narratives. These published sources offer richly textured firsthand accounts of the experiences of individual slaves that showcase their voices, even when mediated by an editor or amanuensis. As a literary genre that emerged from Anglo-American Protestant abolitionist movements, however, they emphasize a trope of personal redemption that did not resonate with French or Catholic antislavery advocates, and no such narratives were created in France or her colonies.[7]

The evidence from French judicial slave testimony more than mitigates this void, offering an alternative set of historical voices and life stories that holds the potential to expand the canon of what we consider slave narratives. What made French law distinctive was that it hinged on testimony as central to judicial procedure. In particular, it privileged confession as the "queen of proofs," since only the defendant was deemed to know the truth. Accordingly, criminal trials in France and French colonies were subject to precise rules and strict guidelines to ensure the careful recording of proceedings. Answers that defendants and witnesses provided during questioning could be as expansive as deponents wished, and the written documents that resulted from this testimony were comprehensive. Depositions were far more detailed, for example, than those of English colonial courts, where, in any case, the testimony of the enslaved was not always permitted. Even when such testimony was allowed, English law did not, as in French law, require a full and accurate rendering of court testimony, so there is no comparable archival body of evidence for North American colonies. Instead of maintaining official court transcripts, there developed in England and her colonies a practice of publishing (for profit, in the commercial press) chronicles and pamphlets based on select trials. Authors purported to have been present during trials (some in their capacity as lawyers or judges) and usually avowed that the transcripts were verbatim accounts, claims that are impossible to corroborate in the absence of official transcripts. These independently published accounts were often laced with preambles, asides, embellishments, and critical commentaries primarily aimed at entertaining the public and, depending on the publication and the author's motive, persuading the reader that justice had been carried out, or not. In contrast, both the legal purpose of testimony in French law and the strict court procedures that regulated how testimony was recorded meant that trials in French courts engendered exceptionally thorough written records. Although colonial and metropolitan officials imposed some limits on the circumstances in which slaves were permitted to testify, they consistently upheld record-keeping requirements, even while they remained committed to the broader project of subjugating enslaved Africans.[8]

Africans were first forcibly taken to Louisiana in 1719, but the slave trade to the colony reached a high point in 1730–1731 and virtually ceased thereafter until the end of the French regime. The last known sanctioned shipment occurred in 1743, when the *St. Ursin* transported 220 slaves from Gorée to Louisiana, 190 of whom survived. More than six thousand men and women were brought from West Africa during those years, though mortality was high. Two-thirds of them came from Senegambia, whose slaving ports were outlets for the exploitation of the members of several distinct African nations, chief among which were the Bambara, Ibo, Mandinga, and Wolof. Sixteen slave ships sailed from Senegambia for Louisiana, one from Angola, and six from Whydah. Other slaves arrived through more opaque, and usually illicit, channels. Their numbers, their identities, and their experiences can only be surmised indirectly, for example, from documents such as baptismal records. Any increase in the slave population after 1731 was thus primarily due to reproduction, resulting in an increasingly creolized populace born in the colony. Already by 1731, when a census was conducted, Africans outnumbered the French by 3,352 to 1,095 for Lower Louisiana alone (an underreported 43 Indian slaves were also enumerated). By 1763, African slaves outnumbered the French 4,539 to 2,966, not including soldiers stationed in the colony.[9]

More than eighty criminal trials involving slaves survive for French colonial Louisiana between 1723 and 1769. Following France's defeat in the Seven Years' War (1756–1753) and the loss of New France, the French crown's interest in Louisiana waned. In 1762, the area to the west of the Mississippi, including New Orleans, was ceded to Spain. It was this half of the territory, representing nearly one-third of the present continental United States, that was to become the basis for the 1803 Louisiana Purchase, three years after Spain had ceded Louisiana back to France. The other half, the area to the east of the Mississippi River, was ceded to Britain in 1763. Although the British were swift to occupy their new possession, the Spanish did not formally take control until 1769, the end date for this study. As a group, these trials preserve the voices of close to 150 enslaved Africans and some Indians who testified as defendants, witnesses, and, more rarely, as victims. With few exceptions, the court cases were tried in the Superior Council of Louisiana in New Orleans. A handful of extant cases were tried in the Illinois Country and Natchitoches (Figure 2).[10]

There was no separate slave court in Louisiana, as the enslaved were tried in the same spaces as colonists, but that did not make for an egalitarian process. Criminal acts, and laws aimed at criminality, are inherently cultural. In ancien régime France, prosecutors disproportionately targeted the poor (including women), one consequence of which was the large-scale penal transportation of convicts and other "undesirables" to the colonies, including Louisiana. The Old World judicial structure was shaped to respond to their crimes. What happened when this judicial model was exported and applied to the colonies is that there was a change in prosecutorial targets, from poor disenfranchised whites in France to enslaved Africans in the colony, especially those without protectors with a vested interest in their persons. Few whites of any rank in Louisiana were accused of theft after the 1720s, not, coincidentally, after the great wave of forced convict immigration to the colony had ended. Soldiers (also of low status) would be the rare exception to this rule.[11]

Most of the extant trial records from Louisiana are complete. There are some caveats; the judicial records for the period from 1756 to 1763 are lost while the number of surviving trial records peaks after 1764. But no French colonial archive in North America or elsewhere around the globe comes close to this mass of extant slave trials, either because the archives have suffered the ravages of time or because, as in the case of the French Antilles, a policy was implemented aimed at destroying judicial records pertaining to the enslaved, whose voices were thereby erased.[12]

Louisiana's extant trial documents are just that—legal records of investigations and prosecutions. They represent only a fraction of the times that colonists and slaveowners sought to punish their slaves, which they could do extrajudicially. Furthermore, this archive is a record of the mechanisms used by colonists to control what they deemed to be criminal and transgressive behavior. Yet the very concept of slaves perpetrating criminal acts is a deeply problematic one, raising questions such as how enslaved persons could be guilty of theft when they themselves were stolen—their time, labor, and even family ties stripped from them. But it was not only those slaves accused of crimes who were brought to court to testify. Slaves were also called to speak as witnesses and as victims, and the resulting archive brims with the sound of their voices and their concerns.

It bears stressing that, as source material, trials have one incomparable advantage in that they showcase a multiplicity of voices, even if those voices are fragmentary. This is especially important because very few individual slaves

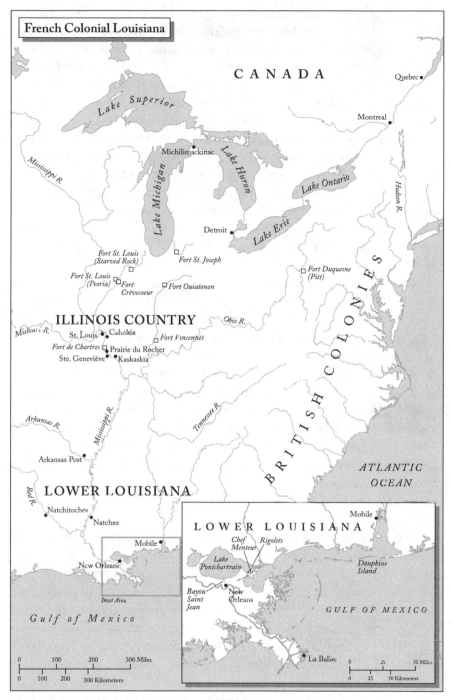

FIGURE 2: "Map of French Colonial Louisiana including the Illinois Country."
Drawn by Alice Thiede

led the kinds of lives that resulted in exceptional archival records of the kind that can anchor full-scale biographies. Though "the success of such studies does not depend on their typicality," as Jon Sensbach points out, those who have left the richest and most fulsome traces in the archives tended to have had atypical life experiences that were far from normative, and Julie Hardwick cautions us to beware of becoming too fixated on these individuals' "beguiling" and "extraordinary tales of mobility, ingenuity, and persistence." As Marisa J. Fuentes puts it, the question might instead be framed as, "How do we construct a coherent historical accounting out of that which defies coherence and representability? How do we critically confront or reproduce these accounts to open up possibilities for historicizing, mourning, remembering, and listening to the condition of enslaved women" and men?[13]

Examining the testimony of enslaved deponents in Louisiana's court cases offers one approach, not least because we can actually hear the voices of individuals who spanned a very wide spectrum. Certainly, those who were accused were primarily male and, often, outsiders who lacked community support. But they were not the only ones to testify. According to Louisiana's code noir of 1724, which set the condition for slave testimony, slaves *had* to testify when accused, but they *could* in some circumstances testify in criminal and civil cases, such as when they were the sole witnesses. There were no constraints against women or children testifying, except when it involved testimony against a husband or parent. Therefore, we find slaves being interrogated because they were suspected of being accomplices or simply because they were privy to relevant information. Still others were brought in as innocent bystanders who had witnessed a crime. A few more testified because they had been victimized. For enslaved women in particular, these interrogatories constitute precious material, since fewer individual women than men were mentioned in records produced in the Atlantic world during the colonial period.

Collectively, the random and not-so-random circumstances that led to an enslaved person's appearance in court as a defendant, accomplice, or witness introduce a broader pool of individuals with a wider range of perspectives and, arguably, more conventional experiences of living in slavery than we might expect if it was only defendants whose words were recorded. Their lives bear writing about, and their lives must be thought about, not least because their own words help us do so. Thanks to the richness of Louisiana's archives, which encompass testimony but also a multitude of other sources that can help us track the biographies of those who testified, the fragments are often enough to bring these lives back to the surface, even when we have only snapshots to work from.

Laws dictated the framework for the testimony of the enslaved and the contexts in which they might appear in court. Testifying was a joint production: both court procedure and the format of judges' questions imposed a structure on these acts of public speech, necessarily framing the answers that the enslaved could provide. Judicial procedure also permitted coercive methods of interrogation that magnified the power of the court. For instance, French law allowed for judicial torture to be triggered in the course of a prosecution. Though it was rarely invoked in Louisiana before 1764, the mere threat of torture was a constant reminder to the accused that they were at the mercy of officials who could authorize, and carry out, state-sanctioned violence.[14]

The French justice system's reliance on confession as the ultimate proof vested enormous importance in the production of court records, especially the accurate rendering of testimony. This premise of French and French colonial judicial law—the accuracy of the trial record—forms the basis of my study. Although trials were not devoid of biases both implicit and explicit, the trial record purported to be a truthful rendering of what had taken place and had been said in court. As in France, justice was rendered, not by juries, but by judges. Judges' deliberations were never made part of the written record. Instead, France's 1670 Code criminel, which governed procedure, required that "conclusions be given in written form and sealed" and explicitly prohibited judges from sharing their reasoning. With this one formal exception, virtually everything else that was said and done during court proceedings was methodically recorded.[15]

The procedure for recording testimony was as follows. During questioning, the clerk of the court *(greffier)* "hastily and in abbreviated form" wrote down the proceedings. Then, at the close of the interrogation, this document, known as the *plumitif*, was read back in court to the deponent and his or her approbation noted—which means that the plumitif was accurate and intelligible enough to be read out, as surviving plumitifs confirm. The greffier then used the plumitif to produce the longhand version that would become the court record. Defendants, witnesses, and victims could be subjected to multiple interrogations, and the greffier repeated the process each and every time.[16]

The clerk did not write down testimony verbatim but usually formalized the French and used the third rather than the first person; no punctuation was included. At the same time, transcriptions consistently captured the words and tone of the speaker. Given the convention for omitting punctuation, reported dialogue was not formally signaled as such, but it is easy to spot since it was almost always rendered as speech: that is, left in the first person with metaphors, turns of phrase, passages in Creole, and other markers of syntax or forms of address intact. For example, in one court case, the clerk switched mid-sentence from formal French to Creole dialogue once he began writing down the reported words of the mother of the enslaved Charlot. Omitting the pronoun, using the incorrect possessive adjective in French, and failing to conjugate her verb—yet clearly communicating her meaning—she had asked him: "Why [you] turn your shirt [inside out] like that?" *(pourquoy tourner ton Chemise Comme Ça?)*. In hewing so closely to the spoken word and allowing dialogue to slip through, clerks enabled the immediacy and spontaneity of original testimony to be preserved, as it was in this passage and as the record of Marguerite's testimony and that of so many others makes clear.[17]

If what they said in court was painstakingly recorded, deponents did change their testimony over the course of multiple interrogations. Sometimes a deponent claimed outright to have lied in previous testimony. When Pierrot, an enslaved man belonging to Joseph Roy de Villeré, was asked anew, during a second interrogation, where he had gotten the cowhide he was accused of stealing, "he said that he had lied previously and that he had taken it from his master" *(il Dit quil avoit menti auparavant, mais quil Lavois pris ches son maître)*. At other times, a change was explained away as a misunderstanding. When twenty-five-year-old Thomas was called out for giving testimony that conflicted with the previous day's interrogation, he "answered that he was telling the truth and that they had misheard what he had said yesterday" *(a Repondu quil a dit La verité Et que Lon a mal Entendu Ce quil a dit hier)*. Deponents changed their testimony for a variety of reasons, including when they realized they needed to shift defense strategies or when they decided along the way to try to save (or betray) accomplices. But, in some cases, it could well be a simple act of miscommunication. Thomas had identified himself in court as Bambara, therefore as being born in West Africa. Though he had been brought to Louisiana from Martinique—suggesting he might have already learned some French—it is feasible that he did genuinely have problems understanding and speaking the language. Alternatively, he could have used his linguistic shortcomings (not to mention his accent) to his advantage in court. The point is that the court scribe took great pains to document these instances of altered testimony. In other words, even when testimony changed over the course of multiple interrogations, we can assume that the written record itself is largely reliable and that witnesses did indeed speak a close version of what they were recorded as saying in a particular interrogation.[18]

Introduction

Judges and court scribes were assiduous in ensuring that the longhand redaction of the initial transcription was as precise as possible, down to noting for posterity any errors that were corrected or passages scratched out. The greffier also made an effort to mention any issues with the document, as seen in the final paragraph of this 1767 interrogation:

> Which is all that she has admitted knowing, her interrogation was read back to her, said her answer contained the truth and persisted in this, and declared not knowing how to write nor read, this enquired of her according to the order. The following [changes] were approved: the word "said" was redone, and one syllable was crossed out above.

> Qui Est tous ce quelle a dit Scavoir Lecture a luy faite de son Interogatoire a dit Sa Reponse Contenir Verité ÿ a persisté et a declare ne Scavoir Ecrire ny Signer de ce enquiz Suivant L'ordonnance, approuvé Le mot Dit, Refait pour valloir et une silabe Rayée desus

Such attention to detail in recording a witness's words was an essential aspect of the process. Though clerks of the court necessarily mediated speech when providing a written record of testimony, they aimed for immediacy in transcribing words: the law required it, justice was believed to depend on it, and the records consistently prove it.[19]

The challenge, then, becomes one of interpreting courtroom testimony, a task magnified when testimony is that of enslaved persons. Because of the inherent power dynamic in the act of testifying, there can be an expectation that testimony, especially that of a defendant, was inevitably framed by a hostile relationship to the law. Though defendants could not speak entirely freely and their answers might put them in jeopardy, the evidence suggests that testimony was not necessarily compelled or exclusively tactical and premeditated. Even when a court appearance was coerced or coached, there was room for redirecting the narrative—the clerk explicitly acknowledged as much when recording what one enslaved witness "said, without being asked" and then "said, again without his being asked," or what another enslaved defendant in a different trial "said, on her own initiative." In other words, appearing before the court provided individuals with an unexpected opportunity to narrate their own stories, to digress, to redirect questioning, and to introduce unrelated matters in an arena where, commanding full attention, they had to be heard.[20]

The records show over and over again that deponents created parallel narratives that did not stay tethered to the investigations at hand and that it was on their own terms, ultimately, that they answered questions. Hence, we need to break away from a preoccupation with intent and strategy when analyzing speech given in court, an approach that can be counterproductive. Instead, the evidence forces us to recognize that, though deponents could have planned in advance what to say, the act of speaking is first and foremost a spontaneous performance that happens on the fly, shifting course along the way. As such, it is also impulsive, subject to different rules and imperatives than written autobiographical narratives. This is especially important given that deponents did not know ahead of time what questions would be asked or what a prosecutor had uncovered in the course of his investigation or while questioning witnesses and suspected accomplices.

Sometimes deponents took the stage with purpose and intent, and sometimes they blurted out things they had not planned to or reacted in some other way in the course of testifying. We see this complicated process at work in other legal regimes. An observer in Suriname described the trial of a convicted runaway slave there who "beg'd only to be heard for a few moments," then proceeded to invoke memories of his honor in battle in Africa and his experience as a slave. His fate was already sealed; his compulsion to speak did not relate directly to the court case or the accusation of running away. Yet he launched into his autobiography, redirecting the narrative toward those selective aspects of his life experiences that were important for him to communicate at that moment in time. The enslaved often saw the occasion to testify, not as an antagonistic ordeal, but as an opportunity for expression. And, sometimes, as Leora Auslander, writing of Parisian Jews after World War II, describes such moments of veering off course, their words became "memory maps," a means of healing psychic wounds, of mourning lives, and of starting "the process of narrativizing loss." Though enslaved individuals were thrust into French colonial courtrooms under vastly different circumstances, they found in the act of testifying motivations other than a single-minded focus on pure self-preservation, and we must heed their words correspondingly.[21]

The work of interpretation rests on knowledge of the archive and the law, it requires detailed linguistic analysis of the text, and it depends on the meticulous contextualization of the evidence against a broad array of other primary sources, including slave inventories, probate documents, manumission records, official correspondence, and even parish registers of slave marriages and baptisms (there are no runaway advertisements of the kind found in British colonies since no newspapers were published in Louisiana during the French regime). Such an approach helps flesh out the lives of the enslaved in Louisiana so that their experiences come more clearly into focus. Though the records from Louisiana during the French regime lie at the heart of this project, it is also sometimes possible, and fruitful, to make direct comparisons between slave testimony in Louisiana and other French colonies. The French Empire was one that aimed for an important degree of centralization, expressed, among other ways, in standardizing laws across its colonies (the 1670 Code criminel and the slave codes are key examples discussed in greater detail in Chapter One). Refracting testimony in Louisiana through the lens of shared slave laws and trials from the same period in France's other colonies in the Atlantic and Indian Oceans brings local particularities into sharper relief.[22]

Yet the snatches of Creole and the passages containing dialogue, the random colloquialisms and the imagery that seep through testimony are most revealing when they are set back into their larger historical and social contexts. Returning to the trial of Marguerite, we must first understand the built environment of New Orleans before we can grasp how she experienced the cityscape and her place within it. When she offered the simile of being "locked . . . up like in a convent" as one motive for running away to the cabin of her male friend, she had literally just been locked up, but in the town jail. How did that experience affect her choice of comparison, especially given the absence of these institutions in West Africa? The prison was located on the Place d'armes (present-day Jackson Square), to the right of the Church of Saint Louis when facing the quay (Figure 3). It was the first major building constructed of brick without a timber frame, covered in masonry. Two stories high, consisting of two separate buildings linked by a walled-in courtyard for the use of prisoners, it measured about six by eight toises (approximately thirty-eight by fifty-one feet). Each cell (on the upper level) measured about two and one half by two toises (approximately sixteen by twelve and a half feet), meaning that these were communal cells (Figure 4). But the prison complex was not just reserved for locking up those being prosecuted and those who had been convicted. It also contained the *"chambre criminelle"* (criminal chamber), where special interrogations *"on the sellette"* (so named for the low stool on which the defendant was made to sit) and judicial torture were carried out and recorded (see Figure 10). A large space, the room measured approximately four by three toises (approximately nineteen by twenty-five feet). Regular interrogations took place in the chambers of the Superior Council, which would have required a defendant to be led out of jail and taken under guard around the block.[23]

That Marguerite had spent time in prison, however, was just one element of her narrative. She specifically mentioned that it was her master and mistress who had locked her up. Though we do not have information on where their residence was located, the architecture of New Orleans allows us to speculate about her experience. When Adrien de Pauger designed New Orleans in

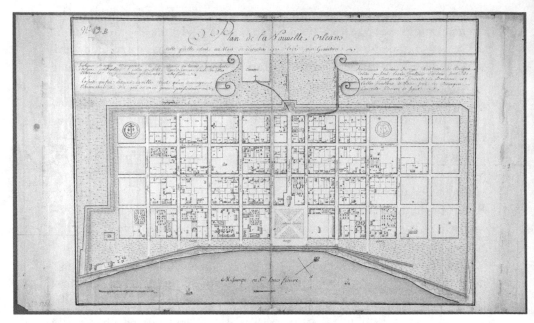

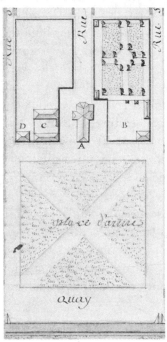

FIGURE 3:

Plan de la Nouvelle Orléans telle qu'elle estoit au mois de dexembre 1731 levé par Gonichon (and detail). FR ANOM 04 DFC 89 B. Courtesy of Archives nationales d'outre-mer, Aix-en-Provence, France

Key C shows the orientation of the prison buildings with the inner enclosed courtyard. A is the Church of Saint Louis, facing onto the Place d'armes and the river, and D is the guard house.

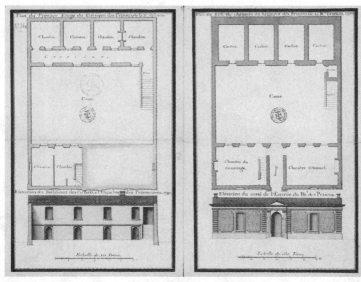

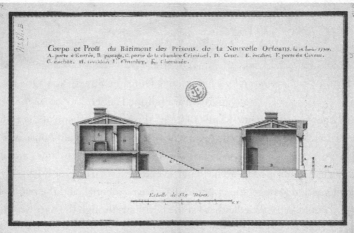

FIGURE 4: Anonymous, *Plan profil et elevation des prisons de la Nouvelle Orleans,
14 janvier 1730*. Watercolor. FR ANOM 04 DFC 84 B. Les archives nationales
d'outre-mer, Aix-en-Provence, France

The top view is of the prison from rue d'Orleans, with the left-hand drawing showing
the upper level and the right-hand drawing showing the street level. The entrance
faced the church. It shows the rear building (accessed from the inner courtyard)
and the floorplan of the upper level. The bottom view shows the prison from the
perspective of rue de Chartre (present-day Chartres Street). It also shows the front
building and entrance from the street and includes the floor plan of the ground level.
The walled-in courtyard measured about six toises by eight toises, or approximately
thirty-eight feet by fifty-one feet. Each cell (on the upper level) measured about two
and a half by two toises, or approximately sixteen by twelve and a half feet, meaning
that these were communal cells. The *chambre criminel* (criminal chamber) was
where interrogations on the *sellette* and judicial torture were carried out; it measured
approximately four by three toises, or approximately nineteen by twenty-five feet.

FIGURE 5: *Madame John's Legacy.* 632 Dumaine Street, New Orleans.
Photo courtesy of Philippe Halbert

Popularly known as "Madame John's Legacy," this site hosted one of the earliest and longest-running inns in French colonial New Orleans. The main house was badly damaged in a citywide fire in 1788 but was reconstructed in the same early French colonial style as confirmed by archaeological excavations. The ground level was used for commerce and storage, the upper levels were residential, and the rear walled-in courtyard could be accessed either via the house or through the narrow side gate.

1722, he laid out the city according to a straight grid anchored by the Place d'armes, with residential lots "of such a size that each and every one may have the houses on the street front and may still have some land in the rear to have a garden, which here is half of life." In other words, the town house lots consisted of dwellings set right on the street with rear courtyards, like the one that Marguerite was made to clear (see, for comparison, Figure 5).[24]

Courtyards were utilitarian, containing vegetable gardens for household use and perhaps housing for the enslaved, but they were also spaces of leisure for the master and mistress of the house. When the elderly Dame Elizabeth Real, Widow Marin (owner of the so-called Madame John's Legacy house), composed her will in 1769, the notary and his attendant had to wait on her at home. They "entered into the hall of the said House in which we have found the said [Dame] Widow Marin, seated between the two courtyard doors in the coolness, who seemed to us to be ill in body because of her great age, but sound in spirit, memory and understanding." After Madame Dufossat beat Marguerite "with a stick, made her work and clear the courtyard, and threatened that if she did not work she would call the slaves to take her to the public square to give her a hundred lashes of the whip," did she, too, like Widow Marin, sit in the shade watching over her slaves? Accessed from the street via narrow side gates, courtyards were generally invisible to passersby, thanks to the high walls that enclosed the properties. Travel accounts emphasized that slaves customarily enjoyed a degree of mobility within the town, but perhaps such statements were hyberbolic. A master who really wanted to control his slaves' access in and out of these sealed-off residences could do so, as Dufossat and his wife seem to have done with Marguerite.[25]

To plumb how Marguerite grasped the concept of cloistering ("locked up" like "in a convent"), particularly given that she identified herself as "of the Congo nation," we also need one final piece of the puzzle—that there was an Ursuline convent right in New Orleans, the buildings visible, the nuns closed off, covered from head to toe (Figures 6 and 7). In fact, the daughter of Marguerite's masters, Françoise Dufossat, would enter that very convent in 1773 to become a nun, suggesting that the household was a devout one that would have very likely sent Marguerite to the Ursulines for religious instruction. Approximately twenty-five years old in 1764, Marguerite could not have come to Louisiana on any known or sanctioned slave ships from the Congo (the only slave ship documented to have done so was *La Néréide*, which transported 294 enslaved persons from Cabinda [Angola] to the colony in 1721), but there were other ways, licit and illicit, for a colonist in Louisiana to acquire slaves, especially through trade with the French islands. Given that Marguerite had sufficient command of French not to need a court interpreter, she was in all likelihood not new to the French colonies but brought in from the islands. Though the ethnonym Congo was ambiguous in terms of her actual origin in Central Africa, it is possible that it was there that she first encountered Christian concepts and imagery, since the kingdom of Kongo had converted to Catholicism in 1481. Yet there were no female convents in the kingdom of Kongo, meaning that it was in the New World that Marguerite initially came into contact with this institution and first saw nuns. If she had come via Martinique, and specifically Saint-Pierre, she might have seen the convent there, which was the only one in the French Antilles. More likely, her earliest glimpse of nuns living in a cloister was in New Orleans.[26]

This understanding of Marguerite's probable origins and the presence of an Ursuline convent in New Orleans helps us interpret her narrative and

FIGURE 6: *Soeur Converse Ursuline de la Congrégation de Paris.*
From Pierre Hélyot, *Histoire des ordres monastiques . . .* , IV (Paris, 1715), x.

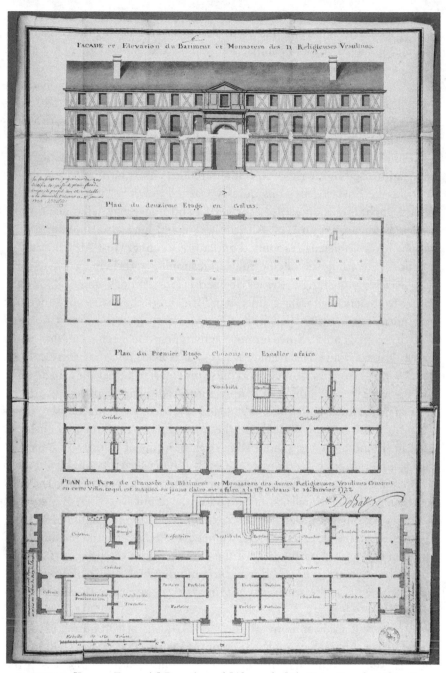

FIGURE 7: [Ignace François] Broutin and [Alexandre] de Batz, *Façade et élévation du batiment et monastère des D. Religieuses Ursulines; Coupe profil du batiment et monnastère des Dames Ursulines de cette ville à la Nlle Orléans le 14 janvier 1732.* FR ANOM F3 290/6. Les archives nationales d'outre-mer, Aix-en-Provence, France

understand what it meant when, seizing the opportunity to voice her outrage, she expressed herself using this particular simile referencing the convent. In her interpretation, it was a comparison that evoked imprisonment but also a lack of access to men, an image that clearly resonated with Marguerite, who had certainly been to the New Orleans convent. Other enslaved individuals brought to bear their own frames of reference, their own motives, and their own particular ways of expressing themselves, based on their worldviews about the places, and roles, they inhabited.

Testimony was a form of speech, and the experience of addressing (and being addressed by) masters and other colonists must have inflected slaves' depositions. Enslaved persons quickly learned how they were expected to behave, including the necessity for verbal and nonverbal deference toward whites. Familiarity with West African laws could have also influenced how deponents in Louisiana responded under questioning. West African judicial practices (including sentencing rules, questioning and divining rituals, and sentences for punishing activities deemed either criminal, immoral, or dangerous to society) might have differed in format, but they were not altogether unfamiliar, not entirely alien from the investigations and interrogations of French colonial courts. Since criminal activity was one mechanism that could lead to captivity and enslavement, it is also conceivable that African-born slaves were personally familiar with these practices, whether they themselves had been subjected to them or simply witnessed them. Knowledge of these judicial procedures, codes of conduct, and sentences were not eclipsed, especially for those born in Africa, and there is evidence that free and enslaved Africans found means to extend West African forms of justice to Louisiana, for example, through secret male societies. The enslaved could also openly co-opt the law for their own purposes (see Chapters Four and Five). They did so when handling internal affairs with other slaves but also when they entered into negotiations with their owners in matters relating to manumission and sanctioned marriage. Accordingly, we need to "reflect on the meaning and function of law, and particularly of the courts, within the lives of slaves" in order to "reflect upon how and why certain individuals and groups, particularly those who are in some way disempowered, regard and use the ideas of law."[27]

Interpreting the testimony of enslaved Africans also requires us to acknowledge a different type of oral communication, that of storytelling. For the enslaved in Louisiana, Ibrahima Seck suggests, storytelling "eased the pain in their limbs and minds and allowed many to deal with their fate instead of crying or drowning in homesickness. Storytelling was also a means for the oppressed to create fictional situations where the weak could overcome

FIGURE 8: Unrecorded artist from Democratic Republic of Congo or Angola,
Divination Basket with Sixty-One Ritual Objects. Mid-twentieth century.
Chokwe style. Plant fiber, wood, animal fur, brass, bird horn, calabash,
gourd, red clay, corn cob, seeds, seed pod, chicken feet, ceramic, antelope
hooves, unidentified ritual powder mixture. Owen D. Mort Jr. Collection,
Snite Museum of Art 2011.036.009. University of Notre Dame

the domination of the powerful," sometimes using humor, including trick-
ster tales. At the same time, differences had to be negotiated. In West Africa,
storytelling was chiefly reserved for the time of day after dusk. For witnesses
appearing in court, choosing when to speak was not a luxury; but that was
also the case for those subjected to divination rituals and judicial practices
in West Africa that likewise required narrating a story (Figure 8). It is inevitable that the conventions of storytelling that developed in Louisiana (as well
as their West African antecedents) informed deponents' conceptions of how
to perform when asked to narrate their explanations. When Marguerite mim-
icked her mistress and openly mocked her, was she invoking a long-standing
West African tradition of using humor to outwit an opponent? What other
insights can testimony provide about the inner lives of individuals?[28]

"OUR PLACE"

Chapter One offers a grand tour of French court procedures. Using particular court cases from Louisiana to flesh out the application of the law in the

colony, it discusses the role of slave codes, especially Louisiana's code noir of 1724, against the backdrop of France's 1670 Code criminel, which dictated in minute detail how crimes were investigated, prosecuted, sentenced, and recorded. Following the chapter on court procedure, this book presents four microhistories that tell the stories of a total of eight enslaved individuals (in addition to Marguerite and François-Xavier, whose stories feature, respectively, in the Introduction and Epilogue). Three of these case studies are anchored by women. Chapter Two focuses on Louison, an enslaved woman belonging to the Ursuline nuns who was stabbed during an incident that escalated when a soldier demanded that she and her companions launder his soiled handkerchief. In her 1752 testimony, we hear Louison insistently communicating her response to a violent act of aggression, making full use of the opportunities available to her to speak: first, in her religion-inflected words to the soldier during their encounter and, second, in her subsequent retelling of the event to court officials. Chapter Three moves to the Illinois Country (Upper Louisiana) in 1748 and explores the contentious relationship between two slaves: Marie-Jeanne, a pregnant woman of African descent accused of infanticide after going into labor, and Lisette, a young Indian girl. Their court appearance afforded them the possibility of narrating their own stories of loss, and, in the fissures between the lines of questioning and their answers, the childless woman and the motherless child interspersed references to work roles, conflicts over authority, and their conceptions of motherhood. A third case study centers on Francisque, an outsider self-described as an "Englishman from Philadelphia" *(anglois de philadelphy)* whose peripatetic life as a slave took him around the British, Spanish, and French Atlantic. Francisque's ostentatious deployment of dress at slave assemblies and in courtship in 1766 left him vulnerable to the enmity of rival slaves, laying bare the artificial cleavages between freedom and unfreedom when the "free" person was a runaway slave. The Igbo Démocrite, in particular, revealed through his words and actions how local enslaved communities—and their leaders, such as Hector—made use of French colonial justice to regulate social, economic, and sexual interactions. Chapter Four is Démocrite's and Hector's story as much as it is Francisque's. Chapter Five shifts the action to 1767 and a swampy bayou beyond New Orleans as it traces the love story of Kenet and Jean-Baptiste and their search for a way to be united. Where enslaved women are concerned, testimony about courtship, love, labor, and longing is especially rare. This man and woman belonged to different owners, and their testimony illuminates the steps they took to secure, over the long term, their affective and physical union and what they envisioned when granted autonomy over two gendered corollaries of spousal relationships: domestic organization and household labor. Finally, the Epilogue foregrounds François-Xavier, whose dogged attempts to get a soldier shamed for a profoundly disturbing act reads at times like a searing indictment of slavery. Individually, each of these microhistories can stand on its own, contributing new biographies of seven enslaved Africans and one enslaved Indian in North America while also introducing Marguerite and François-Xavier. An emphasis on different facets of intimate encounters, from the intimacy associated with courtship, marriage, and procreation to that forged through acts of violence, is the thread that links all of these chapters together.[29]

The questions that court officials selected for interrogation show that they were acutely aware of the affective worlds that slaves created for themselves. But, in the court records, it was enslaved individuals who repeatedly brought to the fore their desires and quests for some forms of intimacy. They also signaled their rejection of other kinds of intimacy (such as sexual advances or demeaning speech and behavior) that evoked the perils to which they were subject because of the special rules that applied to slaves' persons. Often, their words indicate that space, place, and tangible things were integral to their experiences, a reminder that material culture can be especially valuable in giving contour to the lives of the nonliterate, not least their emotional lives.

Slaves were denied the right to own the properties where they were forced to labor. Yet each case study shows how enslaved individuals harnessed colonial spaces and sometimes even commandeered them. They imbued their environment with significance, whether it was the New Orleans riverbank by the convent-hospital where enslaved women laundered; a stable in Kaskaskia, where an enslaved African went into labor; a plantation outside New Orleans, where one runaway ran afoul of locals; or even the domestic space that two lovers coaxed out of a simple dwelling at swampy Chef Menteur, an area isolated from other French settlements but proximate to and in communication with Indian settlements around Lake Pontchartrain. Marguerite juxtaposed the convent-like confinement she felt at her masters' residence with the release of running away to be with Janot at his plantation, though that space would not prove safe to her since it was where she was captured. Those who testified tell us how important place was to them, sometimes obstructing and containing them, other times binding them together, as when one group of slaves claimed rights over the plantation on which they toiled when they called it "our place" ("*chez nous*"). It is clear in the way that enslaved individuals spoke about space that, for them, it was not an abstraction; it held meaning physically, culturally, and emotionally.[30]

Slaves' insistence on understanding their environment in terms of their intimate lives tells an important story, one in which we see not only how profoundly the forced intimacy of slavery affected these individuals but also how they fought to establish boundaries. Sometimes they succeeded in enacting changes in how their masters treated them, such as when masters acknowledged (sometimes only indirectly) a choice of partner or when they turned a blind eye to laws that sought to control the movement of their slaves. Masters might have acquiesced to slaves' requests because they deemed it in their interests to placate their workforce. But it was at the urging of the enslaved themselves that such demands were met, and it was they who determined the contours of the customary practices that emerged as a result of their negotiations with masters.

The stories told and the sources analyzed in this study might be from Louisiana, but they tell us about experiences that were pervasive across the African diaspora. What is remarkable in Louisiana is that it is slaves' own words that give us access to such insights, if only we lean in and make the attempt to hear.

"Only in Default of Whites"

Slave Testimony and Court Procedure

On April 24, 1738, Attorney General François Fleuriau laid out before the Louisiana Superior Council the charges to be brought against Pierrot, a thirty-five-year-old enslaved man who had been arrested the previous Sunday for "carrying a bundle of stolen tablecloths and napkins that he had snatched and taken in spite of the young *negresse* belonging to Sr. Favrot officer" who had tried to stop him. Though Pierrot had abandoned the bundle, thinking he was being pursued, the court deemed that he should be prosecuted regardless, reasoning that it was "necessary to punish him as befits the case." Accordingly, the attorney general proceeded to dictate a set of questions with which he proposed to interrogate Pierrot, which the clerk of the court duly recorded:

Where he was the previous Sunday?
What he was doing at Mr. Favrot's?
If he knew the *negresse* of Mr. Favrot?
Where he took the bundle of tablecloths and napkins that he was taking with him?
If he did not throw the *negresse* into a ditch?
If he did not defend himself against Mr. Thomelin who wanted to arrest him and if he did not knock him over?
If he has committed other burglaries?
What he wanted to do with the tablecloths and napkins and to whom was he going to sell them?

---

ou il fut dimanche dernier
ce quil fut faire chez m. faverot
sil connoist sa negresse
où il prit le paquet de napes et serviettes quil emportoit

Sil ne jetta pas lad. negresse dans un fossé
sil ne se deffendit pas contre Me thomelin qui le voulu arrester et sil
ne le renversa pas
sil a fait dautres vols
ce quil vouloit faire des napes et serviettes et a qui il devoit les vendre

Per procedure, Pierrot was not in the courtroom while this motion was recorded, since prisoners were not apprised of the investigations conducted
against them. But, later on that very day, the prison guard fetched him from
his detention cell in the small prison building and walked him around the
block to the chamber of the Superior Council, which served as the courtroom for both slaves and colonists (Figure 9). After Pierrot was made to
identify himself and to swear to tell the truth in the presence of a crucifix, his
examination began. One after the other, in sequential order, the questions
that Fleuriau had devised were lobbed at him. One after the other, Pierrot
answered them. As each spoke, the scribe made a written record of question
and response.[1]

Judicial laws, slave codes, and court procedures all structured the testimony that a slave could provide once a prosecutor began to probe and prod.
These laws also gave the enslaved a place in which to speak as well as the
space to sketch out, and stretch out, their own narratives. But access to that
space was itself subject to the vagaries of a justice system that was anything
but blind.

RULES OF TESTIMONY

That the enslaved could testify in court was not a given. Their access to testimony, as the accused or as a witness or victim, was a function of the code
noir (or slave code). This law determined whether slaves could testify, in what
circumstances, and in what capacity. Once a decision was made, court procedure adhered to France's 1670 Code criminel, which the crown ordained for
all criminal matters (civil matters were governed by the Coutume de Paris).[2]

Until the introduction of Louisiana's own slave code in 1724, the colony
was governed by the 1685 code noir written for the Antilles (New France, of
which Louisiana was a province, had no code noir). Comparison of the two,
especially the revisions and additions contained in the 1724 code, has provided rich material for assessing the role of French Caribbean slave codes in
laying a foundation for slave laws in another Atlantic colony. Yet the enactment of the 1724 code noir also offers evidence that legal documents transcended the Atlantic. The 1724 code noir was virtually identical, word for

Slave Testimony and Court Procedure

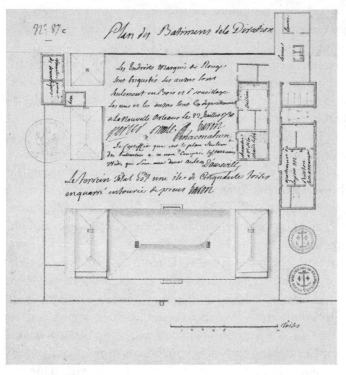

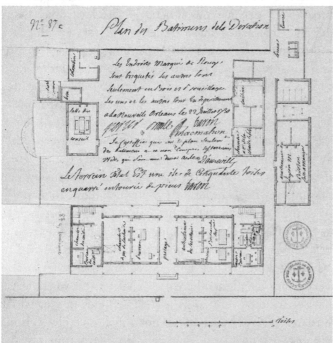

FIGURE 9: [Pierre] Baron, *Plan des batimens de la direction [de la Nouvelle Orléans]*, . . . *July 22, 1730.* Watercolor. FR ANOM 4 DFC 87C. Courtesy Archives nationales d'outre-mer, Aix-en-Provence, France This plan of the government buildings was made with flaps that lift up to show both the aerial view and the rooms within. The chamber of the Superior Council ("*salle du conseil*"), where trials were conducted, is on the left, a rectangular room approximately four by two and a half toises (equivalent to twenty-five by twelve feet) with two long and two shorter tables arranged in a square.

word, to the 1723 code noir pertaining to African slavery in France's East African island colonies in the Indian Ocean, specifically the Isle de France and Isle de Bourbon (present-day Mauritius and La Réunion, in the Mascarene Islands, seven hundred miles east of Madagascar). Both the 1723 and 1724 codes simultaneously initiated the use of the race-based terms "black" and "white" as opposed to the status terms "slave" and "free" found in the 1685 code. Drafted by the governor and intendant in Martinique, the 1685 code was based on local jurisprudence that had developed over nearly half a century in the French Caribbean islands with only minimal revisions in France. The 1723 and 1724 codes heralded, instead, a moment when "the French Empire became the first European overseas empire where slave law emanated from a metropolitan edict," even as they reflected the application of the law and the ebb and flow between colony and state, or the push and pull between local elites and court officials.[3]

Given the successive enactment of the code noir in colonies throughout the French Empire, it is important to recognize the tension inherent in the imposition of external rules on local institutions and officials whose job it was to interpret and apply those rules. It is just as significant to acknowledge that these external codes reflected not just an Atlantic but also a global vision of the French Empire. Nor did the code noir preclude the formulation of local laws, such as the police code enacted in New Orleans in 1751, which focused on providing ways to control specific types of behavior that local officials and elites found threatening. Channeling these anxieties, the 1751 law imposed strict restrictions on the movement of slaves, including their participation in commerce as both consumers and providers. Although it included some oversight of poor whites, the main emphasis in its thirty-one articles and twenty-eight pages lay in exerting control over enslaved and free Africans.[4]

The 1685 and 1724 codes are broadly similar, covering topics such as Catholic instruction, slave marriage, and hereditary status. Above all, they sought to establish the means of controlling and subjugating the enslaved. Both codes identified crimes specific to the enslaved and set out rules pertaining to their civil status and the conditions under which they could appear in court. Article 26 of the 1724 code stated that "Slaves may be prosecuted criminally, without their masters being made parties to the trial, except in cases of complicity." It further stipulated that "the accused slaves will be tried . . . with the same rules, formalities, and proceedings observed for free persons, save the exceptions mentioned hereafter." Actions for which slaves could be tried, but not whites, were addressed in Articles 27–36, which specified that the enslaved could be prosecuted not only for statutory crimes such as theft, *marronnage* (running away), and giving refuge to runaways but also for behaviors that were not necessarily criminal per se but were considered particularly threatening when committed by the enslaved, such as holding assemblies, committing acts of insubordination, or physically assaulting free persons.[5]

Whether under the terms of the 1685 code or the 1724 code, Louisiana's enslaved people were always required to testify when accused. The 1724 code, however, granted the enslaved new authority as witnesses. Both codes prohibited them from serving as "arbitrators or experts," but Article 24 of the 1724 code allowed for them to be called as witnesses in civil or in criminal cases: specifically, "when it shall be a matter of necessity, and only in default of whites, but in no case shall they be permitted to serve as witnesses either for or against their masters." When it was discovered that Jean-Louis was the sole witness to a colonist's accidental death, for example, the court allowed him to testify. The prohibition on slaves testifying against their masters was simply a conflict-of-interest clause, derived from the same prohibition in French law against servants bearing witness against their employers or masters.[6]

As a whole, the conditions set forth in the 1724 code under Article 24, dependent as it was on the absence of white witnesses, nonetheless constituted an improvement over the previous 1685 code. The earlier code had held that testimony by the enslaved could be heard in court but could serve only as a memorandum to help the judges, who were instructed not to "draw any presumption, nor conjecture, nor corroborative proof" from this testimony. To testify while black was hardly equal to testifying while white, yet, whatever the place of slave testimony in judges' deliberations, the fact remains that in certain circumstances the enslaved could appear as witnesses, have their testimony heard, and have their words recorded and archived in the Superior Council of Louisiana. No restrictions were placed in the law on the authority of free blacks as witnesses. But it would not take long for race to also be inscribed on the bodies of free blacks within the court system.[7]

Unlike colonists, the enslaved could not bring suit in either civil or criminal cases. Article 25 of the 1724 code specified that the enslaved could not "be parties to civil suits, either as plaintiffs or defendants, nor to parties [as complainants] in criminal cases, except their masters shall have the right to act for them in civil matters, and in criminal ones, to demand punishment and reparation for such outrages and excesses committed against their slaves." So, even though a slave could not lodge a complaint, his or her master could, and they sometimes did. In 1746, it was Jean-Baptiste Raguet who went to the Superior Council to file a report that his slaves' cabin had been broken into and their clothing and household effects stolen.[8]

As a rule, the Superior Council showed no interest in upholding the law when it meant investigating and prosecuting cases where slaves were the victims of ill-treatment, dereliction of duty, torture, or murder by masters, even though they were required to under Articles 20, 21, 38, and 39 of the 1724 code noir. Such willful negligence stands in stark contrast with the plethora of criminal investigations brought against the enslaved. It is a finding that underlines just how aspirational the code was and how ineffective it could prove to be in practice.

Once the 1724 code noir was introduced, the Superior Council seems to have observed the new rule that the enslaved could serve as witnesses "only in default of whites." In 1751, a well-connected officer, Pierre Henri d'Erneville, interceded in a court case involving his slave Charlotte, who was also his daughter. She had run away to be with her French lover, and the guards tracked her down to the house of one Batard in whose bed she was found hiding, wearing only a short skirt and claiming that no less than the governor's wife had promised her mercy. And, indeed, official correspondence stated as much, accusing Madame de Vaudreuil of meddling and using her patronage to maneuver behind the scenes to try to settle matters informally and extra-judicially. The case was a civil suit instigated by d'Erneville against Batard. D'Erneville asked the court to allow two female slaves to testify, but the court refused on the basis that there were already enough white witnesses, stating that there was therefore no need to invoke Article 24 of the code noir. This case was a particularly thorny one, not least because d'Erneville's father-in-law was Attorney General Fleuriau, but, as with every case in which the Superior Council was asked to bend the rules about slave testimony, the councillors steadfastly refused.[9]

Colonists seem to have quickly recognized the protections that the law afforded them in prohibiting slaves from testifying against whites, except when they were the only eyewitnesses. Even then, there was a certain flexibility in how the attorney general and the councillors applied the rules. In a 1747 letter to the minister of the navy, for example, Vaudreuil described a fight between two colonists where the only witnesses were slaves, but he concluded, despite the provision in the 1724 code noir allowing slaves to testify in the absence of white witnesses, that their depositions were insufficient, since "they can prove nothing against a white per the code noir." Notwithstanding the occasional sleight of hand, after the passing of the 1724 code noir, the archive becomes a rich repository of the testimony of enslaved persons: as bystanders, as the accused and their accomplices, and as witnesses testifying against other slaves and sometimes, if only occasionally, against colonists.[10]

Slave Testimony and Court Procedure

Though the code noir established the rules for slave testimony in the colony, the procedures for initiating an investigation and carrying out a prosecution adhered to France's 1670 Code criminel and were the same as those involving French subjects. Louisiana did not have a separate slave court to prosecute the enslaved, and their trials were integrated within the mainstream judicial system. In Louisiana, investigations and prosecutions were carried out by the Superior Council, which had the power to decide "in the last resort" (in other words, with no right to appeal) all civil and criminal cases. Cases could also be tried in the colony's outposts, with the post commandant overseeing the legal proceedings for those deemed straightforward or referring them to the Superior Council as needed.[11]

A Superior Council was first established in Louisiana in 1712, and, like all French colonial councils, this body was charged with administering justice in civil and criminal matters in accordance with the laws of France. It was originally composed of the governor, the *commissaire-ordonnateur*—the highest ranking civilian authority who served as first councillor and presiding judge—three other councillors (later expanded to six), the attorney general, and a clerk (or scribe). The members of the Superior Council decided whether there was sufficient cause to prosecute a criminal case and oversaw every step of the process through to sentencing, a decidedly discretionary power that allowed for the kind of backroom maneuvering that was not made a part of the official record. As in French courts, there were no juries; justice was determined by judges (whose deliberations were sealed). In Louisiana, this role was exercised by the councillors of the Superior Council. The concurrence of five sitting judges was required for conviction in criminal cases, but only three were necessary in civil cases.[12]

Defendants in Louisiana had no legal representation, since lawyers were prohibited in the colony (and in the Mascarene Islands) as part of an attempt by the crown to curtail litigation in its overseas possessions. Some officials had legal training, such as Fleuriau, who was an attorney practicing before the Parlement de Paris when he was nominated attorney general of Louisiana in 1722, but he did not practice as a lawyer in the colony. Of course the accused and witnesses might have received advice and direction through informal channels. Some coaching must have come from owners, since the conviction of a slave was of direct financial consequence for them. In other cases, the enslaved coached each other. In New Orleans in 1765, twenty-three-year-old Louis claimed that the *negresse* Marguerite had told him to deny everything or they would make him die, a statement that the twenty-five-year-old woman refuted. Meanwhile, in 1757, Estienne, an enslaved boy accused of theft in Natchitoches, stated that he had taken his orders from Marion — who was the ringleader of a wide-ranging illicit trade network within Natchitoches and with the neighboring Spanish settlement at Los Adaes — and that she had "forbidden him from talking about the theft, even to his mother, under threat of not letting him have any corn to eat; she had added that, even should the theft be discovered, it was best to suffer death than to talk about it" *(Elle luy avoit fait defence d'en parler à Personne meme à sa mère sous les peines qu'il ne mangeroit plus de Mahy et que quand bien meme ledt vol viendroit à se decouvrir qu'il falloit Plustot souffrir la mort que d'en Rien dire).* Neither Louis nor Estienne followed these women's orders, but others surely did allow themselves to be guided.[13]

Though the enslaved were tried in the same spaces as colonists, they were already treated differently at the point of investigation with the end result that the enslaved were disproportionately prosecuted compared to colonists. This was a distinct departure from both New France and metropolitan France, where the poor continued to be targeted for prosecution and punishment. In France, a poor Frenchman's theft of four handkerchiefs might carry a sentence ranging from three years in the galley to hanging (though a death sentence often meant serving in the galleys rather than execution). The same pattern can be discerned in the judicial records of New France, where poor whites remained the main subjects of judicial prosecution.[14]

As for punishments, those that prescribed mutilation of the body targeted the enslaved and sometimes soldiers but almost never colonists. The redirection in New Orleans toward the prosecution and sentencing of Africans not only relied on fresh ways of applying existing laws but also on new laws, including rules pertaining to testimony or the possibility that a free person of color could lose their freedom if convicted of a crime. When in 1743 the free black Baptiste was convicted of theft, for instance, his punishment was to be reduced to slavery and sold at auction for the benefit of the hospital (no reference was made to Baptiste's wife, Marie, who was also a free person). Yet, even as these distinctions were drawn, there was one constant: court procedure as enunciated in the 1670 Code criminel.[15]

Criminal trials underwent three distinct phases: the information-gathering stage, the preparatory instruction, and the judgement. When in 1753 Claude Joseph Villars Dubreuil's slave Joseph was prosecuted for theft, the procureur general made an inventory of every document produced for each stage of the procedure in conformity with the 1670 Code criminel:

Slave Testimony and Court Procedure

The complaint
    First Interrogation
    Information
    Arrest
    Second Interrogation
    Information
    Verification
    Confrontation [between accused and witnesses]
    The Prosecutor's Conclusions
    Interrogation on the *sellette* [a special interrogation conducted in the prison so named for the low stool on which the defendant was made to sit]
    Definitive Judgment

Every slave trial in Louisiana followed this same general outline, with some variations dictated by the law.[16]

If tried, a defendant had a minimum of three opportunities to speak in court. The first interrogation was intended to determine if the court wanted to pursue a prosecution. If so, the defendant was interrogated a second time, after further inquiries were made. At this point, any witnesses (both bystanders or potential accomplices) were assigned to appear. Witnesses testified "secretly and separately," without the accused being present in the courtroom. Afterward, their testimony was read back to them for verification of the accuracy of the transcript, and they were asked if they persisted in that testimony. Only after this was done was the defendant brought back into the courtroom to listen while the testimony of each witness was read back to him or her a second time. The accused was then required to confront each witness in turn, and each was given the chance to address one another directly and interrogated as to whether they agreed with one another, wanted to rebut the other's deposition, or wished to modify their original deposition. Each and every one of these interrogations was scrupulously recorded, first in shorthand, then in longhand. After the latter version was approved by the deponent, it was made a part of the trial record.[17]

After the formal confrontation, if the judges so decreed, the accused could be subjected to a fourth interrogation "on the sellette." Whereas a defendant usually stood behind the bar in court, however, the interrogation on the sellette took place in the *chambre criminelle* (criminal chamber) in the prison and required that he or she be questioned while sitting on a low stool that was intended to psychologically belittle the defendant visually and spatially.

Though intended to be physically harmless, that this interrogation took place in the prison might have facilitated the use of nonjudicial threats and physical violence to extract testimony. The defendant could also at this point be sentenced to judicial torture, known as *"la question,"* which constituted a fifth interrogation and was classified as a penalty even though it was a trial procedure. Judicial torture took place in the same room where interrogations on the sellette were carried out (see Figure 10). As with the earlier interrogations in the court, the words spoken during these special interrogations were also meticulously recorded.[18]

Court-mandated judicial torture was distinguished from the nonjudicial and illegal torture of slaves, which, in theory, at least, was explicitly banned though seldom prosecuted. As enunciated in Article 38 of the 1724 code noir:

> We also forbid all our subjects in this colony, whatever their condition or rank may be, to administer, or have administered, on their own private authority, torture to their slaves, under any pretext whatsoever, nor to mutilate their limbs; under penalty of the confiscation of the slaves, and a criminal prosecution: we only permit masters, when they believe their slaves have deserved it, to have them put in irons, or beaten with switches or ropes.

So, masters could with impunity and at their own discretion (and as often as they deemed necessary) inflict corporal punishment so long as it did not rise to the undefined level of torture or mutilation. The only justification needed was a suspicion of guilt.[19]

❧❧

LA QUESTION: JUDICIAL TORTURE

Judicial torture was a feature of Latin Catholic countries, where it derived from Roman law. Torture had been suspended in England in 1166 and finally abolished there in the 1650s. Sentences of judicial torture were used sparingly on the enslaved in French colonial Louisiana, with the exception of the years 1763–1765. This departure from usual practice was the result of a brutal but short-lived law-and-order campaign that occurred at a moment of crisis for the planter class, as they confronted France's cession of Louisiana to Britain and Spain. The event led to the only time during the French regime when judicial torture was applied systematically, although almost exclusively, to the enslaved. In earlier periods, the courts argued for a more pragmatic approach that reflected their priorities. In the Illinois Country in 1725, for instance, the slave Perico was convicted of theft, but local authorities sought permission to whip him over several days instead of enforcing his sentence of judicial

Slave Testimony and Court Procedure

torture. They justified this based on the Company of the Indies's "pressing" need for slave labor, the assumption being that a body that had been whipped was in better condition for labor than one that had been subjected to judicial torture. The same reasoning might explain the generally low rate of judicial torture in a colony that, with few exceptions, did not see the arrival of slave ships after 1731 and could not risk losing its slaves.[20]

Judicial torture came in two variants that were carefully outlined in the 1670 Code criminel. The *question préparatoire* was reserved for capital offenses where guilt was inferred but there was insufficient proof to convict. Since it was intended to elicit a confession, it was applied prior to final sentencing. The *question préalable* was reserved for those already convicted of a capital offense but whose testimony under torture might elicit evidence against accomplices. Either way, there was a presumption that an accused person sentenced to judicial torture was guilty.[21]

If judicial torture was decreed, the law mandated three interrogations, before, during, and after torture. The final interrogation, or "interrogation on the mattress," was conducted after the accused was released from torture and laid onto a mattress. If he or she had confessed under torture, then the confession had to be reiterated on the mattress in order to be binding (and incur the death penalty). If not, only afflictive penalties, in other words those that caused corporal pain, but not death, could be handed down.[22]

Judicial torture was usually preceded by an interrogation on the sellette. As the 1764 court case against the enslaved Jacob and colonist Pierre Degouté dit Fleury demonstrates, this allowed for a smooth transition between the two types of ordeals (Figure 4). During an investigation for cattle theft, Fleury, a butcher, incriminated two accomplices. One of those accomplices was Jacob, an enslaved cowherd belonging to Jacques de la Chaise. Jacob and Fleury were both subjected to judicial torture after undergoing an interrogation on the sellette. During his judicial torture, Jacob was first made to kneel, bareheaded, while the judgment was read to him, which decreed that "the accused shall be presented to the ordinary *question* [torture] and interrogated on the facts resulting from the trials. Which defendant having sat on the sellette, we have proceeded to his interrogation after making him swear to tell the truth." The clerk then wrote down question and answer until page three, whereupon things took a different turn. For the second interrogation, he noted, "the defendant was undressed by the torturer, and put on the ordinary seat for torture, his arms and legs bound, in the usual manner, and we made him reiterate his oath to tell the truth." After this interrogation, in which Jacob denied some accusations and gave fuller answers to other questions, the judicial torture ended. His answers were read back to him, and he was asked one final time if he persisted in his answers and stood by them (no reference was made to a mattress, but he was no longer being tortured during this phase). He said yes and was released and handed over to the jailer. Fleury's judicial torture followed the same script. Although a sentence of judicial torture was a rarity for a French person, especially a civilian, Fleury's torture took place in 1764, in the midst of Prosecutor Nicholas Chauvin de La Frénière's law-and-order campaign.[23]

To apply judicial torture was a specialized profession. In France, the acts of inflicting pain for judicial purposes were reserved for court-appointed executioners and tormentors whose work turned them into social pariahs, paralleling the social death of a criminal condemned to be executed. This stigma made it hard to secure an executioner, and, in Louisiana, beginning in 1725, that role fell to a former slave, Louis Congo, who negotiated his manumission along with that of the woman he wished to marry as a condition of becoming executioner. The standard method of torture in Louisiana was the use of the leg brace *(le brodequin)*. Another accepted method, water boarding *(la question de l'eau avec extension)*, does not appear to have been used in the colony. The leg brace entailed having the defendant sit on the sellette while four planks of wood were placed on the inside and outside of each leg, from the feet to above the knees (Figure 10). The executioner secured the planks "by ropes passed through holes at their ends, and the ropes were then wound tightly around the planks to form a casing for both legs." Pain was inflicted and controlled by means of wooden wedges. The executioner hammered them between the two planks inside each leg, from the knees down to the ankles. Each wedge increased the pressure. For the "ordinary question," four wedges were applied; for the "extraordinary question," eight. After each wedge was driven in, the judges posed questions concerning the crime and the culpability of the defendant until the interrogation was deemed complete. Though the brodequin did not physically injure or permanently mutilate the accused, the pain and sensation it produced were especially acute, akin to having limbs broken.[24]

✄✄

"HIS MASTER'S GRACE": EXTRAJUDICIAL VIOLENCE

Prosecutions were just one means of rendering and seeking justice. The court system was not the only mechanism for identifying and chastising slaves, and the trial records are sprinkled with references to extrajudicial punishments or unofficial bargaining over perceived wrongdoings. Such evidence comes to the fore, for example, through references to masters policing their slaves' conduct and imposing corporal punishment. Extensive evidence also exists of

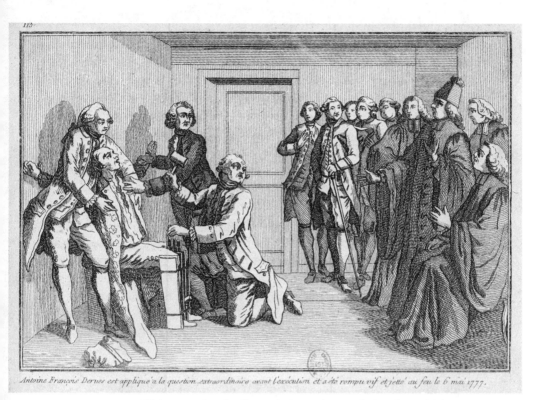

Antoine François Derues est appliqué a la question extraordinaire avant l'exécution et a été rompu vif et jetté au feu le 6 mai 1777.

FIGURE 10: Unknown, *Antoine François Derues est appliqué à la question extraordinaire avant l'exécution et a été rompu vif et jetté au feu le 6 mai 1777.* From *Portrait de Desrues et quarante planches relatives à la vie, aux crimes et à l'exécution de ce scélérat.* 1777. Engraving. Département Estampes et photographie. RESERVE QB-201 (110)-FOL. Courtesy of Bibliothèque nationale de France, Paris

In this engraving from a set about an infamous French court case, the accused is shown undergoing judicial torture using the method known as the brodequin.

the enslaved contesting this regime of violence by preemptively entering into negotiations with their masters (often via intermediaries) to secure their pardon and a lighter punishment. Echoing the way this was done in the French Antilles, they deployed gestures of contrition and submissiveness in a carefully honed performance between slave, master, and mediator.[25]

In September 1765, the aforementioned Louis, who had been arrested for theft and marronnage, claimed that he had wanted to return the items he had stolen and beg his master for mercy. He testified that he confided in Marguerite and that she advised him against doing so: "He had come to town to the house of his master with the blanket, three shirts and three handkerchiefs, and told Marguerite, 'Here, I can't stay in the woods, I need to speak to my master, and he can do what he wants with me,' that Marguerite told him that [his master] was much angry, and that out of fear he returned to the habitation" *(qu'il etoit venu avec La Couverte trois chemises et trois moucheoirs en ville à La maizon de son Maitre que La il dit a margueritte tiens je ne puis pas rester dans Le Bois il faut que je parle à mon maitre qu'il fasse Ce quil voudra que Margueritte Luy dit qu'il etoit beaucoup faché que La peur Loblige de sen Retourner à l'habitation).* She then promptly took possession of some of his stolen goods. A few days later, he tried again to have her arrange an intercession, stating "that he wanted to ask for his master's grace but that she did not want him to" *(quil vouloit demander grace à son maître mais quelle ne Le voulut pas).* Although Marguerite steadfastly refused to mediate, choosing instead to profit from Louis's situation by relieving him of some of his ill-gotten gain, Louis twice tried to find an intermediary to negotiate his return and punishment. And it would have been perfectly legal for his master to discipline his slave himself, to "do what he wants with me," so long as he followed the guidelines for extrajudicial retribution prescribed by the code noir.[26]

The 1753 case against Dubreuil's slave Joseph for theft was a highly unusual one. Dubreuil, the largest slaveowner in the colony, initiated the prosecution when he wrote to the Superior Council about his slave Joseph's constant thefts and asked that the court issue an order that the man be punished and sentenced to have his hamstring cut. Joseph's father was the overseer on the plantation. When asked in court why he had hit his father before running away, Joseph answered "that he had not hit his father in any way, he had had a dispute with him one day over work and his father gave him the whip, that this made him upset and angry and out of anger he decided to run away and wanted to break into the hut to get his blanket to go to Barataria" *(qu'il n'a point battu son pere en aucune maniere, qu'il a disputé un jour avec luy pour le travail et que son pere luy donna le fouet, qu'etant fasché et en colere il eut dessein d'aller maron Et il voulut Couper la Cabane pour prendre sa Couverte pour aller à Barataria).* By resorting to the official judicial system, Dubreuil was in effect rebuking his overseer, Joseph's father. It was also an extreme measure, invoked only because previous attempts to control and punish Joseph from within the plantation system had failed. Joseph was prosecuted again in 1753; and, in 1755, a judge on the Superior Council complained that, though Joseph had been condemned to have his hamstrings cut, this had not been done correctly, since it had not prevented him from running around at night. The councillor requested that the sentence be executed correctly.[27]

Notwithstanding Article 38 of the 1724 code noir, which prohibited mas-

Slave Testimony and Court Procedure

ters from "torturing their slaves or mutilating any limb, under any pretense whatsoever," no master was ever prosecuted in Louisiana for abusing his or her slaves. The code noir was ambivalent at best in such cases. The next clause prescribed the criminal prosecution of masters suspected of killing or mutilating their own slaves and mandated they be punished "according to the atrocity of the circumstances." Yet it allowed that masters and overseers could, in some instances, be absolved of guilt and pardoned. In practice, therefore, masters enjoyed vast latitude and protections when they sought to investigate, question, or punish their own slaves. If it is not surprising that masters took advantage of this laxness, it is still jarring to see not only how endemic extrajudicial violence and investigations were but also how frequently they are alluded to in passing in court testimony.[28]

In 1764, "Jean of the Nago nation belonging to Mr. Mandeville" *(Jean de nation nago appartenant à Mr Mandeville)* was caught and questioned about his activities while on the run. At one point, he admitted to the theft of apparel and gave an account of what happened next: "Said he had taken three pairs of breeches, five handkerchiefs and seven shirts that he carried to the plantation, that the overseer had taken all the clothes and given them to the manager, who gave them to his mistress and she had him whipped" *(a dit quil a pris trois cullottes, cinq Mouchoirs et sept chemises quil a porté à labitation que [le commandeur] luy avoit pris toutes ses ardes les avoit donné à L'econome qui les donna à sa maitresse laquelle le fit foueter pour son vol).* Another witness specified it was two hundred lashes. Summoned to testify, the enslaved overseer *("nègre commandeur")* gave a fuller reply that speaks to the informal surveillance and policing networks that were pervasive within plantations:

that on arriving at the plantation Jean Pierre *nègre* belonging to his mistress led him to his cabin and said "come, listen" and that he told him at once, "Jean has just done a bad thing, he has stolen linens and clothes that he has put in my cabin"; to which deponent said to him, "Where are the clothes?" That the said Jean Pierre answered him that the said Jean had come to get them, on hearing which he had told him off for having let [Jean Pierre] take them; that the said deponent, after searching the cabin, found four shirts that he took, and that the said Jean the accused had gone into town with the rest of the goods and that early the next day he had returned to the plantation with the said goods and had come to the cabin of the deponent who lit a fire and questioned him about where he had put the effects that he had stolen, and Jean the accused did not want to admit the truth, but pressed by the deponent he gave him two shirts that were wrapped in some handkerchiefs, that the deponent said to him that "that is not all, that one had to answer the truth," to which [Jean Pierre] said that the shirt he had on his body was among those [stolen] and he gave it to him along with two pairs of breeches and a white waistcoat, the said handkerchiefs mentioned above numbered six. That the said deponent immediately called the white manager, and gave him all the goods, which is all that he said.

---

que en arrivant à l'habitation jean pierre negre appartenant à sa maitresse le mena dans sa Cabanne et luy dit tien Ecoute et quil luy dit tout de suitte jean vient de faire un coup il a vollé du Linge et des ardes quil a mis en ma Cabanne, lequel deposant luy dit où Estoitent les hardes, que le dit jean pierre luy Repondit que led. jean Estoit venu les prendre sur quoy il l'avoit grondé pour les avoir laissé Emporté Que led. deposant apres avoir cherché dans la Cabanne il trouva quatre chemises quil Ramassa et que led. jean accusé Estoit venu En ville avec le Restant des Effets et que le lendemain bon matin il Estoit Retourné a l'habitation avec lesd. Effets et seroit Entre dans la Cabanne du deposant qui dans linstant auroit alumé du feu et l'auroit interrogé où il avoit mis les Effets quil avoit vollé lequel jean accusé ne voullu point luy avouer la verité mais pressé par le deposant il luy Remit deux chemises qui estoient envopée [sic] dans des mouchoirs quil avoit sur Luy que le deposant luy Repliqua que ce netoit pas la le tous quil falloit avouer La verité sur quoy il luy dit que la chemise quil avoit sur le corps etoit du nombre quil luy Remit avec deux paire de culotes et une veste blanche lesquels mouchoirs mentionnes cy dessus consistoient au nombre de six que le dit deposant appella sur le Champ L'econome blanc qui y Estoit et luy Remist tous les dits Effets qui est tous ce quil a dit

The slave driver seems to have been very successful in getting Jean Pierre to talk, though he did not give details of his methods beyond stating ominously that he had "lit a fire," "questioned," and "pressed" the man. The mistress and her white overseer undoubtedly planned to carry out Jean's punishment in-house: they had him under their control on the plantation. But a legal complaint had already been lodged, setting in motion an investigation, and Jean Pierre's eventual arrest and trial led to the court convicting him of theft and running away. The judges sentenced him to be beaten with switches *(verges)*, to have his hamstring cut, and to be branded with the letter "V" (for *voleur*, or "thief") on his cheek.[29]

Slave Testimony and Court Procedure

The presumption has to be that, most of the time, owners routinely disciplined their own slaves informally and independently of the court system and that criminal trials were just one rather exceptional mechanism for controlling, subjugating, and punishing the enslaved. Conversely, as explored in Chapter 4, testimony also reveals evidence of the enslaved policing each other and meting out justice among themselves, independently of masters and overseers. The irony is not lost that it is in trial records that the enslaved offer glimpses of the pervasiveness of a range of extrajudicial surveillance, prosecution, and corporal punishment that is not documented elsewhere. Violence was not restricted to punishments but was integral to the brutality of a labor system in which a slave like Jupiter dit Gamelle, who did not produce enough for his master, "was shouted at, threatened and sometimes ill-treated" *(Grondé Et Menacé Et quelques fois Maltraité)*. Here, scattered throughout the trials, is evidence of endemic violence of the most intimate kind—up close and personal, commonplace, mentally and physically coercive, and invasive. The legal justice system shared some of these features.[30]

SENTENCES AND AFFLICTIVE PENALTIES

There was one arena in which the enslaved did not have the opportunity to speak before the court, and that was at the point of sentencing and punishment. After all interrogations were complete, the judges deliberated and pronounced their verdict. On September 10, 1764, they rendered judgment in a complex case with multiple defendants, accomplices, and witnesses. The chief defendant, thirty-five-year-old Louis (also known as Foÿ), was convicted of running away and theft and condemned to the most agonizing of capital punishments: to be broken on a wheel and then left on a pole on the road to Bayou Saint Jean. Since Article 36 of the code noir stipulated that an owner was entitled to financial compensation for the economic loss of a slave, Louis was appraised as to his value, in this case, an artificially low price of five hundred livres. Louis's sentence called for him to first atone before the parish church by begging pardon with a rope around his neck while holding a lit torch, on his knees, his head bare, stripped down to his shirt. Those words, if he ever uttered them, were not recorded. Next, he was to be conducted to the public square where he would be bound to a Saint Andrew's cross, which represented the X-shaped cross on which the saint was martyred. This particular cross was a symbol that would have resonated with Kongo belief systems, raising the question whether the executioner Louis Congo ever noted this parallel. The executioner was to then break Louis's legs, thighs,

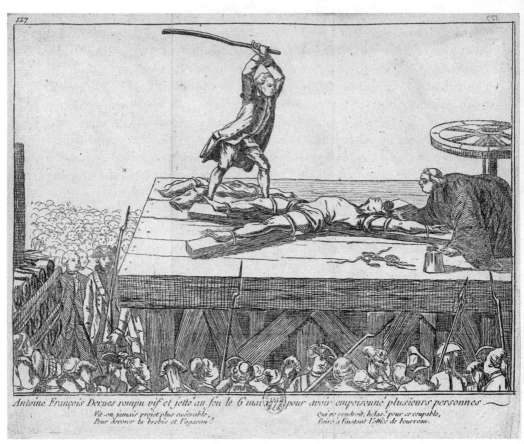

Antoine François Derues rompu vif et jetté au feu le 6 mai 1777 pour avoir empoisonné plusieurs personnes —

Vit-on jamais projet plus exécrable,
Pour dévorer la brebis et l'agneau ?

Qui ne voudroit, hélas, pour ce coupable,
Faire à l'instant l'office de bourreau.

FIGURE 11: Unknown, *Antoine François Derues rompu vif et jetté au feu le 6 mai 1777 pour avoir empoisonné plusieurs personnes*. From *Portrait de Desrues en quarante planches relatives à la vie, aux crimes, et à l'exécution de ce scélérat*. 1777. Engraving. Département Estampes et photographie. RESERVE QB-201 (110)-FOL. Courtesy of Bibliothèque nationale de France, Paris

In this engraving, the executioner is shown breaking the body of the condemned on the cross. A carriage wheel is shown on the scaffold, at the ready if the condemned had been sentenced to have his body left exposed on the wheel.

and back, after which he was to be tied to a carriage wheel, face upturned "to heaven," until he died. Finally, his body was to be taken to the Bayou road and left exposed on the wheel until it was consumed by wild animals or rotted, whichever came first (Figure 11). The court showed Louis some mercy, adding a *retunta* (or secret instruction) as a codicil to the judgment. It was not uncommon for an executioner to finish a victim off before tying him or her to the wheel, and, in this case, the retunta decreed that Louis should not

Slave Testimony and Court Procedure

feel any blows while alive but that he should first be strangled in secret. Every single one of these steps conformed to those prescribed by French law and applied in criminal cases prosecuted in France.[31]

In addition to sentencing Louis, the court convicted Cézar as Louis's accomplice, and he, too, was given the death penalty. Another accomplice, Marie-Jeanne, was convicted of receiving the stolen clothing and sentenced to be beaten with switches throughout the town and branded with the letter "V" for *voleuse* (meaning "thief") on her right shoulder. The hot iron used for branding (which had a diameter about the size of a large coin) was supposed to be applied after the flesh had been deadened to minimize the pain. As a form of punishment, its chief function was to stigmatize the victim and serve as a useful identifier in case of recidivism. Finally, the court pronounced its sentence against two other enslaved women, Louison and Comba, for aiding and concealing Cézar and Louis. The women were condemned to a standard defamatory (rather than physical) sentence but one that must have been especially difficult to undergo: they were to be present as witnesses at Louis's execution. All the other slaves implicated in the case escaped conviction and were sent back to their masters, who were likely relieved to have their slaves returned to them unscathed but who were just as likely to chastise and punish them for having gotten embroiled in the court case.[32]

The sentences in this case might seem random, but they were, in fact, consistent with the law: each one of the penalties fit one of the nine levels (and twenty-five subgroups) of punishments itemized in the 1670 Code criminel. Outside the military, however, afflictive punishments incorporating mutilation of the body were rarely imposed in France by the late seventeenth century. Not coincidentally, in France's colonies, convicted slaves bore the brunt of afflictive punishments. As outlined in Articles 27–32 of the 1724 code noir, whipping and branding with the fleur-de-lis were mandated in convictions for theft, but the death penalty could be imposed for serious thefts. Running away for longer than one month incurred a sentence of having the ears cut and branding on the shoulder, second recidivism meant having the hamstring cut and branding on the other shoulder, and third recidivism resulted in the death penalty. Capital punishment was also prescribed when a slave struck his or her master or a member of their master's family.[33]

The Superior Council decreed sentences and sometimes commuted them, occasionally as the result of an intercession made by an influential figure. In 1730 in the Illinois Country, Mamantouensa, the chief of the Kaskaskia Illinois Indians, stepped forward to ask for clemency when the African Jean Baxes was convicted of assaulting a colonist. Instead of the death penalty, to which he was originally sentenced in accordance with the code noir (see

Articles 27 and 28), he received a sentence that combined afflictive with defaming punishments: he was beaten on three different days, but he also had to get on his knees and present a public apology to the aggrieved party and bow before the victim each time he encountered him.[34]

One unquestioned benefit of the court commuting the death penalty was that the accused lived another day to labor as a slave. Self-serving colonists spoke openly of the need to spare slaves' lives, even when they thought them guilty. Antoine-Simon Le Page du Pratz believed that there was "nothing surprising in seeing Negro thieves when they are short of everything, as I have seen them badly nourished, badly dressed and made to sleep on the ground." This view of slaves as intrinsically criminal — even if only as a result of necessity — was widespread enough that the Superior Council invoked it in 1733 when that body handed down a reduced sentence to two slaves convicted of stealing sacks of rice. The council justified its decision by arguing that, "If we were to hang all the slaves who are thieves not one would have his life saved, for they are all, more or less, thieves."[35]

Not only death sentences were commuted. In 1765, the court issued its judgment against Babette, convicted of stealing sixteen piastres, which she used to go shopping for clothing and treats consisting of "a cotton skirt and a jacket from Sr Nicolet and another skirt from Mistress St Martin; a gold cane handle from La Rochelle, the army drummer; a silk handkerchief and a blue handkerchief from the merchant next to the jail, known as Cassale; some confectionery and pecans from Mistress de Lorier; and a pair of shoes for one piastre from Mistress Olivier Pecherit" *(une Jupe de Cotton et un Cazaquin ches Le Sr Nicolete et une autre Jupe chez Made St martin, et un Joug D'or quelle a Dit avoir acheté de La Rochelle tambour, un mouchoir de soye et un Mouchoir Bleu, du nommé Cassale, Marchand à Côté de La prizon, des Dragées pour Cinquante sols chez La Dame de Lorier et Cinquante sols de pacanes, une paire de souliers chez La Dame olivier pecherit pour une piastre Gourde).* Because of her young age, the court commuted her punishment to forty lashes to be administered in the public square for all to see. She was all of eleven years old.[36]

✂✂

CONCLUSION

It is impossible to know just how the child Babette responded to the court's judgment, to her sentence, or to the punishment meted out to her. Court transcripts were selective soundscapes. Although they aimed to constitute a true and accurate record of words spoken, specifically in the back-and-forth between questions and answers, they were not records of the whole per-

Slave Testimony and Court Procedure

formance of justice. They did not seek to capture every element of a trial or every feature of testimony. Nor did they record defendants' reactions to judgments, such as whether or not they sat in stony silence, gasped, cried tears, or hurled insults when their sentence was pronounced. Nor did trial records make note of whether the accused begged forgiveness, as Louis (Foÿ) was expected to do, following stated convention, when he was taken to the entrance to the church before being broken on the wheel. Finally, transcripts did not include the agonizing sounds of convicted felons being put to death nor did they make note of the noises produced during judicial torture: the creaking sound of the leg brace as it was cranked more and more tightly during the hour or so that the ordeal lasted or the victim's cries of pain. Court records omitted these sounds of suffering, just as they were devoid of deponents' gestures, looks, mannerisms, facial expressions, accents, and intonation during their testimonies. These, too, were components of the performative aspects of court procedure, a performance shaped by words, by sound, by the spatial environment, by sartorial conventions, by gestures, and by the rituals of the court. What testimony does offer is access to the words of the enslaved, allowing the biographies of enslaved individuals to be uncovered virtually as they themselves narrated them.[37]

CHAPTER 2

"It's Only from God That We Ask Forgiveness"

Louison

DEPOSITION OF LOUISON, NEW ORLEANS, JUNE 13, 1752

Told us that eight or ten days ago, while doing the laundry by the riverbank, in front of the house of the nuns, along with some other *negresses,* both those who serve the hospital and those who belong to the nuns, she saw the said Pochenet come, whom she knew for having been sick at the hospital for a very long time, who had a bayonet in his hand and who approached the *négresse* Babet, that she saw that he was tinkering with a piece of wood with the bayonet, by cutting the wood, and that she did not hear what he was telling her. That a moment later, she saw this man giving her a blow of the bayonet on the stomach, that she ran to this *négresse* to rescue her, that this man began to swear and to get angry with her because she was telling him, "Why did he want to assassinate this *négresse?*" That then he gave her blows with the bayonet on the head and the body, but that having a hat on her head and a corset of good [strong] cloth, that meant that she was not very injured that time; that is why she began to flee to reach the convent. She fell, the said Pochenet then gave her more bayonet blows to her body and her arm, which pierced her. In spite of that, she wanted again to flee. The said Pochenet said to her, "Go on, kneel and ask my forgiveness." She replied, "It's only from God that we ask forgiveness." That in spite of this, she got on her knees and said to him, "Sorry, Sir." That in spite of this, he gave her two or more blows with the bayonet. And during that time, all the other *négresses* fled toward the convent and the hospital screaming, "Help, we are being assassinated, there is a soldier who is chasing all of us with a bayonet." That in that moment Baptiste, her husband, with a young Frenchman and others from the hospital, ran to her aid. And when they reached her and the said Pochenet, he gave blows of the bayonet to her husband and this young Frenchman, who both evaded his blows. And that having resisted to try to catch and seize this mad man, he gave a blow of his bayonet to the hand of the said Baptiste, her husband, from which he is very injured. And as other people were coming, they seized him and took him to the hospital where he was swearing excessively while still acting the madman, after which the guard came and took him and she was bandaged. Which is all that she remembers of the affair in question, affirming that it is the truth.

Nous a dit quil y a huit ou dix Jours Etant à laver au bord du fleuve vis à vis la maison des dames Religieuses avec plusieurs autres negresses tant Celles servant à Lhopital que Celles appartenant aux Religieuses Elle vit venir led. pochenet quelle Connoissoit pour avoir été malade à Lhopital tres Longtemps qui avoit une Bayonnette à la main, Et qui aprocha de la Negresse Babet quelle vit quil Badinoit sur un Bois avec sa bayonette En Coupant le bois Et quelle N'entendoit pas Ce quil Luy disoit qu'un moment apres Elle vit Cet homme qui luy porta un Coup de bayonnette sur LEstomac, quelle Courut à Cette Negresse pour la secourirc que Cet homme se mit à Jurer Et à s'emporter Contr'elle parce quelle Luy disoit pourquoy il vouloit assasiner Cette femme, que la dessus il Luy donna des Coups de bayonette sur la teste Et sur le Corps mais qu'ayant un Chapeau sur la teste Et un Corset de bonne Etoffe Cela fit quelle ne fut pas beaucoup blessé [dans] Ce temps la, C'Est pourquoy Elle Se mit à fuir pour gagner le Couvent, Elle tomba, led. pochenet Luy donna alors plusieurs Coups de bayone dans le Corps et dans le bras qui Entrerent malgré cela Elle Voulut Encore fuir, led. Pochenet Luy dit, allons met toy à Genoux Et demande moy pardon; Elle Luy dit L'on ne demande pardon qu'à dieu, que malgré Cela Elle se mit à genoux Et Luy dit pardon Monsr que Malgré Cela Il Luy porta Encore deux ou trois Coups de bayonnette Et pendant Ce temps là toutes les autres Negresse se sauvèrent En Criant au Couvent Et à Lhopital au secours on nous assassine, Voila un soldat qui Court après nous touttes avec une bayonnette, que dans Ce moment Baptiste son Mary avec un jeune françois Et autres de Lhopital Coururent à son secours, Et lorsqu'il furent aupres d'Elle Et dudt Pochenet, il porta des Coups de bayonnette à son mary Et à Ce jeune francois qui Evitèrent ses Coups, Es qu'ayant Resisté pour tâcher de prendre De saisir Cet homme furieux il En porta un Coup de sa bayonnette dans la main dudit baptiste son mary dont il Est fort blessé Et Comme il y vint d'autres

personnes on Le saisit Et on l'amena a Lhopital où il juroit extrême-
ment en faisant toujours le furieux, ensuite de quoy la garde vint qui
L'Emmena Et on la fit panser qui Est tout Ce quelle se souvient de L'affaire en question nous Nous affirmant que Cest la verité.[1]

On June 13, 1752, officials from the Superior Council of Louisiana made
their way to the Ursuline convent in New Orleans to hear the testimony of
two enslaved African women, Babette and Louison, belonging to the nuns.
The previous week, Pierre Antoine Pochenet, an inebriated French soldier,
had attacked them in broad daylight, leaving one severely injured and the
other near death. The prosecutors, for a change, were not soliciting the testimony of slaves as defendants, accomplices, or witnesses, but, instead, as
the aggrieved parties. The investigation is therefore highly unusual in that it
documents an act of violence committed by a French person against enslaved
Africans whose deposition the court sought out, an exceptional circumstance
not because of the law, which allowed such investigations and testimony even
when French men or women committed crimes against slaves, but because
this aspect of the law was rarely invoked.[2]

The assault occurred around two o'clock on the afternoon of Wednesday,
June 7, while Babette and Louison were doing laundry for the convent on
the riverbank in front of the convent-hospital complex where they lived and
worked (Figure 12). The attack by the drunken Pochenet was unprovoked.
The twenty-four-year-old soldier hailed from Mondidieu in Picardie, northern France, and was a member of Augustin Le Pelletier de la Houssaye's
company. He had been recently discharged from the hospital, otherwise he
would have been with his unit, stationed at the English Turn. He had at some
point during the day gone to the barracks and grabbed his bayonet, which
was a removable, dagger-like blade that could be used as a hand weapon but
was intended to be attached to the end of a musket so that the gun could be
used interchangeably to fire or to pierce (Figure 13). The bayonet was small
enough for him to slip under his waistcoat, and it was with this weapon that
he stabbed both women.[3]

Babette did not testify; she was too delirious and incoherent for speech,
so the burden would fall to the injured Louison to bear witness to the violence at the core of the investigation. But, over the course of her testimony,
she also referenced medicine, clothing, family formation, community ties,
labor practices, labor relations, and Catholicism. These details provide further layers of insights, telling not only about her experience that day but also
about how she made sense of her world. At the same time, her deposition
reveals the scope she had for voicing her reaction to this act of aggression,

FIGURE 12: *Ursuline Convent*. New Orleans, facing the quay.
Photo courtesy of Philippe Halbert

FIGURE 13: *Art Militaire, Exercice,* Plate I (detail). From Denis Diderot and Jean le Rond d'Alembert, *Encyclopédie, ou dictionnaire raisonné des sciences, des arts, et des métiers; Recueil de planches,* I (Paris, 1762–1772). Reproduced from the original held by the Department of Special Collections of the University Libraries of Notre Dame Figures 6 through 8 show a soldier attaching his bayonet.

whether during her actual encounter with the soldier or in her retelling of the event to court officials.

Two other slaves who were not connected to the convent, Manon and François, were later brought in to testify about their own violent encounters with Pochenet that late spring day. In each case, Pochenet had foisted himself onto the slave in question and made a demand, and, each time, the slave rebuffed him, causing him to escalate to an act of physical aggression. Acts of verbal and corporal violence are inherently intimate in that they aim to shatter physical and emotional boundaries between attacker and victim. In their encounters with the soldier, Louison, Manon, and François showed themselves unwilling to submit passively to the forced intimacy he sought to impose on them. In the way they narrated and characterized these interactions, they reveal how well the enslaved grasped that they need not be submissive to all whites. Though they lived in a slave society, they recognized the power differentials among colonists and understood that soldiers were among the

Louison

most marginalized of whites. Louison's testimony, in particular, shows how religion could become enmeshed in that power dynamic. Her professed faith proved key to how she articulated her individuality and projected her character. Drawing on Catholicism as a means of asserting her moral authority over the soldier, she subverted the balance of power, claiming for herself a role, not as submissive victim, but as respectable guardian of the faith.[4]

THE DAY'S EVENTS

Here was a fairly straightforward case whose factual details were widely corroborated. Events had transpired in public places, and they were witnessed by many more onlookers than those who testified. The case against Pochenet provided the judges with a surprisingly clear-cut basis for their decision and sentence: unambiguous signs of injury from a long sharp object, a damaged bayonet, numerous eyewitnesses, and an accused who did nothing to refute his guilt beyond invoking his drunkenness in denying his recall of the day's events. The defendant was interrogated twice. The first interrogatory took place in the courthouse on June 12. He began by stating that "he does not remember and he has not done what he is being questioned about" (*A dit qu'il ne se souvient point de cela et qu'il n'a point fait ce dont on l'interrogé*). He continued to maintain that he had no recollection of the events of that day beyond going to the canteen with his friend and that he did not have his bayonet with him at that time, adding that "they could question him all they wanted, he would still not remember anything on the subject, having been dead drunk when they put him in prison" (*qu'on a beau le questionner qu'il ne scauroit rien dire à ce sujet étant yvre mort lorsqu'on la mis en prison*). During his interrogation on the *sellette* (a special interrogation conducted in the prison so named for the low stool on which the defendant was made to sit), he once again denied any recollection.[5]

Louison and Babette were the only two victims cited in the formal complaint. Though Babette's physical and emotional state prevented her from testifying, Louison was able to make a statement about the assault. As the investigation proceeded, seven others were called to testify: four soldiers (including one who worked as a surgeon's aid at the hospital) and three slaves. Jean-Baptiste, Louison's enslaved husband, was not called to testify, since he was related to one of the victims — that is, to one of the parties in the case. Nor was he included in the suit. Despite Louison's description of his hand as "very injured," the surgeon did not submit a report about his injury. Of the three other slaves called as witnesses, one, François, owned by the Ursulines, only testified about what he had seen. The other two, another François and a woman named Manon, had interacted with Pochenet one-on-one. Pochenet had victimized these two in different ways and had also drawn his bayonet against them, but he had not succeeded in injuring either, and they were likewise not made party to the suit, though they were called to testify. Legally, only one denunciation was sufficient for the investigation to proceed.

The main point of deliberation for the Superior Council was to decide whether Pochenet had acted with premeditation. Whether the women lived or not—in other words, whether it was murder or attempted murder—was not a determining factor from a French legal standpoint. The principal issue, according to the 1670 Code criminel, hinged on whether the action was premeditated. Given this legal context, the lines of questioning sought to determine the timing: had he retrieved his bayonet before or after getting drunk? Pochenet, in a rare moment of recollection (or an attempt at self-preservation), asserted that it was the latter. As for those testifying as victims and witnesses, they would meander along in their own fashion, hewing to their own logic rather than that of the court.[6]

The day probably started calmly enough. It was washing day for both the hospital and convent slaves, and the women were at the river that Wednesday afternoon doing the laundry. This could have included washing the linens for the hospital and the convent and perhaps also articles of clothing belonging to paying customers, which constituted a side business for the Ursulines. Laundering was arduous work that involved three key steps. First, the linens were boiled in tubs of water mixed with homemade or imported soaps. This took place in the convent's washhouse (Figure 14). Then the women went down to the river to submerge the linens and scrub and pound them on the riverbank—a particularly important step for linens soiled from use in a hospital. Last, they left the clothes out to dry. On that rainy day, Louison, Babette, Manon, and sundry other enslaved women were absorbed in scrubbing and pounding, physically demanding labor that nonetheless allowed for sociability as they worked communally and unsupervised by the river's edge in front of the convent. As they labored, they were oblivious to the series of events being set in motion across town that would shortly upend their own lives.[7]

Those events began, by all accounts, with Pochenet getting prodigiously drunk ("pissed" [gris] and "dead drunk" [yvre mort]) at the canteen within the barracks, which flanked the Place d'armes (now Jackson Square) (Figure 15). By early afternoon, he had left the canteen and wandered toward the river, perhaps stopping at one of the city's many inns or taverns on his way; such establishments were not supposed to serve soldiers (or slaves or Indians), but they did. François, a Creole slave belonging to the Widow Broutin,

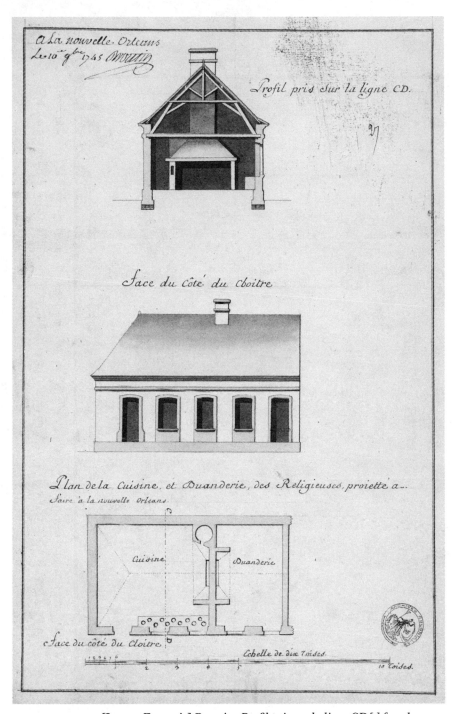

FIGURE 14: [Ignace-François] Broutin, *Profil pris sur la ligne CD[,] face du côté du cloître [et] plan de la cuisine, et buanderie, des Religieuses, proietté [sic] a faire à la Nouvelle Orleans.* Nov. 10, 1745. FR ANOM F3 290 27. Courtesy of Les archives nationales d'outre-mer, Aix-en-Provence, France The washhouse *(buanderie)* shared a wall (and fireplace) with the kitchen *(cuisine)*.

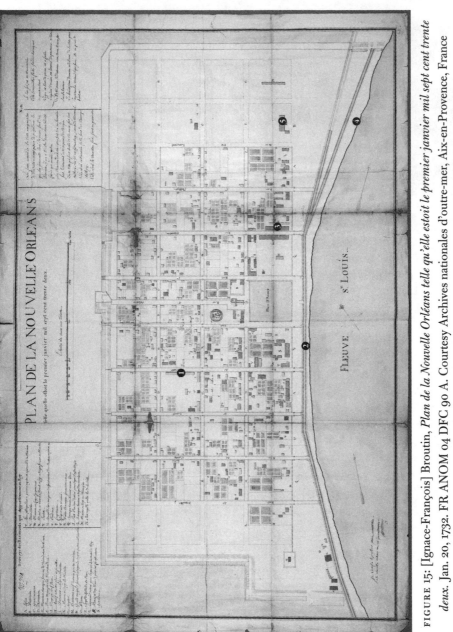

FIGURE 15: [Ignace-François] Broutin, *Plan de la Nouvelle Orléans telle qu'elle estoit le premier janvier mil sept cent trente deux. Jan. 20, 1732.* FR ANOM 04 DFC 90 A. Courtesy Archives nationales d'outre-mer, Aix-en-Provence, France The key superimposed on the map marks the places Pierre Antoine Pochenet stopped and his movements on June 13, 1752: 1 shows the canteen, 2 the market, 3 the king's warehouse, 4 the riverbank in front of the Ursuline convent, and 5 the Ursuline convent and hospital.

was returning home from the riverfront, where he had bought plums for his master. The market was located on the levee to the left of the Place d'armes, in front of the government building, and it was there that he had the bad luck to run into Pochenet. Though perfect strangers, Pochenet apparently demanded, "Give me some plums" *(Donne moi des prunes)*. When François told him (obsequiously but not without some bravado in the circumstances), "If you want some, Sir, they sell them there, you could buy some" *(sy vous en voulez Monsieur on en vend là vous pourrez en acheter),* Pochenet knocked the plums out of his hand, slapped him, then, drawing a "naked bayonet from underneath his waistcoat" *(de dessous sa veste une bayonnette toute nüe),* tried in vain to strike him. François concluded his account by stating that he managed to escape and went in search of the police, whereupon Pochenet ran off in the direction of the king's warehouse.[8]

The tale was then taken up by "Marianne, known as Manon, creole of this colony, belonging to the estate of Kintrec known as Dupont" *(Marianne, ditte Manon Negresse Creolle de Cette Colonie appartenante à la Succession de Kintrec dit Dupont).* Though she did not give her age, when Joseph Le Kintrek dit Dupont's first wife died, in 1747, an inventory of their assets was produced, and Manon was listed among the slaves in their possession:

> Item a *negresse* named Manon aged twenty years old and her two children, namely Marie aged five and Julie two years old, appraised together three thousand livres.

Manon would have been twenty-five in 1752 and her daughters aged ten and seven years old. No other information about her is known, including whether she had more children.[9]

Manon recounted how she and two other enslaved women were doing the laundry on the riverbank "across from the barracks on one side of the *habitation* [plantation]" *(vis a vis les Cazernes dun Cote de l'habitation)* when Pochenet, whom she knew from sight, approached them asking that they wash his handkerchief. The women refused, whereupon he took out his bayonet and pursued them deep into the river. Unable to reach them, he came back to the riverbank and trampled their washing. Observing that they, too, planned to call the guard, he fled again, toward the king's warehouse (Figure 15). It was following this second incident that Pochenet, continuing along, ended up in the vicinity of the convent, setting the stage for a third and final violent episode with Babette and Louison.[10]

According to Louison, Pochenet first approached her companion, Babette, while carving a piece of wood with his bayonet and spoke to her, though "she did not hear what he was telling her." The next thing she knew, he had thrust Babette in the stomach with the blade. It was then that Louison ran to Babette's aid while the other women hastened toward the convent. But Pochenet now turned on her. As she fled from him, Louison stumbled and fell, and he stabbed her with the sharp point of the bayonet, piercing her body and her arm, before delivering another two or three blows. Help eventually came from the convent and hospital. Louison's husband, Jean-Baptiste, was among the rescuers, along with "a young Frenchman and others from the hospital." Together, they eventually managed to subdue Pochenet and hold him, pending the arrival of the guard. Jean-Baptiste suffered an injury while trying to restrain the soldier.

Four witnesses corroborated this final chapter, all of whom were present in front of the convent-hospital complex by the quay. The enslaved François, who belonged to the Ursulines, was called to action from the pharmacy where he was working, and he witnessed Pochenet trying to strike Jean-Baptiste and cut his hand. The other three witnesses were French. One was on sentry duty at the hospital; he only saw some slaves drag the drunken, swearing Pochenet into the hospital yard. Another soldier, a patient at the hospital, was sent out by Mother St. Magdelaine to investigate and only got there in time to see the drunken Pochenet attack a sentry. He recognized Louison and Babette as they were brought into the hospital, "dangerously wounded," for treatment. Joseph Badon, a young surgeon-soldier, was the sole white eyewitness to the attack against Louison. He testified that he had seen Pochenet assault the women by the water's edge and then strike one of them with the bayonet. According to the 1724 code noir, that there was a white eyewitness meant that no slaves needed to testify, and Badon could have filed the deposition instead of Louison. He had not, however, witnessed Pochenet's attack on Babette.[11]

It ultimately took three men (Louison's husband, Jean-Baptiste, plus the sentry and the convalescing soldier) to subdue Pochenet. To disarm him, they had to throw wood and bricks at him. Then, once they had overpowered him, they had to literally drag him kicking and screaming into the hospital. But his "horrendous swearing" led the nun in charge to order him taken back outside, where two sentries stood guard over him until the police arrived to take him away to jail.[12]

"SHE DID WHAT OUR MOST LOWLY SLAVES DID": THE URSULINE CONVENT

Court officials waited a week before proceeding to the convent to solicit depositions from Babette and Louison, one day after receiving the surgeon's report on their wounds and conducting their first interrogation of Pochenet.

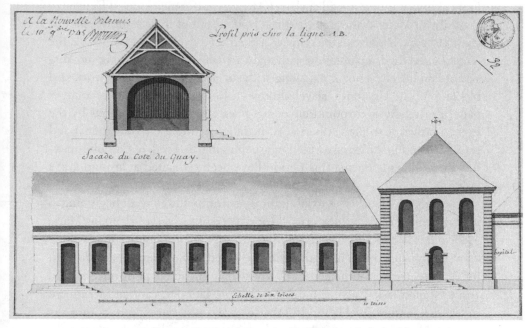

FIGURE 16: [Ignace-François] Broutin, *Profil et facade du coté du quay [du couvent des religieuses ursulines].* Nov. 10, 1745. FR ANOM F3 290 32.
Courtesy Archives nationales d'outre-mer, Aix-en-Provence, France
When the 1745 convent was built, the facade facing the quay was the front entrance.

Because of the victims' injuries (and the fact that the Ursulines, the slave-owners, were a cloistered order), the court officials had to walk the four blocks to the hospital to record their statements in the presence of the nuns, rather than have them appear before the Superior Council as was the norm.

As they made their way onto the convent-hospital grounds, entering on the quay side, which was the main entrance, the officials would have taken note that the building was brand new. Designed in 1745 to replace the earlier, crumbling structures from 1733, the new convent, of plastered brick (the only edifice to survive to the present-day virtually intact from the French colonial period), was completed in the early 1750s, just about the time Pochenet went on his rampage (Figure 16).[13]

Though the Ursulines were a teaching order, the nuns arrived in New Orleans in 1727 charged not only with educating girls but especially with overseeing the military hospital (which is shown on the right-hand side of Figure 16, abutting the Ursulines' chapel). They were to care for soldiers, sailors, the king's workers, and slaves as well as indigent colonists. The New Orleans Ursulines differed from their counterparts in France (and in New

France) in that they also had enslaved Africans and some enslaved Indians to assist them. Many of these individuals labored out of their sight. As part of the nuns' agreement with the crown for their establishment in Louisiana, the king granted them a plantation with eight arpents of frontage along the Mississippi on the city's outskirts, along with six enslaved Africans to work said plantation. The Ursulines' slaveholdings in Louisiana were part of a larger pattern of religious corporations being given slaves and plantations by the French crown with the explicit goal of underwriting their educational and hospital commitments; slaveholdings belonging to French Catholic institutions worldwide during this period have been estimated at around 2,282 slaves.[14]

The nuns also had slaves to labor for them within the convent beginning in 1727, when the convent took on a "Moor" servant to "serve" them, as Marie Madeleine Hachard, Sister St. Stanislas, one of the founding members of the convent, explained it to her father. She exhorted him to "not be scandalized, for it is the manner of the country." These convent slaves performed skilled and unskilled tasks such as food preparation, laundry, care and treatment of the sick, and manual labor. In other words, these slaves were not for the Ursuline sisters' personal use but for the labor associated with the plantation, hospital, and school.[15]

In France, the kind of domestic work done by slaves in the colonies would have been carried out by the convent's servants. The New Orleans convent did have white servants who undertook various auxiliary tasks. Anne Galbrun, widow of Barthelemy Dubic, for example, lived in the New Orleans convent and did yardwork, though she also conducted business on the Ursulines' behalf. Religious orders also had other means of securing manual and household labor, including the use of converse (also known as lay or domestic) nuns charged with the more menial tasks. In the eighteenth century, the Ursuline order formally distinguished between three categories of nuns: choir nuns, converse nuns, and *soeurs tourières* (mature single or widowed women who served as intermediaries between the cloistered sisters and the outside world). Both choir and converse nuns took the three ordinary vows of poverty, chastity, and obedience. But only choir sisters took the fourth vow of education, a fundamental distinction among the members of this teaching order. Although choir sisters might be called on to perform household tasks (and might be exalted for doing so), they were primarily charged with singing God's praises and educating their charges. In contrast, converse sisters were explicitly associated with domestic work and denied the right to sing in the choir and take on teaching duties. As early as 1618, the papal bull establishing the Ursuline congregation of Bordeaux enunciated that converse nuns, after having taken their vows, "will only be occupied with housework." It is notable, therefore, that within the New Orleans convent, one choir nun, Renée Yviguel, was praised by the other sisters for doing "what our most lowly slaves did. She ground corn and rice, chopped wood, and did the washing." Not only does this comment illustrate some of the activities that enslaved women were customarily charged with, it is also significant in that it singles out Yviguel for seeking out occupations "most humiliating and disgusting," which would have been unimaginable if she had been a choir nun in a convent in France. The local work environment provided the broader context for the convent labor regime to which enslaved Africans had to adapt.[16]

When the attack occurred in 1752, there were fourteen nuns in the New Orleans convent, together with an unknown number of their convent-based slaves. Rounding out the population of the convent were an indeterminate number of boarders and day students, some of whom were enslaved Africans and Indians sent to the convent for religious instruction. They all lived within the same walled compound. Like the 1733 convent, the 1745 buildings were designed for function but simultaneously established and upheld hierarchical distinctions between nuns, paying boarders, indigent orphans, and enslaved workers, down to separate eating and convalescing spaces for the various categories of residents (see Figure 7). This ostensibly female space was disrupted by the presence of the occasional orphan boy, enslaved males, and, especially, the fluctuating gaggle of sick and convalescing soldiers, sailors, workers, and poor whites who took up temporary residence in the hospital as they sought treatment and healing. In other words, the nuns could not leave the confines of the convent, but outsiders—including males—could and did enter. This was the environment in which Babette and Louison lived and toiled.[17]

Babette and Louison were brought to the convent under different circumstances that would prove relevant to the outcome of the court case. The Ursulines owned Babette (the mortally wounded woman) outright. Louison, who would testify, and her husband, Jean-Baptiste, had been granted to the Ursulines in 1744 under the terms of an agreement with the crown to work for the hospital. In addition to Louison, her husband, and their children, three other enslaved Africans were included in this contract: Pierrot; his wife, Jeanneton; and another older man, Sans Quartier. Together, this little group was separated from their kin and community on the king's plantation and moved across the river to the town of New Orleans. Their perspective shifted with the move; no longer did they look out toward the town from the opposite bank (Figure 17). Now, it was from the quay close by the convent that they

FIGURE 17: [Jean Pierre Lassus], *Veüe et perspective de La Nouvelle-Orleans*. 1726. FR ANOM 04 DFC 71A.
Courtesy Archives nationales d'outre-mer, Aix-en-Provence, France
Taken from the bank opposite the town, the right foreground shows enslaved Africans clearing the land that would become the Company of the Indies's plantation.

looked out across the river toward their former place of captivity and those who still lived there, whom they only saw sporadically, perhaps on Sundays for church or during other gatherings. They were one-off donations; the only slave whom the king contractually agreed to replace in the event of his death was Jean-Baptiste.[18]

The 1744 agreement reveals that Louison would have been thirty-eight years old at the time of Pochenet's attack and that she served as the hospital's cook, which granted her higher status. Given colonists' frequent fears of being intentionally poisoned by their slaves, she must have enjoyed the Ursulines' trust to be assigned the task of preparing food. Her enslaved husband, Jean-Baptiste, who was the same age, had even more authority as an apothecary (pharmacist) and surgeon's aide. As such, he worked closely with the Ursuline medical practitioners.

Louison and Jean-Baptiste were baptized and married according to Catholic rites, and they had at least three children. In 1744, they were listed as the parents of a five-year-old son, Nicolas (who had died by 1760), and a two-and-a-half-year-old daughter, Marie Josephe; Louison was pregnant with a third. Jean-Baptiste might have also fathered other children, as suggested by testimony from a 1748 murder trial. During the course of that investigation, René Millet mentioned that "Joseph mulatto son of Baptiste from the Hospital" *(joseph mulatre fils de Baptiste de l'hospital du Roy)* had been sent for to bleed the victim, suggesting that by this date there was no longer a surgeon in residence on the king's plantation. How Jean-Baptiste came to have a son in 1748 described as "mulatto" is hard to fathom (and might have been an error

Louison

or was meant to signal some other kind of kin relationship), but this snippet is the only clue left regarding Joseph's possible paternity.[19]

If the attack had not occurred and if the code noir had not permitted slave testimony, there would be precious little else to know about Louison and even less about Manon or François. There would be no record of their own words or how they conceived of themselves, and their grasp of how and where they fit in New Orleans's slave society would be a matter of speculation. Though, collectively, their words add up to little more than a few pages of transcribed testimony, the details Louison, Manon, and the two men named François provided interrogators offer information that goes far beyond that strictly related to their activities and movements that day. To varying degrees, all four enslaved witnesses introduced a range of details about their daily lives, material worlds, and relationships, even if, at first glance, what they conveyed seems irrelevant or superficial at best. Pochenet's series of attacks proceeded via a sequence of events marked by verbal exchanges and physical actions or reactions. In effect, each blow-by-blow installment of Pochenet's violent rampage acted as a catalyst that led his victims to reveal more—both to Pochenet and to court officials— about their inner and outer worlds than they might otherwise have done.

❧❧

"ONE OF THE GOOD SURGEONS OF THE COLONY"

When court officials were led to Louison, they found her in the process of having her wounds dressed. Both Babette and Louison were being treated by the Ursuline nuns in conjunction with the surgeon's aides—which included Jean-Baptiste, Louison's husband, and possibly his son, Joseph. The convent was, to be sure, an unconventional setting for witness interrogation; it was only Louison's precarious health that compelled the court officials to question her there, where she lay in her cabin situated within the courtyard. But, as they recorded Louison's words and noted her condition, court officials also documented information about healing arts and the opportunities it could afford the enslaved.

If Babette and Louison were bled according to conventional European medical wisdom, then Jean-Baptiste was probably the one to perform the procedure, since other records note that he treated others this way. That Jean-Baptiste's son, Joseph, bled the victim (who died after losing consciousness) in the 1748 murder case suggests the primacy of this technique for those suffering from wounds.

Acquiring the skill to perform a procedure such as bleeding secured material benefits for practitioners. Jean-Baptiste had trained in the European medical arts while on the king's plantation. Situated straight across the river from New Orleans, in present-day Gentilly, the plantation complex was substantial and carefully planned. In addition to a hospital for slaves, it included a separate cabin reserved for medicines and for immediate care, where Jean-Baptiste lived (Figure 18). A post-in-the-ground construction with a brick chimney, the building was one of two cabins located directly outside the securely fenced-in slave camp, flanking the locked gate. The other cabin was reserved for the overseer (see bottom of Figure 19). In 1731, these two cabins were appraised at 420 livres, as compared to 2,240 livres (or 70 livres each) for the thirty-two slave cabins within the palisade, giving a sense of their importance. Though Antoine-Simon Le Page du Pratz, who managed the plantation from 1726 to 1734, did not name the individual, he described the presence of one young male slave who "followed the Surgeon, slept and lived in this cabin, in order to be within reach for blood-letting or for putting on a first dressing if the case was pressing. I learned some years later that this *negre* was one of the good surgeons of the colony." Jean-Baptiste was about twelve years old in 1726, making him twenty when Le Page du Pratz left the plantation for the last time.[20]

Jean-Baptiste, in turn, trained others, including his presumed son, Joseph, and at least one other young enslaved African sent by his master to the hospital to be taught surgical arts. But, of course, Jean-Baptiste's adhesion to conventional European medical remedies of course does not eliminate the possibility or likelihood that he supplemented French medical care with treatments of his own. Similarly, when the slave François made *tisanes* (a herbal tea with medicinal properties) for the patients in the pharmacy—the very task he was occupied with when the attack occurred—perhaps he incorporated ingredients guided as much by the nuns' knowledge as his own or other slaves'.[21]

If this particular set of records elides the matter of non-Western healing and medicinal techniques, a court case from 1770 Natchitoches includes the testimony of an enslaved man known as Christophe who described how his white overseer had hit him "on the loins with a stick," leaving the area "very swollen." After the surgeon failed to diagnose a hernia (or to provide any treatment whatsoever), meaning that Christophe would not be let off from work, Christophe resorted to the ministrations of "Jacob, Mr. Pain's *nègre* [who] treated me for that, and I am a bit better"; he certainly believed he had improved from the healer's cures. The slave driver Mercure then sent Christophe broth to aid in his recovery. Jacob was not the only enslaved African solicited for his medical knowledge in Natchitoches; in the same court case, another witness described "Constance, a *nègre* from the other side of the river," fetching herbs for a young slave who was ill. Neither wit-

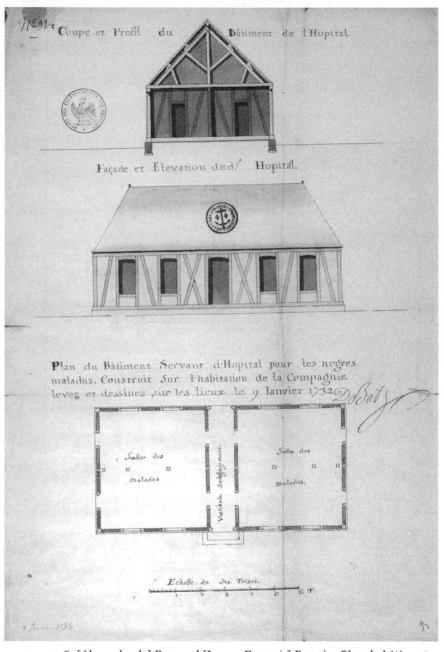

FIGURE 18: [Alexandre de] Batz and [Ignace-François] Broutin, *Plan du bâtiment de l'hopital des nègres construit sur l'habitation de la Compagnie levez et dessinez sur les lieux à la Nouvelle Orléans le 13 janvier 1732.* FR ANOM F3 290 36. Courtesy Archives nationales d'outre-mer, Aix-en-Provence, France The drawing shows the plan of the slave hospital on the Company of the Indies's plantation.

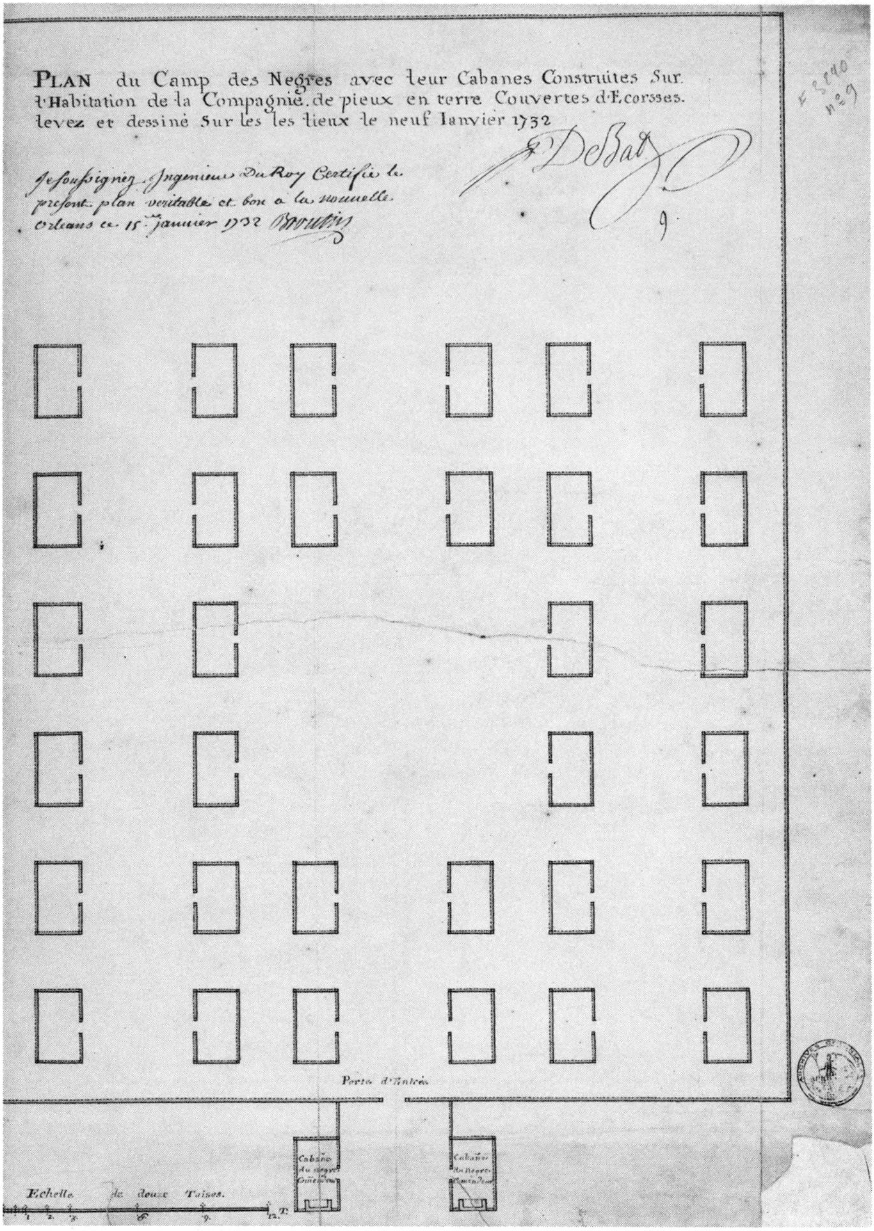

FIGURE 19: [Ignace-François] Broutin and [Alexandre de] Batz, *Plan
du camp des nègres avec leur cabanes construites sur l'habitation de la
Compagnie de pieux en terre couvertes d'ecorsses, levez et déssiné sur
les les [sic] lieux le neuf janvier 1732.* FR ANOM F3 290 9.
Courtesy Archives nationales d'outre-mer, Aix-en-Provence, France
The drawing shows the enclosed compound where the group of slave cabins were
located on the Company of the Indies's plantation. Just outside the gate stood
two cabins identified as those of the overseer, though one was for the surgeon.

ness, however, provided any details of the precise treatments, medical techniques, healing practices, or other tools of the trade used beyond references to medicinal plants. Nor, in another case, did the soldier André Baron specify what he meant when he alluded to his accuser, François-Xavier, as not having "cured him."[22]

Jean-Baptiste could help care for his wife's injuries in his dual role as her medical caregiver and her husband, but he could do so more easily because of the spatial arrangement of the adjacent convent-hospital complex. Just as when he lived on the king's plantation, Jean-Baptiste again enjoyed better housing than most slaves. As noted by court officials, they visited Babette and Louison in two separate cabins located within the hospital courtyard (they specified that Louison's was at the bottom end of the courtyard). In an inventory taken in 1744, there were only two slave cabins associated with the hospital, minimally furnished with "six beds of cypress wood garnished with only six mattresses of canvas [toile de halle] in poor condition." The distribution of the beds between the two cabins was not stated, nor was the configuration of the cabins. In 1744, there were seven slaves belonging to the king living at the hospital, consisting of two family units and one single male — all told, five adults and two children. The Ursulines themselves possessed outright an unknown number of slaves (Babette among them) at the convent-hospital complex as well as the field slaves who worked the nuns' plantation on the outskirts of the town. By 1752, there might have been additional slave cabins built within the courtyard.[23]

By virtue of his special status, it is likely that Jean-Baptiste had the use of one of the cabins, shared with his wife, Louison, and their children but not the other adult slaves. This proximity was a crucial feature of the couple's working lives, enabling Jean-Baptiste to come fairly quickly to his wife's aid when she was being attacked outside the hospital on the riverbank. Though Louison and Jean-Baptiste were of the same age and had borne and raised children together, it is impossible to know the circumstances of their marriage beyond that they had married in the church and that it was a legitimate marriage from a French standpoint. It is unclear, for example, if they had been coerced to marry nor is it possible to know how they felt about their union. But Jean-Baptiste's actions do give some sense of their closeness and reveal his devotion to his wife and the mother of his children.[24]

Jean-Baptiste's care of Louison derived partly from his training and partly from their spousal relationship, but, considered alongside other testimony gathered in the wake of Pochenet's attacks, it makes sense to view this care as falling on a larger spectrum in which enslaved Africans could expect to give and receive aid. In their testimony, both Louison and the other witnesses made scattered references to giving and receiving aid. After Pochenet drew his bayonet on François and then Manon, they each independently ran for help to the *corps de garde* (the police), revealing an expectation that the police were supposed to offer them protection. Babette and Louison's cries brought out a plethora of saviors who helped contain and disarm Pochenet, then dragged him to the hospital courtyard and on to the prison. Others carried the injured women into the hospital. Louison herself described how she immediately rushed to Babette's defense, even at the cost of her own safety. This was followed by the description of Jean-Baptiste (accompanied by a young French man and others from the hospital) putting themselves in harm's way to come to their assistance, which resulted in the injury to Jean-Baptiste's hand.

In other words, Babette and Louison were not left to deal with Pochenet on their own. Beyond the role of sentries and other whites, information about kin relations and peer cohesion among the enslaved is evident in this narrative and confirmed in the spatial and architectural record, fleshing out questions about family formation and community support networks that help illuminate the lived experience of individual slaves. In their testimony before the court, whether as witnesses or accused, slaves peppered their accounts with references to relationships (whether family, kin, affective, sexual, or even economic relationships). Since not all members of a community of enslaved individuals forged bonds with one another, it is noteworthy that Louison's testimony signals that there had developed a sense of conviviality and community among the enslaved inhabitants of the convent as well as among the slave women owned by different masters who met regularly at the riverbank to do laundry.

WASHERWOMEN, A HANDKERCHIEF, AND A SOLDIER

Beyond this evidence of cohesion and community, what seems especially striking in Louison's, Manon's, and the first François's testimony in this court case is the way they described their reactions to Pochenet's demands, whether for plums or for laundering services. Their behavior provides evidence about how enslaved Africans interpreted their position with respect to colonists and how they developed ways to gauge the relational importance of individual Frenchmen, such as soldiers.

In Louison's telling, the attack seemed random. Spotting Pochenet, she immediately recognized him as having been in the care of the hospital "for a very long time," for which privilege he would have had two *sous* retained from his pay and given to the nuns for his board, in addition to the sum that the king disbursed to the convent for his care. She then watched as the soldier approached Babette, carving a piece of wood using his bayonet; spoke to her, though she could not hear their conversation; and, just one moment later, pierced Babette in the stomach with the bayonet. At that point, she informed the court, "she ran to this *negresse* to rescue her, that this man began to swear and get angry with her because she was telling him, 'Why did he want to assasinate this woman?'"[25]

In her testimony, Manon likewise provided very specific details of her altercation with Pochenet. What she focused on in her narrative was labor and the customary right to control (and earn from) work done on the side:

> She was laundering with two *négresses* [illegible] across from the barracks on one side of the habitation when a soldier that she only knows from sight came along, that if she saw him she would recognize him. That he said to her and to the others to wash a handkerchief which they did not want to do because it was raining a lot and they did not have the time, that the soldier took out a naked bayonet that he had under his arm and ran after them to hit them, which obliged the said *négresses* to walk far into the water to avoid his fury, that the soldier also went into the water to hit them which he was not able to do because they were too far in, and out of anger he began to walk on their washing and spoil it, and the deponent wanted to go to the barracks to complain, which, seeing, the said soldier ran off toward the King's warehouse, that the soldier seemed drunk.

> Elle Etoit à Laver avec deux Négresses [illegible] vis à vis les Cazernes dun Coté de l'habitation il vint un soldat qu'elle ne Connoist que de Vue que sy Elle le voyoit Elle Le Connoistroit bien quil Luy dit à Elle Et aux autres de Luy laver un mouchoir Ce qu'elle ne voulurent pas faire parce qu'il pleuvoit Beaucoup Et qu'elles n'avoient point le temps, que Le soldat tira une bayonette toute nue quil avoit sous son bras Et Courut apres Elles pour En fraper, Ce qui obligea Elles Négresses d'avancer dans LEau bien avant pour Eviter sa furie, que Le soldat se mist aussy à L'Eau pour les fraper Ce quil ne put parce qu'elles Etoient trop avant dans LEau, Et de Colere il se mit à marcher sur leur linge Et le gater, et que la deposante voulut aller au Corps de Garde pour se plaindre, ce que ledt. Soldat voyant il s'en fut du coté des magasins du Roy, que ce soldat luy parut soul

Like François, who spoke back when faced with Pochenet's demand for plums, Manon and the other women point-blank refused to launder Pochenet's handkerchief, a rejection of his demands that set off a violent rage, causing him to trample all over the laundry, ruining their work. The excuse that Manon voiced to court officials for not acquiescing to launder his handkerchief was that "it was raining a lot and they did not have the time" given their regular workload. But there was also a pointed undertone to their refusal, one that the women did not voice directly but could only allude to. In demanding that they launder his soiled handkerchief, Pochenet was attempting to assert his authority as a Frenchman and a male. From the soldier's perspective, washing was women's work, both poorly paid and low status, thanks to the association of laundering with filth and the unclean. In Louisiana, slave women were taught this work, for which they served their masters and mistresses or for which their owners hired them out by the day; enslaved women also hired themselves out for their own profit. Left unclear from the testimony was whether Pochenet had offered to pay for the laundering service. The women would have expected payment, given the unspoken rules of an informal economy in which slaves in New Orleans, as elsewhere in colonial societies, worked on their own account to provide a range of apparel-related services (sewing, laundering, and so forth) to colonists, free blacks, and fellow slaves.[26]

Manon's account jars with the prosecutor's initial interrogation of Pochenet, where the lines of questioning centered on sex. In European consciousness, laundering was also associated with prostitution, as borne out by a suit filed in Louisiana by the laundress Madame La Chenay, who demanded a public apology for having been accused of keeping a brothel. The connotation of sex with laundresses also manifested itself in the practice of French bachelors keeping Indian slaves for illicit sexual relations on the pretense "that they can't do without them for their laundry and for their food, and to keep house." This association seems to have played a part in Pochenet's motives and in the prosecutor's reasoning. The town was small enough that the prosecutor could have been aware of sites and people known to engage in prostitution, and, if not, his investigation (for which no records were ever generated) might have brought this information to light. Certainly, colonists themselves occasionally alluded to their easy access to enslaved women's paid sexual services. The first questions Commissioner Jean-Baptiste Raguet directed at Pochenet made an explicit reference to sex, not laundry, as the motive for both his approach to the laundresses and the attack itself:

Interrogated if before this attack he had not wanted to seduce the *negresses?*
Said no that he does not remember this.

Interrogated if it was not the refusal of the *negresses* that forced him to hit them with his bayonet?

Answered no.

Interrogé sy avant de faire ce coup il n'avoit pas voulu seduire les negresses

A dit que non qu'il ne se souvient point de cela

Interrogé sy ce n'est pas les Refus que ces *negresses* luy firent qui l'obligerent de les fraper de sa bayonnette

A repondu que non

Here were leading questions peppered with sexually charged words ("seduce," "the refusal of the *negresses* that forced him to hit them") that seemed to offer Pochenet a route to redemption, or at least justification for him as a Frenchman to feel aggrieved in the face of rejection at the hands of enslaved women. Later in his questioning, the prosecutor returned to the subject of sexual aggression but changed tacks, probing the soldier about his background and signaling that his investigation had generated new, damning information that eerily echoed the Louisiana attack:

Interrogated if he had been prosecuted in France or in the troops for some unfortunate action?

Answered no.

He was remonstrated that he does not tell the truth since he only came to this colony to save himself, that he had knifed a woman in France in the town of Metz where [illegible].

Said that this is false that no such misfortune happened to him and that he came only for desertion as his sergeant knows well.

Interrogé s'il n'a pas été repris de Justice en france ou dans les troupes pour quelque action malheureuse

A repondu que non

A luy remontré qu'il ne dit pas la verité puisqu'il n'est venu en cette colonie que pour se sauver qu'il avoit donné des coups de couteau à une femme en france dans la ville de Metz ou [illegible]

A dit que cela est faux quil ne luy est jamais arrivé de pareils malheurs et qu'il n'est venu que pour la desertion ainsy que son sergent le scait

The prosecutor dropped the topic of sex altogether in subsequent interrogations of the accused, victims, and witnesses.[27]

Neither Louison nor Manon made any reference to sexual connotations, but, perhaps, they chose not to talk about that topic in court. Louison claimed not to have overheard the exchange between Babette and Pochenet. As for Manon, she presented the situation as one that was innocuous enough, justifying the women's denial of his demand that they launder the handkerchief as a sensible decision about refusing to do unpaid labor—not a rejection of an offer for sex. In his testimony, Pochenet claimed simply that he must have acted out of drunkenness. Nevertheless, there was a power dynamic inherent in his verbal demand that the women cleanse the article in question. A "mouchoir," or handkerchief, in a male wardrobe was an item of clothing used by the lower sorts to adorn the head or neckline. It was not necessarily used to blow one's nose (a sleeve usually did the trick for that), but it was a useful cloth for wiping the mouth after meals or the sweat off a brow. Given Pochenet's illness as well as his drunkenness, his handkerchief might well have been visibly (and perhaps olfactorily) soiled with unsavory bodily excretions.

Manon knew Pochenet by sight, though she did not explain how she knew him. By all accounts, he had been in the hospital for a lengthy period. His illness is not specified, but perhaps it was a venereal disease. If so, his illness would have been commonly known within the convent walls, since the nuns kept a separate lodging for those patients, and he would have continued to carry its stigma after being discharged. Depending on how widely the enslaved discussed such information among themselves, this news could have even circulated beyond the convent walls, reaching the ears of women like Manon. This kind of information was probably especially valuable if Pochenet was known to solicit women. Such an illness would have added a level of revulsion to Manon's and Louison's reactions to the man.[28]

In any case, it would have been clear to Manon's interlocutors that the laundresses felt that it was safe for them to reject a demand from a soldier. They knew that, in telling them to launder his handkerchief, he had transgressed economic norms by trying to avail himself of labor that belonged to another master. It is particularly noteworthy that at no point were Manon or François taken to task for their failure to display submissiveness toward Pochenet in spite of a new police code for the colony promulgated in 1751. Echoing the 1724 code noir's injunctions to show submission to whites, Article 28 of the bylaw warned that "all *nègres* and other slaves . . . who fail to show the respect and submission due to whites; in other words who are insolent enough to accost them in the streets by taking up the path; and who, forgetting they are slaves, in some way fail to show them respect, will be punished with fifty lashes and branded with a fleur-de-lis on the buttocks, so that the quality of their crime be known should this be needed."[29]

Louison

The new 1751 code was widely and assiduously disseminated in February and March of that year in each neighborhood across town and dispatched to every outpost in both written and oral form with the intent that "no one can be excused by claiming ignorance of it." In other words, this local code was a response to existing practices and infractions. At the same time that the enslaved no doubt were made familiar with, and discussed among themselves, all the novel ways in which their social and economic activities were to be curtailed and all the new punishments that could be inflicted on them for perceived transgressions, they might have appreciated the following restriction on colonists' actions provided in Article 30:

> We have just explained all the obligations of *nègres* toward whites, and especially toward their masters. It will be good to instruct the public that this does not extend indiscriminately to everyone, in particular, soldiers and all others do not have the right to ill-treat a *nègre* who says nothing to him or does not show them a lack of respect. He can in certain cases have him arrested and demand justice of him, given that the *nègre* is only subject to the justice of his master or of the police. Consequently, and in accordance with His Majesty's orders, we prohibit anyone from taking such license, under the penalty deemed appropriate.

Although it does not appear that this protection was systematically afforded to the enslaved, the case against Pochenet and the testimony of slaves against this soldier provide evidence of the subtleties embedded within this law, especially in terms of the risks slaves incurred when speaking to whites. François did not know Pochenet, Manon only knew him from sight, but both knew that he was a soldier. Consequently, they fathomed instantly that his status within colonial society was a lowly one and that he was not in a clear position of authority over them. This knowledge lay at the root of François's expectation that he could refuse to be bullied into giving Pochenet some of his plums and could in fact tell him to buy his own in a manner bordering on insolence, even as he said "Sir." Meanwhile, Manon also apparently felt fully justified in spurning the soldier's demand to launder his handkerchief. And neither balked at repeating their responses to the court or appeared to fear repercussions from those in authority for talking back to Pochenet.[30]

François and Manon's testimony reveal that they knew how to judge hierarchies among colonists, and even Louison, who was not privy to the original exchanges about the plums or about the handkerchief, verbally resisted Pochenet and fearlessly answered him back. But, unlike François and Manon, the form taken by her resistance to his demands was a very particular one inflected by religion, specifically Catholicism.

At the height of Pochenet's attack, after he first stabbed her, Louison stumbled. As she was trying once more to flee, the soldier addressed her directly. This is how she described their exchange:

> Pochenet said to her, "Go on, kneel and ask my forgiveness." She replied, "It's only from God that we ask forgiveness." That in spite of this, she got her on her knees and said to him, "Sorry, Sir." That in spite of this, he gave her two or more blows with the bayonet. And during that time, all the other *négresses* fled toward the convent and the hospital screaming, "Help, we are being assassinated, there is a soldier who is chasing all of us with a bayonet."

Louison knew to be afraid. She had just witnessed Pochenet stab Babette in the stomach. Yet she was brave enough to run to Babette's rescue without thinking of her own safety and to confront him about his actions. She would confront him again when he asked her to kneel before him, even though by then he had already stabbed her multiple times, or so she asserted; Pochenet himself had nothing to say about his actions in court, claiming not to remember anything of his behavior, hence neither denying nor corroborating her statement. The court scribe followed convention by converting Louison's oral testimony into formal written French. But, her intended meaning is not lost as a result of this switch to grammatically correct syntax in the third person, especially as the scribe left the dialogue intact (as seen in the retention of "we" and "us"). Her transcribed words show, for example, that Pochenet used the familiar second person pronoun "tu" (rather than the formal "vous") to address Louison, a slave. Exactly like François, she claimed that she responded using a more formal and deferential tone, addressing him as "Monsieur," or "Sir," as she must have known to do with all French persons, whatever their status.

Other investigations document the same grammatical hierarchy. The trial of Jupiter dit Gamelle for robbery included testimony by a colonist who reported a conversation with the enslaved man's owner, Jean-Charles de Pradel, in which he seemed to insinuate that allowing a slave to use the familiar "tu" when addressing whites was clearly a warning of worse things to come:

> "Your slave is very familiar with the sailors from the small vessel that is anchored in front of Mr. Prevost's property. I have seen them together at their table they take [liberties], use "tu" in addressing each other and he is father and companion to them. Beware of him do not trust him."

Whereupon the sieur Pradel told him "I am not one of those men who take offense when they are warned of such things but he gives me good account and I am happy with him."

It was expected that the enslaved would address each other using "tu," even in Creole, a convention widely observed when clerks transcribed speech. When the enslaved Pluton began to quote from his conversation with the slave Charlot dit Kakaracou, in the middle of his 1744 interrogation, the clerk followed his lead and rendered the dialogue in first person and the original Creole, showing that the two slaves had addressed each other using the familiar second-person pronoun: "Replied that Charlot had rubbed mud into his clothes and that he had asked him 'Who you kill, Charlot' and that Charlot answered him 'Me not kill anything'" *(a Repondu que Charlot avoit Barbouillé son habit avec de la Boue Et que la dessus il Luy demanda qui toy tuer Charlot Et que Charlot Luy repondit Moy N'a Rien tué).* In contrast, Louison's testimony signals her recognition that whites could address slaves using the familiar pronoun "tu" but that slaves had to show deference verbally, such as through the use of "Monsieur" or "Madame" and the formal pronoun "vous." Similarly, the thirty-four-year-old Alexandre, who self-identified as of the Senegal nation, reported a verbal exchange he had had with a French female retailer in which he addressed her using the term of deference "Madame" and the formal second-person conjugation: "Saying to her 'see there Madam, there is a *nègre* who wants to buy buckles and rings'" *(Luy disant tenez madame voila un Negre qui veut ajetter [sic] des Boucles et des Bagues).*[31]

One might presume that Louison and the other hospital slaves used the same deferential and formal tone in addressing the soldiers and other low-ranking colonists in their care at the hospital. Yet, perhaps Louison's history of helping rehabilitate the soldier had given her standing to speak back to him, for healers (and cooks) had inherent power over those in their charge. Indeed, Louison and Pochenet were no strangers: she recognized him from his long stay at the hospital, and, in his interrogation, he asserted that "the *negresses* that he is said to have injured are not his enemies that on the contrary having been sick at the hospital they nursed him" *(que les negresses que l'on dit qu'il a blessé ne sont point ses ennemis que bien au contraire étant malade à l'hopital elles ont eu soin de luy).* Asked about causing injury to Jean-Baptiste's wrist, Pochenet likewise responded that "he knows nothing of this that if he injured him he is very upset because he is very obliged toward him and being at the hospital [Jean-Baptiste] saved his life many times" *(A repondu quil ne sçait rien de cela que sil l'a blessé il est bien fasché parce quil luy a beaucoup d'obligation et qu'etant à l'hopital il luy a sauvé plusieurs fois la vie)*. Here was a very different tone that muddies readings of Pochenet's actions and his perspective. When sober, the soldier expressed gratitude, stating that he was "very obliged" toward the enslaved men and women who had nursed him and saved his life. But, when drunk, he felt a sense of entitlement, whether to a slave's plums, labor, sexuality, or respect. Where Louison was concerned, the soldier felt entitled to her repentance.[32]

Given the sheer violence and the immediate danger inherent in Pochenet's armed attack, Louison had no real option but to do as she was told, to kneel, and to simulate begging Pochenet's forgiveness. Asking for forgiveness was part of the rhetoric and ritual of slavery, of the debasement that demanded that the enslaved show submission and contrition to all whites, not just their masters. In 1766, for example, judgment was rendered against the enslaved man Antoine Paul, a Creole from Martinique belonging to Sieur Loyola, for simply defending himself in the case of an attack by a white man who was not his master. Multiple white witnesses testified about an incident where a man named Sieur Rivière began hitting Paul with a stick. The slave managed to seize hold of the stick and tried to break it in two, but bystanders swiftly apprehended him and took him to jail. Convicted of lack of respect toward free persons *("Excès et manque de respect aux personnes Libres"),* he was condemned to twenty-five lashes. But, first, he had to demonstrate contrition and proclaim his sin in public by walking bareheaded while carrying a metal bar on his shoulders *("la barre au Col")* as a warning to other slaves.[33]

Like submissiveness, begging forgiveness also played a widely acknowledged role in extrajudicial negotiations between masters and slaves throughout the French Empire. In Martinique, the Creole runaway Michaut rendered an account of the delicate negotiations that sometimes took place, often mediated by white and black intercessors. In his case, it was Sieur Deloré on whose cassava plantation he was hiding (obviously in plain sight) who let it be known to him that, if Michaut worked for him and revealed the location of a maroon camp, then Deloré "would obtain grace for him" *(il luy feroit avois la grace)*. In the same court case, the runaway Jeannot added that Deloré let him know that, if he handed in his gun, Deloré "would bring him back very gently [or quietly] to his master" *(le rameneroit tout doucement à son Maitre),* which Jeannot said "he really wanted" *(avoit bonne envie)*. In early nineteenth-century Isle de Bourbon (present-day La Réunion), and likely earlier, runaways similarly relied on masters but also on priests to serve as intermediaries. Back in Louisiana in 1748, the slave François dit Baraca, who ran away after murdering his wife, was urged by his friend Joseph Laoursot, the plantation's cowherd, to ask for his master's forgiveness ("trust me, cross to the other side [of the river] and beg forgiveness of your master *[croy*

moy passe de l'autre coté demande pardon à ton maître]). And, shortly thereafter, Baraca did indeed solicit the help of Laoursot in doing so, informing
the court that "he [Baraca] asked the cowherd [Laoursot] to tell the overseer to come and talk to him, but that the overseer did not want to come" *(il
demanda au vacher de dire au commandeur de luy venir parler, que le commandeur ne voulut pas venir)*. As for François (who had run away because
his master was going to whip him for spending the night at a dance), when
asked in 1764 if he was "happy" with his master, he answered in the affirmative (what else could he say?), adding that he planned to return and that
"he intended to find Sr. Laval whom he trusted to obtain his master's grace"
*(A dit qu'il ne venoit qu'en l'intention de trouver le s. Laval auquel il avoit
confiance pour obtenir la Grace à son maître)*. This convention of slaves acting contrite and asking forgiveness of their masters was so well and so widely
established as to be part of customary tactics for negotiating with masters and
other whites. In ordering Louison to kneel and ask for his forgiveness, Pochenet was laying claim to this privilege and authority of masters. But Louison
had another, higher authority in mind.[34]

GOD

In Louison's telling, she did in fact kneel before Pochenet as he commanded,
but not before first upbraiding him by reminding him to heed God. She reiterated her expression of religious beliefs one week later for the court officials and bystanders at the convent-hospital when they came to take down her
statement. Enslaved Africans' professions of faith are neither straightforward
nor uncommon. But Louison's words stand out because she definitively spoke
them. Most descriptions of slaves' religious beliefs derive from missionaries'
accounts, which were produced to generate support for their activities. It is
unclear whether missionaries really heard such professions of faith from converted Africans or if they invented or embellished them for a receptive public.
In contrast, archival records from criminal courts represent actual cases that
were investigated and prosecuted, and there is no question that Louison testified. Court officials in Louisiana were not defensive about their activities, and
they had no reason to invent or imagine her testimony. Even though judicial
convention required that they write down her words in legal form, the speech
she is credited with is the one she actually spoke. The case against Pochenet
was about a series of assaults that had nothing to do with religion or Catholicism; Louison, and no one else, brought those particular subjects into view.[35]

Louison was not the only Catholic convert who invoked her faith in God
in the course of testifying. Testimony in court required swearing an oath to

tell the truth *("faire serment de dire verité")* before a crucifix, and this formula appeared at the start of interrogatories. Occasionally the enslaved invoked God with greater rhetorical flourish, as Joseph Pantalon did in 1743. A free black who identified as a Catholic man from Senegal, he proclaimed in his defense "that he is telling the truth and that if he were before God he would say the same thing" *(quil dit La vérité Et que sil Etoit devant dieu il Le diroit de même)*. Perhaps he hoped to garner special consideration from his appeal to religion. If Louison was not the only one to profess her faith to court officials, however, the case remains that her words and actions were extraordinary ones on the part of an enslaved woman, and this only become intelligible within the context of the history of slave evangelism in New Orleans.[36]

Both the 1685 and 1724 slave codes enshrined Catholicism as the only religion permitted by law in France's colonies; laid out provisions for the baptism, instruction, marriage, and burial of slaves; and required that masters respect holy days when assigning their slaves' labor. With notable exceptions, most masters were given much latitude with respect to enforcing these prescriptions, many going no further than sending their slaves to be instructed prior to their baptism, despite the risk of fines or the confiscation of their slaves. Furthermore, the work of conversion was not without its challenges, especially in the context of differential power relations. Many slaves must have resented the imposition of Catholic values, and some of them articulated their feelings in court testimony, as did the twenty-five-year-old Marguerite who, accused of marronnage in 1764, complained that she had run away because her mistress beat her and "every night they locked her up like in a convent" *(tous les Soirs ils la faisoient Renfermé comme dans un Couvant)*.[37]

If many masters blatantly ignored the code noir's prescriptions for baptism, or worse, forced it on their slaves, baptism and attendance at Mass for those who labored for the Ursulines (like those who labored for the Jesuits) would have been virtually inevitable. Surviving sacramental records confirm that they were baptized and brought into the faith, that they married in the church, as Louison had, and that they identified in other formal ways with Catholicism. And significant segments of the population of enslaved Africans in Louisiana were drawn to Catholicism, finding purpose therein. Enslaved women in New Orleans, in particular, experienced conversion and baptism very differently in large part because of the Ursuline convent.[38]

The letters of the Ursuline nun Hachard, Sister St. Stanislas, show that she was certainly preoccupied with skin color. Writing in 1728 to her father, she noted humorously that, had Africans wanted to wear beauty patches (small black velvet beauty spots that fashionable women wore to "make their complexion seem whiter," as *Le Mercure galant* noted), they would need white patches, "which would create quite a funny effect." Yet her letters also expressed a clear preference for African over Indian women in the missionizing endeavor: "What pleases us is the docility of the children, whom one forms as one wants. The blacks are also easy to instruct once they learn to speak French. It is not the same for the *sauvages*, whom one does not baptize without trembling because of the tendency they have to sin, especially the women, who, under a modest air, hide the passions of beasts." The striking appreciation for enslaved African women that Hachard communicated in this letter was to continue, laying the groundwork for the rich intertwined history of Africans and Catholicism in Louisiana.[39]

The Ursuline convent was the primary venue for the instruction of female slaves in New Orleans. But, beyond catechizing activities at the convent, Ursuline nuns sought to develop additional mechanisms for evangelizing slaves. For example, they joined with local (secular) women to found a lay-women's confraternity, the Ladies' Congregation of the Children of Mary. It was run under the auspices of the convent from 1730 until 1744 (the very year Louison arrived at the hospital), but its effects extended well beyond this period. The confraternity had broad religious goals aimed at instituting greater morality within the colony. It also enabled French and enslaved women to participate side by side in activities that vigorously promoted the evangelization of slaves –with Catholic slave women serving as godparents to new slave converts, for example, as seen in the parish registers. Where the Ursulines' own slaves were concerned, the nuns made it a priority to create a community of slaves who adhered to the ideals of a moral Catholic family, not only encouraging sacramental marriage but making business decisions that effectively kept family units intact while also giving great weight to how they perceived their bondspeople's sexual behavior.[40]

Just two years before the demise of the confraternity, the nuns marked the passing of their own Sister Cécile des Ange, who was charged with "instructing our class of day students and with catechizing black men and women." In the obituary they wrote following her death, they described her "boundless zeal" for this responsibility. They particularly lauded how she "contributed well to the establishment of piety in families, as much the whites as the blacks. There were a number for whom she procured by her instruction the good fortune to receive the sacraments of baptism and of the Eucharist, which they approached with edification having been, by her care and upheld by the grace of God, rid of their libertine ways." The mother superior ended her letter with a plea that "whatever virtues our dear sister showed us during the course of her life of holy missionary work, we do not ask you the sufferance of our order to pursue canonization for this dear departed one."

Perhaps there had been some talk at the time of Sister Cécile's qualities warranting nomination to canonization, but the superior tamped this down. Yet this obituary contained another unusual element, a reference to the words of the slaves she had instructed: "Thus these good people showed their feelings upon her death in a manner that was most touching and full of gratitude. These poor black women added to their tears and sorrow the care to pray to God for her, forcing the one who took her place to receive considerable sums, in view of their limited means, to say masses for the repose of her soul. They said that they could not do enough for her."[41]

Although missionaries existed in all the French colonies throughout the Atlantic and Indian Oceans and nuns could be found in convents in New France, Martinique, and Pondicherry, few seem to have matched the success of the Ursulines in New Orleans in converting and catechizing enslaved African women. Isle de Bourbon offers evidence of the Lazarist priests' assiduous attempts to convert their slaves and have them conform to Catholic strictures, including the imposition of sex-segregated slave quarters intended to quash nonmarital sexual activity. In contrast, the record in Isle de France (modern-day Mauritius) is more ambiguous. The extant parish registers occasionally give a glimpse of select French women who were active in godparenting duties for the enslaved such as Anne Vigoureux, whose signature is sprinkled through the register of "Baptêmes, mariages, and sepultures: Blancs, Libres, et Esclaves" for Port Louis. However, she seems to be the exception, and random testimony by enslaved women in Mauritius suggests that religious instruction and baptism for slaves was either a low priority for masters or that it might have even been imposed. When asked about her religion, one runaway, Thereze, who identified as Malagasy, replied "that she does not know what religion she is, that her master had led her to the Church like the others, that she has not been baptized, or at least that she does not remember this" *(quelle se ne sais de quelle religion eslle est, que son maistre la mené à l'eglise comme les autres, quelle n'a pas été baptisé, qu'en tout cas elle ne sen souvient pas)*. Another runaway, Rose, testified that her master "had had her baptized when she had been ill" *(A Repondu avoir été baptizé par son maître dans une maladie)*, possibly during illness thought at the time to be fatal (enough justification for a priest to comply). In both cases, the passive voice used by these women ("had led her" "had had her baptized"), signals their apparent lack of agency and suggests their inability to resist some level of Catholic instruction. It also reveals that they viewed religious instruction and baptism as aspects of their lives that fell within the purview of their masters' control. In contrast, Louison's words, spoken in New Orleans, anchored her squarely within the religious environment specific to Louisiana.[42]

Though the Ursuline convent has not been subject to a thorough archaeological analysis, other sites provide tantalizing glimpses of slaves' deployment of Catholic objects in the context of West African religions. The excavation at the St. Peter Street Cemetery in New Orleans is particularly instructive in this respect. This was the primary burial place for New Orleans's colonial-era population between 1724 and 1789, with intermittent use thereafter until 1800 or 1801. The excavation unearthed an important burial (no. 11) from circa 1770–1790 of a man aged forty to forty-nine years of age at death. Based on his dental modifications—incisors notched centrally (rather than filed to points), he has been identified as originating in Central Africa or the kingdom of Kongo. He was interred in a well-made coffin, with evidence of flowers having been placed on top, and, most significant among the other burials, he was interred with a "rosary, including a silver-plated wooden crucifix and a suite of religious medals linked by a woven silver chain and chaplet. It was accompanied by a second oval medallion with a glass face covering an etching on a copper plate." (Figure 20) Two shells were also interred with him, objects that had spiritual symbolism in the kingdom of Kongo (which converted to Catholicism in 1491, thanks to Capuchin missionaries, at the behest and under the control of the king of Kongo). The medals represent Saint Joseph, Saint Camillus of Lellis (a Capuchin saint), and Saint Andrew (whose popularity in the Kongo was owed to being championed by the Capuchins). Based on the identification of the Saint Camillus medal, it has been surmised that the burial was associated with the Charity Hospital, which was run by the Capuchin fathers, a Franciscan order dedicated to care of the sick. The burial has tentatively been identified as that of "Francisco Congo," who was interred in August 1775 at age forty after receiving the sacraments and extreme unction. Collectively, the items with which he was buried evoke a special status associated with caring for the ill. From a formalist perspective, the rosary-medal suite conforms to the visual lexicon of the kingdom of Kongo, with its emphasis on assemblages of saints. The lozenge-shaped element on the silver mesh chain evokes, in particular, the x-notches associated with Kongo religious thought, especially as found in crucifixes. Here, then, is an object that embodies in material form the symbiosis of Kongo and Catholic cosmologies and iconographies.[43]

Aside from references to baptism and other Catholic rites, Louisiana's court records reveal very little about Catholic or West African belief systems. Yet Louison's own words, given in testimony during a trial that was not about religion but about physical assault, provide another point of entry to understand the religious life of one individual woman and her relationship to Catholicism. In Louison's telling, Pochenet, in phrasing his demand, spoke

FIGURE 20: Suite of Religious Medals. Recovered from burial no. 11, St. Peter Street Cemetery (16or92), Orleans Parish, Louisiana. Courtesy Archaeology Lab of The University of New Orleans Department of Anthropology

in a non-specific way that *he* did not frame as religious. To modern eyes, his words evoke the imagery, familiar from abolitionist texts and art, of the prostrate slave forced to submit physically to his or her master, usually in a kneeling position (Figure 21). Louison would have been familiar with the ways that the French exacted corporal punishment over slaves and with the convention of the enslaved submitting to whites. But, she makes clear in her testimony that quite another image sprang to her mind. Louison's reply, "It's only from God that we ask forgiveness," reveals not only how she interpreted Pochenet's command but how Catholicism mediated her interpretation. What she saw was a parallel between Pochenet's demand that she kneel and beg pardon ("Go on, kneel and ask my forgiveness") and prayer. Perhaps, more specifically, she saw a parallel between his demand and the posture (kneeling in the confessional, facing the priest behind a privacy screen) and purpose (confession of sins; asking for pardon, and absolution; reciting the act of contrition; and receiving absolution and forgiveness) of the Catholic sacrament of penance.

That Louison recognized the parallel between prayer and the rite of confession is to be expected, given her ownership by the Ursulines. The order as a rule placed great emphasis on preparing girls for confession and Communion. In New Orleans, the attention given to these two sacraments in particular was enshrined in the laywomen's confraternity, and, at least once a year, before Easter, baptized slaves would have gone to confession (Figure 22). This was the imagery that colored Louison's response to Pochenet. Nonetheless, Louison's statement about religion should also be read in the context of her nonverbal expressions (specifically the way she expressed herself through clothing), for these bolstered the image of piety and moral authority that emerges from her narration of her verbal altercation with Pochenet.[44]

OF CORSETS AND RESPECTABILITY

In recounting the attack, Louison volunteered a seemingly superfluous and superficial detail: that the first time Pochenet aimed his bayonet at her, "having a hat on her head and a corset of good [strong] cloth meant that she was not very hurt that time." Her reason for making this practical observation about her clothing seems straightforward, showing how she avoided being as badly wounded as Babette. Indeed, the surgeon's report corroborated her interpretation, for he made no mention of any injury to Louison's head, though Pochenet's interrogators specified that he had attacked her with his bayonet "on the head and back." The surgeon's report did note that Louison had sustained a number of cuts including a wound above her right clavicle about

FIGURE 21: Charles Melchior Descourtis, after Jean Frédéric Schall,
Paul et Virginie Obtaining the Pardon of a Runaway Slave . . . Plate 2.
From a set of six plates depicting scenes from Bernardin de Saint-
Pierre's *Paul et Virginie.* 1795/1797. Color aquatint. Prints and Drawings
1895,0617.471. AN479703001. © The Trustees of the British Museum
In this engraving of Bernardin de Saint-Pierre's wildly popular enlightenment
abolitionist novel published in 1788, which takes place in Mauritius, Paul
and Virginie are seen seeking the pardon of a runaway female slave, depicted
prostrate before her master as he, "lifting up his stick, swore, with a terrible
oath, that he pardoned his slave, not for the love of Heaven, but of her
who asked his forgiveness." In the novel, it is Virginie's idea, and Virginie
herself (accompanied by Paul), who seeks the pardon of the slave.

FIGURE 22: Unknown Maker, *Cypress Confessional*. 1730–1760, Pointe Coupée, Louisiana. Photo courtesy of Philippe Halbert

three inches deep (presumably avoiding any arteries), but there was no injury to the area that would have been covered by her hat or bodice. In contrast, Babette had sustained a puncture wound in the area around her sternum, creating a serious and now infected cut about two inches deep into her chest.[45]

In bringing up her hat and corset, Louison hinted at the economic cost of the damage done by Pochenet to her apparel. Certainly, these particular garments on the body of a slave should raise questions. But perhaps Louison was also conveying something less obvious, and her insistence on providing these unusual sartorial details, ones that imbued her characterization of herself with European connotations of propriety and morality, should be carefully probed.

Hats provided protection against the elements, but they also concealed the hair and, as such, conformed to generic Christian conventions requiring married women to cover their heads when in public. In the eighteenth century, stays likewise connoted female propriety and morality. By the French term "corset," Louison actually meant a padded or quilted bodice (sometimes made of leather), known in English as jumps, rather than the fully boned stays with which the term is now associated. Though corsets lacked the tightly packed whalebone strips characteristic of stays (*corps* in French), the firm, padded fabric—which helped protect her from the bayonet—and the insertion of individual strips (or small areas) of whalebone in the lining shaped the chest and pushed back the shoulder blades to provide correct posture and, to some degree, the approximation of a fashionable outline (Figure 23).[46]

In Louisiana, neither jumps nor hats are commonly listed among the garb that masters provided to their slaves. The only item that comes close appears in a 1736 slave lease that specified that an enslaved woman was to be given a camisole (which was similar in construction to a corset, though lacking any boning) along with a shift and a skirt. Under the terms of the Ursulines' 1744 agreement with the crown by which Louison and other slaves were assigned to work at the hospital, the nuns agreed to provide them with clothing, but no specifics were mentioned. The theoretical issue of what clothes were to be supplied to slaves was dealt with in the slave codes. The 1685 code noir mandated a yearly provision consisting of either two linen suits or four ells of cloth for each slave, but the 1724 code remained vague as to specifics. Article 18 dealt with the subject of clothing alongside the other major component of a slave's maintenance—food—and merely specified that apparel was to be issued on a yearly basis, pending the council's advice as to what exactly to provide; the type of cloth to be used was also left vague. The basic function of clothing as a necessity was reiterated in Article 20, which granted slaves recourse to the law should their masters fail to adequately meet their needs,

Louison

FIGURE 23: *Corset* (jumps or waistcoat). Circa 1745.
Silk and linen, hand-sewn with silk thread. England.
Photo © Victoria and Albert Museum, London
Note the quilted fabric and the insertion of boning visible on the back panel.

though no such cases were ever prosecuted. Runaway slaves did cite a lack of food and clothing as a motive for fleeing, but no defense succeeded on this basis. In any case, Article 24 forbid slaves — like servants — from testifying for or against their masters on this or any other matter.[47]

Most slaves in Louisiana and beyond found manifold ways to supplement their wardrobes, which included hand-me-downs from masters (a classic European perquisite of domestic service), bequests, exchanges, thefts, and gifts given in courtship. Yet only a few other corsets are mentioned in the written record as belonging to a slave. Among the items included in a report filed by Superior Council member Raguet in 1746 concerning the theft of goods from his slaves' quarters was a corset. The other items consisted primarily of clothing but also bedding, cooking utensils, and a gun. The 1744 interrogation of thirty-four-year-old Alexandre, who identified as of the Senegal nation, with regard to his interactions with another slave, Jupiter, who had been accused of stealing money, references a corset used in the context of gift giving in courtship. Working on the assumption that Alexandre was an accomplice to Jupiter, the prosecutor asked Alexandre point-blank if he had given "clothes such as skirts and corsets and other things" *(des hardes Comme jupes et Corsets Es autres Choses)* to the woman he was in a relationship with. Alexandre denied doing so, admitting only to the gift of a handkerchief, a response that illustrates that a gift of a corset, like that of a skirt, was considered out of the ordinary, if only because of the cost of the item compared, say, to a handkerchief.[48]

Like any other nonelite group, the enslaved in Louisiana invested in the power of objects, in ways and for reasons that often had little to do with functionality or necessity. They also quickly became acclimated to European conventions of dress and actively consumed French and imported textiles and apparel. Certainly, when Louison deliberately made note of these garments, she was telling her interlocutors that they were meaningful to her. Louison's explanation about her corset and hat signaled her interest in high-status European markers of femininity. Nevertheless, she was also a slave who lived within the convent, and this particular experience shaped her sartorial expressions.[49]

The Ursulines, motivated as they were to convert and catechize Africans, could have ensured that their own slaves within the convent dressed in conformity with religious beliefs centered on European standards of female modesty that called for adequate covering of the body and the head. The description Louison provided was too sparse to enable much more in the way of inference about her work apparel that day at the riverbank; she did not feel the need to describe her overall appearance. She would have certainly worn a shift under her corset and skirt, and, although her corset might have been hidden, its presence would have been made visible by the tell-tale shape it conferred on her body. Onlookers would have seen in her dress the reflection of her privileged status as a cook, as the wife of the most important slave in the convent-hospital complex, and as a figure endowed with some authority and responsibility with regard to hospital patients. She was also implicitly signaling to court officials that she, though a slave, not only had access to material goods but also grasped their meaning. Rather than a superficial comment about dress, Louison's reference to her corset and hat were part of an attempt to draw on material culture to visually invoke her religious moral authority. Head coverings and corsets, as Louision knew well from her immersion in the world of the Ursulines, were key markers of feminine propriety and respectability, of the kind of woman who could upbraid a young male for acting like God. Not only did these garments serve to deny any association of laundering with prostitution, they proclaimed that she recognized the value inherent in dressing in conformity with French norms of piety, propriety, and gendered respectability.

In Louison's telling, she boldly challenged Pochenet twice, and she replayed their verbal exchanges for the court. The first time was when she stepped forward to ask him why he wanted to murder Babette. The second time was when she took Pochenet to task for daring to compare himself implicitly to God. Pochenet was Catholic, and Louison knew he would understand her point. In asserting moral authority over the soldier, Louison publicly claimed and proclaimed a fervent religious conviction. Her words bring to light how religious belief might have provided slaves with a reason for defiance. But her testimony also shows that religion could offer a rationale for publicly articulating defiance toward a French man, in spite of injunctions in the 1724 code noir and the 1751 police code (not to mention customary practice) that required all slaves, and even manumitted slaves, to constantly perform their submissiveness when in the presence of colonists.[50]

Did Louison feel moved by Catholic faith, and can her testimony shed light on this question? She certainly protested Pochenet's demands in a bold manner reminiscent of the proclamations of faith and self-sacrificing acts of resistance found in accounts of martyred women saints, staples of Catholic instruction with which she would have been familiar. But these narratives served up gendered ideals of resistance that were more problematic for women subject to the additional burdens of slavery. Religion offered Louison a way to claim an affinity with Catholics, and it allowed her to verbally assert, and righteously justify, her resistance to being demeaned and attacked by a colonist. For most enslaved men and women, it would prove untenable to resist the violence that was directed at them, let alone to openly discuss this violence in court. The testimony of Louison, Manon, and François offers rare evidence of how the enslaved handled violence and victimization and of how they chose to articulate their response to the authorities. But, as reflected in their testimony, the precise form taken by their resistance was mapped onto their particular worldviews.

✕✕

"THEY WOULD RATHER THEIR SLAVE DIE"

What about those that Louison, Manon, and François lived alongside who subjugated them on a daily basis: Did they acknowledge their slaves' worldviews? Louison's verbal and nonverbal expressions of piety surely should have pleased the Ursulines, but, in the proverbial narrative twist, the nuns chose not to support her in the case against Pochenet. They did not change their mind even after hearing Louison's testimony, and it was unlikely the first time they had heard her and other witnesses tell of the harrowing attack. Eight days had passed between the brutal incident and the deposition, meaning that they were intimately familiar with what Louison and Babette had suffered and the physical pain and emotional trauma they continued to endure as they nursed their broken bodies.

Under French law, a criminal investigation had to begin with a denunciation. According to Article 25 of the 1724 code noir, however, the enslaved could not represent themselves in civil or criminal matters: "Slaves cannot be parties to or in judgment over civil suits, either as plaintiffs or defendants, nor be parties in civil or criminal matters; except that their masters shall have the right to act for or in their defense in civil matters, and, in criminal matters, to demand reparation for the outrages and excesses committed against their slaves." Because Babette was owned by the nuns outright, while Louison, her husband, and their children had been granted to them by the king to work in the military hospital, Councillor Raguet, in conformity with the code noir, pressed the sisters for a formal statement, as they should have been the ones to pursue justice and reparation for crimes committed against their slaves. But the nuns, Charlotte Hebert, Sister St. François Xavier, and Marguerite de Belaire, Sister Ste. Madeleine of Jesus, declared that "neither their community nor they themselves wanted in any way to get involved in this affair, neither as accusers nor as defendants; that on the contrary, if they could save the life of this man, they would ask for it" *(Elles nous ont dit que Leur communauté Ny Elles ne Vouloient En aucune façon se mesler de cette affaire Ny En demandant ny en deffendant qu'au contraire sy Elles pouvoient sauver la vie de Cet homme Elle Le demanderoient).* They then added that "they would rather lose their slave than do anything against the charity owed to others" (*qu'elles aimaient mieux perdre leur négresse que de rien faire contre la charité de son prochain*).[51]

The nuns' refusal to cooperate was not the outcome that court officers had anticipated the day they transported themselves to the convent. Since the code noir only allowed slaveowners, and not slaves themselves, to pursue justice, the Ursulines' lack of cooperation in signing the deposition could have led to the prosecution being dropped. Yet the prosecutor general obviously considered the crime to be of sufficient import that he proceeded with the case. He even came to identify the document bearing Louison's deposition as the official denunciation of Pochenet's crime, even though it went against the code noir for a slave to act as denunciator.[52]

Why did the nuns decline to prosecute? After all, other slaveowners in the colony assiduously pursued claims for damages whenever other colonists injured one of their slaves. For example, in 1738 in the Illinois Country, Father Antoine-Robert Le Boullenger filed a suit against a man named La Croix who had broken the arm of one of the slaves on the Jesuits' plantation (La Croix unapologetically claimed in his own defense that the slave had insulted him, clearly considering himself justified in meting out punishment). The court ordered that La Croix compensate the Jesuits for damages to their property, requiring that he furnish a temporary replacement, cover the surgeon's fees, and pay further damages if the slave became permanently crippled. The Ursulines' refusal to act was all the more significant when viewed from their economic perspective. Under the terms of their 1744 agreement with the crown, any slaves who died (except for Jean-Baptiste) would not be replaced at the king's cost nor could they claim compensation from him. Rather, they would have to substitute slaves of their own. To put it bluntly, in the harsh, purely economic terms of the language and laws of slavery: if the nuns had agreed to lodge a complaint, then, according to Article 25, the prosecution of Pochenet could have opened the door to procure damages from the king for harm caused by one of his soldiers to their movable property. So why did they not proceed?[53]

Given that the Ursulines had authority over their own internal matters and that they deliberated over them as a community, it is perplexing that there are no entries about the matter in the 1752 register that they kept to record their discussions and decisions. But other documents show that at the time of the attack the New Orleans Ursulines were in a particularly precarious political position. In addition to managing the hospital, they were also responsible for running an orphanage for girls and educating the daughters of colonists. To enable the convent to be financially self-sufficient, the king was meant to make annual disbursements for the orphans' care, and the nuns also drew income from the plantation (and slaves) that the king granted them on the outskirts of town to operate. But payments from the crown were not always prompt or forthcoming, and financial conditions in the colony were onerous. Additionally, the Ursulines had become embroiled in contentious discussions with the governor and *commissaire-ordonnateur* over their contract to administer the hospital, specifically over how they had accounted for revenues and whether or not the sisters were required to furnish their own slaves to work in the hospital.[54]

All of these disagreements and intrigues about the Ursulines' finances and reputation undoubtedly provided the political backdrop for their decision not to sign Louison's statement and thus not to risk further antagonizing the king's representatives over compensation for Babette's and Louison's injuries. Yet the nuns' actions (or lack thereof) in the court case against Pochenet seem to have achieved no long-term improvement in their relations with the governor and ordonnateur. In December 1752, a full six months after the trial, the New Orleans Ursulines were still defending their reputation as stewards of the hospital. Their proxy in France, the Abbé de Lisle-Dieu, was called to speak for them against charges of fraud, and, in so doing, he outlined a serious complaint about the surgeons' lack of respect toward the nuns. He pointedly noted that the use of gendered slurs affected the dynamic between healers and their patients, for it:

> takes away the credit and authority that they should have over the patients to control them and rather than lending a favorable ear to their complaints it seems on the contrary that the patients are authorized to show a lack of respect, especially if it is true (as it is said) that the surgeons from the hospital itself say, in speaking of the nuns to the patients, that they are girls and to just let them say what they want.

Though Governor Louis Billouart de Kerlérec praised the Ursulines' zeal the following year, and showed some sympathy to their needs, by 1754, the ordonnateur was again accusing the Ursulines of fraud and repeating an earlier suggestion that the hospital pharmacy be removed from their control.[55]

These disputes and demeaning slights ("girls" not worthy of respect and authority) must have stung the Ursulines but also undoubtedly influenced their decision, providing sound strategic reasons for them to withhold their formal backing from Louison's deposition. At the same time, their tone and their choice of words give a parallel set of insights into the nuns' broader mindset. They could have simply refused to sign the statement. Instead, they went to the trouble of adding, and specifying, that "they would rather lose their slave than do anything against the charity owed to others." Their statement does not read as a generic declaration made by nuns about charity and forgiveness but as one that reflected the hierarchy between an enslaved woman's life and that of a French man's.

The nuns' words seem to strike a discordant note, given the Ursulines' enthusiasm for evangelizing slaves, but this ambiguity was not an anomaly. Furthermore, Marie Turpin, Sister Ste. Marthe, a half-Indian and the first woman to be consecrated as a nun in the New Orleans convent (and the first nun to be consecrated in territory that would become part of the United States), had been living among them since taking her vows in 1751. Born in the Illinois Country in Upper Louisiana to a French colonist and his legitimate Illinois Indian wife, Turpin was only granted the status of a converse or lay nun despite meeting the qualifications of literacy and dowry that were the preconditions for attaining the status of a full choir nun. As a converse nun, Turpin wore a differentiated habit and was prohibited from teaching; she could never have acceded to the rank of mother superior nor could she vote in the community chapter, for example, about the court case against Pochenet. The racial overtones in the way the nuns worded their refusal to sign Louison's deposition are further compounded by the knowledge that Sister Madeleine (who was one of those representing the Ursulines before the court officials) had heard the attack when it happened and was troubled enough to ask Mathieu Mulquet, a soldier in the care of the hospital, to run and find out what was going on. She had been present to see the wounded Louison and Babette being carried into the hospital and to witness first-hand Pochenet's violent cursing and yelling once he was apprehended and dragged onto the hospital grounds, and she would have examined and tended to the many stab wounds that were incurred, witnessed the victims' pain, and seen Manon's delirium.[56]

Given this context, what did—what could—Louison make of the nuns' refusal to sign her declaration and to validate her testimony by stamping it with the convent's approval? She surely heard the two nuns decline to sign and, harder yet, listened as they stated that they would rather "lose their slave" than take any action against Pochenet. She lived with the nuns, worked alongside them in the hospital, and prayed with them. Had she expected more from them, and did their refusal come as a surprise, or did she already recognize that her status as a slave (even if a privileged slave) trumped all other measures of worth? Did they trust and respect her enough to explain their position to her, or did she remain invisible to them? Her repeated assertiveness before Pochenet and the court; her assumption of a mantle of authority, not that of a victim; her claim to morality; even her sartorial self-presentation all suggest that she found ways in her life to uphold and project a modicum of self-respect. The daily ongoing depredations of slavery aside (and the Ursulines certainly drew on violent means of managing their slaves), it is difficult to imagine that the Louison who addressed Pochenet in such strong terms and spoke so evocatively about herself to the court officials could have imagined overhearing the nuns deny her personhood with such raw bluntness. But she did hear them.

Louison survived the attack and was still assigned to the hospital in 1760. Though Babette was still alive ten days after the assault and four days after the court officials had declared that she was delirious and near death, her fate is unknown beyond June 17, 1752, when both women were identified as "the two injured *négresses*" *(les deux negresses blessés)*. Three weeks after Pochenet's attack, thirteen days after Louison and Manon gave their testimony, the soldier was convicted and sentenced to be hanged and strangled, a sentence consistent with the military regulations that governed capital crimes and attempted crimes committed by soldiers. But, some time after he received his death sentence, an official missive from the commissaire-ordonnateur to the minister of the navy reveals that his sentence was commuted. He was condemned instead to the galleys, which meant banishment for life from the realm and, in effect, civil death — making him a second time lucky if the prosecutor was right that he had evaded a capital sentence for knifing a woman in Metz by becoming a convict soldier.[57]

Pochenet was shipped out of New Orleans on *Le Rhinoceros* in September 1752. No explanation was given in the official missive from Louisiana to France commuting his sentence, but a copy of the trial record was included, and Pochenet's crime was tied to a broader critique of "the excess with which *guildive* [alcohol] is distributed in the canteen, a drink that completely ruins the soldier and renders him furious." Perhaps some time after the original sentencing some authority higher than the Superior Council had prevailed, or perhaps the Ursuline nuns had interceded on his behalf, though no record attests to such intercession beyond their expressed desire that no harm come to their fellow man. But, like enslaved Africans (some of whom also avoided the death penalty), French soldiers constituted a valuable commodity, part of a flexible workforce that could be deployed, often forcibly, to serve throughout the French Empire. Pochenet was worth more to the crown alive, even drunk, dangerous, and diseased, than dead.[58]

What Louison thought of the sentence is not known, but it is impossible to sidestep the reality, then or now, that this case was not so much about the suffering of slaves than about the maintenance of state control over soldiers and damage done to "property." The court officials' probing of the Ursuline nuns' wishes in their capacity as Babette and Louison's mistresses and owners as to how to proceed makes this explicit. Even though the Ursulines refused to sign the declaration of a woman who had lived among them for eight years and even though Pochenet's sentence was commuted, the court tacitly upheld Louison, François, and Manon's right to challenge the physical (and potentially sexual) assault made on them by one individual French male as they went about their work on June 13, 1752. For Louison, redirecting the narrative meant framing her response to Pochenet in terms of her religious beliefs, her standing, and her appearance. In so doing, she transformed her testimony from one of being attacked to one centered on the avowal of her superior morality, as she made sure to convey verbally and visually.

"Not So Denatured as to Kill Her Child"

Marie-Jeanne and Lisette

TESTIMONY OF MARIE-JEANNE, JULY 17, 1748

Interrogated why she had not told Matis and Dame Braseau that she was pregnant when they asked her?

Said that when she was asked if she did not feel anything move in her stomach she told them no and that those who asked her these questions said that it must be a mole [molar pregnancy] and that she did not know what a mole was, that she does not know this.

Interrogated why she hid from Dame Beauvois that she had brought a child into the world before the mole, the said Dame Beauvois had told you that you could well have given birth to a child before the mole?

Said that she does not know if she gave birth to a child, lots of stuff came out of her body but having fainted she did not know what happened to her since then, that having come to she found next to her lots of stuff that had come from her body, and having said to the little *sauvagesse* [female Indian] of Mr. Braseau's to go warn her mistress, which she did not want to do, and having gathered into her apron everything that was around her that was left from what she had delivered from her body, she went to the house as best she could.

Interrogé pour quoi elle n'a pas dit à Matis et à la dame Braseau quelle etoit grosse après qu'ils lui ont eu demandé

A dit que lorsqu'on lui demandoit si elle ne sentoit rien remuer dans son ventre elle leur a dit que non et que ceux qui lui faisoient ces questions disoient qu'il falloit que ce fut une molle es quelle ne sçaoit pas ce que setoit qu'une molle qu'elle ne connoissoit point cela

Interrogé pourquoi elle a caché à la Dame Beauvois quelle avoit mis un enfant au monde avant la molle, Laquelle dame Beauvois t'a dit que tu pouvoit bien avoir accouché dun enfant avant la molle

A dit quelle ne scait pas si elle a accouché dun enfant qu'etant dehors il lui etoit sortie bien des choses du corps mais qu'ayant tombée evanouy elle ne sçu ce qui lui etoit arrivé depuis, qu'etant revenue de son Evanouissement elle trouva aupres d'elle bien de choses quelle avoit rendu et ayant dit à la petite sauvagesse de Mr. Braseau d'aller avertir sa maitresse ce quelle ne voulu point faire et ayant ramassé es mis dans son tablier ce quelle avoit autour d'elle qu'etoit sortie de son corps elle se rendit à la maison comme elle pu[1]

TESTIMONY OF LISETTE, JULY 15, 1748

On this day, Lisette Indian slave belonging to Dame Braseau residing with her in this town of Kaskaskia parish of the Immaculate conception, aged nine to ten years old who is of the Odawa nation, not speaking French whereupon we have ordered that the information that she gives us will be explained to us by Joseph Petit, interpreter of this language, whom we have named to this office and to whom we have made swear to well and faithfully in his conscience explain the deposition of the said Lisette, appointed to this office for the deposition relating to Jérôme Matis's denunciation.

Deposes on the facts mentioned in the denunciation of Jérôme Matis which we have read to her and had explained to her in her language by Joseph Petit, he told us that she had said that Marie-Jeanne being in the stable near the house, she deponent being outside at a breach, she saw her with a child in her hands that was crying, and that the said *negresse* held it by the throat to strangle it, and she deponent told her not to kill it, and the said *negresse* told her to go away, and that if she did not go away that she would beat her. And that the said *negresse* having smothered her child tore it into pieces and quartered it, and put it in a hole in the stable, where there were two pigs, and that she, the deponent, having left, she knows nothing more.

Du dit jour Lisette esclave indienne appartenante à la Dame Braseau demeurante chez elle en cette ville des Cas psse de L'immaculée conception, agée de neuf à dix ans laquelle es outa8oise de nation n'entendant pas le français, surquoy Nous avons ordonné que l'information qui nous sera par elle faite nous sera expliqué par Joseph Petit interprette de cette Langue, que nous avons nommé d'office auquel nous avons fait faire serment de bien et fidelement en sa conscience expliquer la deposition de la dite Lisette à ce mandé d'office pour deposer à la denonciation de Jerome Matis

Depose sur les faits mentionnez en la denunciation de jerome matis dont lui avons fait faire lecture et expliqué en sa langue par le dit joseph Petit lequel nous a dit quelle disoit que Marie Jeanne etant dans l'étable près de la maison elle deposante etant dehors à une brêche, elle lui vit un enfant entre les mains qui crioit et que la dite negresse le prit à la gorge pour l'etrangler et quelle deposante lui disoit de ne point tuer et que la dite negresse lui disoit de s'en aller et que si elle ne s'en alloit qu'elle la battroit et que la dite negresse ayant etouffée son enfant l'a dechiré par morceau et mis en quartiers es la mis dans un trou dans la dite etable, ou il y avoit deux cochons et quelle deposante s'etant retirée elle ne sçait rien de plus[2]

In July 1748, a charge of infanticide was brought against an enslaved African woman, Marie-Jeanne, just twelve days after she had gone into labor. The twenty-year-old baptized Creole, who lived in Kaskaskia in the Illinois Country, remained under the shadow of this accusation for the next twelve months. The case was first prosecuted in the Illinois Country, where she was interrogated and witnesses heard, then in New Orleans, where she (alone) was sent one year later so that the Superior Council of Louisiana could further investigate her case and render judgment. In their efforts to reach a verdict, officials questioned Marie-Jeanne four times.[3]

When the case came to trial in Kaskaskia, six witnesses were called to testify, but only one was alleged to have seen Marie-Jeanne in the act: Lisette, a nine- or ten-year-old Indian slave girl identified as Ottawa who did not speak French and lived with her mistress Dame Braseau in Kaskaskia. Lisette attested via an interpreter that she had been present with Marie-Jeanne in the stable and saw her "strangle her child, she tore it apart into pieces and quartered it and put it in a hole." Speaking in her own defense after her arrest, Marie-Jeanne repudiated the allegation, explaining that she had fainted after going into labor and woke up surrounded by fetal matter that was taken at the time as evidence of a doomed molar pregnancy. She further protested her innocence by asserting that "she did not have a heart hard enough to kill her own child, that it is too hard for her" (quelle n'auroit pas le Coeur assé dure pour tuer son enfant que cest trop fort pour elle). She reiterated her assertion before the Superior Council in New Orleans but added a telling new adjective, "that she is not so denatured, nor so bad as to destroy her child, if she

Marie-Jeanne and Lisette

had seen one in what she had delivered" *(quelle n'est pas sy denaturée ny sy mauvaise pour detruire son enfant sy elle y avoit vu un parmy ce quelle a rendue)*. This is as close as the testimony goes in addressing her feelings about her situation or whether she grieved her loss.[4]

Marie-Jeanne was the only woman—slave or free—interrogated about infanticide (or abortion) in Louisiana. Although the lines of questioning the judges pursued focused on determining her guilt, Marie-Jeanne's and Lisette's appearances before the court also provided them with an unexpected opportunity to narrate a different story that was not necessarily centered on the purported crime. Throughout their testimony, they each interspersed references to a special kind of intimacy, that which accompanied a close working relationship and that touched on conflicts over authority among the enslaved. In the two women's responses to court officials, it is possible to glimpse the toll of slavery on reproductive rights and parent-child relationships and to hear how a childless woman and a motherless child fought to communicate their conceptions of the maternal.

✕✕✕

A PREGNANCY? MARIE-JEANNE

Following convention, the court in Kaskaskia asked the defendant to identify herself, and she answered that "she was named Marie-Jeanne, that she is aged twenty years old or so, that she is the *negresse* of Miss Marie Vinsenne, that she is leased to Jerôme Matis resident in this town" *(A dit quelle sappellé Marie-Jeanne quelle est agée de vingt ans ou environ quelle est negresse de Damoiselle Marie Vinsenne quelle est louée à Jérôme Matis demeurant en cette ville)*. Jérôme Matis and Marie-Jeanne resided with Joseph Braseau and his wife Françoise Dizier, who kept lodgers. Their precise living arrangements were not specified, but the Braseau house measured twenty-five by twenty feet when it was built in 1739, with four windows and two doors. Neither Marie-Jeanne or Matis stated how long she had been with him, but he did add in his testimony that she was already pregnant when he leased her, though she would later deny that she was.[5]

The circumstances that led to Matis leasing Marie-Jeanne were circuitous. She actually belonged to the young Maric Vincennes. Vincennes's father, the officer François-Marie Bissot de Vincennes, was the founder of the Vincennes Post. He had legally married Marie Du Longpré in Kaskaskia in 1733. His bride was the legitimate daughter of a Frenchman and his Kaskaskia Indian wife, Marie Ma8e8ence8oire (because the phoneme "8" or "8" was shorthand for the sound "ou" in French or "w" in English, the letter combination "8e" in her name was pronounced like "way" and "8oi," "wah"). His marriage fit within a highly distinctive pattern in the Illinois Country whereby Frenchmen, including prominent ones, contracted legal Catholic marriages with Indian women or their mixed-heritage daughters. These women were deemed worthy marriage partners, for intermarriage with Indian widows and their daughters came with financial and social benefits. Beyond any advantages he accrued from marrying into a Kaskaskia Indian network, Vincennes received a substantial dowry from his bride's parents consisting in part of land. Vincennes died in 1736 after being captured during the Chickasaw War, leaving behind a widow and two daughters, Marie and Catherine. His widow died in 1747. It was Marie who inherited Marie-Jeanne. The young Vincennes girl was around sixteen when the infanticide case was prosecuted. Since she was an unmarried minor, her appointed tutor managed her affairs, and it was her acting guardian, Dame Lasource, who arranged to lease Marie-Jeanne to Matis. Nowhere was it specified why Matis leased her or what labor he required from her beyond the reference to her being in the stable when she went into labor. What duties would he have assigned her if she had given birth? Would he, for example, have hired her out as a wet nurse or kept her entirely focused on fulfilling her usual workload?[6]

Details in the archives pertaining to the circumstances under which Marie-Jeanne came to be owned by the Vincennes are few. Marie and Catherine's maternal grandfather had arranged in 1730 that his Indian widow would be bypassed so that he could leave equal quantities of livestock and slaves to his children on his death. However, the donation was rendered void, since it contravened the Coutume de Paris, which regulated civil law in Louisiana and stipulated that a surviving husband or wife was entitled to half of their deceased spouse's estate with the remaining half being shared equally between any children. Marie-Jeanne might have been among those slaves and could have been passed down to Marie from her grandmother; alternatively, she could have entered the Vincennes household in 1736, when Dame Vincennes acquired a family of enslaved Africans from Jean Lalande.[7]

The court case against Marie-Jeanne hinged on determining whether she had had a molar pregnancy, which would have been doomed from conception, or whether she had given birth to a live baby, then killed her newborn and covered up her actions by burying the body and simulating having had a "mole." In the eighteenth century, a mole or molar pregnancy was understood as an abnormal "mass of flesh without form and inanimate that pregnant women sometimes carry instead of a child." The investigation centered exclusively on infanticide, not feticide. At no point was Marie-Jeanne accused of having induced an abortion.[8]

It is impossible to know what actually happened, but one snippet from the investigation seems to support Marie-Jeanne's denial that she had given birth to a live infant. This was a reference to a conversation she had had the day before, during which Marie-Jeanne denied to her mistress that she was even pregnant and added that she had not felt any movement in her stomach ("that when she was asked if she did not feel anything move in her stomach she told them no"). In her testimony, she added, "Those who asked her these questions said that it must be a mole and that she did not know what a mole was, that she does not know this." In other words, it was not Marie-Jeanne but her interlocutors who first speculated that the pregnancy was a problematic one, using a term that "she did not know." Additionally, this was not her first difficult pregnancy. In later testimony before the Superior Council, she spoke of having miscarried once, long before *("quelle a fait il y a Longtemps une fausse couche")*.[9]

Dame Marie Louise La Croix, wife of Jean Baptiste Beauvais, the midwife who examined Marie-Jeanne shortly after she had gone into labor, noted at the time that Marie-Jeanne's birth canal was very open (the description changed to "extraordinarily open" *[extraordinairement ouverte]* in the New Orleans transcript of her deposition) but did not probe further. In her testimony, which was notable for its defensive tone, she described going to see Marie-Jeanne, who was very sick following the labor:

> Dame Braseau showed her a piece of flesh that the slave had delivered and that the deponent took for a damaged mole, not having paid much attention to it given that the said Braseau told her that she did not think that [Marie-Jeanne] had delivered a child along with the mole, though the said deponent had said that she could well have brought a child into the world along with the mole, since the *negresse* was very open, however, trusting everything that she was told, she concluded that she could well have been pregnant only with a mole and finally, thinking in good faith that she had not given birth did not examine her enough for [illegible], not having been been asked to do so by the said lady [illegible] thinking also that she was pregnant just from [illegible] and in any case since the said *negresse* kept falling [out of consciousness] she could not have done an examination as required if they had absolutely believed that she was pregnant with a child.

---

la dame Braseau lui presenta un morceau de chair quelle dit que ladite negresse etoit delivrée es que la dite deposante pris pour une molle corrompu ny ayant pas fait grande attention attendu que la dite Braseau lui dit qu'elle ne Croyoit quelle Eut rendu avec ladite molle un en-

fant Comme ladite deposante avoit dit qu'elle pouvoit bien avoir mis au
monde un enfant avec ladite molle Etant ladite negresse fort ouverte, es
que cependant s'en rapportant à tout ce qu'on lui dit elle conclut quelle
pouvoit bien etre grosse que d'une molle et enfin pensant de bonne foÿ
quelle navoit point mis au monde [illegible] ne l'ayant pas asses exami-
née pour [illegible] ayant point été requis par ladite dame [illegible]
pensant aussi quelle n'etoit grosse que de [illegible] et que dailleurs la
dite negresse tomboit en [illegible] à tous momens elle ne put en faire
la visite comme il seroit convenue si on lavoit absolument crue grosse
d'enfant[10]

The matter might have gone away but for the fact that the landlady, Dame
Braseau, discovered an infant's skull and an arm bone that had been dug up
by dogs in the days following Marie-Jeanne's going into labor. It was this discovery that set off the investigation. As Dame Braseau testified:

That the following Sunday the seventh of the present month, Dame
Braseau, leaving her house in the early morning, she saw on her door-
step the arm of a newborn, from the shoulder to the hand which was all
in one piece, and a piece of the skull which seemed to be from the same
child as the arm, which was at three or four steps from the door, where
the pigs were digging. Thinking immediately that they were pieces of
the body of the child of the said *negresse,* she told this to the said Jerôme
Matis, who was home and who came looking around the house to see
if he could find any other debris from the body, assuming that the said
negresse had destroyed her child, and all the deponent's other lodgers
made the same assumption, and finally, the said Jérôme Matis having
entered the stable near the house, found in a pile of manure a kind of
pit or hole where the child could have been buried, where there was a
piece of skull that the pigs were digging up, and blood on the stable's
stakes in the ground, which seems to have gotten there after the arms of
the said child had been freshly pulled from the body by some dogs that
had dragged it from [the pit] to the door. And the said deponent, filled
with angry outrage, went to find the said *negresse* to reproach her about
the apparent crime, that the said *negresse* has always denied.

Que le dimanche sept de ce mois sortant de chez elle le matin elle trouva
sur le pas de sa porte le bras d'un enfant nouvellement nay, depuis
l'épole jusque à la main qui y etoit tout entier, et une partie du crane
qui parroissoit être du meme enfant que celui du bras, qui étoit à trois
ou quatre pas de la porte, que des cochons fouilloient, pensant aussi-

tôt que c'etoit des parties du Corps de l'enfant de la dite negresse elle fit avertir le dit Jerome Matis qui etoit pour lors chez lui, lequel étant venu roder autout de la maison pour voir s'il ne trouveroit quelque autre debris dudit corps presumant que la dite negresse avoit detruit son enfant et toutes autres pensionnaires de la deposante firent le meme jugement et enfin ledit Jerome Matis etant entré dans une Etable pres de la maison, trouva dans un tas de fumier comme une fosse ou trou où pouvoit avoir ete enterré ledit enfant où il y avoit un morceau de crane que les cochons fouilloient, es du sang aux pieux de la dite etable, qui parroissoit y avoir été mis par les Bras dudit enfant fraichement arraché de son corps par les Chiens qui l'avoient emporté par cet endroit à sa porte. Es la dite deposante outrée de colere fut trouver ladite negresse pour lui faire reproche de cet apparent crime, que la dite negresse a toujours niée

Though she had no cause to mention it, Dame Braseau had given birth herself not long before, and her eldest son, Louis, was around three years old when these events that filled her with "angry outrage" took place.[11]

It was at this point in the trial, after the discovery of bones, that Lisette was first mentioned. As Dame Braseau continued with her narrative, she stated that:

A little Indian slave belonging to the deponent made her understand by sign, not being able to speak French, that the said Marie-Jeanne had smothered her child by strangling it at the neck, and had told her not to say anything, and told her by sign to go away. And finally, the said little *sauvagesse* made it known that she had seen and heard the said child and that she did not know where it was. After she [the deponent] buried the child's arm and pieces of skull in her garden, and that two or three hours later she went to the area where she had buried the bones of the said child, and that she did not find them there. Having called the little *sauvagesse* to see if she did not know who had removed them, she made [the deponent] understand that she had seen Marie-Jeanne scratch around in that area, and finally this morning, looking around the area where the child or the bones could have been taken, she [the deponent] found a piece of skull that she brought to us.

---

une petite sauvagesse esclave de ladite deposante lui fit entendre par signe ne pouvant parler francais, que la dite Marie Jeanne avoit etouf-fée son enfant lui serrant le col avec les mains, lui disant de ne rien dire, es lui faisant signe de s'en aller et enfin la dite petite sauvagesse fit entendre quelle avoit veüe es entendu ledit enfant et quelle ne sçaoit où il avoit été mis. Apres que la dite deposante fut enterer le bras et les morceau du crane dudit enfant dans son jardin et que deux ou trois heures après, elle fut voir l'endroit où elle avoit enterré les os dudit enfant, et quelle ne les y a plus trouvé, ayant appellée la petite sauvagesse pour sçavoir si elle ne sçauroit pas qui les auroit oté, elle lui fit entendre qu'elle avoit vue Marie Jeanne grater en cet endroit, es enfin ce matin rodant aux environs des endroits où lenfant ou ses ossement pouvoient avoir été portez ou tenus, elle a trouvée un morceau du crane quelle nous a apportée

In other words, it was not Lisette's testimony but the finding of physical evidence that triggered the investigation and ensuing prosecution, one that would last nearly a year. As it turned out, the physical evidence would be the least pertinent aspect of the prosecution's case.[12]

✂ ✂

THE COURT CASE

Though the vast majority of slave prosecutions were tried in New Orleans, court cases could also be heard in the colony's outposts, as Marie-Jeanne's was. Post commandants typically oversaw legal proceedings for cases deemed straightforward, but trickier cases were referred to the Superior Council in New Orleans. Once the investigation was launched, Lisette quickly emerged as the lead witness. French law did not prohibit children, no matter their age, from testifying in criminal cases, and the young girl, whose French name was a diminutive of Elizabeth, appeared twice before the court: once in her role as a witness and once for a formal confrontation with the accused. Both times, her words had to be translated by an interpreter, Joseph Petit, who was "made [to] swear to well and faithfully in his conscience explain the deposition of the said Lisette." Joseph Petit fulfilled his court-appointed role to translate her words, but he was not alone in mediating for her. Other witnesses would step forward, as Dame Braseau had, to provide the court with their own interpretations of Lisette's gestures and her attempts to communicate by sign at the time that the events originally took place.[13]

Throughout the trial, Lisette remained consistent in her testimony. During her first appearance before the court as a witness, she began by relaying the events that took place on the day Marie-Jeanne went into labor, stating:

that Marie-Jeanne being in the stable near the house, she deponent being outside, she saw her with a child in her hands that was crying, and that the said *negresse* held it by the throat to strangle it, and she

Marie-Jeanne and Lisette

deponent told her not to kill it, and the said *negresse* told her to go away, and that if she did not go away that she would beat her. And that the said *negresse* having smothered her child tore it into pieces and quartered it, and put it in a hole in the stable, where there were two pigs, and that she, the deponent, having left, she knows nothing more.

But, Lisette did not end her deposition there. Instead, she went on to describe a subsequent encounter with Marie-Jeanne sometime after, which revolved around the bones and fetal matter that their mistress had disposed of by burying:

> Her mistress having buried an arm and the bones of the head of a child in her garden plot, the said Marie-Jeanne, being seated a little after in the area where the bones had been put, she deponent told her and made her understand that she was not well there, and the said *negresse* told her it was to take the air, and she said to the deponent to go away, which she did, that however she saw the said *negresse* scratch the earth at that spot and saw her with bones in her hands, that she does not know where [Marie-Jeanne] put them
>
> ---
>
> En outre depose que sa maitresse ayant enterré un bras avec les os d'une teste d'enfant dans son jardin, ladite Marie-Jeanne, etant assise peut de temps après à l'endroit où les ossements avoient été mis, elle deposante lui dit et fit entendre quelle n'etoit pas bien là, et que la dite negresse lui dit quelle y etoit pour prendre le frais, et quelle dit à la dite deposante de s'en aller ce quelle fit, et que cependant elle vit ladite negresse grater la terre à cet endroit et quelle lui vit des os entre les mains qu'elle ne sçait où elle les a mis

Once the bones were rediscovered a few days later, Lisette was the only witness who claimed to have seen Marie-Jeanne retrieve and rebury them.[14]

During the subsequent formal confrontation with Marie-Jeanne, Lisette stated again, first, that she had seen Marie-Jeanne give birth to a live infant while they were both in the stable; second, that she had witnessed her kill the baby girl and tear apart the body; and third, that she watched her bury the evidence. The court record further referenced the young girl asserting that she had tried to prevent Marie-Jeanne from hurting her child, asking her if she could hold it; that the child had cried at birth; and that the baby was female. For her part, Marie-Jeanne denied any knowledge of a live birth. She stated that she had gone to the stable to urinate and found herself suddenly feeling sick. She insisted that, having fainted from the pain, she woke up to find "pieces of flesh and clotted blood underneath her" *(des morceaux de Chair et de sang Caillé sous Elle),* which she gathered as best she could to show her mistress. In her fight for the moral high ground, she maintained that she was incapable of murdering her child.[15]

The case against Marie-Jeanne was both complicated and confounding, and it stumped the judges who first heard it. Initially prosecuted in the Illinois Country, it was referred to the Superior Council in New Orleans, where Marie-Jeanne, apparently pregnant once again, was shipped along with a copy of the entire court record, including the witness testimony and the skull fragment. The other bones were not mentioned—had they disappeared or had they already been consumed by the pigs? Marie-Jeanne was interrogated twice more in New Orleans, once in court and once within the prison complex on the *sellette* (a special interrogation conducted in the prison so named for the low stool on which the defendant was made to sit). At no point during any of her interrogations or confrontations with witnesses did she confess nor did Lisette ever recant or waver in her testimony.[16]

❧❧

FROM THE ILLINOIS COUNTRY TO NEW ORLEANS

It could have taken Marie-Jeanne as little as fifteen days to reach New Orleans (the more arduous return trip took closer to three or four months). She would have journeyed on a convoy of flat-bottomed boats and large dugout canoes known as pirogues, traveling past the "patchwork of Native and colonial communities" that stretched along the Mississippi River. Depending on where in Louisiana she had been born, Marie-Jeanne could have been returning to a familiar place or encountering New Orleans for the first time. It was likely that she had heard tales of the town from the slaves and free blacks who worked the convoys between the two settlements. Kaskaskia was a tight-knit community. Did she know Marie Turpin, the "sainted girl" born in Kaskaskia to a French father and Indian mother who, just a year earlier, had also gone down to New Orleans, though voluntarily, to become a nun? As she wound her way through town, did she try to work out which building was the convent, hoping for a glimpse of a familiar face?[17]

From the landing point in New Orleans, which was just a little upriver from the town, she was remanded straight to prison, so her impression of the colonial capital would have been a quick one (especially given the small scale of the settlement) but one that nonetheless allowed her to notice that the urban center was laid out on a grid and the houses built right on the street (see Figure 35, key 14, for the landing point). She would have spotted, too, that the residents of New Orleans dressed differently than did those in the

Illinois Country, though she might not have understood that this was because the styles in New Orleans hewed more closely to French metropolitan fashions than to the lingering influence of French Canadian dress. Did she spot any Indians on her way through town? In 1748, there were few Indian slaves left in New Orleans, but there remained neighboring Indian settlements whose members continued to trade and otherwise interact with the resident colonial population of settlers, soldiers, and slaves.[18]

She would have noticed straightaway that there were no fields in town, no stables like the one where she had birthed the mole. Perhaps, as she passed through the capital, she caught a glimpse of walled courtyards at the rear of many of the houses, but she would have been hard pressed to guess that they contained household vegetable plots (see Figure 5). Once she arrived on the imposing Place d'armes (present-day Jackson Square), she must have been struck by its panoramic view of the river and the whitewashed brick barracks and government buildings that flanked the square, and she could not have missed the church of Saint Louis, which was planted near the brick prison (see Figure 35). No architecture of this scale or type existed in the Illinois Country.[19]

Though Marie-Jeanne would lose sight of these visual features once she was locked up, except when she left the prison to be led the short distance to the chambers of the Superior Council, the smells and sounds of a buoyant, hot, humid settlement would have seeped in and enveloped her. These sensations would have added to the alienation and fear she felt at having finally arrived in New Orleans after being taken hundreds of miles away from the Illinois Country as she waited for her fate to be determined.

These were very different worlds. The Illinois Country, that area in the upper Mississippi Valley known by the French as the *pays des Illinois,* had been populated since at least the mid-seventeenth century by groups of Algonquin people known as the Illinois (see Figure 2). Among the Illinois who had converged in the upper Mississippi Valley in this period, the most important were the Kaskaskia, Cahokia, Tamaroa, Michigamia, and Peoria, numbering around ten thousand in the 1670s, when the French first encountered (and quantified) them. From 1673 onward, French explorers, missionaries, and fur traders from New France had been establishing missions and settlements in the upper Mississippi Valley with a view to expanding the reach of France to the Gulf of Mexico (achieved in 1699 with the founding of Louisiana). Claiming this land for New France, the French found a region in flux owing to disease and prolonged incursions into the territory by members of the Iroquois Confederacy and a people already invested in trade and eager to interact as regional middlemen with new potential military and trading allies. The French established the first permanent settlement at Cahokia in 1699, followed by Kaskaskia in 1703. In 1717, after decades of intermittent French activity in the region, primarily by missionaries and fur traders, the pays des Illinois was removed from New France's direct control and granted to the French colonial province of Louisiana. In 1719, Fort de Chartres was established, followed by the settlements of Prairie du Rocher in 1722, Ste. Genevieve in the early 1750s, and St. Louis in 1764. In 1762, the settlements of Ste. Genevieve and St. Louis, which lay west of the Mississippi, were ceded to Spain. The territory on the east bank, including the other French colonial settlements, was ceded to Britain in 1763.[20]

The first French settlers in the Illinois Country resided within Indian villages, but, in 1719, the French carried out a far-reaching policy of removing those Indians who were not spouses, offspring, or slaves of Frenchmen from French settlements and creating separate French and Indian villages. As seen in Thomas Hutchins's 1771 map of the Illinois Country, which shows the continuing separation of colonial and Indian villages at Kaskaskia and Cahokia, this division remained intact throughout the colonial period (Figure 24). Though this policy did not prevent contact or exchange between members of the two villages, it did alter the dynamics in the region as well as the spatial and environmental features of the French settlements.[21]

The new French colonial villages were compact, centered on the parish church and surrounded by a system of open-field agriculture, features that further contributed to creating cohesive, nuclear communities. The houses were made in the distinctive colonial style that developed in the Illinois Country (Figure 25). Within the houses were French-style furniture and household effects interspersed with indigenous ones. This was the environment that Marie-Jeanne and Lisette inhabited, albeit as slaves.[22]

Following the ceding of Louisiana to the Company of the Indies in 1719, African slaves were brought into the Illinois Country, where they worked side by side with Indian slaves. By 1726, when the first census was conducted, the population of the Illinois Country villages stood at 334 individuals. It was already a slave society: 25.2 percent were enslaved Africans, with a further 12.8 percent consisting of enslaved Indians. In 1752, just two years after the investigation against Marie-Jeanne was initiated, the total population in the French colonial villages in the Illinois Country had reached 1,360, and just under half that number were enslaved (see Table 1). The 1752 census shows that, of the 167 heads of household accounted for, 69, or 41 percent, owned at least one enslaved African. These figures were bolstered by the seasonal availability of slaves and free blacks who manned the convoys from New Orleans and usually joined the labor pool while waiting for the return of the convoy

Marie-Jeanne and Lisette

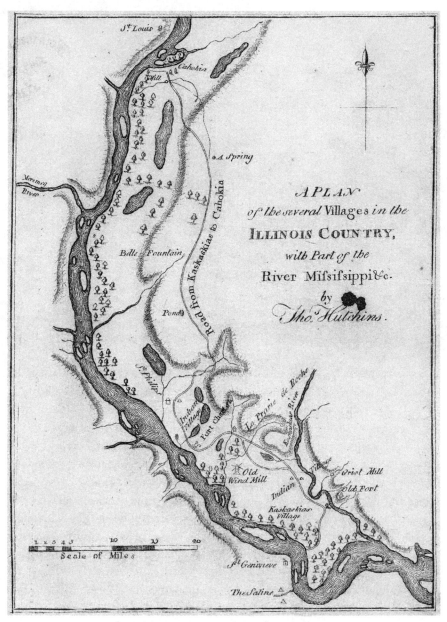

FIGURE 24: Thomas Hutchins, *A Plan of the Several Villages in the Illinois Country, with Part of the River Mississippi &c.* From Hutchins, *A Topographical Description of Virginia, Pennsylvania, Maryland, and North Carolina* (London, 1778). Courtesy of the American Philosophical Society, Philadelphia Note the separation of Indian from French villages, as begun by the French in 1719 and signaled here by the distinction between the French colonial "Kaskaskia village" and the Kaskaskia Indian village just north.

FIGURE 25: *Cahokia Courthouse* (post-on-sill style). Circa 1740, Cahokia, Illinois.
Courtesy of Illinois Department of Natural Resources

French colonial houses in the Illinois Country were constructed in one of two
dominant styles: with vertical logs that were either planted in the earth palisade
fashion (*poteaux-en-terre,* or post-in-ground), or placed upright on sills (*poteaux-sur-
sole,* or post-on-sill), as in the circa 1740 Cahokia Courthouse. The areas between the
logs were filled with a mixture of mud and straw or clay and pebbles; both types of
houses were whitewashed. Beginning in the 1730s, wealthier inhabitants built stone
houses. A distinctive feature found on all of these types of houses was the *galerie*
(wraparound porch), which could run along two, three, or four sides of a house.

to the capital. Out of the 1,360 total persons living in the French-controlled
areas of the region enumerated by the census, there were 445 enslaved Africans, with a preponderance of males, and 147 enslaved Indians, with an in-
verse preponderance of females (see Table 2).[23]

Conditions for slaves in the Illinois Country seem to have been margin-
ally better than in Lower Louisiana in terms of food and other basic necessi-
ties. The majority of enslaved Africans are thought to have worked alongside
French settlers in agriculture farming according to European methods and

Marie-Jeanne and Lisette

TABLE 1: *Population of the Illinois Country, 1752*

	Number
Enslaved Africans:	445
Enslaved Indians:	147
French Population (including Indian wives of Frenchmen):	768
Population of the Illinois Country	1360

Source: Census of villages in the Illinois Country, [1752], Vaudreuil Papers, O/S LO 426, Huntington Library, San Marino, Calif.

TABLE 2: *Population of Enslaved Africans and Indians in the Illinois Country, 1752*

	Enslaved Africans	Enslaved Indians
Adult male	187	
Adult female	113	
Prepubescent male	83	
Prepubescent female	62	
Male		60
Female		87
Total	445	147

Source: Census of villages in the Illinois Country, [1752], Vaudreuil Papers, O/S LO 426, Huntington Library, San Marino, Calif.

were chiefly engaged in the cultivation of wheat for the flour trade with Lower Louisiana. Although there is little information about the gendered division of labor around the time of the court case, there is some evidence that men and women were made to adhere to different activities stemming from European notions of gender-appropriate work but that enslaved women (Indian or African) were also required to do field labor. A petition in 1747 to lease an Indian female slave and her infant noted that she "is infirm not being able to work in the fields or to do the laundry," clearly indicating that these duties would ordinarily fall within the purview of enslaved women. Spring wheat was planted in March and harvested in July. Cattle were put out to pasture during the remaining months on the fallow common fields following the custom of *"l'abandon,"* which was a Northern European system that intertwined grain production with animal husbandry. A 1737 decree confirmed that communal grazing would take place each year from November 1 (All Saints' Day) to April 15. The month of July, when the events surrounding the delivery transpired, was harvesttime; the inhabitants probably knew already that the harvest that year, the summer of 1748, would be a terrible one.[24]

Though enslaved women in the Illinois Country performed agricultural labor, no reference was made to Marie-Jeanne or Lisette working the fields. It is possible that this was not a regular part of their labor or that the events had taken place after field work was done for the day, leaving them to other duties. The court case reveals that Lisette and Marie-Jeanne were at work together in the stables, tending to livestock, namely the hogs that, once transformed into cured hams, would constitute another large-scale staple traded to Lower Louisiana. They were both enslaved and labored side by side, but their work life was hierarchical and gendered: Marie-Jeanne supervised Lisette's work while Dame Braseau (not her husband) oversaw Marie-Jeanne's.[25]

LISETTE

In contrast to enslaved Africans like Marie-Jeanne, only a tiny handful of Indian slaves testified in criminal trials in French colonial Louisiana, and Lisette was the only one to do so in a trial conducted in the Illinois Country during the French regime. That Lisette chose other subjects to raise before the court besides those details directly pertinent to the accusation suggests that the child evidently did not see the requirement to testify as either frightening or pointless. Rather, profiting from the opportunity that the court case provided, she eagerly sought to communicate — enthusiastically even.

Assuming Lisette was still enslaved in the Illinois Country in 1752, she would have been one of eighty-seven enslaved Indian females listed in the census. Before 1717, the Illinois Country was part of New France, but after this date the region was formally transferred to Louisiana (though technically the colony remained a province of New France). Indian slavery had been permitted in New France since 1709, but in Louisiana the situation was more amorphous. For example, from 1706–1713, the king refused repeated requests from Louisiana settlers to allow the trade in Indian slaves to the Caribbean. Nevertheless, Indian slavery was never banned as such in the colony, though, in 1720, the Company of the Indies (unsuccessfully) sought to halt Louisiana's Indian slave trade, "having learnt that the *voyageurs* [fur traders] who go to the Missouri and Arkansas rivers for the trade, seek to sow division among the Indian nations and incite them to go to war in order to procure the slaves that they then buy from them, which is not only contrary to the King's Ordinances, but also prejudices the commerce of the Company and the establishments it hopes to make in this country." In any case, especially after the Great Peace of Montreal in 1701, the French avoided enslaving allies. For example, a new ordinance was enacted in 1739 that banned Indian slavery in the Caribbean (the Indian slaves being exported via New France and Louisiana) but was modified to allow the enslavement of those Indians who were not allies of the French. Most Indian slaves in the Illinois Country were Plains Indians, usually acquired through trade with Indian allies.[26]

Given her inability to speak French, Lisette must have been a recent arrival. In the year leading up to the court case, voyageurs came to Kaskaskia from many points in New France, including Detroit and Michilimackinac. They also returned from trading expeditions to the Missouri and Fox (Meskwaki) Indians. Any of these journeys could have resulted in Lisette being sold in the Illinois Country. Among France's staunchest allies, and, therefore, especially unlikely subjects for enslavement in French settlements, were the Ottawa, the very nation that Lisette was identified as belonging to, making it doubtful that she was in fact Ottawa.[27]

Lisette herself did not directly enlighten her audience as to her identity. In contrast with court procedures in slave trials in New Orleans and Natchitoches, the child was not asked to identify herself in her own words. That the court record repeatedly labeled her as Ottawa ("outa8oise"), however, suggests that it was not a mistake and that officials in the Illinois Country accepted the identification. They did not question having an enslaved Ottawa in their midst. The 1747 ordinance prohibiting the importation of African slaves from Lower to Upper Louisiana was similarly bypassed, suggesting a local flexibility and pragmatism about matters pertaining to slavery.[28]

Rather than being Ottawa, it was more likely that Lisette had been traded to the French by the Ottawas, leading French colonists to associate her with that nation. Or perhaps Lisette identified herself as Ottawa. If the Ottawa had taken her captive, then they might have ritually adopted her (a very real possibility given that she was a young girl). As a result, Lisette, familiar with the process of ritual adoption in her own nation, might have understood herself as having become Ottawa, providing a rare window into the mind-set of an enslaved child making sense of her place and identity in the worlds she traversed.

Lisette's dual status as a slave and as an Indian carried particular significance in the Illinois Country, where other Indian women regularly appeared in legal records pertaining to civil matters. These women did so in their capacity as legitimate (in the eyes of French law) wives and daughters of French men. Most of them were Kaskaskia Indians, among them the grandmother of Marie Vincennes; a few others were themselves former captive Plains Indians. These Indian wives of French men, many of them slaveholders, were systematically counted as colonists in census records, and local officials upheld their right to that status. The authorities' support of the half-Indian Agnès Philippe, who sued to initiate one of the earliest land surveys in the area, for instance, illustrates how they legitimized the power of these women to act in a legal capacity with all the rights of French women.[29]

The rights extended to free Indian wives and daughters of Frenchmen, however, did not extend to the enslaved Lisette. Though Marie-Jeanne's access to testimony was regulated by the 1724 code noir, the code noir applied only to *"les esclaves nègres."* As an Indian slave and not an African one, Lisette's access to testimony was framed by the legal limbo that existed between the general rules that governed testimony (contained within France's 1670 Code criminel) and the laws that concerned African slaves but that were silent about Indian slaves. Unfortunately, the record of Marie-Jeanne's trial does not indicate if Lisette's status as a slave trumped her identification as an Indian, suggesting that court officials in the Illinois Country and New Orleans did not deem the issue worthy of deliberation. The record made no mention of the code noir, but, since Lisette was the only eyewitness, she was qualified to testify whether according to France's 1670 Code criminel or the 1724 code noir. Though enslaved, her testimony in court as a witness carried weight in the French judicial system.[30]

According to Petit's translation of her words, Lisette never vacillated in her testimony. Marie-Jeanne had claimed that she had fainted with pain and woke to find herself surrounded by clotted blood and "matter," fetal matter that the midwife ruled was the result of a molar pregnancy, though she also pronounced her to be "very open." Lisette offered a drastically different account, gesturing that she had seen Marie-Jeanne "strangle her child, she tore it apart into pieces and quartered it and put it in a hole in the said stable, where there were two hogs." Though she begged Marie-Jeanne not to kill the child, Marie-Jeanne told her to "go away and that if she did not she would beat her." Then, once the bones were discovered a few days later, Lisette was the only witness to state that she had seen Marie-Jeanne retrieve the bones and rebury them. The court record further referenced the young girl declaring (during the formal confrontation of the accused with the witnesses) that she had tried to prevent Marie-Jeanne from hurting her child, asking her if she could hold it, that the child had cried at birth, and that the baby was female.[31]

In one way, the trial was a classic "she said, she said" case that hinged on opposing testimony. That the two protagonists were enslaved and that one of them was a child of nine or ten years whose testimony was filtered by an interpreter made the case even more complicated. The physical evidence did

Marie-Jeanne and Lisette

not help matters, for it was virtually irrelevant to the outcome; the surgeons did not examine the skull until after the judgment was pronounced. During the Kaskaskia portion of the trial, Lisette was the only witness whose testimony Marie-Jeanne rebutted, thrice calling the young girl "a liar" *(menteuse)*. In her first interrogation in New Orleans, which took place in the jail, Marie-Jeanne continued to rebut Lisette's testimony, adding "without being prompted that if the little *sauvagesse* made this report, it is that because she is stupid and does not speak French, she [Marie-Jeanne] had to shout at her all the time to make her work" *(dit de son Chef que sy la petite sauvagesse a fait des raports comme on luy a dit, c'est que comme elle etoit bête et quelle ne parloit pas francois elle la grondoit toujours pour la faire travailler).*[32]

The adults around Lisette probably paid little attention to her as a rule. After all, she was enslaved, female, and a child (though at nine or ten years old she was not far from the age at which French girls in the Illinois Country were considered *"nubile"*). Clearly, making signs and gesticulating were the modes of communication that she usually relied on. Like Marie-Jeanne, Dame Braseau similarly underscored Lisette's linguistic shortcomings, relaying how the girl "made her understand *by sign,* not being able to speak French, that the said Marie-Jeanne had smothered her child with her hands, telling [Lisette] not to say anything, and *making a sign* for her to go away and then the little *sauvagesse made it known* that she had seen and heard the said infant" *(lui fit entendre par signe ne pouvant parler français, que la dite Marie Jeanne avoit etouffée son enfant lui serrant le col avec les mains, lui disant de ne rien dire, es lui faisant signe de s'en aller et enfin la dite petite sauvagesse fit entendre quelle avoit veüe es entendu ledit enfant).* Nevertheless, Lisette's interlocutors seemed confident in their ability to understand her "signs," even if they might have missed the fact that some of her gestures were not just ad hoc means of communication in the absence of French but stemmed instead from a wider Amerindian kinetic communication system. That Lisette described an unusual method of infanticide lends added credibility to her testimony. The vocabulary used by Lisette's interpreter, Petit, undoubtedly reflected his knowledge base and his particular exposure to Indian languages, but the young girl was fairly graphic and certainly specific in her description of Marie-Jeanne's act of infanticide.[33]

Lisette's experience as a captive provides another way to read the girl's description of Marie-Jeanne taking apart her baby limb from limb. Dismemberment rituals were associated with captivity and warfare within native societies, and adults and children would have experienced or witnessed such acts. If Lisette had indeed been an Ottawa captive, she would have lived through the violence of capture (in the context of warfare or a slave raid)

FIGURE 26: Louis Nicolas, *Figure d'une femme prise à la guere à qui on avoit arraché avec les dans toutes les ongles . . . .* (detail). 1664–1675. "Codex canadensis" 4726.7.022, plate 22. Gilcrease Museum, Tulsa, Okla. On the left is a woman taken captive during war who has had all her nails pulled off with teeth. The caption reads that the author saw her being burned "for six hours during which she was skinned by fire." On the right is the executioner who has "volunteered to burn and make suffer the prisoners of war."

followed by the ritual mutilation and torture that slaves underwent as they were incorporated or underwent symbolic death (Figure 26). Whether or not Lisette had personally suffered mutilation and abuse, she would have witnessed these acts being inflicted on fellow captives, and she would have anticipated these as her fate, for they were familiar rituals also practiced by her own people against their enemies. Read in this context, the specifics of her accusations, centered on strangling, tearing into pieces, and quartering, take on added nuances that raise the question whether the ten-year-old's memory of captivity inflected how she made sense of Marie-Jeanne's actions and how she explained them.[34]

In the legal space provided by the court, Lisette found an unexpected chance to redirect the court's focus so that her viewpoint was aired. Ironically, it might be because she finally had access to an interpreter, thanks to

French judicial practice, that she seized the chance to speak up. She had kept silent while witnessing the alleged infanticide, but her court appearance emboldened her to communicate. It is possible to read through her testimony to decipher what her response reveals, not so much about the crime itself, but about the life experiences that colored her interpretation and her presentation of the crime.

When Lisette's testimony is foregrounded and contextualized, the courtroom recedes into the background, allowing her understanding of her past and her present to take center stage. For Lisette, appearing before the court enabled her to narrate her story over and over to a captive audience. But that story was not simply about witnessing an extraordinary act of infanticide. It was perhaps even more about a child who had been ripped apart from her own kin wanting to speak of her own story, to confront childhood memories, and to bring to the fore what troubled her in her life as a slave. Above all, it meant telling her history of antagonism with the older African Creole Marie-Jeanne, a history that included the regular and constant threat of verbal and physical violence, as Marie-Jeanne herself confirmed.

Marie-Jeanne spoke of Lisette, not as a child, but as a worker. She had supervisory authority over the girl's physical labor and justified her treatment of Lisette by referring to her difficulties in communicating with the girl. She accused Lisette of being "stupid and [she] does not speak French, so that she had to shout at her all the time to make her work." In Marie-Jeanne's telling, it was frustrating to have to oversee the girl's labor, and she resorted to verbal threats to make her work as needed. In contrast, in her testimony, Lisette emphasized the threat of physical, not just verbal, violence: Marie-Jeanne had told her "to go away and that if she did not go away she would beat her." There to testify about the crime of infanticide, Lisette unexpectedly found a forum in which to repeatedly express her grievances at her mistreatment.[35]

Lisette did not implicate her mistress as being at the root of this abuse (testimony that would have been problematic to convey). The mistreatment that the girl aired was less straightforward because it was inflicted by Marie-Jeanne, a fellow slave. It was the result of a power dynamic that fostered in Marie-Jeanne, not a sense of fellowship with another slave nor those maternal instincts she kept alluding to, but instead animosity toward a young Indian girl who could not yet speak French, for whose labor she was held accountable, and over whose day-to-day life (in her capacity as the senior female slave in the household) she held sway. The girl's testimony shows how preoccupied she was with her relationship with Marie-Jeanne and how direct she could be in expressing her disillusionment. Marie-Jeanne's testimony was just as blunt in showcasing her hostility and frustration with the young girl; to her, Lisette was insignificant, and her low status meant that she was the one witness whose testimony Marie-Jeanne felt she could easily dismiss.

INFANTICIDE

The case against Marie-Jeanne is perplexing and difficult to interpret, but this investigation did not exist in a vacuum. The accusation against Marie-Jeanne stemmed from French historical and cultural conceptions of infanticide, abortion, and reproduction. Between 1565 and 1690, for example, prosecutions for infanticide reached a fever pitch, constituting two-thirds of all death sentences pronounced against women in Paris. At the same time, it was selectively applied, uniformly targeting women (usually poor and single) who had conceived a child illegitimately and feared the shame and dishonor associated with extramarital pregnancies. These were not circumstances that applied to Marie-Jeanne nor were such factors particularly applicable to enslaved women, since their access to marriage was tenuous. Yet African women were prosecuted in the colonies for infanticide, reflecting the emergence of widespread tropes about enslaved African women.[36]

The prosecution of Marie-Jeanne took place in 1748. By that date in France, suits involving infanticide had dropped dramatically, culminating in a gradual shift in thinking about fallen women (including those guilty of infanticide) as victims rather than criminals. In Louisiana, the movement away from targeting the sexual transgressions of poor white women seems to have occurred sooner. Just three decades before Marie-Jeanne's trial, Louisiana had experienced a wave of forced French emigration to the colony that had included a highly publicized contingent of prostitutes (Figure 27). The arrival of these *"filles de joie"* (pleasure girls) coincided with that of the *"filles du roi"* (daughters of the king), indigent women of ostensibly better repute sent by the crown to the colony to find husbands. This demographic policy, aimed at increasing the colonial population, took place against the backdrop of a long-running debate about the desirability of encouraging intermarriage between French men and Indian women.[37]

It is not coincidental that it was in 1727, in the midst of this mass immigration of women, that officials in Louisiana deemed abortion and infanticide of sufficiently pressing concern that they issued a new edict reaffirming French law on the subject. The local 1727 edict mandated that "all girls and women without husbands who find themselves pregnant make a declaration at the office of the clerk of New Orleans or in the other posts to the judge, as soon as they have noticed their pregnancy, under threat of being sentenced to death."

Marie-Jeanne and Lisette

FIGURE 27: Unknown, *Le triste embarquement des filles de joye de Paris et leurs adieu fait à Messieur les Apotiquaires et Chirurgiens ainsy qu'a leurs Amans*. 1726. Engraving. Courtesy of the Bibliothèque nationale de France, Paris This engraving, produced at the height of forced French emigration and mass deportation to Louisiana, shows "the sad embarkation of the pleasure girls of Paris, and their goodbyes to the Apothecaries and Surgeons as well as to their lovers." Though a caricature, the image has some poignancy, with the reference to apothecaries, surgeons, and the tools of their trade suggesting their role in aborting pregnancies but especially because of the personalization of the women, many of them named or otherwise identified.

Gender-specific, the law aimed at both population growth and social control ("the preservation of subjects and the repression of the disorders that are committed in the town when the most enormous crimes are hidden through destroying their children"). Its timing was also not an accident in that the edict was passed during a period of high mortality for colonists and slaves alike. But it was race-neutral, suggesting that when it was conceived in 1727, the main targets, and therefore those suspected of such crimes, were, not so much enslaved women, but single French "girls and women separated from their husbands."[38]

Marie-Jeanne's defense in the New Orleans courtroom, where she asserted "that she is not so *denatured,* nor so bad as to destroy her child, if she had seen one in what she had delivered," took place within this broader context. When first interrogated before the court in the Illinois Country, Marie-Jeanne denied the accusation with different words, saying that "her heart was not hard enough to kill her child, that it is too much for her." Although it was not unusual for testimony to change across investigations, the word "denatured" is a very particular one that complicates the assessment of her testimony, for it was not the kind of word that would have been in common usage for an enslaved African. According to the definition included in the *Dictionnaire de l'Académie française* (1694), a "denatured" person was someone "who lacks affection and tenderness for their closest parents." A "Denatured Child" or "Denatured son" was one " who mistreats his father and his mother." A "Denatured father" or "denatured mother" was someone "who lets their children die of hunger." The word also signified "that which is contrary to the natural feelings of affection and tenderness." The dictionary further stated that, "for a father to kill his son is an action that is very barbarian and very denatured." Marie-Jeanne's usage of this specialized term strongly implies that she had received some coaching in the intervening months between her prosecution in the Illinois Country and her prosecution in New Orleans.[39]

Though there were no lawyers in the colony, Marie-Jeanne might have received advice and direction through informal channels. The trial lasted an unusually long time, which would have facilitated such coaching, and her owner was from a prominent and well-connected family and therefore able to demand access to her slave. Indeed, it would have been in the Vincennes family's best interest to prepare Marie-Jeanne, as her conviction would have had a direct financial impact on them as slaveowners. Whoever coached Marie-Jeanne or introduced her to the concept inherent in the term "denatured" could well have known that such precise, loaded language would resonate with a French audience used to judging women based on their aptitude for maternal feelings and, specifically, with the members of a Superior Council preoccupied with controlling those women who fell short. At the same time, accusations of abortion and infanticide, or simple neglect, were common themes in European stereotypes about enslaved African women and their ostensible lack of maternal feelings, a topos that frequently resulted in criminal prosecutions for abortion and infanticide. Among the methods they accused these women of using to accomplish abortion or infanticide were poisons and other drugs. Physical dismemberment of the type that Lisette described was less commonly mentioned.[40]

Marie-Jeanne and Lisette

Though Marie-Jeanne was the only woman prosecuted for infanticide or abortion in Louisiana, it was another story in France's other colonies. Stereotypes about African parenting echoed around the French colonial world, finding resonance in the questions posed to enslaved women in judicial prosecutions ranging from crimes of *marronnage* (running away) to infanticide. Ultimately, these cases speak to the challenges and perils of parenting under the duress of slavery.[41]

In 1734, fourteen years before Marie-Jeanne was arrested, a case against seven runaways in Isle de France (present-day Mauritius) ushered in a pattern of maroons on that island being accused of infanticide. Among the seven accused were two West Africans, "François Sarra noir de Guinée" and his wife, "Jeanneton de Guinée." Not found among the group was their three-month-old child. He had, by his parents' account, died twenty days into their escape. The prosecutor would accuse Sarra of killing his "Christian child" *(enfant chrestien)*. Jeanneton was repeatedly asked to acknowledge that she had seen her husband in the act, but she consistently denied the accusation, stating instead that it was the other runaways who told her that Sarra had killed their baby. Only once did she seem to slip and acknowledge seeing him strangle the child, but she added that she had not dared stop him out of fear that he would do the same to her. She swiftly rebutted that testimony, though not before mentioning that she had seen "nail scratches around her baby's neck" *(des coups d'ongle au col de son enfant)*. She also inserted one detail, a small, innocuous detail but one that allowed her to convey to listeners a different narrative about her husband and child, one that emphasized their closeness and evoked parental love and responsibility toward their son: that on the night that he had died, she had placed him to sleep between herself and her husband, presumably as she always did. When François Sarra was asked what happened to the child, the father answered that "God had taken him and that when his child died all the others were near. . . . Interrogated if he had cut the throat of his child, or drowned him? He responded that he had not done anything to his child" *(a Dit que Dieu l'avoit pris, Et Lorsque son Enfans mouru Tous les autres y Etoient. . . . Interogé Syl a coupé le Col a son Enfans, Egorgé, ou Noyé, a dit quil n'a fait aucun mal à son Enfans)*. The touching anecdote about co-sleeping with the baby, along with Sarra's repeated use of the possessive noun to describe his child, were not material to the court case. These elements did nothing to overturn the accusation, but they did help to project an alternative image of this family's emotional and affective ties to one another.[42]

Following this lead, it is possible to hear other fathers agonize over having to cut ties to their offspring, such as when they ran away. In Louisiana, François dit Baraca, who fled from the king's plantation in 1748 after murdering his wife, Taco, stated in court that, whenever he ran across his friend Joseph Laoursot, he would always ask what had happened to his children. Laoursot would respond that Baraca ought to circumvent judicial prosecution and go "beg his master's pardon" *(demande pardon à ton maître)*, and Baraca did, in the end, attempt to do so. The passage makes clear that his children were foremost in his mind, offering a counterpoint to colonial narratives that sought to discredit slaves' parenting.[43]

Baraca's motives for leaving his children behind were exceptional. But others, such as Lafleur and Catherine Marie, also left their children behind when they ran away. Just two weeks after the couple had run away, in January 1746, they were spotted opposite the church of Saint Louis. They had shown forethought by taking an iron pot with them, yet they did not take their fourteen-year-old son (no longer considered a child by the measures applied to the enslaved). The precise reasons why Lafleur and Catherine Marie acted as they did are unknown, and even less is known regarding how they felt about it.[44]

One court case from 1773 in Ste. Genevieve in the Illinois Country, however, offers a glimpse into the thoughts of an enslaved Indian woman about the children she left behind when she ran away. Marianne had become involved with a Frenchman, Céladon, who had convinced her to run away with him. Though Marianne would remain free (under the control of Céladon), her boys would remain enslaved. But, as her son Jean-Baptiste testified when he recounted the night his mother ran away, she had planned a different outcome for them:

> [Marianne] said to Baptiste her son to "come with her"; he said that he refused saying that he did not want to go without his little brother, which his mother had not wanted, saying he would hinder them too much. But that since he [Baptiste] did not want to come he just had to stay quietly and that she was going back to her country, that this winter she would come back with some Indians [from her country] to fetch him.

> _____

> [Marianne] dit audit Baptiste son fils de venir avec elle; ce quil a refusé disant quil ne voulait pas y aller Sans Son petit frere; ce que Sa mere

Marie-Jeanne and Lisette

> N'a pas voulu disant qu'il l'embarrasserait trop, mais que puisqu'il ne
> voulait pas venir il navoit qu'a rester tranquille et quelle allais dans Son
> pays, que cet hiver elle reviendrait le chercher avec des Sauvages

Marianne had not dared take her younger son; it was too risky, and the elder
brother stayed behind rather than abandon the boy. What is especially noteworthy in this account is that the woman still felt a kinship with her original
nation (likely a Plains nation), even after a lifetime as a captive of the French.
Marianne had already experienced being permanently wrenched away from
family and kin once before, when she was first made captive, and she seems
to have realized that her current condition (as an escapee dependent on a
man who would never allow her to return to "her country") would also keep
her permanently separated from her sons. Yet she did not forget them. Six
months after her escape, Ste. Genevieve resident Jean-Baptiste Becquet came
across Céladon and Marianne at their encampment. He later testified that,
on seeing him, she immediately entreated him for news of her sons, and she
seized her opportunity to assert an indirect link to the boys' upbringing: she
asked Becquet to help ensure that her sons' owners raised them as Catholics.[45]

Such evidence complicates, and enriches, understandings of parenting
under the duress of slavery. Enslaved parents recognized that to run away was
risky, for themselves and their children. But there were other layers underneath these considerations, layers of meaning and layers of feelings that colonists did not always want to recognize. Instead, the French more commonly
projected their assumptions onto the enslaved. For example, from the Dutch
occupation onward, maroon women on the Isle de France were regularly accused of infanticide as part of a broader framing of enslaved women as unfit
mothers. Their alleged motivation, according to missionaries visiting in 1732,
was to prevent babies from "imped[ing] their flight or reveal[ing] their location through their cries."[46]

Citing two prosecutions from 1746 and 1751–1752, Meghan Vaughan argues that these court cases involving maroons also signaled a shift in the sex
of the perpetrator, from maroon women to maroon men accused of infanticide. In both trials, enslaved women accused of being runaways instead
claimed that maroon men had forcibly abducted them and killed their babies;
Monique described how she watched her abductor as he speared her baby to
death, and Magdalene Marena detailed how she gave birth in the woods only
to have her abductors kill her baby and throw away the body. The 1734 court
case against François Sarra anticipates by twelve years this shift from female
to male perpetrators of infanticide.[47]

There might well have been some instances of infanticide among maroon bands. Certainly there was scope for violence in such communities. Testifying in a court case from Martinique in 1711, the runaway Laurence was asked why she had not fled the maroon gang, knowing that if she had been captured she would be sentenced to death. She replied that "the woods are big, that she would not be able to get out, and that the said Hierosme had threatened her that if she left, he would kill her on the road" *(le bois est grand, qu'elle n'auroit pas peu en sortir et que le dit hierosme l'avoit menassé que si elle sortoit, il la tueroit dans le chemin)*. Yet maroon bands operated primarily as communities that did include children. Children were present in maroon bands on the Isle de France, and they did not necessarily present a risk to those communities.[48]

When, in 1749, Suzanne and Rose were arrested alongside Jasmin, the latter stated that the maroon band had captured him when he was no more than twelve. The court accepted his version of the facts and returned him to his master without any punishment (unlike the adults, Suzanne and Rose, who were sentenced to be whipped then branded with a fleur-de-lis). Younger children were also present in the bands. In 1739, a maroon camp was discovered and, though most escaped, their leader was captured, along with three women "and a little girl aged two years old" *(une petite Negritte agée de deux ans)*. Furthermore, in a 1745 court case, Margot was arrested along with her child, Zaza. It is not insignificant that, when questioned, Suzanne and Rose, whose marronnages had lasted approximately nine years, were each pointedly asked if they had given birth while they were living in the woods. Both women denied ever having children, but, given the length of their marronnage and references by Rose to a husband who was a maroon with her, it is possible that children were born, that they were never at risk of infanticide, and that their mothers actually protected them by concealing them within the maroon band.[49]

❧❦

"THE CHILDREN FOLLOW THE CONDITION OF THEIR MOTHER"

In their dealings with runaway women, officials betrayed their negative assumptions about enslaved women's mothering, barely masking their anxieties about mothers who fought to retain control over their fertility. The ubiquity of such beliefs and the circulation of such views shaped the accusation against Marie-Jeanne, as did the broader matter of reproduction. The prosecutors in the case against her followed a line of questioning that emphasized her fertility. They did not give their rationale for asking Marie-Jeanne if she had been pregnant before, if she was currently pregnant, and who had impregnated her. But a judicial interrogation that veered toward the subject of

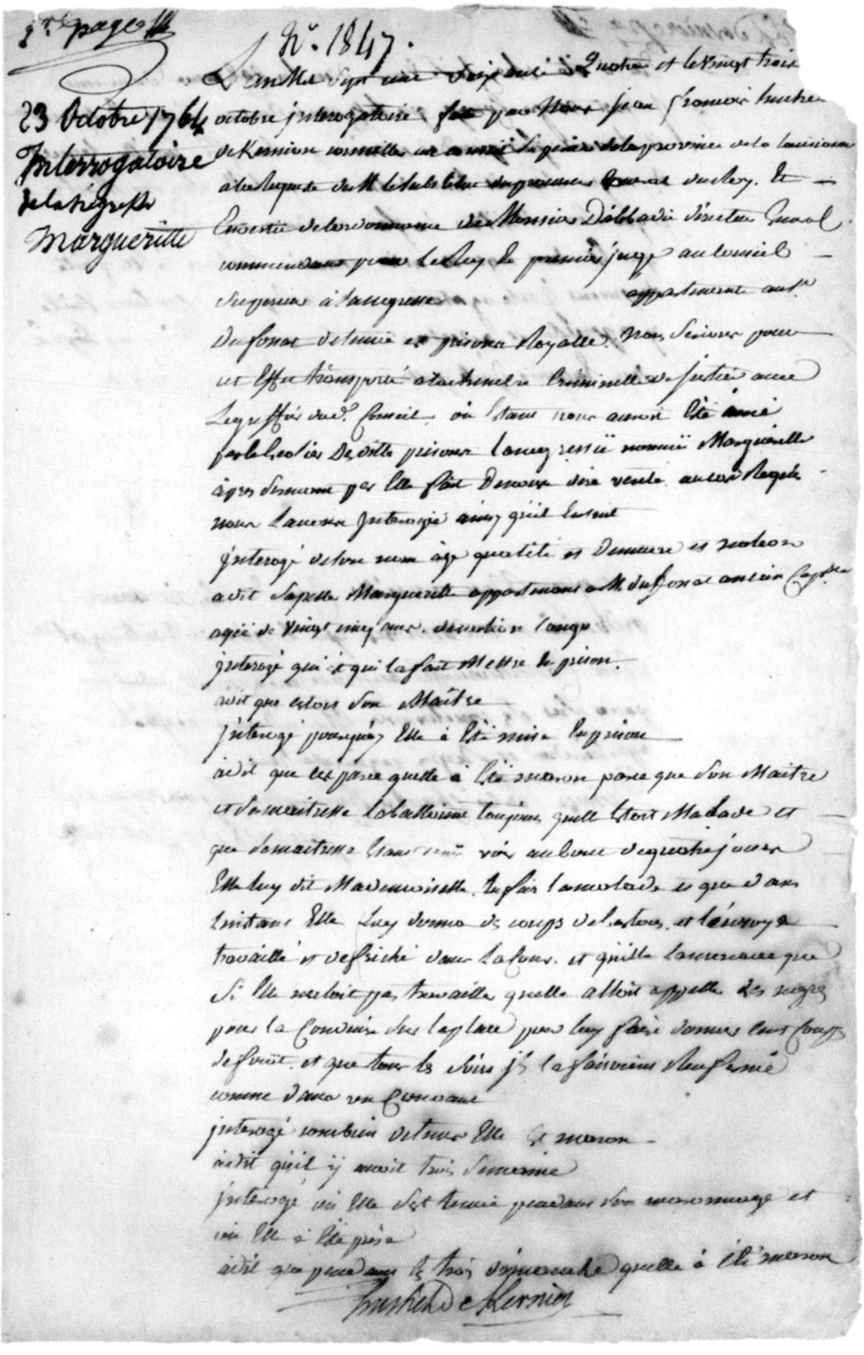

1re page

N°. 1847.

23 Octobre 1764
Interrogatoire
de la negresse
Margueritte

L'an mil sept cent soixante quatre et le vingt trois
octobre interrogatoire fait par Nous Jean François Huchet
de Kernion conseiller au conseil supérieur de la province de la Louisiane
à la requête de M. le Substitut du procureur general du Roy. En
Execution de l'ordonnance de Monsieur Dabbadie directeur general
commandant pour le Roy et premier juge au conseil
supérieur à la negresse [illegible] appartenant au S.
Dufossat detenue es prisons Royalles. Nous sommes pour
cet effet transporté [illegible] chambre criminelle de justice avec
le greffier dud. conseil où étant nous avons [illegible]
[illegible] de ditte prison la negresse nommée Margueritte
après serment par elle fait de dire verité [illegible]
nous l'avons interrogé ainsi qu'il suit
interrogé de son nom age qualité et demeure et religion
a dit s'appeller Margueritte appartenant à M. Dufossat ancien capne
agée de vingt cinq ans [illegible]
interrogé qui est-ce qui l'a fait mettre en prison.
a dit que c'est son Maître
interrogé pourquoy elle a été mise en prison
a dit que c'est parce qu'elle a été maron parce que son Maître
et sa maitresse la battoient toujours qu'elle étoit malade et
que sa maitresse étant venu voir [illegible]
elle luy dit Mademoiselle je suis malade et que dans
l'instant elle luy donna des coups de baton, et l'envoya
travailler et defricher dans la [illegible] et qu'elle la menaçoit que
si elle ne vouloit pas travailler qu'elle alloit appeller des negres
pour la conduire sur la place pour luy faire donner cent coups
de fouet. et que tous les soirs [illegible] la faisoient renfermé
comme dans un [illegible]
interrogé combien de temps elle est maron
a dit qu'il y avoit trois semaines
interrogé où elle s'est tenue pendant son maronage et
où elle a été prise
a dit que pendant les trois semaines qu'elle a été maron
Huchet de Kernion

PLATE 1: Interrogation of Margueritte. RSCL 1764/10/23/01, 1.
Courtesy of Louisiana Historical Center, Louisiana State Museum, New Orleans

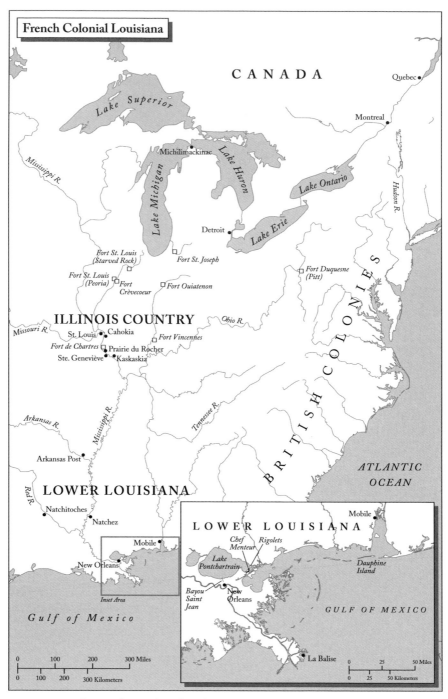

PLATE 2: "Map of French Colonial Louisiana including the Illinois Country."
Drawn by Alice Thiede

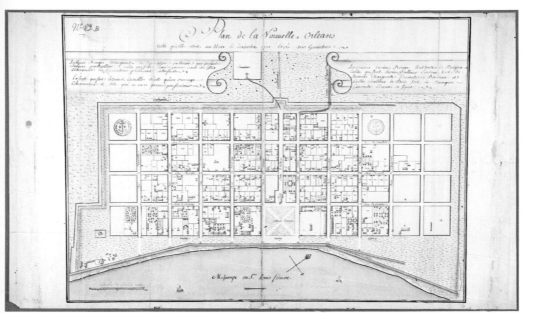

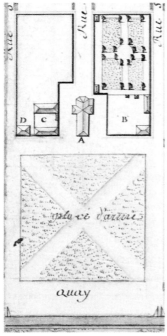

PLATE 3:

Plan de la Nouvelle Orléans telle qu'elle estoit au mois de dexembre 1731 levé par Gonichon (and detail). FR ANOM 04 DFC 89 B. Courtesy of Archives nationales d'outre-mer, Aix-en-Provence, France

Key C shows the orientation of the prison buildings with the inner enclosed courtyard. A is the Church of Saint Louis, facing onto the Place d'armes and the river, and D is the guard house.

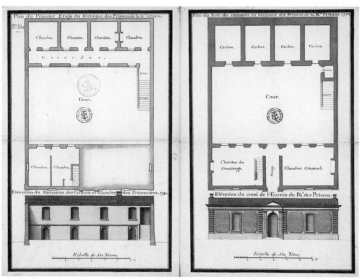

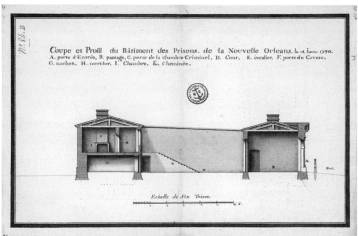

PLATE 4: Anonymous, *Plan profil et elevation des prisons de la Nouvelle Orleans, 14 janvier 1730*. Watercolor. FR ANOM 04 DFC 84 B. Les archives nationales d'outre-mer, Aix-en-Provence, France

The top view is of the prison from rue d'Orleans, with the left-hand drawing showing the upper level and the right-hand drawing showing the street level. The entrance faced the church. It shows the rear building (accessed from the inner courtyard) and the floorplan of the upper level. The bottom view shows the prison from the perspective of rue de Chartre (present-day Chartres Street). It also shows the front building and entrance from the street and includes the floor plan of the ground level. The walled-in courtyard measured about six toises by eight toises, or approximately thirty-eight feet by fifty-one feet. Each cell (on the upper level) measured about two and a half by two toises, or approximately sixteen by twelve and a half feet, meaning that these were communal cells. The *chambre criminel* (criminal chamber) was where interrogations on the *sellette* and judicial torture were carried out; it measured approximately four by three toises, or approximately nineteen by twenty-five feet.

PLATE 5: *Madame John's Legacy.* 632 Dumaine Street, New Orleans.
Photo courtesy of Philippe Halbert

Popularly known as "Madame John's Legacy," this site hosted one of the earliest and
longest-running inns in French colonial New Orleans. The main house was badly
damaged in a citywide fire in 1788 but was reconstructed in the same early French
colonial style as confirmed by archaeological excavations. The ground level was used
for commerce and storage, the upper levels were residential, and the rear walled-in
courtyard could be accessed either via the house or through the narrow side gate.

T. IV. p. 166.

Soeur Converse Ursuline,
de la Congrégation de Paris.

39.

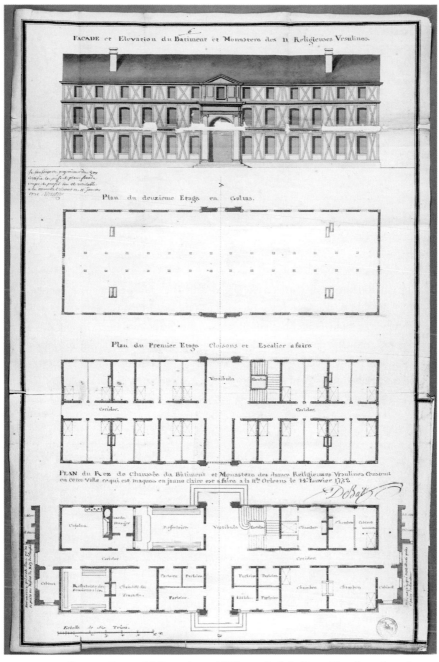

PLATE 7: [Ignace François] Broutin and [Alexandre] de Batz, *Façade et élévation du batiment et monastère des D. Religieuses Ursulines; Coupe profil du batiment et monnastère des Dames Ursulines de cette ville à la Nlle Orléans le 14 janvier 1732.* FR ANOM F3 290/6. Les archives nationales d'outre-mer, Aix-en-Provence, France

PLATE 8: Unrecorded artist from Democratic Republic of Congo or Angola, Divination Basket with Sixty-One Ritual Objects. Mid-twentieth century. Chokwe style. Plant fiber, wood, animal fur, brass, bird horn, calabash, gourd, red clay, corn cob, seeds, seed pod, chicken feet, ceramic, antelope hooves, unidentified ritual powder mixture. Owen D. Mort Jr. Collection, Snite Museum of Art 2011.036.009. University of Notre Dame

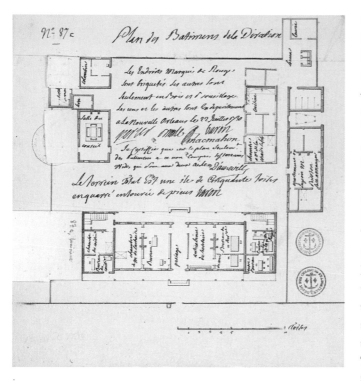

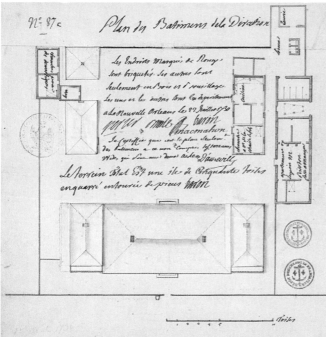

PLATE 9: [Pierre] Baron, *Plan des batimens de la direction [de la Nouvelle Orléans]*, . . . *July 22, 1730.* Watercolor. FR ANOM 4 DFC 87C. Courtesy Archives nationales d'outre-mer, Aix-en-Provence, France This plan of the government buildings was made with flaps that lift up to show both the aerial view and the rooms within. The chamber of the Superior Council (*"salle du conseil"*), where trials were conducted, is on the left, a rectangular room approximately four by two and a half toises (equivalent to twenty-five by twelve feet) with two long and two shorter tables arranged in a square.

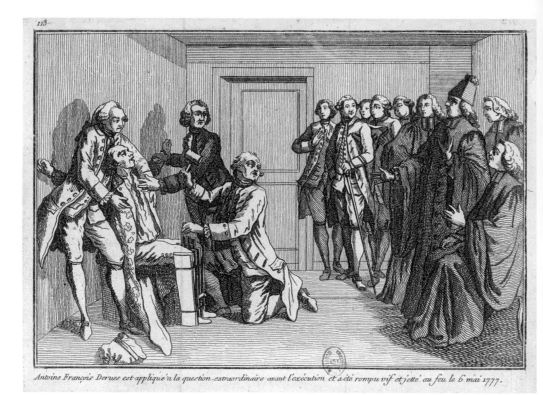

PLATE 10: Unknown, *Antoine François Derues est appliqué à la question extraordinaire avant l'exécution et a été rompu vif et jetté au feu le 6 mai 1777.* From *Portrait de Desrues et quarante planches relatives à la vie, aux crimes et à l'exécution de ce scélérat.* 1777. Engraving. Département Estampes et photographie. RESERVE QB-201 (110)-FOL. Courtesy of Bibliothèque nationale de France, Paris

In this engraving from a set about an infamous French court case, the accused is shown undergoing judicial torture using the method known as the brodequin.

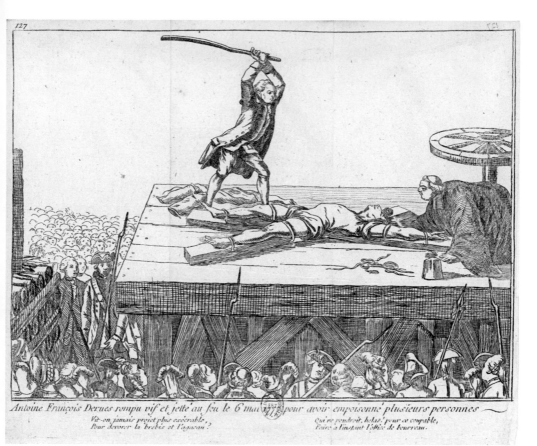

Antoine François Derues rompu vif et jetté au feu le 6 mai 1777 pour avoir empoisonné plusieurs personnes

Vit-on jamais projet plus exécrable,
Pour dévorer la brebis et l'agneau ?

Qui'ro voudroit, hélas! pour ce coupable,
Faire à l'instant l'office de bourreau.

PLATE 11: Unknown, *Antoine François Derues rompu vif et jetté au feu le 6 mai 1777 pour avoir empoisonné plusiuers personnes.* From *Portrait de Desrues en quarante planches relatives à la vie, aux crimes, et à l'exécution de ce scélérat.* 1777. Engraving. Département Estampes et photographie. RESERVE QB-201 (110)-FOL. Courtesy of Bibliothèque nationale de France, Paris

In this engraving, the executioner is shown breaking the body of the condemned on the cross. A carriage wheel is shown on the scaffold, at the ready if the condemned had been sentenced to have his body left exposed on the wheel.

PLATE 12: *Ursuline Convent.* New Orleans, facing the quay.
Photo courtesy of Philippe Halbert

PLATE 13: *Art Militaire, Exercice,* Plate I (detail). From Denis Diderot and Jean le Rond d'Alembert, *Encyclopédie, ou dictionnaire raisonné des sciences, des arts, et des métiers; Recueil de planches,* I (Paris, 1762–1772). Reproduced from the original held by the Department of Special Collections of the University Libraries of Notre Dame Figures 6 through 8 show a soldier attaching his bayonet.

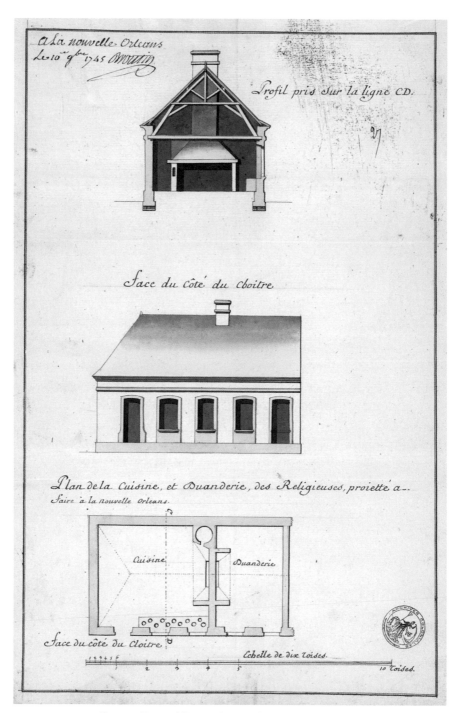

PLATE 14: [Ignace-François] Broutin, *Profil pris sur la ligne CD[,] face du côté du cloître [et] plan de la cuisine, et buanderie, des Religieuses, proietté [sic] a faire à la Nouvelle Orleans.* Nov. 10, 1745. FR ANOM F3 290 27.
Courtesy of Les archives nationales d'outre-mer, Aix-en-Provence, France
The washhouse *(buanderie)* shared a wall (and fireplace) with the kitchen *(cuisine)*.

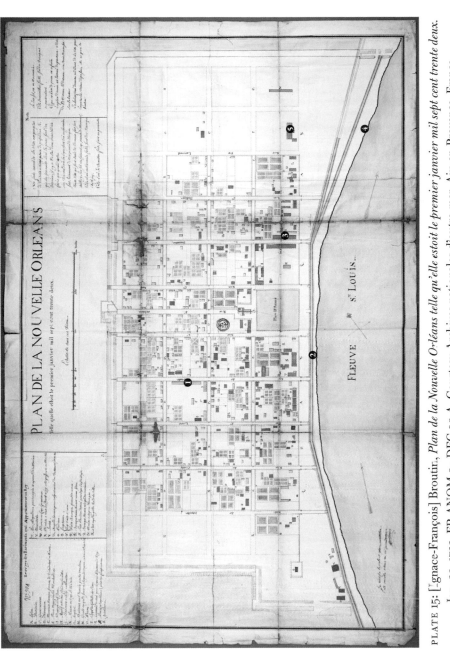

PLATE 15: [Ignace-François] Broutir, *Plan de la Nouvelle Orléans telle qu'elle estoit le premier janvier mil sept cent trente deux.* Jan. 20, 1732. FR ANOM 04 DFC 90 A. Courtesy Archives nationales d'outre-mer, Aix-en-Provence, France

The key superimposed on the map marks the places Pierre Antoine Pochenet stopped and his movements on June 13, 1752: 1 shows the canteen, 2 the market, 3 the king's warehouse, 4 the riverbank in front of the Ursuline convent, and 5 the Ursuline convent and hospital.

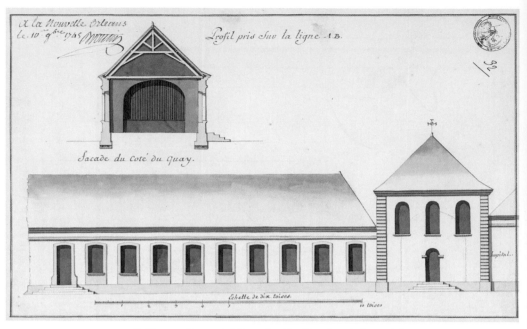

PLATE 16: [Ignace-François] Broutin, *Profil et facade du coté du quay*
[du couvent des religieuses ursulines]. Nov. 10, 1745. FR ANOM F3 290 32.
Courtesy Archives nationales d'outre-mer, Aix-en-Provence, France
When the 1745 convent was built, the facade facing the quay was the front entrance.

PLATE 17: [Jean Pierre Lassus], *Veüe et perspective de
La Nouvelle-Orleans.* 1726. FR ANOM 04 DFC 71A.
Courtesy Archives nationales d'outre-mer, Aix-en-Provence, France
Taken from the bank opposite the town, the right foreground shows enslaved Africans
clearing the land that would become the Company of the Indies's plantation.

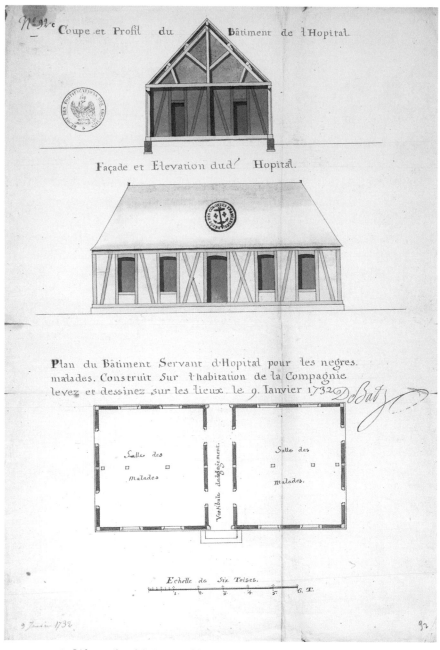

PLATE 18: [Alexandre de] Batz and [Ignace-François] Broutin, *Plan du bâtiment de l'hopital des nègres construit sur l'habitation de la Compagnie levez et dessinez sur les lieux à la Nouvelle Orléans le 13 janvier 1732.* FR ANOM F3 290 36. Courtesy Archives nationales d'outre-mer, Aix-en-Provence, France The drawing shows the plan of the slave hospital on the Company of the Indies's plantation.

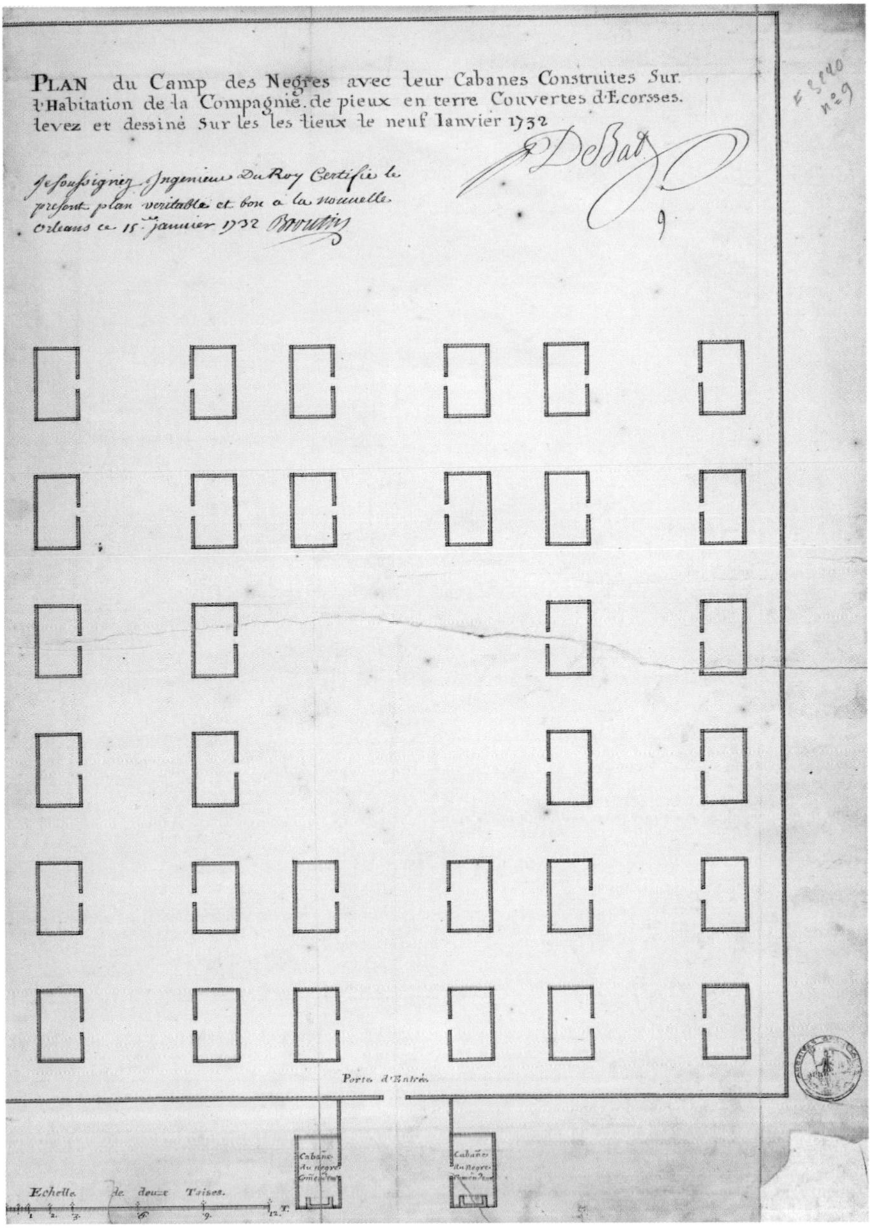

PLATE 19: [Ignace-François] Broutin and [Alexandre de] Batz, *Plan du camp des nègres avec leur cabanes construites sur l'habitation de la Compagnie de pieux en terre couvertes d'ecorsses, levez et déssiné sur les les [sic] lieux le neuf janvier 1732.* FR ANOM F3 290 9.

Courtesy Archives nationales d'outre-mer, Aix-en-Provence, France

The drawing shows the enclosed compound where the group of slave cabins were located on the Company of the Indies's plantation. Just outside the gate stood two cabins identified as those of the overseer, though one was for the surgeon.

PLATE 20: Suite of Religious Medals. Recovered from burial no. 11, St. Peter Street Cemetery (16or92), Orleans Parish, Louisiana. Courtesy Archaeology Lab of The University of New Orleans Department of Anthropology

PLATE 21: Charles Melchior Descourtis, after Jean Frédéric Schall,
Paul et Virginie Obtaining the Pardon of a Runaway Slave . . . Plate 2.
From a set of six plates depicting scenes from Bernardin de Saint-
Pierre's *Paul et Virginie*. 1795/1797. Color aquatint. Prints and Drawings
1895,0617.471. AN479703001. © The Trustees of the British Museum
In this engraving of Bernardin de Saint-Pierre's wildly popular enlightenment
abolitionist novel published in 1788, which takes place in Mauritius, Paul
and Virginie are seen seeking the pardon of a runaway female slave, depicted
prostrate before her master as he, "lifting up his stick, swore, with a terrible
oath, that he pardoned his slave, not for the love of Heaven, but of her
who asked his forgiveness." In the novel, it is Virginie's idea, and Virginie
herself (accompanied by Paul), who seeks the pardon of the slave.

PLATE 22: Unknown Maker, *Cypress Confessional*. 1730–1760, Pointe Coupée, Louisiana. Photo courtesy of Philippe Halbert

PLATE 23: *Corset* (jumps or waistcoat). Circa 1745.
Silk and linen, hand-sewn with silk thread. England.
Photo © Victoria and Albert Museum, London
Note the quilted fabric and the insertion of boning visible on the back panel.

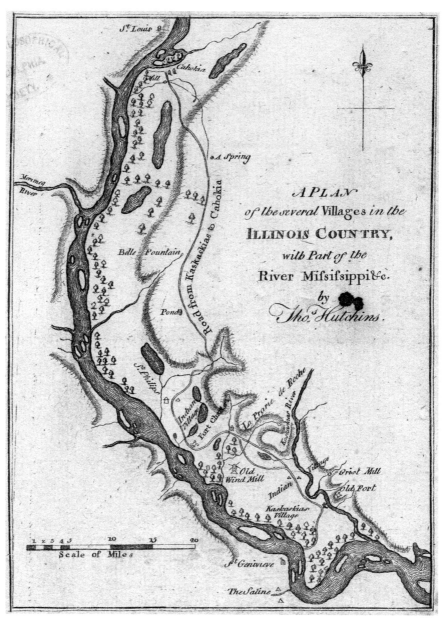

PLATE 24: Thomas Hutchins, *A Plan of the Several Villages in the Illinois Country, with Part of the River Mississippi &c.* From Hutchins, *A Topographical Description of Virginia, Pennsylvania, Maryland, and North Carolina* (London, 1778).
Courtesy of the American Philosophical Society, Philadelphia
Note the separation of Indian from French villages, as begun by the French
in 1719 and signaled here by the distinction between the French colonial
"Kaskaskia village" and the Kaskaskia Indian village just north.

PLATE 25: *Cahokia Courthouse* (post-on-sill style). Circa 1740, Cahokia, Illinois.
Courtesy of Illinois Department of Natural Resources

French colonial houses in the Illinois Country were constructed in one of two
dominant styles: with vertical logs that were either planted in the earth palisade
fashion (*poteaux-en-terre,* or post-in-ground), or placed upright on sills (*poteaux-sur-
sole,* or post-on-sill), as in the circa 1740 Cahokia Courthouse. The areas between the
logs were filled with a mixture of mud and straw or clay and pebbles; both types of
houses were whitewashed. Beginning in the 1730s, wealthier inhabitants built stone
houses. A distinctive feature found on all of these types of houses was the *galerie*
(wraparound porch), which could run along two, three, or four sides of a house.

PLATE 26: Louis Nicolas, *Figure d'une femme prise à la guere à qui on avoit arraché avec les dans toutes les ongles . . . .* (detail). 1664–1675. "Codex canadensis" 4726.7.022, plate 22. Gilcrease Museum, Tulsa, Okla. On the left is a woman taken captive during war who has had all her nails pulled off with teeth. The caption reads that the author saw her being burned "for six hours during which she was skinned by fire." On the right is the executioner who has "volunteered to burn and make suffer the prisoners of war."

PLATE 27: Unknown, *Le triste embarquement des filles de joye de Paris et leurs adieu fait à Messieur les Apotiquaires et Chirurgiens ainsy qu'a leurs Amans*. 1726. Engraving. Courtesy of the Bibliothèque nationale de France, Paris
This engraving, produced at the height of forced French emigration and mass deportation to Louisiana, shows "the sad embarkation of the pleasure girls of Paris, and their goodbyes to the Apothecaries and Surgeons as well as to their lovers." Though a caricature, the image has some poignancy, with the reference to apothecaries, surgeons, and the tools of their trade suggesting their role in aborting pregnancies but especially because of the personalization of the women, many of them named or otherwise identified.

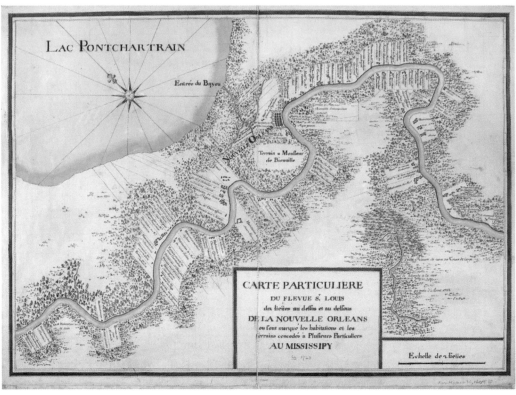

PLATE 28: Unknown artist, *Carte particuliere du flevue [sic] St. Louis dix lieües au dessus et au dessous de la Nouvelle Orleans u sont marqué les habitations et les terrains concedés à plusieurs particuliers au Mississipy.* Circa 1723. Edward E. Ayer Manuscript Map Collection. Vault drawer Ayer MS map 30 sheet 80.
Courtesy The Newberry Library, Chicago

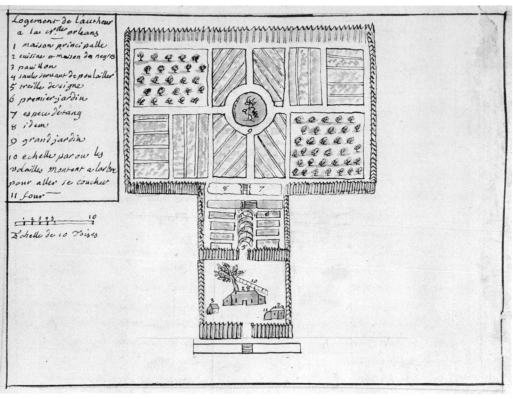

PLATE 29: Jean-François-Benjamin Dumont de Montigny, *Logement de l'autheur a la N[ouve]lle Orleans*. Circa 1733. Vault oversize Ayer MS 257, map no. 8.
Courtesy The Newberry Library, Chicago
Key 1 shows the main house, key 2 the kitchen and slave quarters.

PLATE 30: Unidentified artist, *Jean Paul Gerard de Vilemont*. 1996.79.1.
Historic New Orleans Collection

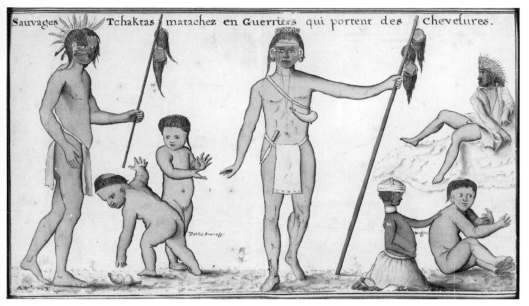

PLATE 31: Alexandre de Batz, *Sauvages tchaktas matachez en guerriers qui portent des chevelures.* Gift of the Estate of Belle J. Bushnell, 1941. PM# 41-72-10/19. Courtesy the Peabody Museum of Archaeology and Ethnology, Harvard University The African figure on the lower right wears a structured head covering.

PLATE 32: Agostino Brunias, *A Negroes Dance in the Island of Dominica.*
Private Collection. Photo © Christie's Images / Bridgeman Images

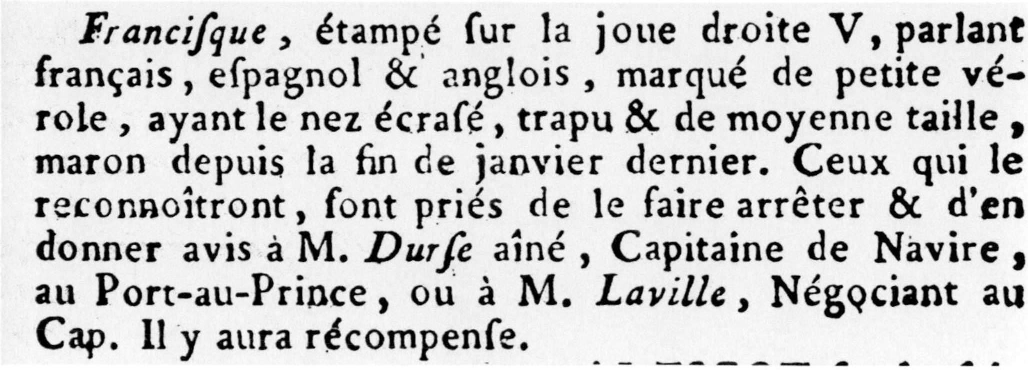

Francisque, étampé fur la joue droite V, parlant français, efpagnol & anglois, marqué de petite vé-role, ayant le nez écrafé, trapu & de moyenne taille, maron depuis la fin de janvier dernier. Ceux qui le reconnoîtront, font priés de le faire arrêter & d'en donner avis à M. *Durfe* aîné, Capitaine de Navire, au Port-au-Prince, ou à M. *Laville*, Négociant au Cap. Il y aura récompenfe.

PLATE 33: Runaway advertisement for Francisque, *Affiches américaines*, Feb. 25, 1767, 64, Le marronnage dans le monde atlantique: Sources et trajectoires de vie, http://marronnage.info/fr/index.html (accessed May 25, 2019)

PLATE 34: Alexandre de Batz, *Dessein de sauvages de plusieurs nations,*
Nlle Orleans 1735. 1735. Gift of the Estate of Belle J. Bushnell, 1941.
Courtesy the Peabody Museum of Archaeology and Ethnology, Harvard University
In his drawing of Indians of various nations, done in New Orleans in 1735,
the artist included the seated figure of a Fox (Meskwaki) female slave. She is
engaged in scraping a hide and lined up beside her are containers of meat, tallow,
and bear oil (used in cooking) and a turkey, all of which were items traded to
the French and that Jean-Baptiste and Kenet could have bartered for.

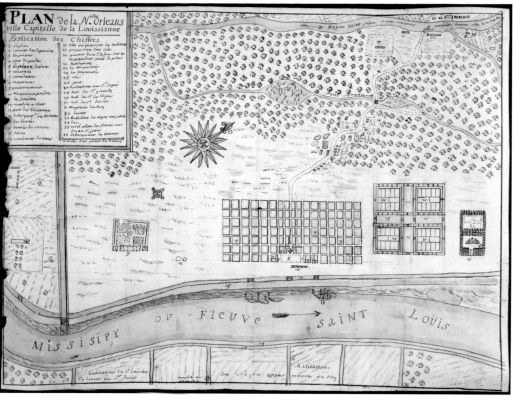

PLATE 35: Jean-François-Benjamin Dumont de Montigny, *Plan de la Nlle. Orleans, ville capitalle de la Louissianne.* [1747]. Edward E. Ayer Manuscript Map Collection. Vault oversize Ayer MS 257, map no. 7. Courtesy of The Newberry Library, Chicago In Dumont de Montigny's 1747 map of New Orleans, the landing point for convoys arriving from the Illinois Country is keyed to no. 14. Bayou Saint Jean is signaled on the upper right

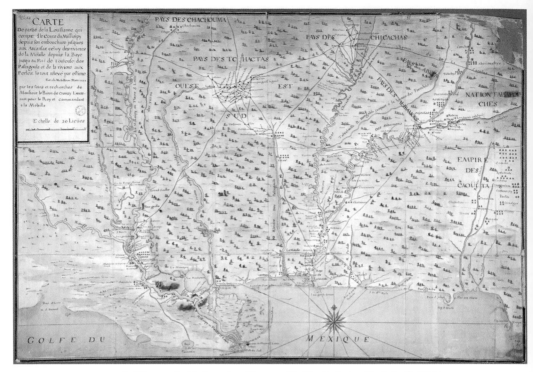

PLATE 36: [Baron de Crénay (ou Cresnay)], *Carte de partie de la Loüisianne qui comprend le cours du Missisipy depuis son embouchure jusques aux Arcansas, celuy des rivieres de la Mobille depuis la Baye jusqu au Fort de Toulouse, des Pascagoula et de la riviere aux Perles . . .* 1733. FR ANOM 04 DFC 1A. Courtesy Archives nationales d'outre-mer, Aix-en-Provence, France

PLATE 37: Unknown artist, *Pierre de Rigaud de Vaudreuil Cavagnial, Marquis de Vaudreuil (1698–1778)*. C147538k-v6. Library and Archives of Canada, Ontario

PLATE 38: Unknown, *Deux Antillaises.* Late eighteenth century. Collection Chatillon
L-29. 2003.4.32. Courtesy of the Musée d'Aquitaine. Bordeaux, France
Though recently titled *Deux Antillaises,* the painting is of a man and woman.

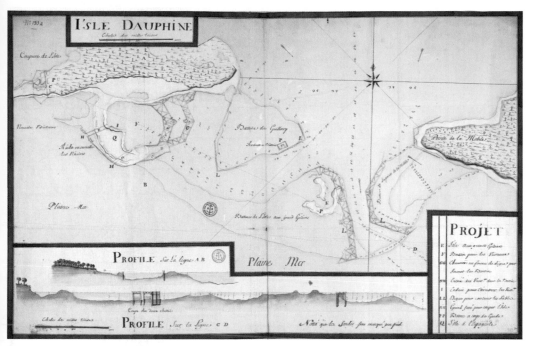

PLATE 39: Unknown, *Plan [et deux profils] d'une partie de l'isle Dauphine jusqu'à la pointe de la Mobile.* Circa 1737. FR ANOM 04 DFC 133A. Courtesy Archives nationales d'outre-mer, Aix-en-Provence, France

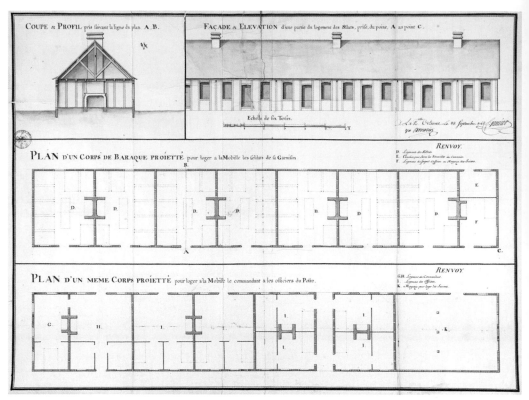

PLATE 40: Saucier, [Ignace-François] Broutin, *Plan d'un corps
de baraque projetté pour loger à la Mobille les soldats de sa garnison.*
Sept. 15, 1745. FR ANOM F3 290 24.
Courtesy Archives nationales d'outre-mer, Aix-en-Provence, France

offspring necessarily evoked the status of the progeny of enslaved women. As first enshrined in Articles 12 and 13 of the Antilles' 1685 code noir (and recapitulated in Articles 9 and 10 of Louisiana's 1724 code noir), any child born to a slave followed the condition of his or her mother and was therefore deemed to be the property of the mother's master.[50]

The scrutiny of Marie-Jeanne's body by her mistress, when probing to see if she could feel any movement in her stomach, was redolent of the scrutiny that servants (and women generally) experienced. But it was especially loaded because of practices inherent to slavery whereby the bodies of enslaved men and women were made intimately available to be inspected by slave traders as well as actual and prospective slaveowners. As Louisiana planter Antoine-Simon Le Page du Pratz explained in his 1758 book on the history of Louisiana, buyers were advised to examine a slave's entire body, down to the genitals: "from the sole of the feet to the top of the head, between the toes and fingers, in the mouth, in the ears, without excluding those areas that are naturally hidden, though they are at that time uncovered." Where pregnancy was concerned, slaveowners believed that it was they who suffered the economic burden from having to lessen the workload of women in the final stages of pregnancy and supporting their children; conversely, it was also slaveowners who ultimately benefited from their slaves' fertility through the natural increase in their slave holdings. These priorities ebbed and flowed in importance according to the time period, tied specifically to factors having to do with the slave trade and the availability of new slaves within the colony.[51]

The 1724 code noir's other main provision concerning offspring centered on protecting the family unit. Article 43 stipulated that, though deemed movables, a husband, wife, and their prepubescent children who belonged to the same master could not be seized and sold separately (see also Article 46). French slave laws were ostensibly more humanitarian than slave laws in English colonies, which offered no protection to married couples and their children; there, masters could legally split husbands and wives and sell children at any age. In French colonies, the special conditions inherent in Articles 7, 8, and 43 (that the parents be legally married and that such marriages could only take place with the master's approval, irrespective of the parents' wishes) meant that the law was more protective in spirit than in practice. Although records of slave sales seem to suggest that the spirit of the law was honored, any slave who became a parent knew that their claim and authority over their own children was superseded, and replaced, by that of their master. The power of slaveowners over their slaves' progeny was fully enshrined in law.[52]

The absence of the father in the case against Marie-Jeanne crystallizes the relative insignificance of enslaved parents' rights to their children before the law. He was left virtually invisible, the archive willfully silencing any reference to his person beyond his act of paternity, just as slave baptism registers usually omitted the names of fathers when the parents were not married (consistent with the code noir's rule about the status of a child deriving from that of the mother). A few examples, all from 1748, exist of the testimony of children who made a point of identifying both their parents, though tellingly they also gave the names of each parent's master. Eighteen-year-old Louis, who belonged to Sieur Dubreuil and identified as Creole, for instance, revealed that he lived with his parents on the same plantation, "having his father and his mother at Sieur Dubreuil" *(ayant son pere et sa mere Chez ledt sr Dubreuil)*. Charlo gave even more detail about his family, which the scribe dutifully wrote down, including the familiar terms the son used for his parents: "Said he was named Charlo as his master calls him, that his dad and mom call him Karacou, that he has not been baptized, that he is a slave belonging to Mr. Raguet, that his dad chops wood and his mom works with the other *negres*. And has promised to tell the truth, is of the Coneda nation, aged about twenty years old" *(a dit se Nommer Charlo comme son maître Lappelle que son papa es maman Lappellent Karacou quil na point Eté Batisé quil est Esclave appartenant au M. Raguet quil a son papa qui Ecarrit du bois es sa maman travaille avec les autres Negres es a promis de dire verité, est de Nation Coneda agé denviron Vingt ans)*. Charlo recognized his master's right to name him, even as he simultaneously made a point of asserting his parents' right to confer the name that he was known by (a name that the court used). A third child, François, did not even know for sure who his father was; in his self-identification, he merely "said that he *thinks* that Scipion *negre* of Mr. La Fresniere is his father, and his mother is named Digueny or Marie who lives with his master Sieur Boisclair" *(A dit quil Croit que Scipion Negre à Mr La fresniere Est son pere Et sa mere se Nomme digueny ou Marie qui Est Chez son maître le sr Boiclair)*. Perhaps enslaved children customarily identified themselves this way in daily life, but, in the eyes of the law, the name of their father was irrelevant and therefore usually omitted from the record.[53]

Marie-Jeanne stated that the man who had impregnated her was an enslaved African. No information contradicts this assertion, but she might have hesitated to name a French man, especially in the absence of a living child and even more so if it was a predatory French man. That only bones were found (with no skin mentioned) further rendered the child's father invisible. His name is never given, they were not married according to French law, and Marie-Jeanne was not asked to identify him or to describe their relationship. Nor was she asked to declare if he was also the father of the child she had previously miscarried "long ago" or if he knew about the pregnancy, questions that might have legitimately borne on the question of whether she had killed her child. She did not volunteer this information. Kaskaskia was small enough that perhaps it was widely known, but it could just as easily have been a secret, open or otherwise. Above all, it is impossible to know if her pregnancy was the result of coercion, though one can hope that she conceived in joy.[54]

❧❧

"SCANDALOUS RELATIONS"

Court cases centered on infanticide, such as that against Marie-Jeanne, necessarily hinged on sexuality, reproduction, and the risks of sexual violence and conception. Prosecutions of maroon men notwithstanding, the greatest risk for enslaved women came from colonists, yet no suit in Louisiana was ever brought against a colonist for sexual abuse of a slave, even when glaring evidence was brought to the attention of the Superior Council, as was the case when a claim of serial feticide stemming from the physical and sexual abuse of female slaves in New Orleans appeared before the court in 1730. The accusation was not part of a criminal trial but an allegation aired as evidence in a civil claim aimed at severing a contractual relationship between Raymond Amyaut d'Ausseville and the overseer of his plantation on the outskirts of New Orleans, Jacques Charpentier dit Le Roy. In other words, it was a civil suit brought by one private party against another in which the evidence of feticide, rape, and physical abuse was pertinent to a claim for loss of property. The claim would neither be investigated nor prosecuted criminally.[55]

In his suit, d'Ausseville accused Le Roy of economic harm by causing the death and injury of his slaves through a regime of brutality, deprivation, rape, and sheer sadism. Among the accusations that d'Ausseville leveled at Le Roy were reports of sustained ill-treatment of pregnant women and the resulting loss of six pregnancies to four women over a four-year period. In one instance, he made an outright accusation of feticide against Le Roy. One woman, Suzanne, he informed the court, had had two stillbirths over a two-year period, and, in one case, the baby was born with "its head crushed, which can only be caused by a violent blow" *(sa tête ecrasée ce que ne peut provenir que d'un coup violent)* in utero. He named Le Roy as the perpetrator. D'Ausseville's statement emphasized the "scandalous relations" *(commerce scandaleux)* that Le Roy had with his slaves in the fields in broad daylight and his ill-treatment of those who refused his sexual predations ("those who do not want to do what you wish" *[qui ne veulent pas faire ce que vous souhaitez])*.[56]

Unlike the accusations against Marie-Jeanne and the maroons suspected of infanticide, d'Ausseville's narrative, registered in the Superior Council of Louisiana where he held the office of councillor, never led to a criminal investigation. Filing suit was a final step. For an entire year after first being made aware of Le Roy's actions, d'Ausseville had exhibited an apparent lack of concern. Rather than taking action or involving the court, he merely wrote to Le Roy to complain about detailed reports he had received of the overseer's ill-treatment of the slaves under his charge. His missive incorporates his slaves' own words on the subject:

> I fail to understand your process, you seek by your process to have the slaves revolt or throw themselves in the river. There are the examples of Blandas and Jean-François, the latter having been fished [from the river] by the Sr. Terrebonne. One of my slaves has died, with furthermore one female slave having died for lack of care and Dorimanie aborted [miscarried] her last, Suzanne has also been ill-treated from which she too aborted. You have as well ill-treated Dorimanie last night without considering that she is pregnant. Here is Bonnet who has come to complain that you have ill-treated him because he did not want to give you a suckling pig, you took it from him, killed it, and ate it in the company of Plaisance. Lafleur and Brunet have told Sr. Terrebonne that soon I will have no slaves left, they ask to be killed rather than be beaten unjustly. Lafleur does not want to drink nor eat, all he does is cry, he laments that you have beaten his wife even though she is pregnant. It is more than a year since I was first warned that you have no scruple in having scandalous relations in the middle of the fields with slave women, that you ill-treat those who do not want to do what you wish.

D'Ausseville's obsession with the fertility of his slaves is starkly obvious from this letter. He ended his admonishment to Le Roy by putting emphasis on how his behavior affected him, "You make me see by your manner the contempt that you have for me," a self-pitying comment that is all the more disturbing when annexed to d'Ausseville's detailed recapitulation of Le Roy's litany of abuses against the slaves. His hijacking of the narrative away from the abuse to his own loss is especially disheartening given that d'Ausseville was a councillor who sat on the Superior Council, the very court that had the authority to investigate cases of slave abuse deemed illegal according to the code noir, laying bare how theoretical the law was where enforcement was concerned. He might well have been appalled by Le Roy's actions, but d'Ausseville's words show that, above all, he was a slaveowner who depended on human chattel for his livelihood.[57]

There were no French eyewitnesses to legally attest to Le Roy's crimes (though a number were willing to come forward, indirectly aware that Le Roy was responsible for the abuses). Article 24 stipulated that slaves could not testify against their masters (a role occupied by Le Roy as overseer), just as in French law wives, children, and servants could not testify against their head of household. Because of the absence of white eyewitnesses, d'Ausseville formally requested that an exemption be made for his slaves to testify in this instance. The court denied the request for an exemption, and no slaves testified. Article 20 of the 1724 code noir mandated legal recourse against masters accused of neglect and of extrajudicial "crimes and barbarian and inhuman treatment" against their slaves. But the Superior Council never acted on the evidence against Le Roy, evidence that one of their own, Councillor d'Ausseville, recognized and presented as barbarian and inhuman. Two other colonists joined him in this characterization of Le Roy's behavior, the surgeon who examined the bodies of the abused slaves and a French widow hired to look after the livestock, who would slip the slaves extra rations and try to stand up for them. The Superior Council investigated d'Ausseville's complaint in his civil suit but never prosecuted Le Roy for his crimes. Again and again, local court officials picked and chose how to apply the code noir, whom to prosecute, and for what crime, thereby laying bare the tensions, in a connected imperial world, between metropolitan edicts, the self-interest of colonists, and the actions and reactions of enslaved individuals.[58]

Given the widespread hearsay about Le Roy's activities, one might wonder if the overseer had an ulterior motive in ending pregnancies that could have been attributed to him, that is, eliminating any evidence of his paternity. Under Article 6 of the 1724 code noir, which also banned marriages between blacks and whites and sought to ban "concubinages" between free persons (white or black) and slaves, Le Roy would have been liable for a hefty fine of three hundred livres if any child had been born from his rapes. No prosecutions are known, but, as d'Ausseville underscored, Le Roy knew well enough not to commit his crimes in the presence of white eyewitnesses who could have testified against him. Though he knew it was highly improbable that he would be prosecuted, he was likely mindful of other potential legal minefields when abusing the slaves he was charged with overseeing and avoided taking unnecessary risks.[59]

Enslaved women never spoke openly in court about the fact that their children were deemed the property of their masters. Their only allusions to having their children taken away from them was that contained in testimony about infanticide perpetrated by enslaved men. In Louisiana's courts, neither enslaved fathers nor mothers offered explicit narratives about masters breaking the bonds of parenthood between enslaved parents and their children. Yet their testimony could evoke the fundamental realities of slavery: that the enslaved could make no legal claim to their own bodies, to their own sexuality, or to their own children. Through their words, even when accused of infanticide, enslaved individuals asserted their right to parenthood. In the testimony of Jeanneton and François Sarra of Monique, Magdalene Marena in Mauritius, and Marie-Jeanne in Louisiana are words of anguish at the loss of a child but also emotional reaffirmations of the maternal and paternal roles that they could not fully fulfill as a result of enslavement. It was the 1724 code noir (and the identical 1723 code noir in Mauritius), with its rules about testimony in judicial prosecutions, that forced these parents and prospective parents to have to defend their identity as parents, just as Marie-Jeanne did by crying out in her first interrogation shortly after her arrest, postpartum, that "her heart was not hard enough to kill her child, that it is too much for her." Ironically, it was the code noir's rules on testimony that allowed slaves the space to narrate their stories of parenthood — of motherhood and fatherhood. It is also what permitted women to allude to, if not directly bring up, their omnipresent vulnerability to the threat of sexual coercion and assault.

On June 21, 1749, a full eleven and a half months from when Marie-Jeanne was first interrogated, the Superior Council of Louisiana in New Orleans pronounced their judgment in the case against her. Since their deliberations were never made part of the record, it is not known how the judges came to their decision. Conviction for the crime of infanticide carried a sentence of death, and she knew the severity of the charge against her. Asked in New Orleans to explain why she thought she had been brought down from the Illinois Country, she answered plainly "that it is to make her die" *(que c'est pour la faire mourir)*. At no point did Marie-Jeanne confess, and the judges pronounced what seems to be an ambiguous judgment, though it was actually a legal one: she was sentenced to have her case "more amply informed within the year." In the meantime, she was to be sent back to her mistress in the Illinois Country. Only *after* the sentencing were the five surgeons brought in to examine the skull, which they declared was not that of a newborn but of a child a few months old, "and even that this bone has been underground for some time, that in addition there should have been membranes adhering to it, which makes them believe that this bone is older than is being said" *(que même Cet os a Resté quelque temps sous terre, que de plus Les membranes devoient Etre adherantes ce qui leur fait croire que cet os est plus ancien qu'on ne dit)*. Testimony was what mattered in passing judgment, not physical evidence.[60]

To have a judge pronounce a sentence of "more amply informed" might seem a cop-out, but it was a standard sentencing option permitted under the 1670 Code criminel. It was pronounced when the facts were not clear or when it was deemed that there was not enough proof to absolve or condemn. The period assigned could vary, from six months to multiple years, and the accused was either remanded to jail or allowed out. The sentence was not in theory to be taken lightly, for it was not absolution but could result in a new sentence, even the death penalty. There was one other detail that the court could have acted on (and perhaps did during the judges' deliberations) but did not take a position on. In her testimony during the trial in New Orleans, Marie-Jeanne claimed to be pregnant again. According to the 1670 Code criminel, had she received a death sentence, pregnancy would have caused her punishment to be deferred until after the birth. Invoking a pregnancy might have been tactical (her owner would have certainly known the law in this respect). But the Superior Council never referenced the pregnancy nor did the judges follow the law by having Marie-Jeanne's condition examined by "expert" matrons. From the perspective of her owner, Marie-Jeanne's sentence of "more amply informed," while neither perfect nor finite (as an acquittal would have been), allowed her to immediately regain access to the labor of her slave. No further information was brought to light during her probationary period, and the court did not take any additional action in the case, which, by default, closed at the conclusion of the year.[61]

How Marie-Jeanne responded to the sentence and how she made sense of such an unusual one can never be reclaimed. The trip that had brought her downriver from Upper to Lower Louisiana would have taken only about fifteen to twenty-five days. If she was taken back to the Illinois Country, she would have had about four months to ponder her situation during the more arduous return trip upriver and to imagine how she would be greeted on her return. Travel would have been a risky endeavor if she was pregnant. Perhaps her owner decided to leave her in New Orleans or even sell her there, although the risk of the case being reopened might have encouraged her to bring Marie-Jeanne back to the Illinois Country.

There is no further trace of Marie-Jeanne's existence in New Orleans or the Illinois Country, not even a birth record resulting from the pregnancy she announced during her New Orleans trial. Likewise, the child Lisette also drops out of the records. Perhaps Lisette acquired sufficient French in the intervening year to use words as well as signs to speak for herself and retell her story. But, thanks to the child's gestures and the interpreter's translations, language acquisition did not prove an impediment to the initial proceedings. Marie-Jeanne was investigated and imprisoned. Most important of all: she was removed from the household and from oversight of Lisette.

CHAPTER 4

"Our Place"

Francisque, Démocrite, and Hector

Interrogated if he knows a *negre* named Francisco?

Said that on Saturday night this *negre* Francisco came dancing at their place, that he did not know he was a runaway, that he paid richly for the drum and courted the *negresses,* that everyone said, "There is a very rich *negre.*" That he danced and then went off. That another day at noon he returned to their place with a basket, saying that his master had sent him to fetch eggs. That we filled his basket and he took a large note from his pocket that we could not change but nonetheless he took the eggs, promising he would come and pay for them as soon as he had changed the note. That another time he came dancing again but that he was impertinent and insulted the *negresses,* which led the *negre* Hector to say to him, "There is a b. [bugger] who we do not know who comes here to be a show-off, leave, go away, we do not need you to pay the drum, keep your money and leave." Whereupon Francisco told him, "If you were at the levee I would eviscerate you," so Hector grabbed the stick that [Francisco] was holding and gave him a good blow, telling him that "the next time he came back to their place he would have him tied up to four posts to have him whipped." That since that time they had not seen him until one day when he met him near where Mr. La Houssaye lives, that he, the deponent, being with another *negre,* heard [Francisco] chatting with a *negresse,* and he said, "Well, there is the *negre* who was being such a show-off at our place, he is a runaway we must stop him," and he immediately jumped on him, and the accused put his hand in his pocket and said, "Leave me, here are six piastres." That he [Démocrite] answered him, "I do not want your piastres" and held him down. But he could not stop [Francisco] from pulling out a large *bucheron* knife [a type of French trade knife with a fixed blade] and trying to stab him. [Démocrite] grabbed his hand and kept the knife in his grip, even though Francisco still wanted to stab him, he used force to get the knife out of the deponent's hand, which cut him. The deponent did not dare hold him any more, especially since the other *negre* had not wanted to help him tie him up, that he deponent went to get help from the camp and rang the bell, and, when they reached him, the accused stopped and, putting his knife in his hand, shouted at them not to approach, that anyone who tried to lay his hand on him, he would slit his stomach with his knife, and no one dared approach him, that he deponent waited for him until daybreak in Mr. Le Breton's mill, but he did not see him and has not seen him since.

Asked if when he met him he was carrying a bundle of laundry?

Said that he did not see any bundle on him, only a large tobacco box trimmed in silver, that when he went dancing he was like a gentleman, with a ruffled shirt, a blue waistcoat, a white hat, and three or four handkerchiefs around his neck, and elsewhere on his body. Added that he paid for the drum with coins and that he had large bills, that however he had not yet paid for the eggs that he had taken.

Interrogé sil connoit un negre nommé francisco

A Dit qu'un samedy au soir Ce negre francisco fut danser ches eux qui ne Le Connoissoit pas pour Marron, quil paÿoit Grossement Le tambour et fezoit La cour aux Negresses, que tous dizoient voila un negre bien Riche, quil Dansa et s'en fut ensuite quun autre Jour en plen Midÿ il Retourna chez eux, avec un panier dizant que son maitre Lanvoÿoit chercher des oeufs qu'on Luy rempli son panier et quil avoir tiré de sa poche un gros Billet qu'on ne peu changer que nonobstant il emporta Les oeufs avec promesse de venir paÿer aussitôt quil auroit changé qu'une autre fois il fut encore danser, mais quil fezoit Limpertinent et insultoit Les negresses ce quil fit que Le negre hector luy dit voila un b. qui vient icy faire Le fanfaron que nous ne Connoissons point, Retire toi, va ten, nous n'avons pas bezoin que tu paye le tambour garde ton argent et Retire toi Surquoy francisco luy dit si tu etoy à la levée je te ventreray alors hector luy arracha un batton qu'il avoit et luy en donna une bonne volée, luy dizant que la premiere fois qu'il reviendroit chez eux il le ferait amarrer pour luy donner le fouet à quatre piquet, que depuis ce tems la il ne l'avoient pas vu jusqu'a un jour qu'il le recontra pres de chez mr. La houssaÿe que luy deposant etant avec un autre negre l'entendirent qu'il babilloit avec une negresse et qu'il dit allors, voila le negre qui fezoit tant le fanfaron chez nous, il est marron il faut l'arreter qu'aussitot il luy sauta dessus, et l'accuzé luy dit attends et mettant la main à sa poche luy dit laisse moy tiens voila six piastres gourdes qu'il luy repondit je ne veux point tes piastres et le tenant il ne put empecher qu'il ne sortit un grand couteau boucheron et voulant luÿ en porter un coup, il se saizit de sa main et tenoit le couteau empoigné, que francisco voulant toujours le poignarder, il tira de force Le coutteau de la main du deposant qui luÿ coupa la main le deposant n'oza pas le tenir davantage dautant que l'autre negre n'avoit pas voulu l'aÿder pour l'ammarrer, que luy deposant fut chercher du monde au camp, et sonnerent et l'ayant joint l'accuzé s'arreta et metant son coutteau à la main il leur cria de ne pas approcher, que celuy qui voudroit metre la main sur luy il luy ouvreroit le ventre à grands coups de coutteau, et aucun deux n'oza s'approcher, que luÿ deposant fut l'attendre jusqu'au jour dans le moulin de Mr. Le Breton et qu'il ne le vit point et ne la plus vu

Interrogé si lorsquil le recontra il avoit un paquet de Linge

A Dit quil ne Luy avoit vu aucun paquet rien qu'une tabatiere grande Garnie en argent que Lorsquil alloit danser il etoit Comme un Monsieur, chemize Garnie une veste bleue, un chapeau Blanc, et trois ou quatre mouchoirs à son Col, et autour de Luÿ, adjoutte quil paÿoit Le tambour avec de Largent blanc et quil avoit des Gros Billets, que Cependant il n'avoit pas encore payé Les oeufs quil avoit pris[1]

In 1766, a case was brought in New Orleans against a thirty-year-old runaway slave alternately known as "Francisque" or "Francisco" (the French and Spanish spellings of Francis). The self-described "Englishman from Philadelphia" *(anglois de philadelphy)* was jailed when Sieur Boré turned him in, accusing him of having stolen from one of his female slaves. Francisque would ultimately be charged with running away, stealing a bundle of apparel from a white laundress, and setting fire to a boat on the convoy that navigated up and down the Mississippi River between New Orleans and the Illinois Country. These offenses were criminal acts according to French law, and Francisque was prosecuted in a French colonial court. But there was a parallel system of informal justice that set his prosecution by the French in motion — that of a group of local enslaved African men who wanted to punish him following a series of contentious altercations during which he had stolen from them, flaunted his stylish and flamboyant appearance, and successfully courted their women. Francisque was at risk wherever he turned.[2]

Runaways were by definition vulnerable; they took a chance every time they were accosted or approached someone. To survive, they had to know, or

Francisque, Démocrite, and Hector

guess, whom to trust. The court case against Francisque inverts this perspective by offering the testimony of slaves who were not runaways but anchored to a plantation or other dwelling. In their telling, they and the members of their community were the ones most at risk from runaways, the ones who had to assess whether or not they could put their faith in a fugitive in their midst. In many ways, though colonists ultimately arrested and prosecuted Francisque, this was a judicial affair that one cohort of plantation slaves initially sought to resolve, and to police, on their own.

Prior to the courts becoming involved, two enslaved men in particular, Démocrite and Hector, worked together to defuse the threat that Francisque posed, not to colonists, but to their local slave community. The men's actions would result in Francisque being isolated and hence vulnerable to prosecution by the colonial justice system. Theirs would be a sustained campaign aimed at getting rid of Francisque. When Francisque turned up at a slave gathering and courted the women and "insulted" them after having stolen some eggs a few days before, Hector, assuming a position of authority, asked him to leave. When Francisque responded by threatening him, matters swiftly escalated. Hector beat him with a stick and went so far as to warn the runaway that they would "have him tied up to four posts to have him whipped" if he dared to return, a threat that suggests that Hector was likely an overseer or slave driver with power over other enslaved individuals on the plantation. It was perhaps not coincidental, given that Francisque had never paid for the eggs, that the judicial punishment for the stealing of "sheep, goats, hogs, poultry, grain, fodder, peas, beans, or other vegetables, produce, or provisions, when committed by slaves," was a lashing by the public executioner. In other words, Hector threatened him with a form of punishment borrowed from the French.[3]

Hector's warning reflected knowledge of the code noir and its application in the colony. But there was more to his posturing than a mere channelling of the colonial justice system. Instead, it becomes apparent that some enslaved men took it on themselves to publicly perform their role as enforcers, to assume a mantle of responsibility for regulating social, economic, gender, and sexual relations within their community. It was a role that owed as much, if not more, to West African judicial norms and practices (including the existence of all-male societies charged with maintaining order) than to French ones.

It was Francisque's transgressions against the inhabitants of the slave camp that caused Hector to threaten him with a whipping and led Démocrite and others to attempt to have him caught and handed over to the authorities, and it was Démocrite's testimony that ultimately clinched Francisque's conviction. Through their actions and their words, these enslaved men, who were well established within the local slave community, emphasized that Francisque had broken *their* rules and that it was within *their* purview to regulate his behavior among them, indeed, that it was their responsibility to render justice and have him punished for what they deemed breaches of order and of trust.

As Démocrite's testimony in particular reveals, emotions ran high. Anxieties about Francisque centered on his style and access to women. But the fugitive's real offense was to flaunt his sartorial and monetary wealth — dressing to seduce and paying for the music at slave gatherings — while at the same time taking advantage of the support that the enslaved community offered him and even stealing from them (eggs, earrings, and a hat). That was the rub. On the one hand, by virtue of being a runaway, Francisque could not avoid being vulnerable to discovery, arrest, and worse. On the other hand, by running away, he laid claim to a special kind of self-determination. To be sure, to be a runaway was a liminal state of being. But it was all the more irritating — and disturbing — to slaves like Démocrite precisely because it showed up *their* condition as enslaved.

The testimony in this court case exposes the cleavages between those who lived within slave communities and those runaways like Francisque who operated, if only temporarily, as virtual free agents. This, then, is not so much the narrative of Francisque as it is the intertwined stories of three men, Francisque, Démocrite, and Hector, one that opens a window into the ways that enslaved Africans perceived those who had seized their autonomy by running away and, in the process, upended slave communities' internal rules regulating property, sexuality, and the policing of social behavior.

ℵ℧ℱ

THE COURT CASE

In the course of a lengthy investigation and trial that stretched from April to August 1766, Francisque appeared in court seven times. Démocrite was called to testify in the case as a witness and appeared again in the formal confrontation with Francisque. Hector was not interrogated, but he played an important role, and his words were recorded as hearsay. A third slave, Jacques, was also interrogated. He was accused of being Francique's accomplice during the thefts. Though charges against Jacques were ultimately dropped, his statement would contradict Francisque's, and his testimony brought to light some important details. None of the women mentioned in the trial record, whether because Francisque had stolen from them or otherwise interacted with them, testified.[4]

Francisque, Démocrite, and Hector

The investigation and court case would end up encompassing multiple crimes, including breaking and entering at night, theft of clothes, running away, and issuing threats. Francisque came to the authorities' attention when his master, Sieur Saroux, seized a bundle of clothes from him. The apparel was identified as having been stolen from a female slave belonging to Sieur Boré. It was not made explicit whether these were Boré's clothes or his slave's. As the investigation proceeded, further crimes were unearthed. The laundress Anne Boyer (wife of Gabriel Soulard dit St. Germain) testified that a theft had occurred on her premises, and she and one of her customers, Jean Rousset, were asked if they could identify any of the stolen clothes from among the goods found in Francisque's possession. In addition, the town jailer testified about Francisque's attempts, while incarcerated, to break out of prison. Francisque denied the accusation, but the trial lasted a long time, and he must have become very familiar with any weak points in the prison and prison courtyard (see Figure 4).[5]

Both the white laundress and her customer made depositions, but the court did not hear the testimony of Francisque's enslaved victims. Boré's unnamed female slave did not testify nor did the unnamed female slave belonging to Sieur Dublanc from whom, according to Jacques, Francisque had stolen earrings and a hat after spending the night with her. The court did briefly interrogate him about the stolen earrings, but no reference was made to the restitution of either of the enslaved women's property. These two victims' absence from the courtroom was not so much gendered as it was a consequence of Article 24 of the 1724 code noir, which stipulated that masters act for their slaves in civil and criminal matters "to demand punishment and reparation for such outrages and excesses as their slaves may have suffered." Such cases were seldom given priority in the courts, but, when in 1765 the slave François was convicted of being a recidivist runaway, the judgment also mentioned that he had stolen a *capot* (a hooded overcoat of simple construction made of cheap wool or a blanket) from another slave. He was sentenced to have his ears cut, to be branded with a fleur-de-lis, and to be exiled from the colony, while his master, Jerome Matuliche, was made to pay his board at the jail and to reimburse the slave from whom the theft was committed.[6]

Prosecutions of slaves for running away and for theft necessarily reveal much about colonists' anxieties, since they were the ones who usually set investigations in motion. Yet it is possible to locate the viewpoint of the enslaved in Francisque's answers to the prosecutor's questions and, especially, in the testimony of those who testified against him. As seen in Jacques's and Démocrite's testimony and their courtroom confrontation with Francisque as well as Hector's reported words, these slaves charted the runaway's movements; argued over his social, economic, and sexual interactions with the enslaved men and women he encountered; and dissected his performance at slave gatherings, where he dressed "like a gentleman," paid for the music, courted the women, and, in so doing, alienated the men.

Their understandings of Francisque's actions were also fused onto notions that had developed within the slave community about what constituted appropriate standards of behavior. Possessiveness over women usually manifested itself on a case-by-case basis. For example, when a woman named Marion in a 1757 court case from Natchitoches was asked when she had last seen her accomplice Pierrot, she answered that "she had not seen him since he left, but she had heard from Rose that he was looking for Gammenon in order to kill him because he had been seeing Rose his former wife / woman *(A repondu qu'elle ne l'avoit point vu depuis son depart, mais qu'elle avoit Sceut par la nommée Rose quil cherchoit le nommé gammenon pour le tuer à Cause quil frequentoit la ditte roze son ancienne femme)*. Similarly, François dit Baraca, who in 1748 would stand accused of murdering his wife, Taco (they lived together and were married according to French law), had accused her of infidelity—and worse. In contrast to these examples of raw emotion linked to specific women, Jacques's, Démocrite's, and Hector's reactions to Francisque were, not focused on his individual conquests, but encompassed all of the women they felt were in their charge. Sometimes, as in the response of the African-born Démocrite, these standards were probably inflected by cultural mores and judicial practices derived from West Africa.[7]

Francisque initially succeeded in building trust as he inserted himself into the community of enslaved Africans on the outskirts of New Orleans with which Démocrite and Hector were affiliated, and he found there both material and social support. But the runaway's subsequent actions betrayed the community's social conventions, and Démocrite's testimony vividly expresses the resentment that male members of his group felt toward the outsider. In particular, Démocrite provided a lengthy statement that supplied far more than the cursory information required by the court and in which he repeatedly singled out for criticism the runaway's financial shenanigans, his ostentatious attire, his lavish spending on music, and his shameless (and apparently successful) flirtations with women.

Dress and appearance were crucial tools that Francisque used to make his foray into this community, highlighting the importance of nonverbal cues in negotiating and maintaining relations among New Orleans's enslaved populations. Yet Francisque's appearance and his performance of masculinity would also become key factors in his eventual capture. They were certainly at the heart of the ill will that he elicited. In Démocrite's narrative, it was Fran-

Francisque, Démocrite, and Hector

cisque's flaunting of material assets, combined with his continual flouting of codes of conduct (also centered on objects, as in the thefts from fellow slaves) and the flamboyant way he courted enslaved women, that caused local enslaved males to turn against him and then try to hand him over to the authorities, a fate that, in Démocrite's telling, Francisque fully deserved.[8]

"THAT *NEGRE* WHO WAS BEING SUCH A SHOW-OFF AT OUR PLACE"

To understand how Démocrite arrived at his assessment of Francisque, it is necessary to first understand the context and circumstances of the two men's interactions. In his testimony, the forty-year-old Démocrite, acting as the de facto spokesman for his immediate community, described four encounters with Francisque. Francisque initially surfaced, a stranger, at a Saturday evening gathering held by Démocrite and his group, and he immediately impressed them all with his munificence. After dancing, lavishing his money to pay for the music, and showering his attention on women, Francisque left, only to return a few days later with a basket to purchase some eggs, ostensibly on his master's account. Offering only a large note in payment, Francisque was allowed to keep the eggs with a promise to return as soon as he had made change, a debt he never settled.

Francisque next appeared at another dance assembly, but, this time, Démocrite asserted, Francisque was both generally impertinent and insulting toward the women. He also carried a big stick (in contravention of Article 12 of the 1724 code noir, which limited slaves' access to "weapons or large sticks, under the penalty of being whipped, and of having the weapons confiscated"). It was during this dance assembly that Hector stepped in, saying, "There is a b. [bugger] who comes here to fool around that we do not know. Leave, go away, we do not need you to pay the drum, keep your money and leave." Hector might have guessed that Francisque was a runaway, though the resumption of the slave trade to Louisiana in the 1760s meant that it must have been difficult to be certain about the identity of a new arrival. But Hector's words expressed in no uncertain terms that he did not trust the stranger, and he consequently moved to protect the members of his group by immediately expelling Francisque rather than risk taking his money. Instead of leaving, however, Francisque raised the stakes, warning Hector that he would have eviscerated him "if you were at the levee." It was then that Hector, once again claiming a position of authority, grabbed the stick that Francisque was brandishing, beat him with it, and warned him that the "next time he came back to their place" he would have him bound and lashed.[9]

Démocrite went on to describe one final showdown. He spotted Francisque some time after while out with another (unnamed) slave. On overhearing him "chatting with"—and chatting up—an unnamed enslaved woman, Démocrite said to his companion, "There is the *negre* who was being such a show-off at our place, he is a runaway we must stop him," and he promptly pounced on him. According to Démocrite, Francisque tried to hold him off by bribing him with six piastres, but Démocrite said he did not want his money. Though Démocrite was holding him down, Francisque managed to pull out a large knife and, in the ensuing tussle, wound Démocrite in the hand so that "the deponent did not dare hold him any more, especially since the other *negre* had not wanted to help him tie him up." Undeterred, Démocrite doggedly went for help from the slave quarters, but Francisque, acutely aware of the danger he was in, wielded his knife again and "shouted at them not to approach, that anyone who tried to lay his hand on him, he would slit his stomach with his knife, and no one dared approach him, that he deponent waited for him until daybreak in Mr. Le Breton's mill but he did not see him and has not seen him since."[10]

Démocrite, Francisque, and Jacques each gave their own version of the last incident. Francisque claimed he had acted in self-defense in wounding Démocrite. Jacques provided one pertinent detail that both Démocrite and Francisque omitted: that Francisque was carrying a bundle of stolen clothes when Démocrite accosted him and that Démocrite had tried to steal it (in his own testimony, Démocrite denied that Francisque had been carrying any goods). It was during Jacques's interrogation that Démocrite was first mentioned and entered the record, so it was thanks to Jacques's testimony that Démocrite was assigned to appear as a witness.[11]

✵

"FRANCISQUE CREOLE FROM PHILADELPHIA"

Though Francisque's clashes with other slaves preceded his arrest and though the testimony at his trial centered overwhelmingly on slaves' interactions with one another, once swept up within the judicial system the case against him followed standard procedures that pitted the slave against the full force of the French colonial justice system. The court case began with a declaration about criminal activity committed by a slave whose identity was not known (later ascertained to be Francisque), and it was followed by the investigation and prosecution. Court procedure dictated that those testifying identify themselves and provide certain standard pieces of information (name, religion, age, and ownership if applicable). It was a requirement that offered each defendant or witness some scope for describing themselves

Francisque, Démocrite, and Hector

as they saw fit at this point in time and in this specific circumstance. Francisque's words demonstrate how he chose to communicate his conception of himself in an official French judicial arena. Namely, his personal statements about his origins hint at the complexity — and the fluidity — of slave identities and gesture toward the complex geographies that the enslaved navigated as a consequence of their enslavement.

Francisque had two occasions in court to introduce himself. In the course of his first interrogation, he identified himself as "Francisque creole from Philadelphia aged about thirty years old field worker" *(Francisque creol de philadelphy agé de trente ans ou environ travaillant à la terre)*. Tied to Francisque's use of the adjective "Creole," which denoted someone of either European or African origin born in the colony, was a claim to have been born in Philadelphia. During his final interrogation on the sellette, on August 2, he gave his age as thirty years old and pronounced his religion as Catholic. This time he stressed his identity not so much as a "creole from Philadelphia" but more pointedly as an "Englishman from Philadelphia." In a later statement, he spoke of having been in Saint Domingue and also asserted that he had been in Louisiana before, having come "with the Spanish frigate and that he had [also] come there various times with the English" *(dans la fregatte espagnolle et quil y estoit venu plusieurs fois avec les anglois)*.[12]

Francisque's testimony does not reveal how a slave from Pennsylvania ended up in Cuba via Haiti. Perhaps he was a runaway, or perhaps he had sailed on a licit or illicit voyage from Philadelphia to Havana. Either way, the court did not judge this pertinent and did not elect to ask him about this aspect of his biography. Rather, the prosecutor simply accepted that he was from an English colony and had some familiarity with a Spanish one (he presumably spoke French with a British accent), asking him at one point if he had ever been prosecuted "during the time he had been in English and Spanish America" *(pendant qu'il a été en l'amerique anglois et espagnole)*.[13]

Communication, both in words and nonverbal expressions, was key to Francisque's ability to navigate his way around Louisiana and the Atlantic. Despite his immediate point of origin in Spanish Cuba and his assertion that he was originally from Philadelphia, all of his interrogations were conducted in French, and no interpreters were called in to translate his words. Démocrite, Hector, and Jacques did not allude to any difficulties communicating with Francisque either. Among other languages, then, Francisque could make himself understood in French and Louisiana Creole, not surprising given that he had lived in Saint Domingue and visited Louisiana. Yet officials and witnesses could not even fix on what to call him; he was intermittently called Francisque, Francisco, or François. Though he did not allude to his linguistic abilities, Francisque did invoke his experience navigating the British, Spanish, and French Atlantic worlds. When asked, for example, if he had offered to show a female slave how to cook some dishes, he readily acknowledged that his specialties included both "English and Spanish stews" *(des Ragouts anglois et espagnols)* — evidence that he had indeed experienced life in both British and Iberian worlds. That he was skilled at cooking is an indication of his privileged access to a more elevated skill set than that of his primary occupation, which he gave as field laborer. Even that he declared he was Catholic reinforces his peripatetic experiences: if he had indeed converted, his baptism (compelled or otherwise) would have taken place in a Spanish or French colony, not likely in Pennsylvania.[14]

When prompted to identify his owner during his first interrogation, Francisque stated that he belonged to Jean Pierre Robert Gérard, Chevalier de Vilemont (see Figure 30). Under the French regime, Vilemont was a member of Louisiana's colonial and military elite and former post commandant of Fort Tombecbé (for which service he was made Chevalier of Saint Louis). After a hiatus in France and Spain, he returned to Louisiana in 1765 under the Spanish flag following the Treaty of Fontainebleau (1762), having negotiated an office as second-in-command with the Spanish crown. By then he had married Françoise Petit de Coulange, widow of Vincent Guillaume Le Sénéchal d'Auberville, the former *commissaire-ordonnateur* of Louisiana, the top administrative official in the colony. Francisque added that Vilemont had purchased him in Havana and that he had arrived in Louisiana on a Spanish frigate. Since Vilemont had arrived in the colony on February 14, 1765, having departed Havana with the new Spanish governor Antonio de Ulloa and sixty Spanish troops, Francisque must have landed in New Orleans not long before his April arrest.[15]

But the interrogators also seemed to be aware that Francisque had been in Louisiana previous to his arrival with Vilemont, something the prosecutor might have discovered when he conducted his preliminary investigation. The judges promptly asked him a leading question about his earlier visits to the colony, which was when he answered that he had come before on the Spanish frigate as well as other times with the English; perhaps during those visits he had been employed as a sailor. Corroborating the fact that he had visited New Orleans with "the English," a story that was not implausible given the existence of illicit trade, Francisque added further biographical details about his life during a second interrogation on the sellette. This new information lends support to his claim to have been in the colony prior to his time with Vilemont: "Says that he had come here sent to Mr. D'Abbadie, and was then sent back to Havana where he was sold about two years ago" *(A dit estre Venu icy et envoyé à mr. Dabadie, et qu'il fut de son tems renvoyé à la havanne où il fut vendu il y a environ deux ans).* As director-general of Louisiana, Jean-Jacques Blaise d'Abbadie had served as first judge on the Superior Council, where he personally oversaw all slave prosecutions until his death in February 1765, about five months before Francisque's trial began. This was the very court poised to pass judgement on Francisque.[16]

Francisque was not listed among the slaves at d'Abbadie's estate sale or in d'Abbadie's diary, but, one of the slaves sold at auction after his death was a twenty-five-year-old woman, Marie, who had a seven-month-old boy named François, and it is not inconceivable that this was Francisque's son. Marie had another daughter, a three-year-old who, in contrast to the infant François, was specified as a *"mulatresse,"* suggesting that the children had different fathers. Marie was not legally married, hence no father was named for either child. Though d'Abbadie's records make no reference to receiving slaves from Havana, his biography and timeline are consistent with Francisque's declaration in July 1766 that he had been in Louisiana with the director-general two years or so before the trial. D'Abbadie had arrived in Louisiana in June 1763, charged with overseeing the transfer of the colony from France to Spain and Britain as a result of the secret Treaty of Fontainebleau (1762) and the Treaty of Paris (1763). Francisque's earlier time in Louisiana, together with his cosmopolitan background and existing familiarity with New Orleans, might have made him seem especially valuable to Vilemont, who likely perceived his background and experience as value-added benefits that set Francisque apart from other slaves for sale in Havana.[17]

Though Francisque identified Vilemont as his owner, court officials had inside knowledge that, at the time of his arrest, Francisque no longer belonged to Vilemont, and they asked the slave to whom Vilemont had sold him. He replied that he "had been sold to be sent to the Illinois and that he does not know if it is Sieur Maxant who had bought him, and that not wanting to go there he had left the boat and had been sold to Sieur Saroux in chains" *(avoit été vendu pour estre envoyé aux illinois et qu'il ne sçait pas si c'est le s. Maxant qui l'avoit acheté et que ne voulant pas y aller il a quitté le batteau et qu'il avoit été vendu aus. Saroux les fers aux mains).* In other words, it was shortly after Francisque's return to the colony that Vilemont had sold (or possibly leased) him; perhaps Vilemont had always planned to sell him for a profit on arrival in New Orleans. Gilbert Antoine de St. Maxent was a prominent merchant and fur trader and one of the founders of St. Louis in the Illinois Country. In fact, Francisque was on his way between New Orleans and the Illinois Country when he deserted the convoy. He might have labored as a rower, since convoys up and down the Mississippi made heavy use of enslaved Africans as such. Though it was physically taxing labor, some free Africans also bound themselves as full-fledged, professional voyageurs (fur traders and those who manned the river convoys), taking advantage of specialized knowledge gained in their homeland navigating the Senegal River to negotiate a more skilled position on the boat. Francisque's convoy was probably the one that was loaded and ready to leave at the end of April 1764, two months before he was captured. Clearly, Francisque did not turn out to be compliant, for, as he explained, having "left the boat," it was "in chains" that a third party, Sieur Saroux, acquired him, undoubtedly for a correspondingly low price. The accusations against Francisque included the charge that he apparently set fire to St. Maxent's boat, presumably at the time that he "left" it.[18]

Having elicited a reference from Francisque to being put in irons, the court asked him if he had ever been prosecuted in either Anglo or Spanish America. Though he answered in the negative, the court ordered that he be stripped and his body searched for marks of previous punishments. None were found, but Francisque could not escape this invasive act by which the court pored over his naked body, one that was not merely investigative, since it simultaneously humiliated and subjugated the accused.[19]

In Francisque's subsequent interrogation on the sellette, the questioning became more probing, probably as a result of the prosecutor finding fresh cause for interrogation based on further inquiries he had made in the interim. Francisque was now asked if it was because he had wanted to poison his mistress that he had been sent from Saint Domingue, a question that provides an ominous context for the earlier exchange about whether or not he could cook (and whether in Louisiana he had taught the *negresse* of Sieur Maxent" how to make "ragouts"). Colonists tended to obsess over fears of their slaves poisoning them, and food preparation provided the ideal opportunity to administer poison. Rather than denying outright that he had tried to poison his mistress, Francisque answered that "he had never had any mistresses but always masters" *(a dit n'avoir jamais eu de Maitresse mais toujours des maîtres),* a fact that the court would have found impossible to check. He then denied any criminality, adding, unsolicited, that "he had been sent here [to Louisiana] only because they had a bad overseer who always beat them, that he used to run away to the Spanish part [of the island] and for that reason they had sent him here" *(il n'avoit été envoyé ici que parce qu'ils avaient un mauvais econome qui les battaient toujours qu'il s'en alloit marron dans la partie espagnole et que pour cela on l'avoit envoyé ici).* In response to a follow-up question as to whether he had committed robberies when in Saint Domingue, he answered, "No, he has never stolen, that in that country they cut the ears as punishment *(Dit que non quil n'a Jamais volé que dans ce pay Là on*

Francisque, Démocrite, and Hector

y Coupe les oreilles pour punir). His reply signaled knowledge of variations in how the judicial systems of Saint Domingue and Louisiana were administered and mandatory sentences applied as seen through the eyes of one peripatetic slave who had moved between the two legal regimes.[20]

Francisque finished chronicling his movements by specifying that he had remained with Saroux two weeks, cutting wood every day by the riverbank. It was then that he ran away from him as well and began to move covertly among the New Orleans slave community. A runaway for about one and a half months before his capture, his peregrinations allowed him to survive by availing himself of the resources that local communities of enslaved persons customarily proffered runaways. His interactions with that community, and with Démocrite and Hector in particular, would pave the way for his eventual prosecution and conviction.

DÉMOCRITE AND HECTOR

Francisque's appearance in court created an opening for him to narrate his peripatetic existence traversing the French, Iberian, and British Atlantic worlds. Motion across the Atlantic, and the written documents that such movement could lead to, has come to define the recent surge in richly textured biographies and life stories of enslaved individuals. But mobility was not the norm. Though sparser information exists for Démocrite, Hector, and Jacques, whose lives were relatively static, the archival record offers tantalizing glimpses of their existence as well.[21]

The thirty-five-year-old Creole Jacques was owned by the Chevalier Alexandre François Joseph de Clouet, who lodged with his wife in New Orleans at the large residence of his mother-in-law, Dame Bruslé (the widow of a former member of the Superior Council). Jacques seems to have been assigned to their plantation outside the city. Asked how long he had been a runaway, he stated that "he had stayed a month without leaving his plantation, where he lived off maize" *(a dit avoir resté un mois sans sortir de son habitation, où il vivoit de Mahis);* he could not have done so without the knowledge and support of other slaves on the plantation.[22]

Démocrite and Hector were owned by another resident of New Orleans, Sieur Jacques Esnould de Livaudais (former captain of the port), but the two men, like Jacques, also lived and worked on an outlying property. It was on Livaudais's plantation that Francisque stole the eggs and in that vicinity that he attended the dances. Both men seem to have lived there for some time, based on their familiarity with the place and its people as well as their expressions of belonging. They would remain fixtures there for years to come, with

Démocrite and Hector being listed on a May 1773 inventory of Livaudais's slaves taken shortly after their master's death.[23]

Hector, appraised in that inventory at two thousand livres, was identified as a forty-five-year-old carpenter who suffered from a hernia *("Un otre negro nomdo Hector carpintero, quarenta y cinco años con una hernia, estimado en dos mil Libras 2000")*, making him about thirty-eight years old at the time of his encounter with Francisque. In all likelihood, Livaudais acquired Hector through his wife, who was the stepdaughter of François Carrière. When Carrière died in 1738, among the records of his slave holdings was one family unit that included "Hector thirteen years old." The French name of Hector's African-born mother, La Petite Jeanneton (Little Jeanneton), is legible, but that of his African-born father is indecipherable except for the first letter, "B." Fleshing out this extraordinary record of his lineage, the document also listed Hector's two siblings, Charlot, two years old, and Celestin, six years old; all three children, because they were born in the colony, would have been baptized.[24]

Démocrite was listed on the 1773 inventory as thirty years old, making him about fifteen years younger than the skilled carpenter Hector, which is consistent with the way that Démocrite in his narrative seemed to defer to the other man's authority. The listing specified that Démocrite's legs were "defective," a condition that was evidently severe enough that he was only valued at one thousand livres, half of Hector's estimate *("un otre negro nombrado Democrite defectuoso de las piernas de treinta a˜, estimado en mil libras 1000")*. The information about Hector's and Démocrite's injuries was included only because it bore on their valuation; tellingly, in the context of the brutality of slavery and of slave labor, no details were provided about the circumstances that led to their ailments.[25]

Though the archival record only affords glimpses of the lives of Démocrite, Hector, and Jacques, the way they saw themselves and understood their role in their world as well as their relationship to the plantation where they lived and labored emerges from their verbal expressions, whether spoken in court or recorded as word of mouth. For both Hector and Démocrite, a clue lies in how they used the possessive noun to describe this space as "their place" and "our place" *("chez eux"* and *"chez nous")*. Démocrite used the expression four times in his testimony. It is unclear if they meant "our place" as a generic reference to the plantation or if they were being more specific in identifying those spaces on the plantation that they considered to be theirs, such as the area where the cabins were located. Either way, Hector and Démocrite were laying claim to the plantation and asserting their right to limit outsiders' access to that space and to control what happened there.

Francisque, Démocrite, and Hector

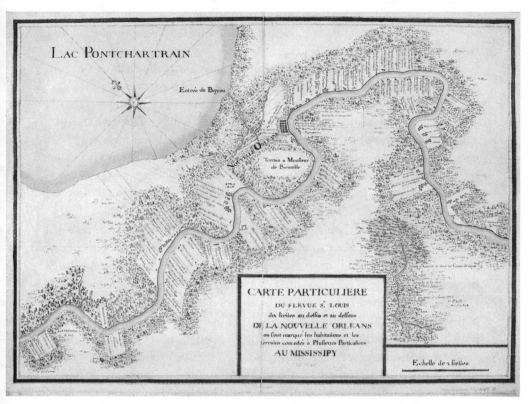

FIGURE 28: Unknown artist, *Carte particuliere du flevue [sic] St. Louis dix lieües au dessus et au dessous de la Nouvelle Orleans u sont marqué les habitativns et les terrains concedés à plusieurs particuliers au Mississipy.* Circa 1723. Edward E. Ayer Manuscript Map Collection. Vault drawer Ayer MS map 30 sheet 80.
Courtesy The Newberry Library, Chicago

Livaudais's plantation was one league (about two and a half miles) upriver from New Orleans, on the same bank as the city, about a forty-minute walk away (Figure 28). Its location serves as an important reminder that the enslaved were not confined to their master's property. Laws, such as the code noir or the 1751 police code, sought to control or at least limit the movement of slaves, but individual slaveowners were the primary enforcers. When Antoine-Simon Le Page du Pratz took over as manager of the Company of the Indies's plantation, he noticed that the plantation was the site for large gatherings of neighboring slaves (by his account, about twice the number of those based on the plantation would come there to attend social events), and he joined with other slaveowners to curb this activity. He also noted that the plantation's slaves had canoes that they used to cross the river into the city for illicit purposes, and he ordered them smashed, though it is doubtful that he succeeded in eradicating their movement. Notwithstanding intermittent and largely ineffective attempts to curtail their mobility, the enslaved circulated on foot, sometimes on horseback, and often by boat along the river (see Figure 17). In this way, they participated in a range of regular or sporadic, licit and illicit meetings that took them away from their living and working quarters.[26]

If the Livaudais plantation was organized like other plantations in Louisiana, the slave cabins were likely situated apart from the main house but "near enough to observe what is happening among them," a practice advocated by Le Page du Pratz. Army officer and long-term resident Jean-François-Benjamin Dumont de Montigny produced a drawing of his residence in New Orleans around 1733. It shows slave cabins set away from the house (Figure 29, key 2), just as his drawing of his plantation ten leagues downstream shows six cabins a short remove from the main house. Masters also granted the enslaved land near their cabins to grow vegetables, raise chickens, and produce other staples (such as eggs) for their own use or for trade.[27]

Slave cabins usually housed multiple families and individuals. For example, Le Page du Pratz had thirty-two cabins built to house the approximately two hundred slaves on the company's plantation; smaller slaveholders adjusted as needed (see Figure 19). Dumont's cabins followed convention in being constructed cheaply, using local techniques: they were post-in-the-ground structures, plastered with mud, roofed with bark or stakes, and fitted with unglazed window openings. Within the line of sight of the main house but beyond earshot, this common kind of plantation arrangement, while not lacking oversight and surveillance, nonetheless facilitated the development of autonomous communities.

Démocrite's testimony shows how such spatial arrangements on plantations could also foster a sense of belonging—even ownership—among the enslaved community. This feeling of attachment was not limited to land and buildings but extended to the material culture contained within those spaces. Slaves' frequent references to their ownership of personal storage containers, such as chests, or even to the fact that cabins were secured by locks underscores that the enslaved deemed goods that had come into their possession to be their personal and exclusive property, even though from a legal standpoint their right to do so was not straightforward. Article 22 of the 1724 code noir forbid slaves from owning or inheriting property of any kind, though the next article moderated this by granting slaves the ambiguous right to acquire and dispose of property, if not to own it. In practice, slaves' private possession of certain household goods—namely clothing—was tacitly acknowledged and underscored a process through which, once in their possession, slaves'

Francisque, Démocrite, and Hector

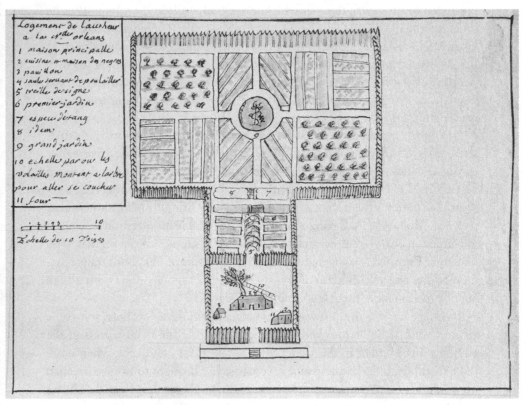

FIGURE 29: Jean-François-Benjamin Dumont de Montigny, *Logement de l'autheur
a la N[ouve]lle Orleans.* Circa 1733. Vault oversize Ayer MS 257, map no. 8.
Courtesy The Newberry Library, Chicago
Key 1 shows the main house, key 2 the kitchen and slave quarters.

goods (even those handed them by their masters) were perceived as their personal and private property. Masters consistently upheld this premise, as was
made implicit when Jean-Baptiste Raguet filed a report in 1746 on behalf of
his slaves, their cabin having been broken into and their clothing and household effects taken.[28]

Accompanying that sense of belonging was a sense of responsibility for
regulating such spaces. To understand what this meant for Démocrite is to
know, first, that he was born in West Africa. Two nuggets of information
that Démocrite provided the court as he took the oath to testify help piece
together his biography: his age and his origins. Following standard procedure, the court asked him to state his name, age, and status. Démocrite responded by introducing himself to the court as a forty-year-old man of the
"nation hibou" (Igbo nation). Democritus, after the ancient Greek philoso-

pher Democritus, was the name his master had conferred on him. That he included the information about his origins means that Démocrite, like Francisque, had traveled the Atlantic. But unlike Francisque, who was born in the Americas, Démocrite had known what it was like to live among his own people in West Africa, and he alone of the three enslaved men who testified knew what it was to endure the Middle Passage, the arduous journeys that preceded it, and the "final passages" that followed.[29]

The Igbo entered the French slave trade at the Bight of Biafra, a distinctive region of Lower Guinea in the Niger delta and the Cross River valley in present-day southeastern Nigeria. By the nineteenth century, the word "Igbo" would become associated with slave; the term could also serve as a generic identifier for the Ibibio, Moko, Ekoi, Essan / Edoid, Bioko, and Calabar peoples. Momentarily leaving aside the more significant question of what it meant for an enslaved individual to self-identify as Igbo, for the French, who like other European slaving nations developed assumptions about traits common to any one African ethnonym, the Igbo were synonymous with a high suicide rate, making them less desirable as slaves.[30]

If the age he gave in court was near correct, Démocrite was born sometime around 1726. If he had arrived in Louisiana during the main period of the colony's involvement in the slave trade, between 1719 and 1731, when more than six thousand men and women were forcibly brought to Louisiana, then he would have been at most five years old when he was taken from the shores of West Africa. After 1731, the sanctioned slave trade to Louisiana virtually ended, with the exception of one slave ship in 1743, which originated in Senegambia, not the Bight of Biafra, making it not at all likely that Démocrite had arrived on that ship. But he could have also arrived in an illegal shipment, or he might have accompanied a colonist, possibly after a stint in another colony. The Igbo were present in substantial numbers in Saint Domingue, so it is not inconceivable that he was rerouted to Louisiana from that colony, though, in contrast to Francisque, no evidence points to this trajectory.[31]

Démocrite would have found few other Igbo or inhabitants of the Bight of Biafra in Louisiana. No other Igbo-identified individual is known to have lived in Louisiana during the French colonial period, and it is not until the Spanish colonial period that the Igbo were identified in any quantity in Louisiana, notably at Pointe Coupée. Given this general context and the lack of an Igbo community in the colony, how strong was Démocrite's Igbo affiliation and what did such an identification mean as he went about his day-to-day life? The question of his age matters in terms of his exposure to Igbo society and his recollection of it. That he identified as Igbo at age forty im-

Francisque, Démocrite, and Hector

plies a continuing association with his origins and suggests, therefore, that he had not arrived in New Orleans as a very young child but after he had already established a basis for his self-conception as Igbo. Although living in Louisiana would have colored his worldview, the memory of what it meant to identify as Igbo could not help but inflect his understandings of courtship, masculine honor, community organization, social interactions, cultural and religious norms, kin relations, and criminality.[32]

As elsewhere in West Africa, among the Igbo, criminal acts, including theft, could result in being condemned to enslavement (other more common routes to captivity included warfare and raiding). The Igbo operated as a patrilineal society, with secret all-male societies charged with maintaining order within each community; like other secret societies, their lore was also encapsulated in their storytelling traditions. Around age thirteen to fourteen, Igbo males underwent a series of rites of passage involving ritual scarification that would eventually secure them membership in the village governing council. Had Démocrite undergone initiation and ritual scarification before leaving West Africa to an extent that was visible to onlookers?[33]

There is other evidence to corroborate the existence in Louisiana of powerful all-male societies whose members claimed a role in enforcing proper behavior in the colony. Following the 1737–1740 Chickasaw War, the French freed enslaved Africans who had served. Along with their manumission, the men received land in 1744 located at the English Turn, just south of New Orleans, where they would establish a settlement. Laying claim to a measure of autonomy and influence, they also started a free black militia that drew on both French models of military honor and their knowledge of various West African military cultures, including the *ceddo* warlord states and the Muslim jihadis familiar from Senegambia, where the majority of Louisiana's African-born slaves were from.[34]

If it is not known whether Démocrite had begun his Igbo initiation before his capture, his reaction to Francisque should be read through the lens of Igbo social and political structures. Rather than a generic response to one slave's infractions, Démocrite's actions and viewpoint provide instead a tantalizing glimpse of the possible presence of West African judicial sensibilities about society, criminality, policing, and punishment in Louisiana.[35]

"HE WAS LIKE A GENTLEMAN"

A close reading of Démocrite's testimony suggests that Francisque's appearance, in particular, did much to erode the goodwill that he initially garnered among New Orleans's local enslaved community. The final question-and-answer segment of Démocrite's interrogation brought to the surface the root of his dislike of Francisque:

> Asked if when he met him he was carrying a bundle of laundry?
>
> Said that he did not see any bundle on him, only a large tobacco box trimmed in silver, that when he went dancing he was like a gentleman, with a ruffled shirt, a blue waistcoat, a white hat, and three or four handkerchiefs around his neck, and elsewhere on his body. Added that he paid for the drum with coins and that he had large bills, that however he had not yet paid for the eggs that he had taken.

The interrogator had asked a question intended to elicit information about the thefts that Francisque had been said to have committed. Among the crimes for which he was prosecuted, Francisque admitted to the theft of bundles of laundry and other clothing taken from Anne Boyer, Madame St. Germain, the laundrywoman, much of which consisted of women's and children's dress but also two pairs of men's trousers (one of them striped red), two handkerchiefs, and three men's shirts—two of them ruffled shirts made of cotton. But Démocrite did not limit himself to a neutral description of Francisque. Instead, he provided a subjective and vivid snapshot of the man as he was dressed for the revelries with his sexual prowess on full display.[36]

What exactly did it mean that Francisque was "like a gentleman"? First of all, it meant that he looked like a person of leisure. There was in this simile a pointed comment on the way that slaveowners did not work—as slaves did—yet benefited from their labor. It was a distinction that must have had particular resonance for an enslaved person observing a runaway who was living free from the rigors of enforced slave labor. Second, Démocrite zeroed in on Francisque's sartorial performance as the key marker of his gentlemanly appearance. He made no reference to the runaway's hairstyle nor did he provide many details, other than color, with regard to his waistcoat and hat, but perhaps he did not have to since these were distinctive articles of clothing in slave dress, where uniformity and standardization were the norm. That Francisque wore a waistcoat was itself unusual. When the enslaved had outer garments, they tended to own a capot, which was ubiquitous among slaves as well as the general population in Louisiana. It was the ruffled shirt, however, that would have stood out. The enslaved were usually given plain shirts. Made of imported unbleached linen, these shirts of simple construction could be sewn locally or imported as ready-made garments for use by slaves, for trade and gift exchanges with Indians, or for sale to poor settlers. Where trade shirts differed from plain shirts was in the quality of the linen and possibly the care with which they were sewn. In addition to being made of more finely woven, bleached linen, a ruffled shirt of the kind worn by Francisque would have been decorated with ruffles at the collar and cuffs, the very best ones being distinguished by sleeves finely pleated with an iron. Francisque wore his without a cravat, meaning that his shirt was left open, revealing a glimpse of his chest as on the man in Figure 32, below.[37]

Where Francisque was "like a gentleman," two of Francisque's owners in Louisiana, Vilemont and d'Abbadie, were quite literally gentleman of high enough caliber to have their portraits painted. Though there is no evidence that Francisque had any personal contact with them, rather than with their agents, he did sail on the same ship as Vilemont. He therefore had the opportunity to look at Vilemont, and possibly also d'Abbadie; to observe them and men like them; and, given his own sense of fashion and his soft spot for fine clothing, to take note of their apparel (and that of other "gentlemen" in Saint Domingue and Cuba). As revealed in their portraits and in their probate inventories, here were men who customarily wore lace cravats, ruffled shirts, and other accoutrements of elite male dress, including wigs; their faces appear framed by hair that was powdered, styled with side curls, and tied at the back with a black bow (see Figure 30). D'Abbadie owned seventy-three ruffled shirts at his death and another thirty-six that were also embroidered. In his portrait, Vilemont wears a blue velvet waistcoat under his white coat with a fine ruffled shirt peeking out from his cuffs, showing exactly what a slave like Démocrite would have recognized as a "gentleman" in 1760s New Orleans. Like Vilemont and d'Abbadie, Francisque wore, not a plain, but a ruffled shirt. His, however, had originally belonged to a non-elite man named Rousset, left by him with a laundrywoman for cleaning; it would not have been as fine as the linen shirts with lace ruffles customarily worn by Vilemont and d'Abbadie.[38]

In contrast to his dress-up garb of ruffled shirt, blue waistcoat, white hat, and multiple handkerchiefs, Jacques described Francisque's everyday dress as consisting of worn-out clothing made of the cheapest fabrics and suitable for laboring in, "one gingham shirt with a vest on top no hat and a torn pair of linen long breeches [trousers], that he had nothing else" *(une chemise de Ginga un gilet par dessus sans chapeau et une Grande Culotte de toile dechirée quil n'avoit pas autre chose)*. This testimony was taken by the court as corroborating evidence that Francisque had stolen the richer clothing he was described as wearing at the dance. The divergence between the description of Francisque in poor, torn workday clothing (worse for his being a runaway) and his flashy appearance at the festivities brings into sharp focus the differences between how slaves dressed in their free time and during their working

FIGURE 30: Unidentified artist, *Jean Paul Gerard de Vilemont.* 1996.79.1.
Historic New Orleans Collection

hours. Two descriptions of another slave, Louis dit Foÿ, likewise accused of
theft of apparel, echo the contrasts in Francisque's appearance. When first interrogated about how he was dressed during his marronnage, Louis answered
that "he had only an old coat that he was wearing when he was arrested, and
large breeches [trousers]" *(quil n'avoit qu'un vieux Capot avec Lequel il a été
arreté et des grandes Culotes).* Yet Jean, an enslaved man of the Nago (Yoruba)

Francisque, Démocrite, and Hector

nation, instead told the court that Louis had been "well-dressed" *(bien abillé)* wearing a white shirt (meaning that it was of high quality bleached linen) and, like Francisque, a hat. As Francisque's and Louis's cases demonstrate, slaves, even runaways, made concerted efforts to procure clothing that could bolster their status among other slaves, notably fine apparel.[39]

Such fine apparel would have been saved for Saturday and Sunday festivities rather than for workdays, thus minimizing the likelihood of colonists being confronted with slaves' conspicuous sartorial displays and reserving this special act of dressing for a nonwhite audience. Francisque saved his flashy dress for his appearance at the slaves' weekly gathering, a private affair shielded from the sight of colonists. Aimed at an audience of his fellow slaves, Francisque's gestures must be interpreted in the context of his attempt at immersion into that community. In Francisque's case, his ostentation at the dances provoked feelings of resentment among the male slaves present, who felt they were being shown up in front of their female audience by someone outside of their usual acquaintance, a rakish stranger who had assumed a position of economic superiority and sexual availability. Many of the women, by contrast, seemed to find Francisque desirable—was it for his physical charms, or his other attributes? The court record is silent about his physique but clearly there was something about Francisque that made him appealing to the wide swathe of women who fell for him. And then there was his sense of style. As Démocrite's testimony makes implicit, many factors were at play in Francisque's success with women, not least his sartorial appearance.[40]

The portrayal of Francisque's dress when out dancing must have been jarring to the French hearing this testimony in the courtroom, for Francisque wore not one handkerchief around his neck, as was usual in European dress, but "three or four handkerchiefs around his neck, and elsewhere about him." What did it mean to them that he had draped multiple handkerchiefs on his body? The judges might have been confounded by this description, but anyone from West Africa or of West African descent would have interpreted his surfeit of handkerchiefs in a specific way. Francisque did not merely flout the standards of behavior of the local slave communities that he associated with. He also sought acceptance by following other codes of conduct, such as paying for the music for everyone's benefit. The handkerchiefs provided another point in common, for enslaved Africans would have recognized this article of clothing as a form of self-adornment that denoted his masculinity and as a material asset he could use to participate in courtship rituals such as gift giving.[41]

In contrast to the *mouchoir à moucher* (handkerchief for blowing the nose), still rare in the eighteenth century since it was customary to blow one's nose on one's sleeve rather than into a handkerchief, the term *mouchoir* (handkerchief) referred to a large square of fabric that could be adapted to multiple sartorial uses. Worn handkerchiefs were large enough to be wrapped around the head or draped around the neckline. They came in infinite varieties of striped, checked, or floral patterns, and they were imported into the colony as lengths of cloth, printed two to a width of fabric. In 1738, the free black "Marie la Negresse" was the successful bidder at auction for two lots of handkerchiefs; both lots involved the bulk purchase of handkerchiefs of printed cotton on a red ground. One of the lots consisted of an uncut length of handkerchiefs; the other lot was already cut (but probably not hemmed) into twenty handkerchiefs. Once cut and hemmed, she could retail them in the local market. The lots purchased by Marie la Negresse came from India, but others were made in France in imitation of India goods. Indian cottons were central to the slave trade, constituting three-quarters of the merchandise used to purchase slaves from West African slavers and reflecting a taste and demand in West Africa for Indian fabrics. In wearing handkerchiefs, enslaved Africans in Louisiana could—and did—draw on a world of goods as consumers.[42]

Beyond the matter of the textile itself, the way the handkerchief was worn was also significant as a repository of West African culture. Specifically, for the enslaved, the handkerchief when worn on the crown was an adaptation of West African sartorial cultures that emphasized the head, whether in the form of hairstyles or head coverings, as seen in engineer Alexandre de Batz's depictions of runaway slaves in Louisiana with their more structured head wraps (Figures 31 and 34). The meaning of Francisque wrapping handkerchiefs around his body is clarified in paintings by artists such as the Italian-English painter Agostino Brunias, the Guadelupean Marie Joseph Hyacinthe Savart, the Martinique painter Le Masurier, the South Carolinian John Rose, and others. In their visual depictions of scenes of daily life for free and enslaved Africans, these colonial artists glossed over the brutality of slavery, offering instead a "saccharine and harmonious image of essentially cruel realities of colonial life." The popularity of such depictions of exotic and erotic enslaved bodies reveals much about how white men's fantasies about enslaved women and free women of color were normalized in the visual record. Yet each one of these artists can also be mined for information about the dress of enslaved and free blacks, including a predilection for headkerchiefs and neckerchiefs.[43]

Brunias, an especially prolific artist and regular visitor to the West Indies, produced repeated images of enslaved and free blacks in Dominica, often featuring the same stock characters wearing the same apparel. One such painting, among many on the same theme, presents a man and woman dancing.

Francisque, Démocrite, and Hector

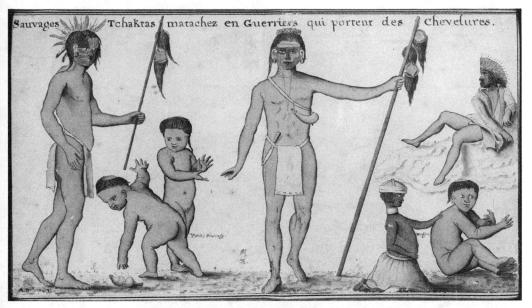

FIGURE 31: Alexandre de Batz, *Sauvages tchaktas matachez en guerriers qui portent des chevelures.* Gift of the Estate of Belle J. Bushnell, 1941. PM# 41-72-10/19. Courtesy the Peabody Museum of Archaeology and Ethnology, Harvard University
The African figure on the lower right wears a structured head covering.

Both are garbed in turban-like head wraps, and the man has another handker-chief wound asymmetrically around his body (another painting that is a vari-ant on this motif, Brunias's *The Handkerchief Dance,* has the woman holding up a handkerchief while dancing with the man). The figures in the back-ground, drumming, clapping, and socializing, are likewise wearing handker-chiefs wrapped around their head, the women with handkerchiefs draped over their necklines while others, men and women alike, have tied even more handkerchiefs around their waists (Figure 32).[44]

The court case against Francisque provides a fresh perspective for in-terpreting the surfeit of handkerchiefs seen in these images. His multiple handkerchiefs underline the sexual overtones of courtship performances of the kind shown in Brunias's paintings and manifested throughout the writ-ten record of slave testimony in Louisiana. Simultaneously a means of self-presentation and presentation, of adornment and tokens he might give to a love interest, Francisque's handkerchiefs were the objects of Démocrite's envy and desire, and he sought to appropriate them, literally and metaphori-cally, by fighting the runaway for possession of the bundle of laundry at the cost of a wounded arm.

FIGURE 32: Agostino Brunias, *A Negroes Dance in the Island of Dominica.*
Private Collection. Photo © Christie's Images / Bridgeman Images

COURTSHIP

Francisque's behavior and his dress at the dances were not anomalous. The way he acted—and dressed—was anchored in well-established patterns of courtship that took place against the backdrop of dances and other assemblies where Africans met up with one another to socialize. Some of these gatherings even required a fee to attend. In 1746, Jeannette, a free woman of color, was brought before the court and reprimanded for holding nightly "assemblies where she clearly provided supper to various *negres* and domestic slaves of this town" *(faisoit des assemblees evidemment à souper à plusieurs negres Es Esclaves domestiques de cette ville).* Though Jeannette's assemblies took place in town, most others took place on plantations where the enslaved lived apart from masters within slave compounds that lent themselves to social activities enjoyed exclusively by Africans (Figure 29).[45]

These communal events were sheltered from the gaze of whites but not concealed from them. In the summer of 1764, for example, twenty-year-old François got into trouble for staying out all night after attending a dance. Ar-

Francisque, Démocrite, and Hector

rested some time after, he was made to answer why he had run away: "Said that it was because he had been dancing at Widow Duval's at Pointe Coupée, that he had been surprised by the dawn and had returned to his master who had had him tied up to whip him, that not being properly tied he had freed himself and gone off" *(A dit que c'estoit parcequ'il avoit été danser chez la Ve Duval à la pointe coupée que le jour l'ayant surpris il avoit retourné chez son Maitre lequel l'auroit fait amaré pour le foueter et que n'estant pas bien amaré il s'estoit defait et s'en est allé)*. François's reply makes clear that it was not because he had attended a dance that his master was going to whip him. It was because he had slept over and did not make it back by daybreak.[46]

Nevertheless, François's master was well within his legal rights to punish him. The 1724 code noir referenced the dangers of slave assemblies and even allowed for fines against masters who permitted them on their property or knowingly allowed their slaves to attend any. Composed in New Orleans, the 1751 police code went further and serves as an especially useful indicator of common violations that authorities deemed threatening. In no less than four separate articles (20, 21, 22, and 26), the 1751 code prohibited assemblies and dances where slaves of different masters might come together and singled out the dangers of slaves roaming the streets at night, including those slaves from plantations who came to town after dark. Notwithstanding these regulations (or rather, as these regulations reveal), attendance at assemblies and dances did not abate; rather, they became customary to the extent that masters turned a blind eye. Most of the time these assemblies took place without incident, but masters could intervene at will and with violence, which they did primarily when they felt their rules (such as curfew in François's case) had not been adhered to. Testimony such as that of François's helps to finesse how the enslaved understood the limits of this customary right at the same time that it also reveals something about how the enslaved conceived of the spaces where they gathered and socialized, including the values that governed these meetings and the authority of those slaves who ensured those values were upheld.[47]

Dances were well established sites of sociability, and those who attended were expected to meet certain standards of behavior and of dress. The correspondence of Jean-Charles de Pradel, a military officer, plantation owner, and slaveholder, helps to illuminate this point. In a 1755 letter to his brother in France, he described the temporary fall from grace of his favorite slave, St. Louis La Nuit (who was so favored that he often conducted business for Pradel, being literate, and had even accompanied him to France). Pradel attributed his slave's downfall to the latter's airs and pretensions: "He acted the little master when he got here and to keep up this condition he stole from me: sheep, poultry of every kind, and maybe even some other things that I did not find out about, although the appearance of this is there to see." But Pradel then narrowed in on what it was about St. Louis's behavior that bothered him. Pradel's plantation, Montplaisir, was situated across the Mississippi River, facing town. He had instructed La Nuit to go each morning to the New Orleans slaughterhouse, but, instead, La Nuit "would go when we had gone to sleep, with two young *negres* to row him there, he danced all night with some free *negres,* and *negres* and *negresses* of the town, paid the violin and collations coming to 150 livres, he could not do it without robbing me." Rather than have him whipped, Pradel smirked that he had found a better punishment in sending La Nuit away from the main house, where he had previously served, to become instead a field laborer and live in the "negro camp," a state of affairs that, he reported, La Nuit, or "Mr Saint Louis," as Pradel called him in jest, was "not very happy about." In the two and a half years that he was sent away, St. Louis was only relieved of the hard labor of the fields when important company came to dine, since Pradel would then summon the man to come and prepare meals for his guests at his richly furnished table. Pradel ended his tale about La Nuit by saying that the man must have heard that he was writing to his brother, for he had come to Pradel's room only fifteen minutes before "to pray that I convey to you his very humble respects." "He is a cunning man," Pradel concluded, "who knows well how to curry favor, but all his efforts are to no avail." Cunning indeed, for, although "Mr. Saint-Louis" might have been assigned to field work, he clearly still found ways to work in the house as a cook, he continued to have access to Pradel's quarters, and he surely carried on attending dances.[48]

Like Francisque, St. Louis assumed specific roles at gatherings of free blacks and slaves—sponsor of the music and refreshments, dance partner, and suitor—roles that proclaimed his identity through a precise execution of prescribed masculine rituals. The close parallel between Francisque's and St. Louis's performances was mirrored in men's behavior at weekly slave gatherings in Louisiana and throughout the Atlantic world. Francisque was familiar with such social events and the gendered acts that they called for. Like Démocrite and Hector, he also knew that these performances of masculinity hinged on dress: articles of clothing displayed on the male body but, just as importantly, used in gift giving to female love interests.[49]

The court records are sprinkled with incidental references to courtships that were lubricated by means of gift giving by men to women, often accompanied by food preparation by women for men. This connection between men offering gifts to women, who in turn offered comfort and sustenance to men, is apparent in the earliest known reference to gumbo *(gombeau)* in the archival record. In 1764, the runaway Louis was asked to confirm "if the *negresse* Comba had not served gumbo to him and another *negresse,* and if he had not slept with her" *(si La negresse Comba ne Luy avoit pas donné un Gombeau avec une autre Negresse, et sil navoit pas Couché avec elle).* He replied that it was false that he slept with her but acknowledged "that he ate with her from the time that her husband lived and before he had gone up to the Illinois Country, but since he has come back he has not set foot there" *(qu'il mangeoit chez elle du tems que son mari vivoit et avant quil ne monta aux illinois mais que depuis qu'il est dessendu il n'y a pas mis Le pied).* Where Louis denied having recently been to see Mama Comba, however, his companion and fellow runaway Cézar confirmed that Louis always slept at her place, adding that she had even told her overseer that "he was a *negre* from the upper area [the Illinois Country] who is of my country" *(cet un negre de La haut qui est de mon pais).* (Mama Comba was Mandinga; therefore, Louis originated there, too).[50]

The back-and-forth continued during the formal confrontation between Cézar and Mama Comba, with Cézar underlining that Louis not only slept at her place but slept *with* her, and often *(qu'il avoit couché souvent chez elle et avec elle).* When Mama Comba finally acknowledged her relationship with Louis, she could not resist highlighting Louis's failings in proper gift-giving etiquette:

> The said Comba said that that was true, that she had even served gumbo to him and another *negresse* and admitted that the said Louis slept with her, and the said *negresse* [Mama Comba] also maintained that she had never received anything from the said *negre* Louis, only a carrot of tobacco, which carrot he had taken back to smoke . . . .
>
> She also maintained that this Louis was not like him [Cézar], who always went to see his mistress, who is the *negresse* Marianne belonging to Sr. Caillé to whom he gave apparel, skirts, and everything he stole and whom he always went to see in Cantrelle's garden and other places.

> ladite comba a dit que cela etait vrai, quelle luy avoit même donné un gombeau avec une autre negresse et a avoué que le dit Louis couchoit avec elle et la negresse luy a soutenu aussi qu'elle n'avoit jamais rien reçu dudit negre Louis qu'une seule carotte de tabac, laquelle carrotte il luy avoit repris pour la fumer . . . .
>
> Luy a encore soutenu que ce Louis ne fezoit pas comme luy, qui

alloit voir toujours sa Maitresse qui est La negresse marianne au sr Caillé et quil Luy donoit hardes Jupes et tout Ce quil vouloit et quil La voyoit toujours dans le Jardin de Contrelle et par tous ailleurs

Her response set up a contrast between her own relationship with Louis and that of Cézar and Marianne, a twenty-eight-year old who self-identified as being from Guinea and acknowledged Cézar as "her suitor" *(son galand)*. If Cézar and Marianne's romance was facilitated by the exchange of food for gifts, Mama Comba and Louis's faltered on the rocks of unmet expectations. As Mama Comba was at pains to explain with her barbed reference to Louis's not giving her anything but tobacco, her suitor had failed to uphold his end of the bargain and added insult to injury when he took back the tobacco he had given her so that he could smoke it himself.[51]

Sometimes questioning about gift giving elicited an explicit admission of a love affair, as in this instance, but, at other times, the meaning was implied. When asked what he had done with the apparel that he had already admitted to stealing, twenty-five-year-old Louis Jupiter dit Gamelle "of the Cere nation" *(de Nation Cere),* slave of Pradel, said "that he wore the shirt, ate the bread, wore the hat, and gave the skirt to a *negresse* of Sr. Lange named Dubet" *(que la Chemise il l'a uzé a Mangé Le pain s'est servy du Chapeau Et a donné la jupe à une Negresse du sr Lange Nomme Dubet).* As for Alexandre, when the court interrogated him in 1744 in the same court case, he was asked outright "with what money he kept the *negresse* known as Pierre who is well kept. Said that he had only ever given a handkerchief to this *negresse,* that if she has a lot of clothes, it is not from him that she has gotten them, having never given her anything else" *(Interrogé avec quel largent Il entretient la Negresse dit Pierre qui est bien Entretenue. A dit quil na jamais donné qu'un Mouchoir à Cette Negresse et que si Elle a beaucoup de hardes que Ce nest pas de luy quelle Les tient qui ne Luy a jamais donné autre choses).* Whether or not the details are correct in terms of the actual items and quantities given, the point is that gift giving was an essential component of courtship and affective relationships, just as it was for those of European descent. Those male suitors, for example, gifted ribbons and other articles of dress to ladies in whom they were interested. Such items could be used to decorate outer clothes, but they could also be deployed on more intimate and unseen parts of the body. Ribbons could be used to hold up stockings; a busk (a stiff long flat insert, sometimes decorated or inscribed by the suitor) was meant to be slipped into the front of a woman's corset to keep the body straight, nestling between her breasts down to her pubic area.[52]

For enslaved men, the gift-giving stakes were high enough that Jupiter

Francisque, Démocrite, and Hector

had even gone into debt to get a "small silver cross" *(une petite Croye dar-gent)* to give to Marie Josephe (the only gift he said he had given her since the time Mr. de Vaudreuil had returned from Mobile) and "that he bought it from d'Ory and that he still owes him for it" *(quil la ajetté d'ory Et quil la doit Encore).* According to Jupiter, he went to visit her at night sometimes, as she had "served him as woman / wife occasionally since about one year" *(quelle luy servoit de femme quelque fois depuis Environ un an).* It was not necessary to make a gift at every visit, but not doing so was worthy of comment. So Jupiter specified that one night, while "every one was sleeping, he spoke to Marie Joseph, he slept with her, and he did not give her anything" *(tout le monde dormoit qu'il parla à Marie Joseph qu'il Coucha avec Elle qu'il ne luy donna Rien).*[53]

During the same interrogation, Jupiter, *"de son chef"* (in other words, on his own initiative, without being asked), reported a lengthy exchange with fellow slave Alexandre (whose beloved belonged to Madame Douville) concerning their plans to purchase gifts for their womenfolk. They bought the gifts from a white female trader named Dusigne; pawning was also mentioned:

Said of his own accord that the said Alexandre had come to find him by the riverbank telling him, there are at Ducinne's some pretty rings, buckles and earrings if you want to do me the favor of going to buy some on my behalf . . . and Alexandre gave him thirty livres in card money to buy a small pair of buckles, that he also gave him thirty livres to have a gold ring, that he, Jupiter, went to Dusigne's to buy the buckles and the ring, they cost sixty livres together, that the next day, Dusigne came to find him on the levee and said my wife gave you a ring of forty livres instead of thirty, give it back to me, and he gave it back, that Dusigne gave him another small one that he said he was selling for thirty livres, that around eight or nine o'clock the said Alexandre came, he gave him the ring and the said Alexandre having told him that he had other silver buckles, Jupiter told him to give them to him as a present, and he gave them to him, that these same buckles are pawned for a pair of breeches that Louis the tailor had sold him along with ten livres that he owed him. That they are still pawned for twenty livres that he planned to get them back when he had the money. That Alexandre told him that he was buying this ring for the *negresse* of Madame Douville, that he saw other money in the wallet of Alexandre when he gave him the sixty livres.

Dit de son Chef que ledt alexandre Etoit Venu le trouver au Bord de leau En luy disant il y a Chez ducinne de jolies Bagues Boucles Et pendant doreilles sy tu Veux me dire le plaisir de m'en aller ajetté Voila aussy une andouille de tabac que je Veux Vendre six Ecalins luy dit sy tu Veux je ten donneray quatre quil luy donna Et qu'etant de lautre Côté il la Coupa Et la trouva pourrie Et que alexandre luy donna trente livres En Cartes pour ajetter une paire de petite Boucles quil luy donna aussy trante livres pour avoir une Bague dor que luy jupiter fut chez dusigne ajetter les Boucles Et la Bague le tout Coûta soixante Livres, que le lendemain Dusigne Vint le trouver sur la Levée quil luy dit ma femme t'a donné une Bague de quarente livres au lieu de trente Rends la Moy Et qu'il luy Rendit que dusigne luy en donna une autre plus petite quil dit qu'il Vendoit trente livre que sur les huit ou neuf heures Le dt alexandre Vint il luy donna la Bague Es le dt alexandre ayant dit quil avoit dautres Boucles dargent jupiter luy dit fais m'en present Et il luy donna que ces mesmes Boucles sont en Gage pour une Cullotte que louis le tailleur Luy a vendu avec dix livres qu'il luy devoit Et qu'il les a Encore En gage pour vingt livres quil contoit les Retirer lorsqu'il auroit de largent qu'alexandre luy disoit qu'il ajettoit Cette Bague pour la Negresse de madame douville, qu'il Vit dans le portefeuille d'alexandre d'autres Cartes quand il luy Eut donné Ces soixante livres

As indicated in Jupiter's account of his conversations with Alexandre, courtships were often collective affairs, subject to discussion, supported by a coterie of well-wishers and gossips, and sometimes critiqued by the odd naysayers.[54]

Courtships were also public knowledge. Explaining why the slave Fabou had run away, a witness stated that it was because of an affair of gallantry: "for no other reason than the embarrassment of having fallen in love, this *negre* is in fact a very good subject, quarterer, and half-carpenter, never having run away before, and only because of the shame he felt toward the other slaves" *(sans autre Raison que la honte davoir atrapé une galanterie Lequel Negre est dailleur tres bon sujet Ecarisseur es demy Charpentier n'ayant jamais fait Le marron ny ayant Eu que La honte qu'il avoit des autres Negres).* Sadly, there are no details of the incident that caused Fabou to feel so bashful and ashamed.[55]

Though a runaway at heightened risk of being caught, Francisque seems to have enthusiastically, and perhaps too brazenly, thrown himself into the pursuit of courtships. In addition to attending dances, he made numerous attempts to initiate intimate contact with women, and at least one of these women became his regular partner. According to the runaway Jacques, "On the second day that [he and Francisque] were together, during the night, Francisco told him that he was going to Mr. Petit's, where he had his mistress" *(que le second jour qu'ils etoitent ensemble dans La nuit francisco Luy dit qu'il alloit chez Mr petit où il avoit sa maitresse).* However, Francisque instead "went to a cabin of Mr. Dublanc where another *negresse* lived, and from her he took the earrings and a white hat" *(que Cependant il fut dans une Cabanne de Mr Dublanc où Logeoit une negresse, et à Laquelle il prit Les pendans Doreille, et un chapeau blanc).* The exact circumstances of Francisque's alleged theft from Dublanc's unnamed enslaved woman are not known. Did Francisque break into her hut? Given that it was nighttime, she would have been there, so it is easy to assume that he gained access to her earrings and hat because she had lain with him that night. In light of his plans to spend that night with a woman (albeit a different woman), the latter seems more likely. Perhaps he had proferred one of the numerous handkerchiefs that he had worn when dancing as a gift to this new love interest.[56]

Francisque clearly had success with women. Although none of the women involved with him left any trace of their feelings in court, their actions, whether their willingness to dance with him or to sleep with him, indicate that they acquiesced to his advances with pleasure and perhaps even initiated intimate contact with this dashing new man on the scene. Dublanc's slave ultimately opted to have her master lodge a complaint for theft against a man who had in all likelihood courted her and then spurned her by breaking her trust and stealing her things. Other men knew of Francisque's liaisons; in fact, these courtships and love affairs were widely known to everyone—how could they not be, given slaves' communal, crowded living conditions. It was not coincidental that Démocrite, when describing the last time he and Francisque met, made a point of adding that the runaway was flirting—with yet another woman.

"HE WOULD HAVE HIM TIED UP TO FOUR POSTS TO HAVE HIM WHIPPED"

Francisque was a runaway for a number of weeks. Though he ended up repeatedly arousing the ire of those he encountered, things might have taken a different turn, for runaways could customarily expect community support in times of need. Instead, as the sequence of events unfolded, animosity, verbal posturing, and physical violence swiftly replaced the support and negotiation with which enslaved Africans in New Orleans first greeted him.

The type of community support that was offered to runaways varied but was neither insignificant nor undertaken lightly. In April 1764, two years before Francisque was brought to trial, sixty-five-year-old Jeanot justified running away on the basis that his master, who had not grown any indigo the previous summer, had switched to maize and then blamed Jeanot, who was in charge of the field, when the crop was ruined because of marauding animals, which meant that "his Master angered and ill-treated him and during the winter he did not give him the slightest thing, neither coat nor shirt to protect himself from the harsh inclement season" (que son Maitre fâché Le maltroitoit et pendant L'hiver ne Luy auroit donné La moindre choze ni Capot ni chemize pour se preserver des inclémences de La Rude saison). He acknowledged being a runaway for about five months. Asked who had fed him and where he had lived during that time, Jeanot answered that "at Bayou St. Jean near the barracks he had run into the slave Jacob belonging to Mr. Dubois, who told him 'stay with me I will feed you and dress you,' he stayed with him for about three months, and afterward he returned to the town to beg for his bread" (qu'au Bayou St Jean pres du Corps de garde il avoit rencontré Le negre Jacob appartenant à Mr Dubois, qui Luy dit Reste avec moy Je te nourrirai et t'abillerai qu'il y avoit Resté avec Luy Environ trois mois, et qu'ensuite il Revint à La ville Mandier son pain). Jacob knew he was taking a risk in helping the runaway, but he nonetheless provided succor to Jeanot, understanding full well that it was his duty and that it was crucial to the elder's survival. As it was, Jeanot broke his trust by naming him in court. Jacob was not prosecuted, but his master undoubtedly punished him.[57]

Instead of investigating Jeanot's claims, the judges convicted him. Despite Article 20 of the 1724 code noir, which required that the council prosecute masters who failed to properly feed, clothe, and provide for their slaves, and Article 21, which stipulated that older and infirm slaves abandoned by their masters be adjudged to the nearest hospital and their masters charged for their food and maintenance, the court showed him no mercy. In conformity with Article 32, pertaining to slaves who had run away for longer than thirty days, they sentenced him to have his ears cut, to be branded with a fleur-de-lis, and to be returned to his master. This was colonial justice at work, pronouncing a sentence aimed not only at punishing Jeanot but at serving notice to any slaves who wanted to provide a means of support to runaways.[58]

Francisque made two references, aside from Jacques, to other runaways inviting him to join them, but he either declined or stayed with them only briefly before parting ways, as he had done with Jacques. Francisque was cautious in his interactions with other runaways, slow to have faith in them and quick to tell on them. Other than Jacques, he stated that he had encoun-

Francisque, Démocrite, and Hector

tered the runaway Nianga, "who was coming to town, and he went his own way and that they did not stay together and that the said *negre* was armed with a large knife in a sack and that his right arm was injured" *(a dit avoir rencontré le nommé nianga qui venoit en ville, et qu'il a suivy son chemain et qu'ils n'ont point esté ensemble et que ledit negre etoit armé d'un grand coutaux dans un sacque et qu'il etoit blessé au droit bras)*. This description was precise enough to help in Nianga's capture, as Francisque knew well. Francisque was later found with a large knife, likely this very one, but he glossed over that specific detail. Then there were two other runaways "belonging to M. Labarre who wanted to take him with them, that they had powder horns without a gun and that he had not wanted to go with them" *(deux à M. Labarre qui ont voulu l'emmener avec eux qu'ils avoient des cornes à poudre sans fusil et qu'il n'a pas voulu les suivre)*. He claimed not to know their names. Such intelligence about the whereabouts and activities of runaway slaves was valuable to the French. A self-reliant stranger in a new place, Francisque needed little prompting to answer nor did he show remorse in providing such information; his survival skills were well honed.[59]

Francisque seems to have preferred to maintain his autonomy, though his was by no means a solitary life given his frequent interactions with other slaves, male and female. Yet to be a runaway was especially risky for outsiders, even multilingual, enterprising ones like Francisque, for they were unknown to all and bereft of kinship or other ready ties to the local community. Such factors meant that outsiders, including unknown male runaways coming to town from outlying plantations, were by far the most likely to be targeted for prosecution in New Orleans. Often, other slaves appear to have found that it was not worth the risk of offering them protection. Added to this were manifold other potential sources of antagonism among the enslaved, whether based on personal animosity, contests over women, competition for resources, or differing religious or cultural practices and linguistic or ethnic origins.

Tensions brought about by differences in the ethnic or cultural background of Louisiana's enslaved population sometimes rose to the surface quite explicitly. Testifying in his own defense in 1748, twenty-year-old Charlot dit Karacou named Pierrot, who identified as Bambara (generic shorthand for non-Muslim), as his accomplice. Pierrot denied that they were accomplices, stating that he had not gone to Charlot's cabin because he, Pierrot, was no friend of the Creole slaves; ironically, Charlot was not Creole—when asked to identify himself, he specified that he was *"de Nation Coneda"* (of the Coneda nation), but he probably associated with Creole slaves. In turn, Charlot accused Pierrot of being a liar because he was a Bambara. But such animosity did not prevent Charlot's sister Marianne from associating with Pierrot and even hiding in his cabin when she ran away.[60]

Testimony like Charlot's and Pierrot's draws attention, quite insistently, to the fact that the enslaved were constantly called on to make judgment calls about who to include or exclude from their circles. Occasionally, these judgment calls fomented a parallel justice system in which the enslaved sought to police and judge each other, a system that could also deploy the French judiciary as a proxy for achieving a desired outcome or sentence. For example, in 1760, it was a slave named Jean-Baptiste who, in an act of self-policing, tracked down and helped capture the runaway Foÿ, after the latter had stolen garments that Jean-Baptiste and an enslaved woman had commissioned bespoke from a French seamstress, the Widow Célain. In effect, Foÿ was imprisoned and later convicted because Jean-Baptiste investigated the matter and turned him in.[61]

To be an outsider was to be in an especially precarious situation that demanded deft handling. If a runaway was known to members of the local community, they might provide him with aid, sometimes even employment. In 1741, the Superior Council initiated an inquiry into the conduct of one enslaved overseer who was suspected of concealing fugitive slaves. Not only did he hide them, but he also offered them work on the plantation. This was a convenient arrangement; the overseer (quite likely with the master's tacit knowledge) found a ready supply of manpower while runaways found a relatively safe means of subsistence. And the overseer's case was not an isolated one. As long as runaways hewed to certain rules and codes of conduct, they could benefit from the help proffered by slaves, thereby increasing their chances of subsisting. The stakes were high for all concerned, but, for the runaway, not knowing the rules of conduct, or worse, violating known rules, could be detrimental, and potentially fatal.[62]

At first, Francisque was able to avail himself of local support networks. And need help, he did, for he was famished. In his final appearance before the court, Francisque acknowledged Démocrite's accusation that he owed the slaves of Sieur Livauday "two piastres in payment for some eggs that he had bought and that he had eaten, being hungry" *(deux piastres en paiment pour des oeufs, qu'il avoit acheté, et qu'il avait mangé, les oeufs, ayant faim).* But his lack of regard for their rules would soon land him in trouble. For their part, whether or not they believed him to be a runaway, Démocrite and his group did not make any concessions to Francisque's circumstances. In initially allowing him to take the eggs, they were not being altruistic; they expected him to fulfill his promise to pay for them in the anticipation that they

Francisque, Démocrite, and Hector

would benefit, at minimal risk to themselves, from the resulting circulation and redistribution of money and goods. That Francisque did not pay would become a bitter point of contention. Though it was a colonist, Sieur Boré, who would ultimately bring Francisque in, accusing him of having stolen from his female slave, it was Démocrite who was instrumental in having the runaway convicted and sentenced. He and Hector ultimately succeeded in having order restored. Démocrite left no further traces after this court case, other than his listing in the 1773 Livauday inventory, but Hector was still alive in September 1819, his age given then as ninety years old.[63]

Born by his own account in Philadelphia, a pawn of English, Spanish, and French colonial forces in Pennsylvania, Cuba, Saint Domingue, and Louisiana, Francisque survived more voyages, and more masters, than it is possible to know about. His undoing would be brought about by his interactions with still others: the enslaved population that he tussled with in Louisiana. Unfortunately for his long-term survival, he broke their rules and their trust, eroding any goodwill he might initially have elicited from them. He began by alienating members of the local slave community that he infiltrated through his ploy to avoid paying for the eggs, in spite of having the apparent means to do so. His theft from a fellow slave, the female acquaintance (and maybe lover) from whom he purportedly stole some earrings and a hat compounded his offense. Finally, instead of contributing to the informal slave economy by sharing the fruits of his thefts, he repeatedly took from other slaves and refused to share unless it was for self-serving courtship purposes that put his needs ahead of those of the other men seeking women. Most egregious of all, he strutted as he displayed his decked-out body, his appearance the direct result of his access to material goods that other slaves could only hope to match and that one slave, Démocrite, tried to appropriate. It was his very ostentation that ultimately cost Francisque his freedom and very nearly his life. He was convicted and condemned to be hung. However, the Superior Council commuted his death penalty, and, on August 2, 1766, he was sentenced instead to receive a beating, to be branded with the letter "V" for *voleur* (thief), and to be banished from the colony.[64]

In February 1767, the following runaway advertisement appeared in Saint Domingue's newspaper *Affiches Américaines*:

Francisque, branded with a V on the right cheek, speaking French, Spanish and English, pockmarked, his nose broken, stocky and of medium height, a runaway since the end of January last. Those who recognize him are requested to have him arrested and to give notice to

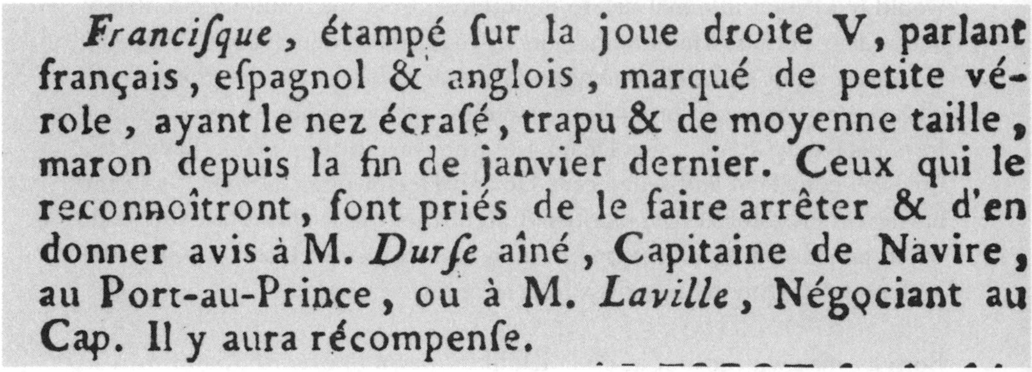

> *Francisque*, étampé fur la joue droite V, parlant
> français, efpagnol & anglois, marqué de petite vé-
> role, ayant le nez écrafé, trapu & de moyenne taille,
> maron depuis la fin de janvier dernier. Ceux qui le
> reconnoîtront, font priés de le faire arrêter & d'en
> donner avis à M. *Durfe* aîné, Capitaine de Navire,
> au Port-au-Prince, où à M. *Laville*, Négociant au
> Cap. Il y aura récompenfe.

FIGURE 33: Runaway advertisement for Francisque, *Affiches américaines,* Feb. 25, 1767, 64, Le marronnage dans le monde atlantique: Sources et trajectoires de vie, http://marronnage.info/fr/index.html (accessed May 25, 2019)

M. Durse the elder, ship's captain, at Port-au-Prince, or to M. Laville, merchant at the Cap [Français]. There will be a reward.

Francisque, étampé sur la joue droite V, parlant français, espagnol et anglois, marqué de petite vérole, ayant le nez écrasé, trapu et de moyenne taille, maron depuis la fin de janvier dernier. Ceux qui le reconnoîtront, sont priés de le faire arrêter et d'en donner avis à M. *Durse* aîné, Capitaine de Navire, au Port-au-Prince, ou à M. *Laville,* Négociant au Cap. Il y aura recompense.

Three years later, another advertisement appeared. Though not as close a match as the first, it, too, seems to describe Francisque:

A creole slave, named Francisque, who has been marked by the hand of the executioner, height of 5 feet 1 or 2 inches, well built and very agile, a little pock-marked, and missing some teeth, he is a runaway since the 17th of the last month. Those who recognize him are requested to have him arrested, and to give notice to M. Longuet, habitant at Grand-Boucan, to whom he belongs.

Un Negre créole, nommé *Francisque,* qui a été marqué par la main du Bourreau, taille de 5 pieds 1 à 2 pouces, bien fait et fort agile, un peu picoté, et lui manquant quelques dents, est maron depuis le 17 du mois dernier. Ceux qui le reconnoîtront, sont priés de le faire arrêter, et d'en donner avis à M. *Longuet,* Habitant au Grand-Boucan, à qui il appartient.

Francisque, Démocrite, and Hector

Fluent in three languages, he was "well built," even "stocky," of medium height at around five foot one or two, and "very agile." Both advertisements mention that he was lightly pockmarked from having had the smallpox, and, by 1767, when the first was printed, he had a broken nose. The advertisements provide details about his build and his facial features, but without the court case it would be impossible to grasp his success with a wide range of women or to know anything of his sense of style, his personality, or his bravado.[65]

The conclusion of Francisque's trial in Louisiana does not mark the end of his story. The advertisements reveal that he landed in Saint Domingue sometime before January 1767 and that, once again, he sought to escape from bondage. His peripatetic life was not yet over, nor, one would expect, his dancing and courtship days, even if the archives tell no more.

CHAPTER 5

"Asleep in Their Bed at the Door of Their Cabin"

Kenet and Jean-Baptiste

Has been brought to us by the jailer of the said prisons the said *negresse* named Kenet to whom we have made swear to tell the truth.

Interrogated as to her name age, quality, and residence?

Said she is named Kenet aged thirty-five years old or thereabouts, laborer, belonging to the estate of Sr. Desruisseau, resident at the bayou.

Interrogated why she is in prison and who has had her put there?

Said that it was because Sr. Brasilier had had her seized by his *negre* named Baptiste.

Interrogated how much time she has been gone from her master?

Said that it was since about a year and that it was the day that Mr. de la Ronde had gone to establish a tar factory with a boat.

Interrogated where she has been led by the said *negre?*

Said that she had been taken to Brazilier's tar factory called the Bayou de Pasquier and that they went there in the boat of Mr. de la Ronde.

Interrogated if she stayed a long time at the tar factory and if they did not go elsewhere?

Responded that she stayed until the end of [the making of] a furnace of tar and that afterward Sr. Brazilier made them go to his plantation at Chef Menteur with the said *negre* Jean-Baptiste.

Interrogated if she stayed all the time at Chef Menteur and who was it who fed them at Chef Menteur?

Responded that she stayed all the time at Chef Menteur and that the *negre* [Jean-Baptiste] went to fetch their provisions from Sr. Brazilier who supplied them.

Interrogated if she worked on this plantation?

Said that she did nothing and that a few times she took care of a garden plot that the *negre* had cleared without Brazilier having ever commanded him to.

Interrogated if Sr. Brazillier had promised that he would buy her?

Responded that Brazilier had never spoken to her and that it was only the *negre* who told her, speaking for his master, that he would buy her.

Interrogated if Sr. Brazilier had seen them at Chef Menteur?

Said that yes that he had seen her a few times but that he had never spoken to her.

Interrogated who it was who had seized them and in what manner they had been led to prison?

Responded that it was Sr. Millon with Vincent Rieux.

Interrogated where they were when they were taken?

Said that they were taken around midnight asleep under their cot at the door of their cabin.

Interrogated if it was the first time that she had left her master?

Responded that they had been runaways near Mobile, that having been arrested they were each sent back to their master and that it is since that time that the said Brazilier had had her seized a second time.

Interrogated who had given them a boat and supplies to go to Mobile?

Said that they took a pirogue boat from the Indians and that they had bought food with money that they had.

Interrogated who had sold them the food?

Said that it is the *negre* André belonging to Madame Poupart to whom they had given money, that he bought bread and rice in town.

Which is all that she has admitted knowing, her interrogation was read back to her, said her answer contained the truth and persisted in this, and declared not knowing how to write nor read, this enquired of her according to the order, the following were approved: the word "Said" was redone and one syllable was crossed out.

Nous a été amené par le Geolier des dittes prisons laditte Negresse nommée Kenet à laquelle avons fait faire serment de nous dire Verité

Interrogé de Son nom age qualité et demeure

A dit Sappeller Kenet agée de trente cinq ans ou environ piocheuse appartenant à la succession du S. desruisseau Demt[eurante] au bayou

Interrogé pourquoÿ Elle est en prison et qui Es qui L'y a fait mettre

A dit que cetoit parce que les. Brazilier la fait Enlever Par son negre nommé Baptiste

Interrogée combien de tems quelle est Sortie de chez Son Maitre

A dit qu'il y avoit environ un an et que cest le jour que M. de la ronde a été former un Etablissement de goudronnerie avec un batteau

Interrogée où Elle a été menée par ledit Negre

A dit quelle a été conduite à la goudronnerie de brazilier appellée Le Bayou de pasquier et quils ont passé dans le batteau de M. de La Ronde

Interrogé si Elle a Resté longtemps à La goudronnerie et Sils n'ont point été ailleurs

A repondü qu'ils ont Resté jusque la fin d'un fourneau de Godron et qu'apres les. Brazilier Les a fait passer sur son habitation de Chef menteur avec ledit negre Jean Baptiste

Interogée si Elle a toujours resté à Chef menteur et qui Est qui les nourissoit à Chef menteur

A repondu qu'elle a toujours Resté à Chef menteur et que le negre alloit chercher leurs vivres chez les. Brazilier qui leur en a fourny

Interrogée si Elle travoilloit sur cette habitation

A dit qu'elle ne faisoit rien et quelle s'occupoit quelques fois à un dezer Que le negre avoit fait sans que Brazilier luy ait Jamais Rien Commandé

Interrogée si les. Brazillier luy avoit promis de L'acheter

A Repondu que brazillier ne luy avoit jamais parlé et qu'il ny avoit que le negre de la part de Son maître luy Dit qui Le l'acheteroit

Interrogé si les. Brazillier Les a vü à Chef menteur

A dit que oüi qu'il L'avoit vüe plusieurs fois Mais qu'il ne luy a jamais parlé

Interrogée qui Est qui Les a pris et de quelle façon est quils ont été menez en prison

A Repondu que c'est le Sr. Millon avec Vincent Rieux

Interrogée où ils Estoient Lorsqu'ils ont été Pris

A dit quils ont été pris vers Minuit Couchez sous leur Bert à la porte de leur Cabanne

Interrogée si cest la premiere fois quelle cest en allée de Chez son maitre

A repondu qu'ils avoient été maron du Costé de la mobille qu'aÿant été arretés ils ont etez Renvoyés chacun à leur Maître et que cest depuis ce tems la que ledit Brazilier La fait enlever une seconde fois

Interogée qui est qui leur a donné une voiture et des vivres pour aller à la mobille

A dit qu'ils prirent une pirogue aux Sauvages et qu'ils avoient acheté des vivres avec quelques argent qu'ils avoient

Interogée qui est qui leur avoit vendu des vivres

A dit que c'est le Negre André appartenant à madame poupart à qui ils avoient donné de l'argent qui luy a acheté en ville du pain et du ris ecarré

Qui Est tous ce quelle a dit Scavoir Lecture à luy faite de son interrogatoire a dit sa Reponse contenant verité y a persisté et a declaré sçavoir ni Ecrire ni Signé ce enquis Suivant L'ordonnance, approuvé Le mot Dit Refait pour valloir et une silabe Reyée.[1]

Sometime during Pierre de Rigaud de Vaudreuil's tenure as governor (1743–1753), Jean-Baptiste and Kenet fell in love. Forming an instantaneous bond, they managed to sustain a profound attachment for at least fourteen years, until 1767, when they were arrested, interrogated, and convicted: Jean-Baptiste for kidnapping and concealing Kenet and Kenet for running away with Jean-Baptiste. It was not the first time that these two, who had different masters, had sought to live together. The previous year, Jean-Baptiste had run off to find Kenet, and they had fled by boat toward Mobile, 140 miles away. Their first documented attempt at living with one another was when Kenet's owner moved her to an island on the bayou; Jean-Baptiste, "who was attached to her" *(auquel ledit negre estoit attaché),* had run away to join her there. On being arrested and jailed in Mobile, around 1766, Jean-Baptiste protested to his captors that he "would rather die than return" *(aimait mieux mourir que de retour avec luy).* No record of a prosecution exists, and the two were sent back to their respective masters and separated once more. But, shortly after their return, Jean-Baptiste's owner, Jean-Baptiste Brazilier, assigned him to live at his isolated plantation at the swampy Chef Menteur on Lake Pontchartrain. He was to work at the nearby tar factory at Bayou de Pasquier.[2]

Soon after his arrival at Chef Menteur, Jean-Baptiste sought out Kenet once again. The precise circumstances would be deliberated in court, but what is clear is that he borrowed a boat from M. de La Ronde and made his way back to Kenet under the cover of darkness. She left with him, and together they went to the tar factory; then, probably about two months later, they moved to Chef Menteur, a swampy area just northeast of New Orleans and Bayou Saint Jean on a waterway that was linked to the easternmost part of Lake Pontchartrain. The area stretching from the Gulf Coast between the Mobile and Mississippi Rivers was populated by ethnically diverse polities (or *"petites nations,"* as the French termed them), and Lake Pontchartrain

FIGURE 34: Alexandre de Batz, *Dessein de sauvages de plusieurs nations,*
Nlle Orleans 1735. 1735. Gift of the Estate of Belle J. Bushnell, 1941.
Courtesy the Peabody Museum of Archaeology and Ethnology, Harvard University
In his drawing of Indians of various nations, done in New Orleans in 1735,
the artist included the seated figure of a Fox (Meskwaki) female slave. She is
engaged in scraping a hide and lined up beside her are containers of meat, tallow,
and bear oil (used in cooking) and a turkey, all of which were items traded to
the French and that Jean-Baptiste and Kenet could have bartered for.

teemed with the presence of small and large groups of Indians who participated in New Orleans's informal economy and sometimes also its social and
political life. Jean-Baptiste and Kenet undoubtedly interacted with some of
them, trading for goods and services and perhaps lighting on an occasional
outlet for sociability (Figure 34). They were sufficiently in evidence that Brazilier complained in court that the nighttime seizure of Jean-Baptiste had left
his property "at the mercy of the sauvages" *(à la mercy des sauvages).* What
the couple did not find at Chef Menteur were many, if any, French. So there
they lived undisturbed for eight months or so until, one night, relatives of
Kenet's owner came to retrieve her.[3]

Kenet and Jean-Baptiste

As both Jean-Baptiste and Kenet poignantly underscored in describing their capture, they were taken in the middle of the night, awakened from their sleep. In Kenet's words, they were "seized around midnight asleep in their bed at the door of their cabin," while, in Jean-Baptiste's telling, it was nighttime and they were "seized from under their cot at the door of their cabin where they were sleeping" *(Saisy sous leur Bert à la porte de leur Cabane où ils estoient couchés)*. They were both in their thirties or forties at the time, and no offspring were mentioned in any of the court records pertaining to their case. When the prosecutor asked Kenet if she wanted to be with Jean-Baptiste, she answered in the affirmative, at some risk to herself since she had in effect pleaded guilty to being a runaway rather than an abductee. But, digressing from the question about her current situation, she immediately qualified her answer, explaining the longstanding nature of their relationship: "Yes and that they are together since [the time of] M. de Vaudreuil" *(a dit que oûi et quils Sont Ensemble depuis M. de vaudreuil)*. Where enslaved women are concerned, such testimony about love is especially rare. This invisibility is a function of the relative absence of enslaved women from the archive but also the result of the silences surrounding certain topics, especially those pertaining to sexuality and emotions.[4]

The trial against Kenet and Jean-Baptiste illuminates the series of steps they took to secure, over the longterm, their affective and physical union. From their answers, it emerges that Kenet and Jean-Baptiste expected their owners to play a role in managing their relationship, if need be by negotiating with the other's owner so that they could cohabit; their masters, too, acknowledged this option. No mention was made of Kenet and Jean-Baptiste seeking a legally sanctioned marriage, but they must have considered it. In French colonies, as articulated in the 1724 code noir, slaves who were baptized were permitted to wed in the Catholic Church, so long as they secured their masters' approval. Church weddings automatically conferred legitimacy on an enslaved couple's union in the eyes of the crown. Such marriages, which were not allowed in most of British America, afforded married couples belonging to the same master certain rights, including protection from being sold separately or having their prepubescent children removed from them — rights that did not exist for slave families, married or not, in the English colonies. Nevertheless, though French law allowed slaves to marry legally, the rights conveyed by marriage made masters cautious about giving permission. Whether Jean-Baptiste and Kenet entertained the idea of a church marriage, doing so would not have precluded them from also entering into another form of marriage, one with roots in West African law and ritual. Perhaps they had already cemented the permanency of their union and "married in the manner of the *nègres" (amanceués à la maniere Des negres)*, even if their marriage was not recognized by the French.[5]

After Brazilier tried and failed to arrange a sale or exchange with Kenet's owner, the two lovers worked yet again to find a way to be together. Their lack of autonomy might have clashed with their urge for intimacy, but their quest to live as a couple was a force that both of their owners had to reckon with on an ongoing basis. The story of Kenet and Jean-Baptiste brings to light the importance for the enslaved of fostering and maintaining affective relationships and how assiduously they sought to achieve them. In asserting their need for intimacy, enslaved couples drove home to masters and authorities what could be gained from displaying a flexibility and pragmatism with regard to their slaves' intimate lives. In hearing about Jean-Baptiste and Kenet's persistent hopes for reunion, it is possible to imagine their constant anguish at their separation and, underlying it, a moving expression of deep attachment and longing.

If Kenet and Jean-Baptiste's story is, first, one about love and commitment, their testimony also reveals that their relationship, like those of so many other couples who fought against the odds to forge longstanding ties, was not just about love, sex, procreation, or even the benefits accruing from public acknowledgment of their union. It was also about freedom from labor norms practiced within slavery. Even more specifically, it was about household formation and African males' control over the labor of their womenfolk. Though very, very few slaves would ever achieve, whether licitly (through manumission, for example) or illicitly, the degree of independence that Jean-Baptiste and Kenet enjoyed for a short time at Chef Menteur, their words reveal what was at stake for them in being together as a cohabiting couple. For them, to be together meant not only gaining autonomy over corollaries of spousal relationships such as sexual, physical, and emotional intimacy but also wresting control from their masters over their domestic arrangements and, specifically, Jean-Baptiste's ability to lay claim to Kenet's labor.[6]

✕✕

KENET AND JEAN-BAPTISTE

Kenet and Jean-Baptiste entered the court record as part of a civil suit between colonists, not a criminal investigation. Kenet's owner had denounced Jean-Baptiste's owner for colluding with the slave to abduct and conceal Kenet and then for giving his tacit approval to their cohabitation. The intricacies of the case, therefore, hinged initially on determining Brazilier's role in the affair, as distinguished from Jean-Baptiste's and Kenet's guilt with regard to the crimes of abduction and *marronnage* (running away), which became the focus of the ensuing criminal trial. Brazilier had undoubtedly colluded with Jean-Baptiste. By allowing his slave to cohabit with Kenet, he ensured Jean-Baptiste's loyalty in not running away, thereby continuing to benefit from his labor as well as Kenet's. In spite of Jean-Baptiste and Kenet's testimony implicating Brazilier, the slaveowner would be exonerated; only Jean-Baptiste and Kenet would be convicted and sentenced. The accused slaves were each interrogated twice, once in court and once on the *sellette* (a special interrogation conducted in the prison so named for the low stool on which the defendant was made to sit). Other than the couple and Brazilier, nine white witnesses appeared, many of whom introduced detailed hearsay from Jean-Baptiste and Kenet concerning their relationship.[7]

Jean-Baptiste and Kenet were known to have formed a strong bond and had previously run away together to Mobile before being returned to their respective masters. Why did it take eight months, "since the start of the tender corn of the previous year" *(dès le commencement du mahy tendre de l'année derniere)*, for Kenet's owner to identify her whereabouts and have her seized under the cover of darkness? Jean-Baptiste's and Kenet's chains of ownership suggest some reasons why it took so long to retrieve Kenet, as does the ancillary testimony of white witnesses who reported rumors that their own slaves had spread about the couple.[8]

Both Kenet and Jean-Baptiste belonged to local elites settled at Bayou Saint Jean outside New Orleans (Figure 35). Jean-Baptiste likely lived his entire life in the area as Brazilier had purchased him from "the old Graveline." Jean Baptiste Baudreau dit Graveline, one of Mobile's founders, had settled at Bayou Saint Jean in 1713, and Brazilier's father had acquired a plantation from him in 1729. Though Graveline might have been a founding figure, his wife sued him in 1752 for separation on the basis of his dissipation of their marital property (which was held in community in accordance with the Coutume de Paris, the customary law that governed civilian matters in Louisiana). Although the litigation brought up his gambling, profligacy, indebtedness, and libertinage, what pushed her over the edge (and tilted the court in her favor) was when he sold the last one of her slaves — perhaps Jean-Baptiste — to subsidize a new trading endeavor.[9]

The varied tasks Jean-Baptiste performed for Brazilier suggest that he was a skilled and valuable slave in the prime of his working life. When the court asked him to identify himself, Jean-Baptiste answered that he was named "Jean Baptiste *nègre* aged twenty-five years old belonging to the Sieur Brazilier, carter, residing at the bayou" *(Jean Baptiste Negre âgé de vingt cinq ans appartenant au Sieur Brazilier, chartier [charretier] demeurant au bayou)*.

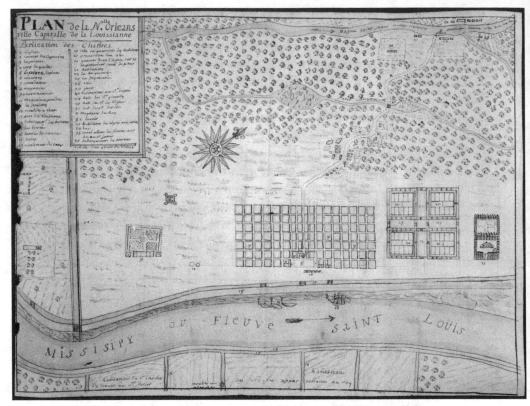

FIGURE 35: Jean-François-Benjamin Dumont de Montigny,
Plan de la Nlle. Orleans, ville capitalle de la Louissianne. [1747].
Edward E. Ayer Manuscript Map Collection. Vault oversize Ayer MS 257,
map no. 7. Courtesy of The Newberry Library, Chicago
In Dumont de Montigny's 1747 map of New Orleans, the landing point
for convoys arriving from the Illinois Country is keyed to no. 14.

In other testimony, he gave responses about his age ranging between twenty-five and thirty-five. And he was more versatile than the occupation of carter suggests—not least, he could navigate a boat. Brazilier seems to have esteemed him highly in spite of the slave's earlier stint as a runaway. He picked him for the skilled work of the tar factory and, more importantly, perhaps, trusted him enough to leave him unsupervised at Chef Menteur. Brazilier was also willing to negotiate with Jean-Baptiste to buy Kenet on his behalf.[10]

As for Kenet, whose name was sometimes spelled Quenet and occasionally Quenel, she stated that her age was thirty-five (a later document put her at forty-five). She further identified herself to the court as Creole, born in

Kenet and Jean-Baptiste

Mobile, Catholic, and a field laborer. She named her owner as the estate of Sieur Joseph Desruisseaux. He and his wife, Marie Françoise Girardy, were also long-term inhabitants of Bayou Saint Jean. But, by February 1767, not long after Kenet had absconded, Desruisseaux had passed away. So, while searches (which included trying to contact Brazilier) were conducted as soon as she disappeared, efforts to locate her might have stalled, sidelined by other more pressing needs linked to the aftermath of Desruisseaux's death. The Coutume de Paris mandated that the surviving spouse (male or female) was to inherit half of any assets after debts were settled while the deceased's children (again, whether male or female) were to obtain equal shares of the remaining half.[11]

The settling of estates could drag on depending on the circumstances, and it was not until July 1767 that the widow Desruisseaux finally finished rendering the accounts for the estate. The last period of accounting is likely what spurred a renewed search for Kenet, since it was around June 10 that the executor, Etienne Maurice Millon (Girardy's son from her first marriage), led the expedition to retrieve and capture her. He might have acted on new information, for there were many routes to obtaining fresh intelligence about runaways. For example, one of the white witnesses mentioned how a neighbor, La Ronde, had described Kenet fighting with his female slaves. Even though the exact timing and extent of this particular skirmish cannot be ascertained, La Ronde's male slaves corroborated that some sort of incident took place. If they were willing to share such information with their master, it probably meant that they were willing to reveal other inside knowledge they might have about her movements. But it is clear that the Desruisseaux household already suspected that Kenet had been with Jean-Baptiste from the start, since they had made enquiries with Brazilier, his associates, and his neighbors when she first went missing, around the time that the tar factory was established. In bypassing Brazilier to capture her in June, they signaled that they believed him to be involved.[12]

In addition to being preoccupied with settling the estate, the Desruisseaux family might have also delayed their search in hopes that they could reach a favorable agreement with Brazilier to buy or trade Kenet, as both parties alluded to a negotiation. They likely considered that the odds of Kenet getting pregnant were more favorable if she lived with Jean-Baptiste for an extended period, a circumstance they would have stood to benefit from: Article 9 of the 1724 code noir stipulated that children born to slaves with different masters belonged to the mother's master. A pregnant slave in Louisiana was especially valuable given that the colony had seen virtually no new slave shipments since 1731. The heirs' expectation that a deal could be reached with Brazilier

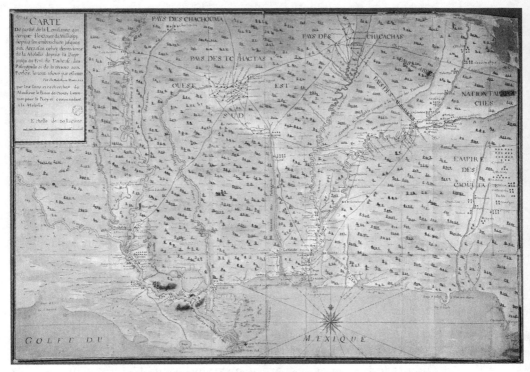

FIGURE 36: [Baron de Crénay (ou Cresnay)], *Carte de partie de la Loüisianne qui comprend le cours du Missisipy depuis son embouchure jusques aux Arcansas, celuy des rivieres de la Mobille depuis la Baye jusqu au Fort de Toulouse, des Pascagoula et de la riviere aux Perles . . .* 1733. FR ANOM 04 DFC 1A. Courtesy Archives nationales d'outre-mer, Aix-en-Provence, France

would have certainly staved off any sense of urgency until such time as the widow Desruisseaux needed to render accounts. It might also explain why no official declaration was filed with authorities attesting to Kenet's disappearance, even though she was a recidivist who had absconded once before.[13]

When the couple ran away the first time, they chose to flee to Mobile. Did they have family and kin still living there whom they missed, who could take them in and protect them? Kenet was born there, and Jean-Baptiste's master hailed from there, so it makes sense to imagine that they had sound motives for choosing that destination. The easiest way to travel to Mobile was via waterways (Figure 36). Interrogated as to who had given them a boat and supplies to go to Mobile, they "said that they took a pirogue boat from the Indians." It was a journey that took four to five days and involved some treacherous waters, notably the passage out of Lake Pontchartrain through

Kenet and Jean-Baptiste

what is now known as the Rigolets (Figure 2). Jean-Baptiste could handle boats, but it would have been easier and cheaper to catch a ride with some of the Indians settled around Lake Pontchartrain who plied the route to Mobile. Either way, the distance and complexity of travel was great enough that it cannot have been an improvised escape.[14]

Beyond the information about their ownership, little else is known about Jean-Baptiste and Kenet. Though the court identified Jean-Baptiste generically as a *"nègre,"* one white witness described him as mulatto. Similarly, where Kenet was characterized as a *"négresse,"* Brazilier used the more precise term for a mulatto woman, *"mulataise [sic]."* Perhaps as a *mulatresse* she was her late master's progeny or relative (if she had been born within his household rather than purchased). At the time she went to Chef Menteur, she was under medical care. The surgeon Montegut provided a certificate in August 1767 attesting that late in the year 1766 he had been called to treat "Guenet," who had considerable sores on both legs, that he treated her several times, but that she had disappeared while still "in a very bad state" *(dans un tres mauvais etat)*. Neither Kenet nor Jean-Baptiste ever mentioned her health nor the cause of the sores, a measure of how the enslaved treaded gingerly when addressing the source of their injuries and other medical concerns in court.[15]

Nevertheless, while little is known about Jean-Baptiste's and Kenet's lives apart from the court case, Kenet's actions reveal something about her fortitude. Here was a woman who twice absconded with the same man and who fought with other women (La Ronde's enslaved women). It was not the only time. Previously, "having had trouble with the *negres,* her master sent her to the other side of the lake to punish her" *(ayant Eü quelques difficultés avec les negres Son maitre la Envoyée de l'autre Bord du lac pour la punir)*. Maybe it was this particular altercation that led Desruisseaux to send her off to his island on the bayou. He might have had other reasons for doing so, but Kenet interpreted his decision as a punitive one. The location of the island is not known but it could well have been on the other side of the lake. What is certain is that, in doing so, Desruisseaux set in motion the chain of events that would lead to her running away to Mobile with Jean-Baptiste, who was "attached" to her, and their finding one year later a means to be together undisturbed at Chef Menteur, where for eight months they formed an autonomous household.[16]

Kenet and Jean-Baptiste were repeatedly challenged in their quest to remain together. They employed a range of strategies to achieve their goal of being united, and these provide significant clues about the meanings they ascribed to their own permanent, monogamous relationship. Yet, like all enslaved people in the colony, they had to contend with the reality that masters could at any point seek to exert control over their love lives. This had repercussions for the types of relationships slaves could enter into, not least whether legal marriage—which hinged on French law and Catholic rites—was an option for them. Though it is impossible to know how Kenet and Jean-Baptiste defined their union, whether they sought a legal marriage, or how closely their concepts allied or diverged from those of the French, their experience invites a consideration of the range of affective and conjugal practices that were possible for people of African descent (enslaved and free) in Louisiana and the rights and privileges that they did or did not confer.

Most fundamentally, Kenet and Jean-Baptiste belonged to different owners and lived on separate properties, the distance between which is unknown. Still, their words allude to a recurring search to find a way to remain physically as well as emotionally linked and to forge a home of their own. Theirs is precious testimony. With the exception of marital relationships that developed among free blacks or between free and enslaved blacks, few traces exist in the written record about affective relationships among those of African origin living in Louisiana, especially testimony about household formation. Through examining those relationships involving free blacks, it is possible to draw parallels with Jean-Baptiste and Kenet's story. In cohabiting, they staked a claim to independence not unlike the kind of autonomy that free blacks sought to secure when they married.[17]

The similarities between Kenet and Jean-Baptiste's story and those of free blacks comes into sharp focus in cases where a free black man and an enslaved woman wanted to marry with the protections that the law granted sanctioned unions (there are no cases of free women negotiating the manumission of their male partner). The first step in such marriages was for the prospective husband to negotiate terms of manumission for the enslaved woman. One such example concerns the English-speaking free black John Mingo and his enslaved wife. After making an arduous overland escape from Carolina, John Mingo arrived in New Orleans in August 1726. He was immediately sheltered by Sieur Darby, manager of the Cantillou concession, who pronounced him free and promptly employed the new arrival. Within a year, Mingo was ready to take a new step in establishing permanent residency in the colony. On November 28, 1727, he entered into a formal, legally binding church marriage with an enslaved African on the same concession known as Thérèse, having already agreed to terms with her owner. John Mingo had converted to Catholicism as a precondition of the marriage, and he agreed to pay for her freedom over time, resulting in Thérèse securing Darby's permission to wed. The process, however, did not go smoothly. In the ensuing contractual dispute, Darby (as the defendant) gave his take on the circumstances of the marriage:

> that the said Jean Mingo having come from the English overland in August 1726, the defendant received him in his house almost naked, and relieved him as much as he could, and even hired him at two hundred and fifty livres per year, but before he had finished his year with the defendant, and having fallen in love with a *négresse* named Thérèse from the concession of Mr. Cantillou . . . , the defendant finally gave in to his pestering and granted him the said *negresse* in marriage before the Church.

The court case hinged on whether the two parties had upheld the terms of their agreement over Thérèse's marriage and manumission. Here, in this civil case, is a snapshot of a couple falling in love and of a free black "pestering" the manager of his beloved's owner to intercede in facilitating and enabling their legal marriage.[18]

Like John Mingo and Thérèse, Kenet and Jean-Baptiste had also fallen in love, and they, too, developed strategies to ensure a long-term solution to their desire to be together. Similar to Mingo's negotiations with Darby, a key part of Jean-Baptiste and Kenet's strategy entailed pressuring and "pestering" their respective owners to reach a deal with one another. Masters had the power and opportunity to compel their slaves, but they did not necessarily find it wise to do so. Brazilier apparently acquiesced to his slave's pleas to be formally united with his partner. But, unlike the case involving John Mingo and Thérèse, it is only possible to go so far in speculating as to whether they, as enslaved rather than free persons, could have, or would have, chosen to be married according to French law and Catholic rites.

For John Mingo and Thérèse, securing a future together meant ensuring that they entered into a legally binding marriage contract solemnified according to the rites of the Catholic Church—and, therefore, crucially, recognized by the French. Likewise, free blacks chose to enter into legal marriages by marrying in the church and signing marriage contracts as Louis Mulâtre and

Rosine did in 1764, the bride contributing five hundred livres and the groom seven cattle and six horses (valued at six hundred livres) to their community property. John Mingo even went so far as to convert to Catholicism so that he could qualify for such a marriage. But what about Jean-Baptiste and Kenet, who were both baptized Catholic? What did they envisage when they imagined being joined together? Did they even consider a Catholic marriage?[19]

In French colonies, in stark contrast to most English colonies, the enslaved were not prohibited from entering into legal marriages. Indeed, in theory, the code noir strongly endorsed sanctioned marriages between baptized slaves as a safeguard against extramarital sex, in other words, for religious and moral reasons (as was also the case in Puritan Massachusetts, which permitted legal marriage). If this did not mean that access to legally sanctioned marriage was always achievable in practice, not least since each slave's master had to grant permission, it was certainly *imaginable*.[20]

Whether or not they contemplated a legal marriage, what steps could Kenet and Jean-Baptiste have taken—and which steps did they take—to safeguard their union in the long term? Their first act of running away, to Mobile, was a bold and risky act of desperation by a couple frantic to find a lasting solution. But their own words speak volumes about their initial and continued hopes to be together and their expectation that it was feasible if only their masters could be persuaded to become involved. And seek to persuade they did, enlisting their masters, and their masters' acquaintances, in their quest to live in the same place, to be physically joined (if not necessarily married in the church) under the same roof.

Both the accused and multiple witnesses mentioned that Brazilier had attempted to negotiate a deal that would unite the couple, and Brazilier himself acknowledged as much. Jean-Baptiste alluded no less than five times to Brazilier's repeated promise "that he would buy her for him" *(qu'il l'acheteroit pour luy)*. When officials asked during his first interrogation what he had done to Kenet to warrant Sieur Millon arresting him, Jean-Baptiste cited Brazilier's involvement, answering that "it was for having taken Kenet *negresse* with him by order of his master who had promised to buy her for him" *(a dit que cestoit pour avoir emmené Kenet negresse avec luy par ordre de son Maître qui luy avoit promis de lacheter pour luy)*. When asked during her first interrogation why she was in prison and who had had her placed there, Kenet, too, mentioned Brazilier, saying that "it was because the Sieur Brazilier had had her abducted by his *nègre* named Baptiste" *(cetoit parce que led. Brazilier l'a fait Enlever Par Son negre nommé Baptiste)*.[21]

Even when testifying a second time on the sellette in the prison, the couple reiterated as their line of defense that Brazilier was involved. Kenet even expanded on her previous testimony, adding that:

> In the time since she has returned from Mobille, the said Brasillier had her seized in her kitchen and she was brought to the other shore, and since her young masters the Millons often came to that area, the *negre* Baptiste belonging to Brazilier said to his master that the *negresse* that he had had brought was there, what did he want him to do with her, that he worried that this would cause a bad affair, that Brazilier told him to finish [the tar] and that he would see about it afterward.
>
> _____
>
> a dit que dans les tems quelle Est Revenüe de La mobille led. De Brasillier la fit prendre dans sa Cuisine et quelle fut ramener de lautre Bord et comme ses petits maitre les Milons venoient dans ces quartiers le negre Baptiste appartenant à brazilier dit à son maître que la negresse qui luy avoit dit damener Etoit la, quest quil en vouloit faire quil Craignoit que cela Luy Cauzat une Mauvaise affaire, que Brazilier luy dit de finir le fourneau qu'il veroit sela apres

In placing responsibility for their actions on Brazilier, Jean-Baptiste and Kenet implicitly recognized his power and his authority in legitimating their relationship, but they also signaled their knowledge that they had a chance to sway him to their point of view.[22]

Traces of hearsay evidence show how widely Jean-Baptiste and Kenet discussed their predicament. Not only did they narrate their story to the court, but the court record referenced other conversations in which the runaways spoke about their fate and their hope that their masters would regularize their situation. Vincent Rieux, who had been among those sent to seize the couple, stated that, when captured, both slaves expressed their conviction that Brazilier intended to buy Kenet so that the two could remain together. Rieux described asking Jean-Baptiste why he had taken Kenet and provided a highly detailed summation, with dialogue, of what he claimed the slave replied:

> That the said *negre* had answered him that it was not his fault but that of his master who had told him to take her, that having represented to his master when they went to make tar that he could not leave without this *negresse* to whom he was attached and that his master had said to him, "Well then bring her but be on guard that she is not seen." That the intention of Millon and the deponent was not to take the *negre* [Jean-Baptiste] with them, and that it was the *negre* who said to them,

"Sirs do not take me, my intention is to come with you to town when you want." That the said *negre* said on top of that that he had made many representations to his master to buy the *negresse* given that a lot of people came to the tar works and that he could be discovered, that his master answered him to "work the tar furnace, I will give you food and a boat you will go to Chef Menteur and only you will be seen here."

que ledit negre luy auroit Repondü que ce netoit point de sa faute Mais Bien de celle de son maître qui luy avoit dit de lemmener que ayant Representé à Son maître lors quils furent faire du godron qu'il ne pouvoit point partir Sans cette negresse à laquelle il estoit attaché et que son Maitre luy auroit dit ait Bien emmene la Mais prends bien garde quelle ne soit vüe, que lintention du deposant et de millon nestoit point d'emmener le negre avec Eux, et que ledit negre leur dit Messieurs ne m'amarré point Mon intention Est daller avec vous en ville quen vous ne le voudrez pas, que ledit negre leur a deplus dit qu'il avoit fait nombre de Representation à son maitre pour acheter cette Negresse attendu qu'il venoit Beaucoup de monde aux godronnerie et qu'il pouroit Etre decouvert que Son Maitre lui a Repondü de finir le fourneau de de [sic] goderon deja emmené Je vous donneray des vivres Et une voiture tu t'en iras à chef menteur et tu sera vü que icÿ

Louis Duvernay, the widow Desruisseaux's brother-in-law, corroborated this statement, recounting how, only two months earlier, Brazilier's overseer had approached him for help in negotiating either the sale of Kenet to Brazilier or Jean-Baptiste to Desruisseaux. Duvernay and Rieux were by no means impartial witnesses, but their testimony accords perfectly with the explanations that both Jean-Baptiste and Kenet presented to court officials.[23]

Not only did the two slaves express their expectation that Brazilier would negotiate Kenet's purchase, but Brazilier himself acknowledged trying to secure a deal:

Interrogated if he had not told Duvernay to speak to Desruisseau about buying the said *negresse?*

Replied no, that he had made no such proposition to Sr. Deruisseau, that in fact he had had his overseer offer his *negre* to the said Deruisseau if he wanted to buy him since he suspected that he had abducted his *negresse,* that the said Deruisseaux offered him such a low price that it is does not deserve repeating, that the said Deruisseau made it known to him that on the contrary if he wanted to give him a *negritte* [girl slave] of fifteen years old he would [in exchange] give him Quenet [sic].

Kenet and Jean-Baptiste

Though he denied complicity in Jean-Baptiste's abduction of Kenet and pointedly emphasized, instead, that his negotiation had failed owing to Desruisseaux's greed, Brazilier did not repudiate his role in seeking to find a permanent solution to the enslaved couple's attachment. Indeed, he seemed self-satisfied that he had done his due diligence and probably took a self-righteous view of his actions as those of a good patriarch.[24]

"YOUR MASTER DOES NOT GIVE YOU A WIFE / WOMAN"

As a slaveowner, Brazilier could expect to play a role in arranging his slaves' relationships, so long as this promoted (or at the very least did not interfere with) his self-interest. Even if relationships among enslaved people in Louisiana were usually initiated by slaves themselves, they could not entirely escape their masters' control. Furthermore, privileged, skilled slaves such as Jean-Baptiste could expect favored treatment and special perquisites. The provision of female partners or wives was viewed by slaves and masters alike as one such recompense. This incentive was granted at the prerogative of the master—and, as such, was revocable.

As Jean-Baptiste and Kenet's story reveals, slaves could find themselves at the whim of masters, and masters did not necessarily plan for the relationships they fostered among their slaves to be permanent or legally binding. According to Article 8 of the 1724 code noir, priests could not marry slaves without proof of the consent of their masters. This authority of masters to legitimize relationships, or to procure female partners for their enslaved men, was easier to accomplish within the same household, since it did not involve negotiations with other slaveowners.[25]

As slaveowners reacted to the halt in slave shipments to Louisiana after 1731 by relying on reproduction alone to increase their slave holdings, their control over their slaves' relationships grew in importance. For example, Sans-Soucy, who identified as Bambara, ran away in January 1741 because his master, Jean Guillaume Lange, wanted him to end his relationship with Jean-Charles de Pradel's slave "who is his wife / woman" *(qui est sa femme)* and give him a different woman. In French, *femme* refers to both "woman" and "wife," making it hard to determine here what Sans-Soucy understood by the term. The case is made more opaque by the fact that Pradel and Lange had been in partnership with joint slave holdings, so perhaps this is when the union between Sans-Soucy and his "femme" started. By the time Sans-Soucy ran away, Sieur Lange seems to have owned the man and Pradel the woman. Though Sieur Lange could have perceived Sans-Soucy's daily visits to his wife as desertion or a variant on the practice of stealing time, he likely also hoped that Sans-Soucy would impregnate a slave belonging to him, not Pradel. Article 9 of the code noir mandated that "children, issued from the marriage of slaves, will be slaves and will belong to the masters of the female slaves, and not those of their husbands, if the husbands and wives have different masters." Lange had incentive in pressuring Sans-Soucy, by beating him, to stop seeing his wife and accept a new woman on Lange's plantation who could bear children belonging to Lange. But there were many factors at play beyond promoting reproduction, and masters seem to have tread carefully as they evaluated the benefits and the risks associated with their slaves' relationships.[26]

Unless slaves married according to French law, masters retained the prerogative to separate enslaved couples and use women as pawns in negotiations with their enslaved men. As seen with Sans-Soucy, women were not the only ones to experience the coercive nature of masters' power over their slaves' relationships. Speaking in 1765 about his capture after eight days as a runaway, Essom, an African-born runaway, explained his motives through a female interpreter who understood Essom's "Nago language" (one associated with the Yoruba language group and the Bight of Benin). Translating his words into French for the court, she reported that he had run away "because his master took away the woman / wife he had given him to prepare his drink and food" *(parceque son maître luy a osté sa femme: qu'il luy avoit donné, pour faire Son Boire et Son mangé).* Essom and his French master seem to have held a shared notion that forming a partnership with a woman was not only about love, sex, procreation, and companionship; rather, they both recognized that women also served important functions in their interlocking roles as wives, mothers, and purveyors of meals.[27]

How one Indian slave's implicit expectation that his master would provide him with a woman played out is revealed in the 1748 testimony of a twenty-eight-year-old Chickasaw Joseph who was put on trial for marronnage. When caught, he reported a conversation he had had with a Meskwaki (Fox) Indian slave, Cocomina, whom he accused of inducing him to make his way to the Choctaw Indians. Cocomina had given him alcohol, gotten him drunk, and then stirred the pot by asking Joseph, "What are you doing here, your master does not give you a wife / woman he wants to sell you to a Frenchman that you do not know" *(que fais tu icy ton maitre Ne te donne point de femme il Veut te Vendre à un françois que tu ne Connois pas).* If Cocomina wanted to needle Joseph and provoke him into running away, he knew the angle to pursue. That he succeeded in doing so suggests that he had found a fertile ground for resentment: Cocomina's belief that his master owed him access to a woman.[28]

Left almost completely unaddressed by the archive is the question of women's input in these decisions, perhaps because both West African and French rules of courtship required that men initiate and contract relationships. Article 8 of the code noir forbade masters "from placing any constraints on their slaves to marry against their will," and it can be hoped that masters or mistresses discussed prospective partners with their enslaved women, whether the outcome was a legally binding or informal union. But the evidence is lacking and instead predominately bears witness to the expectations of men such as Cocomina, Essom, and Jean-Baptiste. And their accounts, their *cris de coeur* (cries of the heart), suggest that women and men were not necessarily consulted, especially on larger plantations where masters and overseers might have felt more free to arrange unions that were convenient for their purposes rather than for those of the enslaved couples themselves, least of all the female partners in such relationships.[29]

Sometimes enslaved women did allude indirectly to how invested they were in their relationships. Marguerite—who in 1764 accused her master and mistress of locking her up like in the convent—stated that on "the three Sundays that she was a runaway, she had been at Mr. Vilars's in the cabin of the Congo *nègre* Janot" *(pendant les trois dimanche quelle a Été maron Elle a été chez led. Vilars dans la Cabanne du nommé janot negre Congo)*. Likewise, in a 1767 case for marronnage against the enslaved Catherine, it emerged that she had run away to be with a Frenchman, Louis Jourdan, and stayed with him covertly until his landlord forbid him from having her on the premises. She claimed to have then gone to live with a slave, Louis, in his cabin (which Louis would vociferously deny) and that Jourdan would visit her there once a month.[30]

At other times, women's voices echoed quite literally from beyond the grave. This was the case with Taco. She was murdered in 1748, after enduring a protracted period of physical abuse from her (legal) husband François dit Baraca. (For the record, domestic abuse among colonists also occurred and included one husband who burned his wife with a hot iron and another who attacked his wife with an axe.) Two witnesses—Joseph Laoursot, a frequent guest of the couple's who identified himself as Turkish *("turc de Nation")*, aged forty-eight to fifty years old, and Catholic, and Antoine Flatagué, the enslaved overseer on the king's plantation where they all toiled—recounted in Creole how Baraca thought that she was cuckolding him. Although Baraca's point of view is represented in Laoursot's hearsay testimony—that he told his wife, "You too whore for me" *(toy trop putain pour moy)*—Taco's words are preserved in Flatagué's recital of events. In the middle of her husband's rant, Taco had walked in, turned to Flatagué, and defended herself, saying, "Here, Baraca always beat me because he jealous, he complains that I always go to see a *negre* and that is not true" *(tiens Baraca toujour Battre moy par-*

ceque luy jaloux il se plaint que je vas [sic] toujours voir un negre et cela n'est pas vray). Though both Laoursot and Flatagué cautioned Baraca (or so they claimed), Taco was killed that night, when Baraca grabbed a log from the fire and knocked her out. She was still breathing, so a surgeon was called for from the Ursuline hospital, but, by the time "Joseph mulatto" arrived from across the river to bleed her, "the *negresse,* having lost all consciousness died shortly after around six in the morning." Taco would speak no more.[31]

In contrast with these snippets of women's voices, Kenet's interrogation is a unique document in Louisiana history in that she not only explained her actions but explicitly stated her feelings about her choice of mate. In the court case against Kenet, evidence of one woman's desires, intentions, hopes, and expectations comes to the fore. When asked if she had voluntarily wanted to stay with Jean-Baptiste, Kenet was unambivalent in her affirmation: she "said yes and that they are together since [the time of] M. de Vaudreuil" *(a dit que oui et quils sont Ensemble depuis M. de vaudreuil).* (Figure 37) She repeatedly acted in ways that showed that she wanted to be with Jean-Baptiste, and her words bore out her actions.

What testimony by Sans-Soucy, Kenet, and Jean-Baptiste offers is a sense of how invested enslaved individuals were in forging their own relationships. Masters held authority over their slaves' ability to contract legally binding marriages, and they could appropriate enslaved women's bodies and reproductive capacities. But enslaved couples remained hopeful and determined even in the face of futility, making protracted attempts to control their intimate lives even as they were forced to reckon with the power of their masters.

✂ ✂

"EN FACE D'EGLISE": LEGALLY SANCTIONED MARRIAGES

In spite of the complications standing in the way, the enslaved fought to express how important marriage was to them, however they celebrated it, according to however many myriad ways they defined it. Courtship was a ubiquitous and valued aspect of life for them. Conducted at dances, in slave cabins, and during nighttime trysts, relationships were facilitated by gift giving from male suitors to their love interests. But, if it was by happenstance that the enslaved felt the pangs of desire or fell in love and entered into short- or long-term connections, only masters could reify conjugal relationships and legitimize them in the eyes of the French. In other words, there were two parallel marital worlds that coexisted, and only sometimes did they overlap.[32]

Neither Kenet nor Jean-Baptiste characterized the nature of their attachment nor did they articulate the type of relationship they envisioned for themselves once united on the same plantation. As Creoles born in the colony,

Kenet and Jean-Baptiste

FIGURE 37: Unknown artist, *Pierre de Rigaud de Vaudreuil Cavagnial, Marquis de Vaudreuil (1698–1778)*. C147538k-v6. Library and Archives of Canada, Ontario

they had been baptized in the Catholic Church, as consistent with the code noir, and were familiar with Catholic marriage. But neither they nor Brazilier addressed whether they anticipated getting married under the church's auspices. Though it is difficult to imagine that Kenet and Jean-Baptiste, given their particular circumstances, would have chosen to forgo the protections granted to slaves in French colonies who legally married, at the same time, slaves could not get married in the church without their masters' support.

Kenet and Jean-Baptiste   { 193

And, for slaveowners, the matter of granting permission was not straightforward precisely because of the benefits that legal marriages conferred on enslaved families. According to the code noir, masters were prohibited from splitting up families for sale, making slaveowners cautious about allowing their slaves to enter into sanctioned marriages.

The code noir included specific provisions for slaves to marry according to French legal rules and religious rites. Baptism was, of course, a prerequisite of such marriages, and Article 2 required that all slaves "will be instructed in the Catholic, Apostolic and Roman religion and baptized." But the code noir upended French legal conventions by displacing parental approval and replacing it with that of the master, as seen in Article 7:

> The ceremonies and forms prescribed by the ordinance of Blois, and by the edict of 1639, for marriages, shall be observed both with regard to free persons and to slaves; but nonetheless without the consent of the father and mother of the slave being necessary; only that of the master shall be required.

As seen in Article 8, the authors of the code noir also envisioned a role for priests in ensuring that enslaved women and men had agreed to a legal marriage:

> We expressly forbid all curates to proceed to marriages between slaves, without proof of the consent of their masters; and we also forbid all masters from placing any constraints on their slaves to marry against their will.

One would like to think that priests sought to ascertain that neither party felt pressured, in the same way that they probed French marriage partners on this question.[33]

Surviving marriage registers do show that priests strictly enforced the rule about masters' consent, thereby upholding masters' authority. Though the records are not complete, marriage and baptismal records provide an important index of church marriage rates and show that Louisiana was exceptional among French colonies in terms of the relatively high rate of legal slave marriages. Twenty-five percent (or sixty-seven) of the marriages that took place between 1759 and 1769 (when marriage registers survive) involved two slaves. Baptismal registers from 1744–1759 flesh out the record, showing that more than 12 percent of enslaved children (397) were born to parents married in the church. Even more notable, all of these marriages appear to have united slaves belonging to the same owner, despite baptismal records attesting to births from relationships that were not coresidential. Though ownership by the same master was not a precondition for marriage according to the code noir, it seems to have emerged as an unspoken rule in Louisiana. Consent was thus the prerogative of masters who alone controlled access to legal marriages celebrated by priests.[34]

Beyond sacramental records, other sources can be mined for data about marriages. The chapter minutes of the Ursuline convent show that the nuns promoted sacramental marriages among their bondspeople, favoring the purchase of slaves who held the potential for creating and maintaining family units and disposing of individuals they felt lived contrary to Catholic ideals (for example, those who engaged in sex outside legal marriage). A similar strategy was employed by Jesuit priests in Louisiana and is also documented in the records of Lazarist priests in Isle de Bourbon (present-day La Réunion).[35]

Listings of slave holdings, which tended to group the enslaved in household units, provide further evidence of the rate of legal marriage among slaves. As a general rule, though the term "femme" could mean either "wife" or "woman," when the possessive was used to describe a patriarchal relationship ("sa femme") it meant that the French inventory takers saw the union as legitimate and binding. For example, whereas Roze Rosalie was described only as "mother of Borgia" in the 1763 inventory of the Jesuits' property (a plantation distinguished by a high rate of sacramental marriage), the women on the plantation who were legally married were itemized in marital groups using the possessive noun. The family unit "Boria ironsmith 30 years old, Fanelon *his wife* seamstress 25 [years old]" appears in the same sentence with Roze Rosalie. That year, appraisers used the identical formulation in inventorying the De Noyan plantation: "Jupiter indigo-maker, confectioner" was listed just before "Jeanne Marie his wife, servant," and "François, butcher" was followed by "Catherine his wife, laundry." These people were itemized like property, serving as a reminder of the hard labor that undergirded the idyllic and not so idyllic features of the De Noyan plantation, with its pecan tree alley and garden flanked by an orchard and a terrace, its fields, indigo factory, bakehouse, blacksmith's shop, coach house, livestock, poultry houses, and washhouses. Beyond inventories, deeds of sale also confirm the existence of recognized family units that were sometimes, if very rarely, multigenerational. Among the numerous family units sold from the Dubreuil plantation in October 1758 were "one negro named François, his wife named Boguio, and his mother named Emé," who, together, fetched a price of seventy-eight hundred livres. Needless to say, such records of family units reveal perhaps more about those who inscribed such roles on enslaved peoples than how enslaved people themselves defined kinship.[36]

With the emergence of pronatalist policies aimed at promoting reproduction among slaves following the virtual end of the slave trade after 1731, masters pushed for the formation of family units among their own slaves. Manager of the king's plantation Antoine-Simon Le Page du Pratz was blunt in advising slaveowners to pair enslaved males on their plantation with a "femme": "Endeavor to assign each of them a wife, to keep clear of debauchery and its bad consequences. It is necessary that the negroes have wives, and you ought to know that nothing attaches them so much to a plantation as children." But his was a slaveowner's pragmatic perspective. Though Le Page du Pratz advocated enforcing monogamy, he did not specify whether he intended these relationships to be legal. Masters hoped that unions between enslaved people would lead to procreation, facilitate cooperation, prevent slave marronnage by keeping them anchored to plantations, and also provide an incentive for desirable behavior. As described by Sans-Soucy, when he narrated his master's attempt to impose on him a new wife from within his own plantation, and anticipated by Article 8 of the code noir, which forbade masters' from forcing their slaves into marriage, however, masters' authority could all too readily lead to coercive measures.[37]

Had Desruisseaux chosen to purchase Jean-Baptiste, he could well have conceived of the slaves marrying in the church. He already owned at least one enslaved couple who were legally married and had two children. Evidently respecting their integrity as a group, Desruisseaux hired them out together in 1744. Article 43 of the code noir prohibited the breaking up of legally sanctioned families owned by the same person, decreeing that "we desire nonetheless that the husband, his wife, and their prepubescent children shall not be seized and sold separately, if they belong to the same master: declaring null and void any seizures and separate sales that may have taken place." But the code noir said nothing about requiring that slaves be *leased* as family units. Even so, Desruisseaux seems to have followed the spirit of the law in this regard.[38]

The enslaved would have noticed how slaveowners kept legal families together. As couples like Jean-Baptiste and Kenet attempted to work within the system in order to live together, they undoubtedly factored in the protections afforded by church marriages. That Brazilier made moves to unite the pair by acquiring Kenet (or selling Jean-Baptiste to Kenet's owner) suggests that he foresaw a legal marriage. But he did not necessarily have to agree to one. Perhaps it was enough to placate Jean-Baptiste with the promise of cohabitation with Kenet on an isolated plot of land far from the curiosity and surveillance of the French.

At the same time that Kenet and Jean-Baptiste might have perceived the benefits of a marriage *"en face d'Eglise"* (in the face of the church) it is possible that they had already entered into another type of marriage, though one not sanctioned or deemed legitimate in the eyes of the French. Enslaved Africans did not merely accept, or adapt to, the imposition of French views of marriage. Instead, they were the bearers of inherited knowledge of forms of marriage originating in West Africa whose rituals and laws were similarly designed to legitimize permanent unions between men and women. These might include polygynous practices among slaves of Muslim ancestry, which also appear to have existed in the colony. The code noir forbid the exercise of any religion other than Catholicism, ordered that any assemblies linked to such religious practices—which of course included marriage ceremonies— be banned and declared seditious, and required that transgressors (and their masters, if they had permitted such assemblies) be punished. Yet there is no evidence that the Superior Council enforced the ban on religious practices, and colonists recognized slaves' participation in non-Catholic religious ceremonies, including those tied to marriage.[39]

When Bernard de Duvergé filed a declaration in 1747 attesting that two of his slaves, Coudou and Geneviève, had run away, he specified that they "are married in the manner of the *nègres"* since three or four months. Speculating about their motives for running away, Duvergé proposed that their action must have been taken out of fear of being whipped for "some fault committed in their work" *(pour faute Commises Dans Leur travail)* and disingenuously claimed not to know of any other possible reason. Leaving aside the reference to violence, Duvergé's choice of words betray another reality of daily life for the enslaved in colonial Louisiana: masters' sexual access to enslaved women, crystallized here in Duvergé's choice of attributes to characterize the runaways' physique. He described the forty-year-old Coudou as *"de moyenne taille,"* translated as "of medium build," but depicted Geneviève, aged about sixteen to eighteen, as *"D'une bell[e] taille,"* meaning she had a fine figure, a gendered and sexualized term that implicitly conveyed the predatory lens through which Duvergé evaluated the girl. The age difference between Coudou and Geneviève also opens the door for modern sensitivities to consider Coudou as a sexual predator. Juxtaposed against the evidence of Duvergé's gaze is proof of two slaves' determination to control their sexual and affective lives. First, they chose to make their union permanent by marrying independently of the consent of their master and of the church. Second, by fleeing

FIGURE 38: Unknown, *Deux Antillaises.* Late eighteenth century. Collection Chatillon
L-29. 2003.4.32. Courtesy of the Musée d'Aquitaine. Bordeaux, France
Though recently titled *Deux Antillaises,* the painting is of a man and woman.

together, they were in effect taking things one step further by planning to lead
an autonomous life together, one that they likely envisioned as graced with
children.[40]

A painting in the Musée d'Aquitaine, in Bordeaux, offers a visual counterpoint to the story of Geneviève and Coudou (Figure 38). Composed by an
unknown artist, it has recently, but incorrectly, been given a new title, *Deux
Antillaises,* that identifies the sitters as two women. Its previous title had been
Antillaise au plateau de fruits, or *West Indies woman with platter of fruit.* The
painting actually shows a representation of a man and a woman. The lighter-
skinned woman in the foreground, carrying two platters of fruit, is wearing a
red petticoat with a shift and bodice that have been pulled down to reveal one
breast. The sleeves of her shift have been fastened decoratively with a ribbon
while her shoulders are draped with a pale blue scallop-edged silk mantle, her

Kenet and Jean-Baptiste

attire accessorized with gold-tone drop earrings, a necklace, and a linen head-dress adorned with flowers. The darker-skinned figure in the background is unquestionably male. Carrying a stick under his arm (an implicitly threatening attribute), the man allows one hand to linger on the woman's shoulder while reaching behind her with his other hand to grab one of the pieces of fruit on her platter. He is wearing male garb, including a man's jacket in blue cloth, and, underneath, a linen shirt with gold tone cufflinks and a standing collar (unlike women's shifts, which had no collar and were cut lower to reveal the expanse of the chest, as seen on his companion). A flowing red hand-kerchief edged with two white stripes dangles from his jacket pocket, and the way he has styled his head wrap is consistent with the way these were worn by men in the Caribbean. Finally, deviating from European convention but likewise consistent with representations of enslaved men, his jacket and shirt are left open to reveal his chest (see Figure 32, for comparison). The painting channels the artist's gaze and, by extension, the gaze of white masters. Here is a representation of a light-skinned woman shown in the act of serving — profferring both fruit, a symbol of fertility in European art, and herself. The man crouches around her, seizing some of the fruit and her arm. At first glance, the man is brushed aside, delegitimized as a suitor: the woman and the platter are clearly not intended for him. Yet he is helping himself to both, lustily and slyly, in the artist's rendering. The humor of this scene notwith-standing, he poses a threat to white male viewers, the intended recipients of the woman's sexual and gustatory offerings, just as Coudou disrupts Duvergés's lusting after Geneviève by running away with her himself, leaving the empty-handed Duvergé to file a declaration of their marronnage. As for the woman in the painting, she looks straight at the viewer while leaning toward the man with a half smile. Neither her identity nor that of the man is known or even the names of the models who posed for the painting. Unlike the court records, which reveal something of Geneviève's and Kenet's emotions, the painting does not focus on how the woman feels.[41]

Though the French generally made explicit whether they were referring to Catholic or non-Catholic marriages, the enslaved seldom differentiated between the two. Interrogated in 1764 in connection with a gunshot fired at a colonist, the aptly named Jean Patissier, pastry maker to Sieur Amelot, gave as his alibi that he had been attending a slave wedding *("noce")*. He stated specifically "that around midnight he was at the back at Sr. Boussineau's to see two *nègres* fight and to separate them at the end of a nuptial, that two *negresses* named Magdelaine and Mathurine had also gone to see the said *nègres* fight" *(que cestoit trouvé Environ Minuit derriere chez le S Boussineau pour voir Battre deux negres et pour les Separer au Sortir d'une Noce, que deux negresse nommée Magdelaine et mathurine auroient été Egallement pour voir Battre les dits Negres).* Though "noce" was the term used for wedding feasts and other celebrations of marriage, it is impossible to know for certain what type of marriage he meant by that expression. When they spoke about their own relationships, enslaved men did, however, draw another distinction: that between the women they considered themselves married to (however they defined marriage) and their mistresses. In other words, they chiefly differentiated between temporary attachments and permanent conjugal-type attachments. One looming factor in this distinction was the inherent difficulty in gaining their masters' approval to contract a Catholic marriage, and it is noteworthy that most short-term relationships and temporary sexual encounters for which evidence remains had one factor in common: the couple belonged to different owners.[42]

In some cases, living on separate plantations might have offered a new set of opportunities, namely with respect to polygyny as practiced in the colony by Muslims or their descendants. Muslims, originating in Senegambia, were present in French Louisiana, though how well they could engage in religious practices is hard to gauge. Sometimes their religious affiliation was visible, as when they retained their names or honorific titles: a male Mamourou or Baraca (a religious title) here, a female Fatima there, names that individuals used when asked to identify themselves in court and that masters validated when they wrote them down in plantation inventories. But other possible identifying markers never surface. Female circumcision, for instance, is not documented, even in the context of masters' unfettered access to their slaves' bodies (for example when assessing a slave for purchase). This likely signifies that the practice was halted in Louisiana, probably as a confluence of slave-owners' overt disapprobation combined with the loss of the literal and metaphorical space for this initiation ritual to take place. Other Muslim or West African religious rites and practices, namely with respect to marriage, could have lingered on in altered form.[43]

Though enslaved individuals might have converted or been made to convert to Catholicism, there is evidence that some continued to find ways to practice polygyny, if unofficially. Joseph Léveillé, the Ursulines' (enslaved) overseer, was legally married to Victoire, one of the convent slaves, with whom he had a son, Louis. But he was also involved during the same time with a free woman, Marie-Thérèse Carrière, with whom he had a child. Emancipated in 1778, Léveillé married Carrière in 1786, following the death of Victoire. Conversely, if Sans-Soucy had been Muslim, he might have welcomed the possibility of forging a polygamous marriage with the woman that his master promised him while continuing his relationship with Pradel's slave, but,

Kenet and Jean-Baptiste

given that he vociferously rejected such a possibility, the odds are that he was not Muslim. If those owned by different masters hoped to regularize their unions according to French law and religion, rather than marry according to their own rites, however, they would find themselves caught in the same trap that Jean-Baptiste and Kenet tried to extricate themselves from.[44]

As enslaved people make clear in their testimony, marriage ceremonies were important not only as ritual observances but also because they served as sites of community support and sociability. Elder males seem to have acted as guardians of morality within enslaved communities, though their presence is only rarely glimpsed in the archives. Antoine Flatagué told court officials that earlier on the night François dit Baraca murdered his wife, Taco, he had first sought him out for marital advice (note the Creole): "That the *negre* Baraca came to find him in his cabin the night of the eighth to the ninth around eleven saying, give me some tobacco and we will smoke a pipe, that, having gone to the cabin of Baraca he [Baraca] cut a pipe of tobacco by the fireplace saying 'my wife always running to see a *negre* named Mamouroux even though I have forbidden her'" *(Que le negre Baraca est venu le trouver la nuit du huit au neuf sur les onze heures dans sa Cabane luy disant donne moy du tabac et nous fumerons la pipe quetant entré dans la cabanne de Baraca il a coupé une pipe de tabac pres du feu et qui luy disoit ma femme toujours à Courir pour voir un negre nommé mamouroux quoy que je luy ay defendu).* Though Baraca did end up killing Taco, he did not do so before reaching out to Flatagué so that the overseer could intercede between him and his wife. And, despite that Baraca was Muslim and Flatagué Bambara (and therefore non-Muslim), the man worked to keep the peace and good order in Baraca's household. Admonishing Baraca in Taco's presence against beating her, Flatagué asked him: "Why you angry since you have seen nothing, why you always shout and beat your wife? That is not good" *(que luy deposant Dit à Baraca pourquoy toy facher puisque tu nas rien Vu pourquoy toujour Crier Et Battre ta femme sans Raison Cela nest pas Bon).* Baraca did not heed the advice, but he did not reject Flatagué's right to counsel him either. Rather, he called him his "great friend" *(grand amy),* even when they were fighting about the murder.[45]

Marriage did not simply matter to masters seeking to assert control over their chattel nor did it only involve those who tied the knot and their offspring. Rather, marriage was a communal affair. It was just as vital for those slaves who witnessed, celebrated, or officiated at marriage ceremonies and for those kin members, elders, and other figures of spiritual and community authority who helped support marriage partners and steer their conduct in their married lives as it was to married couples themselves. When the enslaved attended marriage ceremonies, it was they who legitimized these unions, the direct involvement of masters in their slaves' love lives and the occasional role of Catholic clerics in sanctifying slaves' relationships notwithstanding.

❧❧

HOUSEHOLD LABOR: "STAYED AT THE
CABIN" AND "DID NOTHING"

At the same time that marriage operated as a tool of social order *within* slave communities, helping to cement and manage relations between a husband and his wife or wives, the testimony of Jean-Baptiste and Kenet suggests something more: that marriage (however defined and however celebrated) was also about domestic space. It was, of course, a site for physical and sexual intimacy, signaled by both Kenet and Jean-Baptiste in their references to their shared bed. Yet, if their depositions primarily narrate a story of attachment and commitment, Kenet and Jean-Baptiste's words also reveal something about how they conceived of work with regard to factors such as the structure of household labor and a man's right to benefit from his wife's labor.

When given the autonomy to create their own household, Kenet and Jean-Baptiste worked together to live according to their cultural understanding of what they considered the natural gendered division of labor in which women's work was primarily domestic, which is not to say easy. According to Jean-Baptiste, when asked "what he did with this *negresse* on Brazillier's habitation" *(cequil faisoit ávec cette Negresse sur l'habitation dudit Brazilier)*, he asserted that Kenet "stayed at the cabin and a few times went to work with him at the furnace" *(laditte negresse Restoit à la Cabane et que quelques fois alloit travailler avec luy au fourneau)*. When Kenet was asked what work she did, she answered "that she did nothing and that sometimes she looked after a desert [garden plot] that the *negre* [Jean-Baptiste] had cleared without Brazilier asking him to" *(a dit quelle ne faisoit Rien et quelle s'occupoit quelques fois à un dezer que le negre avoit fait, sans que Brazilier luy ait Jamais Rien Commandé)*. "Stayed at the cabin" and "did nothing": neither Kenet nor Jean-Baptiste claimed that she did any real labor, beyond the few times she went to work at the furnace. Perhaps they did not want to implicate Brazilier (who benefited from her labor). But there was a contradiction in how they characterized her work and the actual activities that filled her day, a distinction that merits closer scrutiny.[46]

When asked later on in the same interrogation to enumerate his master's livestock, Jean-Baptiste listed twenty-two head of cattle at the Chef Menteur plantation, along with nine goats, six laying hens, and a cockerel. In accordance with both African and European notions of the gendered division of labor, Kenet was likely the one who took care of the livestock, just as it

Kenet and Jean-Baptiste

was she, by her own account, who cultivated their garden plot, once Jean-Baptiste had cleared the land. Indeed, while Kenet spoke of working on their "dezer," Jean-Baptiste did not bring up that detail when asked about her activities, an omission that took place in a very specific context structured by the forced labor exacted from enslaved women in Louisiana.[47]

When prompted to introduce herself at the onset of her interrogation, Kenet listed her occupation as "piocheuse," loosely translated as one who digs (a *pioche* is a pickax). It was not a term in common usage in Louisiana's written records, but it clearly represented the way she and her master understood her primary occupation. As a field laborer, Kenet was relegated to the bottom of the occupational hierarchy, tasked with hard labor, deemed unskilled, and deprived of formal authority. Slaveholders (and managers or overseers) controlled their slaves' labor and allocated their tasks and responsibilities. Typically, masters upheld European notions of sexual difference when assigning slaves supervisory positions or occupational specialization. With few exceptions, women were excluded from most positions of leadership (and never put in charge over men). They were also seldom given training in the kinds of occupations that conferred status as a result of being deemed specialized or skilled and reserved for men. Slaveholders did, however, suspend their own cultural beliefs about what constituted appropriate gendered divisions of labor when it meant they could extract the maximum productivity from their slaves, irrespective of their sex. So, if they could not as a general principle imagine most European women capable of hard labor, they gradually allowed themselves to believe that African women were. As Kenet, "piocheuse," experienced in mid-eighteenth-century Louisiana, masters did not exempt enslaved women from the same hard physical labor to which they subjected their enslaved males.[48]

Kenet's occupation as an enslaved female field laborer provides the context for the way the couple defined her activities when "free." In portraying her as not engaged in productive labor of any sort (staying at home and doing nothing), the couple was implicitly commenting on the divergence between Kenet's work practices when under the direct yoke of slavery and those when she was cohabiting with Jean-Baptiste. In effect, by leaving her master's household to go settle with Jean-Baptiste, Kenet accessed a different cultural compass for women's productive labor. Though both Kenet and Jean-Baptiste were born in the colony, living together at Chef Menteur enabled them to recreate West African domestic arrangements and gendered work practices that were also similar to ones that their masters performed in their own households. White women (depending on their status) might engage in the often arduous and certainly monotonous drudgery of food preparation, cleaning, laundry, tending vegetable plots, and caring for livestock. But, as a rule, they were not put to work doing the hard labor of the fields and plantations. Kenet and Jean-Baptiste's narratives offer clues about how this enslaved couple envisioned an appropriate domestic arrangement as one in which women's work was limited to household activities.

Kenet's and Jean-Baptiste's labor preferences find sometimes surprising and uncanny echoes in the records pertaining to other slaves who found ways to construct autonomous households. Among these were maroons in the French colonies of the Caribbean and Indian Ocean. Their testimony provides a broader sweep from which to consider Kenet and Jean-Baptiste's experiences. The French distinguished between two types of running away. *Grand* (major) marronnage was used when fugitives, who had no intention of returning, grouped themselves into bands, in contrast to shorter-term, or *petit* (minor), marronnage. But the distinction was only encoded in the code noir with reference to the length of time a slave had run away; the expressions "grand" and "petit" marronnage do not appear in that document, and these precise terms were not in common usage in Louisiana. The concept of marronnage relied on stereotypes that seep through the documents, informing the actions of investigators and the questions of interrogators. Yet the testimony of maroon men and women signal that maroon bands enforced their own, very specific gender roles, and that these had cultural meaning for them, distinct from the way the French interpreted such actions.[49]

In Martinique in September 1711, Laurence, a twenty-five-year-old Creole, was captured along with eight other maroons, one of whom she designated as her mate. She stated that she had run away about a year earlier after her master had burned down her cabin. Her testimony was not clear-cut. On the one hand, she spoke of being confined under threat and duress (whether real or not, it must have seemed a reasonable defense to proffer), saying that "the woods are big, that she would not be able to get out, and that the said Hierosme had threatened her that if she left, he would kill her on the road" *(le bois est grand, qu'elle n'auroit pas peu en sortir, et que le dit hierosme l'avoit menassé que si elle sortoit, il la tuëroit dans le Chemin)*. On the other hand, she seemed to accept the need to follow the rules of the camp, as seen when the interrogation veered toward elucidating what they had subsisted on during their marronnage. Laurence stated that they had stolen plantains and bananas until such time as they had made a "garden in the woods" *(un jardin dans le Bois)*—just like Kenet and Jean-Baptiste had cleared a vegetable patch. When the interrogators, possibly drawing on prior knowledge, followed up by asking her a leading question about the maroons trading some of their produce—"with which of the *nègres* from this borough did they trade for vegetables from their garden?" *(avec quels negres de ce bourg ils negotioient les legumes de leur jardin)*—Laurence claimed she did not know:

> Answered that she does not know where the *negres* went when they left [the camp] because when they returned they did not want to tell the women, and that she, respondent, and the two other *negresses* never left their dwelling.

> A repondu qu'elle ne sçait pas où les negres alloient quand ils alloient dehors parcequ'ils ne leur voulloient pas dire à leur retour, et qu'elle repondante et les deux autres negresses ne sortoient jamais de leur ad-joupa

Laurence had originally run away of her own volition, but, once in the maroon camp, she seemed to acquiesce to males imposing limitations on her movements when it was for the good of the maroon community, such as provisioning the camp.[50]

Laurence was not the only maroon woman who spoke of being confined by maroon men to camp. In the former French colony of Isle de France (present-day Mauritius), a similar occurrence seems to have developed in which women likewise claimed to have been sequestered, sometimes by force. In that colony, there was a long-term pattern of court cases in which enslaved women accused of marronnage instead described themselves as powerless to resist physical and sexual subjugation within communities of maroon slaves. Much of this testimony was questionable and smacked of strategic maneuvering, but not always. In a 1751–1752 case, the Malagasy slave Cupidon stated that his assignment in the maroon band was to stand guard over an abducted woman he identified as the "femme" of the chief of the maroon camp (she had ostensibly been seized from another maroon band after a battle over her):

> Interrogated, speaking through the interpreter, if he had not been at Sr. Desvaux's with the others?
>
> Responded, speaking through the interpreter, that he had not gone there, that he along with a Mozambique [slave] had stayed at the hut to keep watch on the woman of Mahere.

> Interrogé par la bouche de l'interprette s'il n'a pas été chez le sr Desveaux avec les autres

A repondu par la bouche de l'interprette qu'il n'y a point été qu'il estoit resté à la caze pour garder la femme de Mahere avec un Mozambique

It was Cupidon who explicitly described the maroon leader, Mahere, putting a woman—specifically, the woman he claimed as his own—under guard. But coercion was not always a factor in these confinements, and other female runaways in Isle de France, just like Laurence in Martinique and Kenet in Louisiana, willingly stayed within their compound and did not partake of the mobility available to male runaways. In 1747, another runaway in Isle de France, who was Malagasy, asserted that she had not gone off to steal food like the others but instead had remained in the hut that the maroons had built in the woods.[51]

What emerges through all of this testimony, time and time again, is a sense of women's acceptance of different rules for male and female maroons. Whatever the motive, whether in Louisiana, Martinique, or the Mascareignes Islands, coerced or not, womenfolk remained in the vicinity of maroon compounds and did not venture out like male runaways. In some cases, there seems to have been coercion. In other cases, the impetus stemmed from notions (ubiquitous across West Africa, East Africa, Madagascar, and their diasporas) about women's roles and women's work also consistent with conventions in parts of West Africa where men conducted long-distance commerce and women local trade. And, if within the space of the maroon band, mobility itself was gendered, there was a practical as well as symbolic purpose to having women who "stayed" at home.[52]

Just as Jean-Baptiste and Kenet sidestepped the matter of her work, none of the testimony presented in the maroon cases above was explicit in describing what exactly these runaway women *did* while they "stayed at the cabin" or "never left their dwelling." But another case involving enslaved Africans provides an explanation of what exactly was in play: cultural understandings originating in West Africa surrounding the organizing principles of their societies as achieved through the gendered way that household tasks were allocated.

"I AM HUNGRY GIVE ME TO EAT"

The 1748 New Orleans court case brought against François dit Baraca for killing his wife, Taco, brings into sharp relief how important it was to the enslaved to maintain cultural and gendered practices pertaining to food preparation and eating. In describing the events that led to Taco's murder, two of

Kenet and Jean-Baptiste

the witnesses referenced the couple's domestic affairs. One was Antoine Fla-tagué, who had sought to counsel Baraca to stop beating his wife. The other was the couple's frequent guest, Joseph Laoursot. Laoursot recounted the events that took place in their cabin on the night of the murder as follows:

> Deposed that the night of the eighth day of this month after work and after the sun had set, the deponent went into the cabin of where he usually went, he found the wife of Baraca who was shucking corn, that her husband having entered at the same time, he said to his wife, "I am hungry give me to eat." That the wife immediately left her work to give him the gruel she had made, that he began to eat and said to Mamou-rou, who was there to eat with him, that the said Mamouroux began to eat with him, that the wife of the said Baraca continued to shuck her corn, that the said Baraca, having eaten, said to his wife, "Give me my pipe so I can smoke," to which the wife of Baraca answered back, "Do I have the pipe? I do not know what you've done with it," that he said to her, "Well then give me yours," that she answered him back, "Go get it from where it is behind the barrel."

> ---

> Depose que Le soir huit de Ce mois apres avoir travaillé Et que Le So-leil Etoit Couché Luy deposant Entra dans la Cabanne de Baraca où il Va ordinairement Il trouva la femme de Baraca qui Etoit apres Egrener du mahy que son mary Etant Entré dans le même moment Il Dit à Sa femme Jay faim donne moy à manger, que la femme quitta à linstant Son ouvrage pour Luy donner à manger de la Boullie quelle avoit fait quil se mit à manger Et dit à mamourou qui Etoit là de manger avec Luy que led. mamouroux se mit à manger avec Luy que la femme dud. Baraca Continua d'egrener son mahy, que led. Baraca ayant mangé dit à Sa femme donne moy ma pipe que Je fume à quoy la femme de Baraca Luy Repondit Est Ce que Jay la pipe Je ne scait pas Ce que tu en as fait quil Luy dit hebien donne moy La tienne quelle Luy repondit Va La prendre là derriere Le Baril où Elle Est

This exchange was rife with tension, yet it also illustrates the rhythm of women's work days, which did not end at dusk as it did for men, since food preparation ensued.[55]

The night she was killed, Taco was engaged in shucking corn (prepara-tory to grinding it for cornmeal), what Laoursot described as her *"ouvrage,"* or housework. Asked by her husband to serve him his food, she immedi-ately did as told, leaving aside the shucking to serve him a meal consisting of *"bouillie,"* a cornmeal gruel that she perhaps seasoned and cooked like the corn, rice, millet, or couscous dishes eaten in Senegambia. She also provided the meal to other enslaved males who had come to the cabin to eat, as they apparently did on a regular, if not daily, basis. Taco did not eat with the men. Though her ethnicity was not given, her husband was identified as being of the Poulard nation (Fulbe). Her husband's given French name was François, but his fellow slaves and officials called him Baraca, an Islamic religious title. He stated that "he has been baptized," but his conversion might have been perfunctory, if not forced, as he seems to have retained his identity and standing as a Muslim spiritual leader. Ironically, though he was Muslim and might have expected, as a male, to be polygamous, it was in fact his wife who seemed to have more than one male sexual partner. Nonetheless, in his household, not only did Taco comply with West African practices pertaining to women's responsibility for food preparation, she also observed the customary segregation of the sexes at mealtimes, waiting for the men to finish eating before she began her meal.[54]

Writing about women from Senegambia (in an account published in 1728), Father Jean Baptiste Labat described how it was their duty to thresh the rice, corn, and millet; prepare all the food; gather the firewood; fetch the water; and clean the house as well as spin and dye cloth, make the clothes, grow the tobacco and crops, and look after the cattle. Pertinently, not only were women "in charge of all the work of the household," but a wife ate "after her husband has taken his supper." Furthermore, "when their husbands are holding conversations," he observed, wives were expected to "chase away the mosquitoes that bother them, and present their pipes and tobacco to them." Nonetheless, he added that, in spite of the supremacy of males, women found ways to assert themselves. He might well have been describing Taco: laboring for the household, dropping everything to serve Baraca his meal, yet haughty enough to talk back to him and tell him to fetch his own pipe. The tension between them might have been long-standing, but, that night, she would die for it.[55]

No other testimony so explicitly documents women's segregation from men. But many other trial records reference women's exclusive responsibility for food preparation and other domestic labor within household spaces exclusively occupied by the enslaved. This gender segregation extended to food consumption practices that were often communal. In the 1750s, many witnesses testified to the activities of Marion, a powerful enslaved Creole woman who ran a well-organized (if illicit) business that traded goods between French Natchitoches and Spanish Los Adaes. As Estienne, one young male accomplice expressed, she "often gave him to eat." He added that he was not alone in this, for, as he relayed, "we often ate at Marion's" *(l'on mangeoit sou-*

vent chez ladtte Marion); and, indeed, among other dishes, she served grilled chicken as well as *croquignole* (biscuits) and beignets (doughnuts) made with flour and sugar stolen from her master. Similarly when the runaway Louis was asked in 1764 to confirm if had slept with Comba (and another woman), they first asked if she had not served him gumbo. He replied that it was false that he slept with her but acknowledged that "he ate with her from the time that her husband lived and before he had gone up to the Illinois Country but since he has come back he has not set foot there" *(a Dit que Cela etoit faux quil mangeoit chez elle du tems que son mari vivoit et avant quil ne montat aux illinois mais que depuis quil est dessendu il n'y a pas mis Le pied).* Sans-Soucy, whose master beat him for going to see his wife everyday (and not accepting a new wife on his own plantation), very likely took his meals during his visits to see her and considered himself head of her household, in contradiction with French views and laws on the matter.[56]

Testimony was sprinkled with such allusions to women providing men, including unattached men, with food that they prepared, seasoned, and served in their own quarters. The conspicuousness of women in this role helps to envisage how the enslaved organized themselves into familial and social units. Demographically, enslaved women were in the majority in New Orleans's urban areas, and men were in the majority in outlying and plantation areas. But if enslaved men had little choice but to come to town for women, they also sought out female companionship as a practical way of accessing tastier cooked meals. If part of a sexual relationship, the gift of food was usually matched by men's reciprocal gift giving of apparel and jewelry. But, as the example from Natchitoches (where Marion fed the young Estienne, among others) shows, the special sociability inherent in these meals was also at times cross-generational and nonsexual.[57]

Women did prepare food for men from outside of their immediate communities, whether these communities were bound by kin or work. But for a man to have his own wife (however defined) cook for him and run his household put him in a separate category. When in his 1765 trial Essom explained through his interpreter that he had run away because his master had taken away his "woman / wife," he was careful to specify her role: she was the one given him to "prepare his drink and food." For Essom, a wife's role as food provider was her chief responsibility; it even explained how he verbalized the loss of her presence, namely, as the loss of a cultural system in which he was the beneficiary of his woman's domestic labor. As for Baraca, he could command his wife, Taco, to drop everything and serve him his food. He could also demand that she feed his guests—Laoursot after all had testified that on the night of the murder "he went to Baraca's cabin *where he usually went*" *(luy deposant entra dans la cabanne de Baraca où il va ordinairement).* He was not alone. Mamouroux (also a Muslim name) was already there, waiting for Baraca's invitation to partake of the food that Taco had cooked, and Baraca did invite him to eat, even though he believed his wife had slept with the man.[58]

This deeply embedded practice of women preparing food for men provides a key backdrop to Jean-Baptiste and Kenet's characterization of her activities at Chef Menteur—that she primarily "stayed at the cabin" or "did nothing"—which stood in stark contrast with the gender-blind workloads that white masters customarily imposed on female slave laborers such as the "piocheuse" Kenet. Jean-Baptiste had been sent to labor on a secluded plantation, his rations given to him once a month in the form of half a barrel of shucked corn and one barrel of unshucked corn. He knew that, among other benefits, once he had secured Kenet and her labor—shucking and grinding maize and cooking their food using the vegetables she had grown in the garden plot he had cleared, supplemented with any fish or game he had caught and other staples traded with the neighboring Indian settlements around Lake Pontchartrain—his meals would be taken care of. It was only together that they could enact the household and gender roles that they deemed appropriate and that allowed them to restore order to domestic arrangements within their cabin. In having Kenet keep house for him, Jean-Baptiste could assert his masculine authority as the head of his household, and, henceforth, it was he who would commandeer all his wife's labor, free of any interference from his or her owners. Aside from their mutual longing for each other, these hard-held cultural conceptions of gender were also factors in the couple's quest to be permanently united.[59]

By having Kenet join him at Chef Menteur, Jean-Baptiste in effect extricated her from the hard labor of the fields and from plantation labor structures as well as from the sexual attentions of any predatory colonists. The contours of their union were sexual and affective but also anchored in a desire for day-to-day companionship and a suitable domestic arrangement; they were, in essence, in a "committed conjugal relationship." If their masters did not acquiesce to a sale that would be mutually beneficial for them both, then they would use any other means necessary to achieve the desired outcome, including highly risky maneuvers that could put them in jeopardy.[60]

"TASKS SUITABLE FOR WOMEN"

In their ability to order the domestic division of labor within their household while at Chef Menteur, Kenet and Jean-Baptiste's circumstances as runaways

Kenet and Jean-Baptiste

were not altogether distinct from those of free blacks who could likewise exert relative independence in terms of managing their own households. In every case where a free black in Louisiana entered into negotiations for his wife's freedom, his first priority was to wrest authority from her master and establish *his* control over her labor. On paper, these contracts were settled by men, not least because in these instances it was the men who were free and therefore the only ones able by law to enter into contracts. There is no reason, however, to believe that women were silent partners in these manumission negotiations.

In 1725, in the midst of a desperate struggle to find an executioner to carry out judicial sentences in a fledgling colony filled with exiled convicts, Company of the Indies officials eventually proposed hiring "Louis Congo *nègre,* belonging to the Company plantation, strong and vigorous" *(Louis Congo negre appartenant à la Compagnie sur son habitation fort et robuste),* to serve as the public executioner. They agreed to manumit him in exchange for taking the position. Recognizing his advantage in the negotiation, Louis Congo refused to accept their offer of freedom unless his wife was also manumitted, and he promptly made a number of specific demands, likely with her input. An official from the Superior Council of Louisiana left a description of the long, drawn-out haggling over terms:

> He requests his freedom and that of his wife, and a complete ration in goods and drink for himself only, also that we give him a plot of land, separate from the habitants which he will work for his own account and on which he will establish himself and his wife, also *negresse* belonging to the King.

> ----

> il demande sa Liberté et celle de sa femme et la Ration complette en vivres et Boisson pour luy Seullement, outre qu'on luy donne un terrain à luy en propre, et separé des habitans sur lequel il s'establira luy et sa femme aussy negresse appartenant à la Compagnie sur lequel il travaillera pour son Compte

After discussing the relative cost of freeing two slaves in light of the urgent need for an executioner, the council agreed to all of Louis Congo's demands They granted him his freedom along with a complete ration plus a plot of land measuring two arpents (about 1.6 acres) and set out a schedule of fees for each type of judicial punishment he would carry out. Finally, they "granted him his wife to live with him without the Company using her at its service" *(luy laisse sa femme pour habiter avec luy sans que la Compagnie l'employe à son service).*[61]

In a separate missive, *Commissaire-ordonnateur* Jacques de La Chaise, the highest-ranking administrator in the colony, commented on the *"belle negresse"* (beautiful *negresse)* who had been freed as part of the deal with the new executioner, omitting any information on the couple's attachment beyond an assumption about physical attraction. But, for Louis Congo, the key factor in his negotiation was for his wife to live with him without having to do any labor for the company. Henceforth, any work she did was for the benefit of his household. This arrangement would have suited both him and his wife, as it was one familiar from their own upbringing in West Africa. At the same time, one can only imagine the satisfaction that Louis Congo and his unnamed wife felt in successfully rejecting the work regime that the French had imposed on her and, by extension, on other enslaved women.[62]

When John Mingo, the free English-speaking runaway from Carolina, entered into his marriage contract with the enslaved Thérèse on November 28, 1727, with the permission of Sieur Darby, the director of the concession that owned her, he also negotiated for her freedom. The document specified the terms whereby Mingo would redeem her at a price of fifteen hundred francs. He would pay as much as he could each year toward her purchase, during which time her owner would cover her food and clothing rations "equal to those of the other slaves of the concession" *(Comme aux autre Esclaves de la dit. Consession).* John Mingo made sure to obtain an English translation of the document, and he was right to have done so, for the contract would become part of the contentious legal dispute with Darby over Thérèse's freedom. Beyond ensuring her manumission, he, too, was preoccupied with his wife's labor. In 1729, before he had finished paying off her freedom price, Mingo entered into a labor contract for himself and his wife in which he stipulated that Thérèse would only "work at tasks suitable for women" *(travailler aux ouvrages convenables aux femmes).* Not only did he subscribe to gendered notions of what was suitable women's work, but he and his wife also sought, through marriage, to extricate her from the hard labor that enslaved women were customarily subjected to. In the process, Mingo reasserted his notion of manhood and of masculine authority, and they each found the means to attain their desired family configuration. Though Thérèse was born in Africa and Kenet was Creole, in the absence of Thérèse's own words in the documentary record, the latter's testimony suggests that women did not contest their menfolk's view that a wife's labor belonged to their partners; indeed, Kenet's words indicate that she and Jean-Baptiste shared this perspective and worked together to uphold it.[63]

There are two other extant agreements in which free black males negotiated the purchase of enslaved women. In 1744, François Tiocou committed to work for seven years at the hospital to redeem Marie Haran. Tiocou had been emancipated as a result of his military service in the 1737–1740 Chickasaw War and was a member of the free black militia in New Orleans. Along with other Africans who had been manumitted for the same reason, he settled on the land granted to these men in 1744 at the English Turn, just south of New Orleans. But, though the French had manumitted the enslaved men who had helped them win a war against Indians, they gave no thought to their women-folk. It was not enough for Tiocou to be free, and it was not by accident that, as soon as he was able, he lobbied and negotiated the terms of his wife's free-dom. Whether there were any children is unclear, as neither the French nor Tiocou mentioned any in their negotiation. Though less is known regarding the story of Jean-Baptiste Marly and his wife, Venus, he similarly agreed in 1745 to work three years as a cook at Pointe Coupée to redeem her.[64]

Although neither of these two manumission documents make an explicit reference to the labor conditions of the women in question, it can be conjec-tured that these men did in fact share the same worldview as Louis Congo and John Mingo: that having a freed wife was not simply about love and attach-ment but also about obtaining the rights to her labor. When given autonomy to regulate their own households, whether legally (through manumission and sanctioned marriage among free blacks) or illicitly (through running away, abduction, or marronnage), African-born males and those of African-descent sought and fought to assume control of the labor of their female partners. It was not a coincidence that free blacks who negotiated for their wives' free-dom also entered into agreements pertaining to their work. That they did so corroborates the evidence that Jean-Baptiste and Kenet linked having a wife with the possession of her labor.

There is nothing to suggest that any of these soon-to-be manumitted women disagreed with their husbands over the cultural appropriation of their labor; on the contrary, they likely were instrumental in laying out the strate-gies for negotiating the terms of their emancipation. As for their adhesion to Catholic marriage rites, was this just perfunctory? Certainly they knew the benefits that accrued in Louisiana to those who married in the Catho-lic Church, and not to do so if given the opportunity would have been fool-hardy. Jean-Baptiste Marly and Venus, François Tiocou and Marie Haran, Jean Mingo and Thérèse, Louis Congo and his "belle negresse" were all mar-ried according to French and Catholic law. Just as these couples resorted to French law to negotiate labor contracts and manumissions, they each looked to church marriages to legitimize their unions in the eyes of the French. In so doing, they ensured that their wives and children could benefit from the vital rights that were laid out in Article 34 of the code noir. Yet, as the free Jean

Baptiste found out in 1743 when he was convicted of the theft of fine shirts and handkerchiefs, in consequence of which his freedom was rescinded, the freedom of Africans was never absolute but conditional and revocable. There is no trace of the words of any of the women manumitted by marriage. Kenet's narrative stands apart. It was with her full cooperation that Jean-Baptiste extracted her from slavery, paving the way for a gendered division of labor that was more desirable and satisfying to both parties because it was compatible with West African norms.[65]

Kenet and Jean-Baptiste could not bear to live without each other. Theirs was a love story for the ages, and they acted truly, madly, and deeply in love. Through their actions and their words, these two individuals articulated how they envisioned freedom when they lived as a family unit. Some enslaved individuals would access a degree of self-determination as a result of manumission or of attaining status as skilled or supervisory workers. Others, like Jean-Baptiste and Kenet, achieved relative autonomy by running away and establishing quasi-independent households. Their story is above all one of long-term attachment, though the intimacy they sought transcended the emotional, physical, and sexual. It is their testimony in court that illuminates the magnitude of what was at stake for them, that which so many other couples might have longed for if not accomplished: emotional attachment, sexual desire, physical proximity, autonomy to organize their household labor, and the ability to sleep together every night "in their bed at the door of their cabin."

The court issued its ruling on August 13, 1767. Jean-Baptiste was convicted of concealment and Kenet of running away. Pending the prosecutor general's ultimate judgment (the final sentence is not known), Jean-Baptiste was given a provisional sentence, one that was psychological rather than physical. He was condemned to be attached to the back of a cart so that he could witness Kenet's punishment up close, a sentence that must have felt unbearable. And this is what he was made to witness: Kenet "beaten with sticks in every corner of the town then brought back to the Place [d'armes] to be branded with a fleur-de-lis on the right shoulder, before being returned to her master." No more is known about Kenet or Jean-Baptiste after this point.[66]

On the same day that the court pronounced its sentence against the lovers, it also rendered judgment in a case against two white men, André Rose and Guillaume Jaisant, "vagabonds sans aveü" (vagabonds of no known abode), who were accused of theft at night. They, too, had been interrogated "on the sellette," and both men were convicted. Jaisant was condemned to perpetual banishment from Louisiana. Rose was sentenced to be beaten with sticks in

Kenet and Jean-Baptiste

every corner of the town, then returned to the main square to be branded with the letter "V" (for *"voleur,"* or thief) and sent to the galleys for five years, which in reality meant that he was condemned to forced labor at the (ostensibly) fortified island of La Balise that guarded the entrance to the Mississippi River from the Gulf (Figure 36).[67]

Kenet's corporal punishment was virtually identical to that of a French man. But there was one key difference in the sentencing of the free and the enslaved. Whereas Jaisant was banned in perpetuity from the colony and Rose sentenced to the galleys for five years, Kenet received a sentence consistent with the differences in how "white" and "black" lives (to hew to the 1724 code noir's terminology) were valued: she was returned to her owner and to hard labor; her enslavement was hereditary and meant to last her lifetime. The stakes for enslaved women and men were that much higher than for whites. Yet, for at least fourteen years, Kenet and Jean-Baptiste took their chances. And, for eight months, Kenet succeeded in living with Jean-Baptiste, "stayed at the cabin," "did nothing," and every night, slept with him "in their bed."

Epilogue
Toward an Intellectual Critique of Slavery?

DEPOSITION OF FRANÇOIS-XAVIER, MOBILE, AUGUST 13, 1753
Deposes on the facts mentioned in the complaint of the acting attorney
general, which we have read to him, that last Saturday 4th of this month
at around four o'clock in the evening the deponent was pulling stakes by
order of his master. He noticed a soldier who had placed his kit around
the neck of a mare belonging to Madame Parent and, having made the
mare drop down into an old lean-to surrounded by stakes that used to
serve as a tannery, tied the said mare to a stake with his kit. The soldier
then climbed onto two stakes arranged [in an "x"] behind the mare.
The said deponent, not knowing what the said soldier intended to do
with this mare, approached the hut quietly and recognized the said
André Baron, soldier in the Company of Favrot, who had his breeches
undone and his organ in the nature of the said mare, holding the tail of
said mare in his right hand. That the said deponent, seized with horror at such an act, wanted at first to throw himself on [Baron] but that,
since he could not do this, he slipped away very quietly. Running into
the said Leidek, he told him to go and see what was going on in the hut.
That the said deponent, having then gone back to his master, recounted
what he had seen in the hut, which made La Ferme, his master, curious
to go the next day to look at the hut, where he saw the heap of stakes in
the same way that the said Baron had put them.

Depose sur les faits mentionnes en la plainte du substitut du procureur
g[eneral] du Roy de laquelle Luy avons fait lecture que le samedy quatre de ce mois environ quatre heures et demy du soir le Deposant etant
apres à arracher des pieux à l'Œ par ordre de son maître il aurois aperçu
un soldat qui avoir passé son fourniment au col d'une jument apparte-

nante à la De Parent qu'ayant fait chuter lade Jument dans un mauvais apenti entouré de pieux servant autrefois de tannerie et ayant attaché lade jument à un pieu avec ledt fourniment auroit ensuite monté dessus deux pieux qui etoit en sautoire derriere lade jument que ledt deposant ne sçachant pas ce que led. Soldat pouvoit faire avec cette jument il se seroit approché doucement de lad'e cabanne et auroit reconnu le Né André Baron soldat de la Comp[agnie] de favrot lequel avoit ses Culottes defaites Et son membre dans la nature de la d[ite] Jument tenant de sa main droite La Queue de la d[ite] Jument, que ledt Deposant saisy d'horreur d'une pareille action Voulu d'abord se jetter sur luy, ce que n'ayant pu faire Il s'eloigna bien doucement et ayant recontré le Né Leidek il luy auroit dit d'aller voir ce qui se passait dans ladte cabanne, que led. Deposant etant rentré chez son maître il luy autoit conté ce quil avoit vu dans ladte cabanne, ce qui donna La curiosité aud. Laferme son maître d'aller voir le lendemain lad[ite] cabanne où il avoit trouvé les echaffaudages en la meme situation que le dt Baron les avoit mis[1]

In August 1753, rumor began to circulate around Mobile that a French soldier, André Baron, had committed the crime of bestiality with a mare. François-Xavier, an enslaved African and the sole eyewitness, had stumbled on the soldier in the act, having first watched perplexed as the soldier led the mare into a hut and tied her up before climbing up behind the animal with his breeches undone. Word had got around town because, while François-Xavier had been so "seized with horror at such an act" that he "wanted at first to throw himself on [Baron]," the slave did not, in fact, confront the soldier at the time but instead "slipped away very quietly" and went on to tell a slew of people about what he had seen. He told a passerby and his master immediately. Several days later, as the news spread through Mobile, Baron sought out François-Xavier to get him to reassure the other soldiers that he was innocent of the crime. The enslaved man, however, related once again, directly to the soldiers this time, what he had seen: Baron poised on stakes behind the mare with his breeches undone. Shortly after François-Xavier denounced him in front of his peers, Baron fled, was captured on neighboring Dauphine Island (Figure 39), and then prosecuted, thanks to the deposition that François-Xavier provided.

In this highly unusual court case, François-Xavier provided his audience with a window into his immediate reaction to Baron's act. François-Xavier's actions—or, especially, lack thereof—signal how he made sense of his world and his place within it and, especially, how well he understood the limits im-

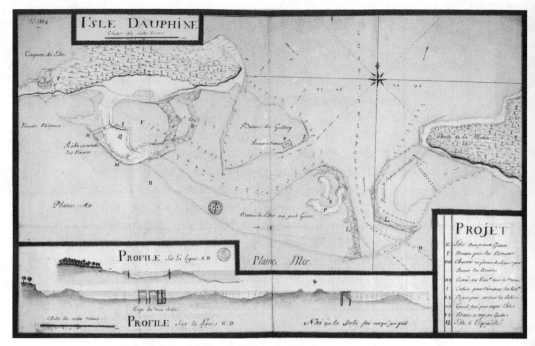

FIGURE 39: Unknown, *Plan [et deux profils] d'une partie de l'isle Dauphine jusqu'à la pointe de la Mobile.* Circa 1737. FR ANOM 04 DFC 133A.
Courtesy Archives nationales d'outre-mer, Aix-en-Provence, France

posed on his person because of his status as a slave. By stepping away from the specific allegation against Baron and parsing what François-Xavier tried to convey about his demeaning day-to-day experiences of enslavement, it is possible to recognize once again how testimony served as a form of autobiographical expression. Clearly this is not autobiography in the strict sense of a literary narrative arc of one lifespan, but it is nevertheless intrinsically personal. Spoken in the moment, often in mere slivers, testimony like François-Xavier's reminds us to consider how—and why—some enslaved individuals spoke, often so candidly, about *themselves*. Each of the various Frenchmen who testified, evaluated the slave's account, or judged the court case acknowledged François-Xavier's role in shaping the narrative. They did so even though his status as an enslaved man would be incessantly invoked as reason enough to discount his word. As for François-Xavier himself, his words reveal how tenaciously he strove to keep the focus on his own humanity, his character, and his honor.

Whether telling his story in the community or in the courtroom, François-Xavier insisted on expressing himself, on conveying—repeatedly—how strongly he had reacted to what he characterised as a horrific act. He did not limit himself to describing but persisted in passing judgement. At every opportunity, he brought up the sight of Baron with his "breeches lowered and in the act" *(ses Culottes bas et étant dans L'action)*. Seizing the moral high ground, he not only testified about Baron's crime in court, but he also informed the court that he had recounted what he had seen to a whole series of colonists: starting with a bystander, Conrad Leideck, then his master, Pierre Ignace Bardet Laferme, the royal surgeon at Mobile. These two individuals testified, and each corroborated that he had talked to them about the incident. Finally, he told his story to a group of soldiers, which they, too, would corroborate. No doubt he told others.[2]

Once he began testifying in court, François-Xavier went further in emphasizing the moral gulf that separated him from Baron by asserting that he had refused Baron's attempt to buy his silence. François-Xavier gave very precise details of that exchange, stating that the accused had come to find him and said to him, "Here my friend, if you want to not tell I will give you one piastre that I earned from Mr. Blouin for eight days' work for him" *(tiens mon amy si tu veux ne le pas dire je te donnerai une piastre que j'ay de gagné chez M. Blouin pour avoir travaillé pres de huit jours chez luy)*. That particular sentence was underlined in the trial record. Baron did not deny offering money but explained that the money was to pay François-Xavier for a "cure," which had failed. Under interrogation on the *sellette* (a special interrogation conducted in the prison so named for the low stool on which the defendant was made to sit), Baron added that "he had told the said *negre* that he would never give him anything because he had not cured him" *(il avoit dit audt negre, quil ne luy donnerois jamais rien parcequ'il ne l'avoit pas guery)*. Baron never did explain what the cure was for or what the treatment consisted of. Baron's master was the royal surgeon, and, perhaps, like Jean-Baptiste at the Ursuline convent, he had received training in French medical techniques or brought his own knowledge of healing practices to his work. It is also conceivable, given the circumstances, that François-Xavier had offered to cure the soldier, not of a physical problem, but one of a sexual nature.[3]

François-Xavier told the court that he had in fact rejected the bribe because the crime was "too atrocious." Yet he seems to have continued to interact with Baron because the two men appeared together to address the soldiers. According to François-Xavier's detailed account, "The following Friday, word having spread of this act, and the soldiers who were [Baron's] friends having reproached him on the subject, the said Baron had come to find the deponent at his master's to beg him to come to the fort to tell his friends that he had only seen him pull horsehair from the tail of the said mare and that he would give him a piastre from his ration" *(que le vendredy ensuivant dixieme de ce mois Le bruit s'etant repandu de cette action les soldats ses camarades luy ayant fait des reproches à ce sujet, le Né Baron serait venu trouvé le deposant chez son maître pour le prier de venir jusqu'au fort pour dire à ses camarades qu'il l'avoit trouvé seulement à arracher du crin de la queue de lade jument et que chemin et qu'il luy donneroit une piastre de son pain).* François-Xavier stated in court that he "did not want to promise to do that" *(que n'ayant pas voulu luy promettre),* however Baron must have been sufficiently reassured, since the two walked together to the fort and to the barracks where a large number of soldiers had assembled to hear the slave speak (see Figure 40). But, instead of repudiating his initial accusation, François-Xavier described, before this new audience, Baron's act with the mare once again. It was at that point that Baron jumped out the window of the barracks, scaled the fortifications of Fort Condé, and ran away because, he later said, "All his friends were against him" *(tous ses camarades étoient contre luy).* Baron was captured on Dauphine Island, about three miles by sea from Mobile. The soldiers found him drying his wet clothes on some vegetation, in other words only partly dressed; no explanation was given as to how he got there. On being captured, Baron, fearing that he would be burned at the stake if brought back to Mobile, begged the guards to kill him on the spot rather than arrest him. These men were brought in to testify; all but one stated that they had interpreted this statement as an admission of guilt. Baron denied this was the case.[4]

No information was provided in the court record about François-Xavier beyond the fact that his master was the royal surgeon. As for the twenty-six- or twenty-seven-year-old Baron, he was a native of Dauphiné in southeastern France who had arrived in Louisiana three years earlier to serve in the Swiss troops. Twice interrogated, the second time on the sellette, he was sentenced to interrogation under judicial torture. Since Mobile lacked an executioner-torturer, he was remanded to prison in New Orleans. There, the Superior Council evaluated the documents sent from Mobile and completed its own investigation, making one change in that the bystander Leideck was now named the first witness and François-Xavier the second. As part of its inves-

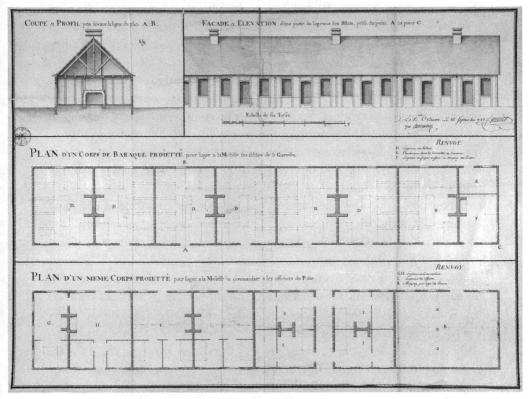

FIGURE 40: Saucier, [Ignace-François] Broutin, *Plan d'un corps de baraque projetté pour loger à la Mobille les soldats de sa garnison.* Sept. 15, 1745. FR ANOM F3 290 24.
Courtesy Archives nationales d'outre-mer, Aix-en-Provence, France

tigation, the court ordered Baron stripped to see if he had been branded on the shoulder, which would mean he was a convicted recidivist; he was not.[5]

François-Xavier was surely aware as the trial proceeded that, according to French law, Baron could be sentenced to death for a crime he himself found "atrocious." Nevertheless, on October 5, 1753, the Superior Council pronounced its verdict and convicted Baron to a sentence of "more amply informed," with the proviso that, during the intervening year before the matter was reconsidered, Baron would remain in prison. This was the same sentence that Marie-Jeanne had incurred in 1748 when accused of infanticide. It was a useful option for the judges when they felt unable — or unwilling — to make a determination of guilt or innocence, for it held the promise that the court case could either be revisited and a new sentence issued or left to expire. Like the soldier Pierre Antoine Pochenet, who had attacked Louison and Babette just one year earlier, Baron seems to have evaded the death penalty. He was in all likelihood made to resume his duties (and labor) as a soldier for France as soon as he was freed.[6]

François-Xavier's testimony, exceptionally permitted under the code noir's rule that the enslaved could testify against whites when they were the sole eyewitness to a criminal act, did not result in the conviction that Baron had feared and that the slave might have anticipated. Yet testify François-Xavier did, and his testimony was not in vain. In speaking out (which he did not have to do, with no one the wiser), he stepped squarely and decisively into the narrative frame, retaining his right to mete out moral judgment while simultaneously pushing back against subtle and not-so-subtle attempts to question his authority and disparage his motives *because* he was a slave.

The trial records document the myriad ways in which the French sought to silence François-Xavier or cast aspersions on his actions. They did so even though the facts seemed to clearly support his veracity. Leideck testified that he had not seen Baron in the act but found the soldier, who "had climbed up on stakes serving him as scaffolding in the hut" *(etoit grimpé sur des pieux qui luy servoit d'echaffaudage dans ladte cabanne)*, and that, as soon as Baron had noticed his presence, "he began to pull horsehairs from the tail of a mare belonging to Dame Parens" *(il se seroit mis à tirer des crins de la Queue d'une jument appartenante à la D[ame] parens)*. More incriminating, Baron followed Leideck back to Corporal Boccart's "and entered all trembling and disheveled and having lots of cobwebs on his back, that the said Bocart having noticed the embarrassment and paleness of the said Baron, had said to the deponent that 'this man seems to have done something bad' and the deponent replied that this man is suspected as much" *(et est entré tout tremblant et défait et ayant derriere son dos beaucoup de toile d'arraignée, que Le Né Bocart s'estant aperçu de l'embarras et de la pâleur dudt Baron avoit dit au Deposant que cet home parroissoit avoir fait un mauvais coup Le Deposant Repondit qu'il en etoit soupçonné)*. Perhaps Leideck had seen more than he was willing to say. The cobwebs on Baron's back — Boccart said they were on his cuffs — came up not a few times, as did the horsehair that Baron had pulled from the tail and was seen fiddling with, but the soldier claimed he had taken them to make a fishing line. François-Xavier's owner, Laferme, confirmed that he found the hut arranged in the way François-Xavier described, down to hoof and foot prints. Even the horse, a red-haired mare *(une jument de poile rouge)* was used as evidence for identification purposes. Though Baron never confessed, these elements, compounded by his convoluted explanation about the money, his running away, and his wish to be killed rather than arrested,

Epilogue

seemed to present a strong case for conviction. But, though the witnesses certainly seemed to corroborate François-Xavier, not one of them missed an opportunity to disparage the man for the sole reason that he was a slave.[7]

Criminal procedure allowed defendants to state if they rejected a witness (for example, if they believed them to be biased). Baron only did so for François-Xavier, saying that "he has nothing to say against the French who made depositions against him, only against the *negre*, who is a rogue and a wretch who wants to do him harm" *(il na rien à dire contre les françois qui ont deposé quil ny a que le negre qui est un gueux et un miserable qui cherche à luy faire de la peine)*. He said nothing against Leideck or Boccart, who made strong statements implying Baron's guilt. It is only to be expected that the accused would choose to disparage François-Xavier, who held power since he was, after all, his main accuser and the only eyewitness. Yet the precise terms Baron used to do so betray a degree of familiarity and intimacy with the slave, even though, tellingly, he did not even use François-Xavier's name, just called him "the *negre*."[8]

Baron was not alone in casting aspersions on François-Xavier's character on the basis that he was a slave. When Leideck described his interactions with François-Xavier, he began with a snippet that puts this into relief. Leideck told the court that when he saw François-Xavier on the road beckoning him to come over to the cabin, "the said Leidek, thinking that the *negre* apparently wanted to show him some *negresse* taking her pleasure, he refused to go" *(pensant Ledt. Leidek que ledt. Negre voulu apparemment luy faire voir quelque negresse y prendre ses ébats il refusa dy aller)*. Leideck suspected that François-Xavier had other motives, salacious, and probably transactional ones, at that. Perhaps they had previously engaged in such an exchange, for colonists certainly sought out paid sexual services. But Leideck's explanation tells us more about himself than about François-Xavier; he certainly appears rather disingenuous in claiming to know, yet be uninterested in, whatever the enslaved man seemed to be offering. As for François-Xavier's master, Laferme, though hanging on his slave's words, he did not trust him to tell the truth but went to the cabin to satisfy his own curiosity and see for himself if it looked like Baron could have committed the crime with the mare. Even the court got involved in discrediting François-Xavier, raising questions about the premise of allowing a slave to make an accusation. That they allowed François-Xavier's testimony suggests that, in spite of their stance, they thought the slave credible, and they point-blank asked the soldier, "Why, if he was innocent, he had not lodged a complaint and had the *negre* punished for what he had said against him?" *(pourquoy est ce que sil etoit innocent, il n'a pas porté ses plaintes pour faire punir ledt negre de ce quil avoit debité contre luy?).* To which Baron answered that "had he known that earlier, he would have lodged a complaint, but he never thought of it at the moment, so he decided to desert" *(que s'il avoit sçüe cela plutot, il en auroit porté ses plaintes, mais que cela ne luy est pas venu dans le moment dans l'idée et qu'il a prit le party de deserter).* In all of these instances, there was an implicit inference that a slave could not be trusted and ideally could and should be punished for daring to say anything "against" a colonist. This was a rare arena in which a soldier, therefore one of the colony's lower-status categories of Frenchmen, could exert a measure of privilege by staking his affinity with other whites. Against this backdrop of slights, François-Xavier refused to stop talking but instead constantly reasserted his right to do so.[9]

OF BOUND BODIES AND UNBOUND VOICES

As we read the voluminous records that this court case generated, we need to pause and move past the circumstances of the trial, past the sensationalism and scandal of an accusation of bestiality. André Baron's anguished explanation that he had fled because "all his friends were against him" evokes his despair and goes to the heart of what was, in the end, the real issue for him. Though his condition was in every respect superior to that of a slave, here was a scared, troubled young man of twenty-six, probably conscripted or otherwise pressed into service, garrisoned with other soldiers, far from home, with few prospects of returning to France and his native Dauphiné any time soon. No matter the disturbing circumstances that brought him to court to testify, he, too, is worthy of being heard.

As for François-Xavier, from a legal standpoint, his declarations of outrage were irrelevant. But if we follow his lead, we can understand more fully what was at stake for him as we imagine the spectrum of emotions that he must have felt in the moment and as he made repeated attempts to be heard, believed, and trusted. The slave had begun his deposition by stating that, "seized with horror at such an act, [he] wanted to throw himself on [Baron] but that, since he could not do this, he slipped away very quietly." He ended his deposition by declaring that "if [Baron] had been a slave, he would have stopped him." What should we make of these two declarations that capped his testimony?[10]

There were dual facets to his deposition. One was centred on expressing his utter shock as he first processed what it was he was seeing before his very eyes. But then he tacked in a different direction. By stating that "if the accused had been a slave, he would have stopped him," was François-Xavier also making a pointed comment about slavery? Namely, was he drawing attention to the expectation that all slaves, and even free people of color, constantly perform their subservience when in the presence of colonists? François-Xavier signaled that he had complied, that he had internalized this code of behavior, even when he held the moral high ground. He had witnessed a disturbing sexual act. He knew that by custom and law *he* was not permitted to avail himself of the intimacy of violence when the subject to be judged and punished was a white person. At the same time, he managed to implicitly throw light on the corruption of this system by demonstrating his powerlessness to act simply because *he* was a slave and the soldier was not. It was a damning intellectual critique of slavery, one that he could not verbalize in court but that hung in the silence.[11]

The trials from colonial Louisiana are full of such moments when words and silences work, not in isolation, or in tension, but together. As Leslie M. Harris reminds us, "The idea of silence, which is often used in discussions about early African American history, in fact can undermine the significance of our projects of historical recovery by implicitly positing a perfect archive." There is no ideal or complete archive, nor do we have the luxury to imagine one. Instead, why not let our guard down, shake ourselves free from assumptions, rethink received wisdom—for example, about what constitutes a slave narrative or what determines the gold standard for autobiography—and allow ourselves to bumble along, immersing ourselves deeper and wider until we see, and hear, in sometimes new and unexpected ways, what was always there in the silences and words.[12]

The records of trials in which the enslaved testify are far from perfect, and their voices are not perfectly free, yet this archive affords us access to a space where the enslaved narrated their own stories, with immediacy, with urgency. Though court officials regulated the proceedings and controlled interrogations and though they and colonists at large used their power to hush certain topics, over and over again, deponents found ways to implicitly condemn a system that sought to reduce them to chattel. Marguerite did so through her critique of violence and of French, and Catholic, models of cloistered sexuality. In Louison's case, words and silences combined to allow us to hear her claim to moral and spiritual authority. With Marie-Jeanne and Lisette, it is their thoughts about the toll of slavery on motherhood and childhood that we glimpse. Démocrite and Hector allow us to see how they co-opted the space of the plantation as their own while Francisque, Kenet, and Jean-Baptiste show us how they fought to establish their right to seek courtship, love, longing, and belonging. Sometimes, testimony even reveals rare moments when the enslaved dared to critique, however implicitly, the premise of their enslavement, as François-Xavier did. Their courtroom narratives tell us that much and yet so very much more, for they lift these individuals from anonymity even as their stories underscore the heart-wrenching banality of the violence of slavery.

The medium of testimony in French colonial courts enabled enslaved individuals to present autobiographical snapshots that illuminate their experiences of diaspora and slavery. In bringing to the fore their character and personality, and at times their emotions, inner thoughts, and intimate worlds, the individuals who testified provide a counternarrative that rebuts slavery's intent to silence them, dehumanize them, and render them anonymous. Sometimes we can trace the arc of their biographies through other records, but mostly we only catch sight of them for brief moments in time. Yet here were real people who lived full lives. We are the richer for having encountered them, however fleetingly. And whenever they did have the opportunity to speak and have their words recorded, we surely owe it to them to listen and to try to hear.

NOTES

INTRODUCTION

1. RSCL 1764/10/23/01 (year/month/day/sequence).

2. Code Noir, 1724, Article 32; RSCL 1764/11/03/03. For Dufossat's wife, see Emily Clark, *Masterless Mistresses: The New Orleans Ursulines and the Development of a New World Society, 1727–1834* (Chapel Hill, N.C., 2007), 128.

3. RSCL 1764/10/23/01, 1. On Dubreuil's father, Claude Joseph Villars Dubreuil, see Henry P. Dart, "The Career of Dubreuil in French Louisiana," *Louisiana Historical Quarterly*, XVIII (1935), 267. A "young negro named Jean" (Janot is a shortened version of the name) was purchased in 1758 by the younger Dubreuil from his father's estate for 3,050 livres (ibid., 318). On Catholicism in the kingdom of Kongo, see Cécile Fromont, *The Art of Conversion: Christian Visual Culture in the Kingdom of Kongo* (Chapel Hill, N.C., 2014).

4. For physical and bodily intimacy, see, for example, Jennifer L. Palmer, *Intimate Bonds: Family and Slavery in the French Atlantic* (Philadelphia, 2016). Palmer's study of race and gender in the French Atlantic "reconceptualizes intimacy to extend beyond blood relations or even the household, considering a broad array of ways in which individuals came into contact and built 'close and deep' personal relationships with each other" in order to rethink "the role that intimacy and family played in the construction of gender and racial norms in the late eighteenth century" (ibid., 13–15). See also Ann Laura Stoler, ed., *Haunted by Empire: Geographies of Intimacy in North American History* (Durham, N.C., 2006).

5. For an introduction to understanding the slave experience in West Africa with a focus on how to articulate slave voices, see Martin Klein, "Understanding the Slave Experience in West Africa," in Lisa A. Lindsay and John Wood Sweet, eds., *Biography and the Black Atlantic* (Philadelphia, 2014), 48–65.

6. For more expansive approaches to what might constitute a slave narrative, see, for example, Sophie White and Trevor Burnard, eds., *Slave Narratives in British and French America, 1700–1848* (Abingdon, U.K., forthcoming). On the challenges of producing slave biographies, see also Lindsay and Sweet, eds., *Biography and the Black Atlantic*; Jeffrey A. Fortin and Mark Meuwese, eds., *Atlantic Biographies: Individuals and Peoples in the Atlantic World* (Leiden, Netherlands, 2014), Part 2; Sue Peabody, "Microhistory, Biography, Fiction: The Politics of Narrating the Lives of People under Slavery," *Transatlantica*, no. 2 (2012); and the papers presented at the symposium on "Voices in the Legal Archives in the French Atlantic," organized by Nancy Christie, Michael Gauvreau, and Clare Haru Crowston held May 28–30, 2018, in North Hatley, Quebec. See also the series overseen by Marie-Jeanne Rossignol and Claire Parfait, which has consciously sought to bring together both "canonical" nineteenth-century published slave narratives

and examples of slave voices from courtroom testimony, https://www.cairn.info/revue
-francaise-d-etudes-americaines-2017-2-page-51.htm?contenu=resume; and Nicole N.
Aljoe, "'Going to Law': Legal Discourse and Testimony in Early West Indian Slave Narratives," *Early American Literature,* XLVI (2011), 351–381. For the twentieth century, there
is rich source material showcasing the voices of former slaves. See the transcriptions of
interviews produced by the Federal Writers' Project in the 1930s, "Born in Slavery: Slave
Narratives from the Federal Writers' Project, 1936 to 1938," Library of Congress, https://
www.loc.gov/collections/slave-narratives-from-the-federal-writers-project-1936-to-1938
/about-this-collection/ (accessed Aug. 24, 2018); and Zora Neale Hurston, *Barracoon: The
Story of the Last "Black Cargo,"* ed. Deborah G. Plant (New York, 2018).

7. Annette Gordon-Reed, "Slavery's Shadow," *New Yorker,* Oct. 23, 2013, https://www
.newyorker.com/culture/culture-desk/slaverys-shadow (accessed Oct. 31, 2017). On
slaves' access to literacy, see Sue Peabody, "'A Dangerous Zeal': Catholic Missions to
Slaves in the French Antilles, 1635–1800," *French Historical Studies,* XXV (2002), 56n.
For a rare exception from Louisiana where one master wanted his slave Doucet, a young
African man apprenticed to a cobbler, to receive instruction in how to read and write in the
first two years, then taught the cobbler's trade, see RSCL 1741/08/09/01, 1741/09/02/02.
For La Nuit, a favored slave of Jean-Charles de Pradel who was literate, see A. Baillardel and A. Prioult, eds., *Le chevalier de Pradel: Vie d'un colon français en Louisiane au
XVIIIe siècle d'après sa correspondance et celle de sa famille* (Paris, 1928), 361. The literature on Anglo-American autobiographical narratives is vast; for a French perspective on
these sources, see Michaël Roy, *Textes fugitifs: Le récit d'esclave au prisme de l'histoire
du livre* (Lyon, France, 2017); and Marie-Jeanne Rossignol and Claire Parfait's series of
works on slave narratives, https://www.cairn.info/revue-francaise-d-etudes-americaines
-2017-2-page-51.htm?contenu=resume. On critiques of the dominance of the slave narrative as a peculiarly Anglo-American autobiographical genre, see, for example, Peabody's
point that, "unlike the English and American abolitionists, the French antislavery lobby
did not seek out slave narratives to publicize the injustices of slavery and so we have no
autobiographical French accounts of the enslaved. Whether this is because the Protestant
literary trope of a bound life freed did not resonate with either Catholic or Republican
France, or because most French opponents of slavery were elites who did not think the
stories of slaves worth telling (except very rarely, in fictional form), this gap has made it
very difficult for historians and the wider French public to imagine the subjective perspective of the enslaved" (Peabody, "Transiting Imperial Boundaries: Slavery and Freedom in France's Indian Ocean Colonies," paper presented at the 127th Annual Meeting
of the American Historical Association, Jan. 3–6, 2013, New Orleans). See also Peabody,
*Madeleine's Children: Family, Freedom, Secrets, and Lies in France's Indian Ocean Colo-
nies* (Oxford, 2017), 3–4; and Deborah Jenson, *Beyond the Slave Narrative: Politics, Sex,
and Manuscripts in the Haitian Revolution* (Liverpool, U.K., 2011).

8. On French law pertaining to testimony in France and her colonies, see Eric Wen-
zel, *La justice criminelle en Nouvelle-France (1670–1760): Le grand arrangement* (Dijon,
France, 2012), 91 (quotation); André Morel, "Réflexions sur la justice criminelle canadi-
enne au 18e siècle," *Revue de l'histoire de l'Amérique française,* XXIX (1975), 242; and Jan
Grabowski, "French Criminal Justice and Indians in Montreal, 1670–1760," *Ethnohistory,*
XLIII (1996), 405–429. On French criminal law, see also Richard Mowery Andrews, *Law,*

Magistracy, and Crime in Old Regime Paris, I (Cambridge, 1994); and François Serpillon, *Code criminel, ou commentaire sur l'ordonnance de 1670 . . .* , 4 vols. (Lyon, France, 1767). There was no such consistency in English colonies. Slaves and free persons of color in colonial Virginia, for instance, were not allowed to testify in court (trials against slaves for capital crimes being the only exception). See Philip J. Schwarz, *Twice Condemned: Slaves and the Criminal Laws of Virginia, 1705–1865* (Baton Rouge, La., 1988), 19. Slaves in the English Caribbean, on the other hand, could testify, but only for or against other slaves, not for or against free persons. See Natalie Zacek, "Voices and Silences: The Problem of Slave Testimony in the English West Indian Law Court," *Slavery and Abolition*, XXIV, no. 3 (December 2003), 24–39, esp. 25. For examples of English trial records that were published and thoughtful explanations of their value and problems as source material, see Serena R. Zabin, ed., *The New York Conspiracy Trials of 1741: Daniel Horsmanden's Journal of the Proceedings with Related Documents* (Boston, 2004); and Zacek, "Voices and Silences," *Slavery and Abolition*, XXIV, no. 3 (December 2003), 24–39. For a classic example of the genre of published trial commentaries, see, for example, Francis Hargrave's pamphlet "An Argument in the Case of James Sommersett a Negro, Lately Determined by the Court of King's Bench: Wherein It Is Attempted to Demonstrate the Present Unlawfulness of Domestic Slavery in England; To Which Is Prefixed a State of the Case," first published in London by W. Otridge [and G. Kearsly] in 1772, reprinted in Boston in 1774, and discussed in Paul Finkelman, *Slavery in the Courtroom: An Annotated Bibliography of American Cases* (Union, N.J., 1998), 21–22. On the trial records of the Old Bailey in London and developments over time in how they were published, see Clive Emsley, Tim Hitchcock, and Robert Shoemaker, "The Proceedings — Publishing History of the Proceedings," Old Bailey Proceedings Online (www.oldbaileyonline.org, version 7.0, accessed Aug. 10, 2018).

9. For a chronological listing of the slavers sent to Louisiana in the French period before 1763, see Gwendolyn Midlo Hall, *Africans in Colonial Louisiana: The Development of Afro-Creole Culture in the Eighteenth Century* (Baton Rouge, La., 1992), Appendix A, "Basic Facts About All Slave-Trade Voyages from Africa to Louisiana during the French Regime," 382–397. It was in Senegal that the Company of the Indies (based at Lorient) held its slave concession and from there that most shipments of slaves to Louisiana were made. For Hall's discussion of the importance of the Senegambia region to the history of Louisiana's slaves, see ibid., 29–34. See also Emily Clark, Ibrahima Thioub, and Cécile Vidal, eds., *Saint-Louis, Senegal, and New Orleans: Two Mirror Cities, 17th–21st Centuries* (Baton Rouge, La., forthcoming). For a discussion of the figures available on the slave trade to Louisiana, see Philip D. Curtin, *The Atlantic Slave Trade: A Census* (Madison, Wis., 1969), 163–202. The bulk of the remaining slaves sent to Louisiana originated in Whydah (see Hall, *Africans*, Table 2, 60). Occasionally, there are references to Africans arriving from the French West Indies or from English or Spanish colonies, including as runaways. See Daniel H. Usner, Jr., "From African Captivity to American Slavery: The Introduction of Black Laborers to Colonial Louisiana," *Louisiana History*, XX (1979), 25–48; Jennifer M. Spear, *Race, Sex, and Social Order in Early New Orleans* (Baltimore, 2009); Thomas N. Ingersoll, *Mammon and Manon in Early New Orleans: The First Slave Society in the Deep South, 1718–1819* (Knoxville, Tenn., 1999); and Jessica Johnson, "Wives, Soldiers, and Slaves: The Atlantic World of Marie Baude, la femme Pinet," in Clark, Thioub,

and Vidal, eds., *Saint-Louis, Senegal, and New Orleans*. On broader demographic trends, see Paul LaChance, "The Growth of the Free and Slave Populations of French Colonial Louisiana," in Bradley G. Bond, *French Colonial Louisiana and the Atlantic World* (Baton Rouge, La., 2005), 232, 243n. For censuses, see Charles R. Maduell, comp. and trans., *The Census Tables for the French Colony of Louisiana from 1699 through 1732* (Baltimore, 1972), 113–122; and Jacqueline K. Voorhies, comp. and trans., *Some Late Eighteenth-Century Louisianians: Census Records of the Colony, 1758–1796* (Lafayette, La., 1973), 5–103. Yevan Terrien has calculated that 977 of the 7,020 Europeans shipped across the Atlantic were soldiers (he counts another 1,338 convicts forcibly transported to the colony). See Terrien, "Forced European Migrants and Soldiers in French Colonial New Orleans / Les émigrants forcés européens et les soldats dans la colonie française de La Nouvelle-Orléans," in Erin Greenwald, ed., *New Orleans: The Founding Era / La Nouvelle-Orléans: Les années fondatrices*, trans. Henry Colomer (New Orleans, 2018), 80.

10. On the records of the Superior Council of Louisiana from the French regime and the records of the Cabildo from the Spanish regime, held together in one archive (which includes the court records in which the enslaved testified), see Greg Lambousy and Emily Clark, eds., "Atlantic World Archives of Louisiana," special issue, *Collections: A Journal for Museum and Archives Professionals*, XI, no. 3 (Summer 2015). On the French records, see, in particular, Sophie White, "Notes from the Field: Lured in by the Archives," *Collections: A Journal for Museum and Archives Professionals*, XI, no. 3 (Summer 2015), 167–170.

11. As Meïssa Niang reminds us, what constitutes criminality in any given society and period depends on cultural values. See Niang, "La Criminalité au Sénégal" (Ph.D. thesis, Université de droit, d'économie, et des sciences d'Aix-Marseille, 1995), 3–4. On convicts transported to Louisiana, see Terrien, "Forced European Migrants and Soldiers / Les émigrants forcés européens et les soldats," in Greenwald, ed., *New Orleans / La Nouvelle-Orléans*, trans. Colomer, 82–83. On Old World judicial targets, see Benoît Garnot, *Crime et justice aux XVIIe et XVIIIe siècles* (Paris, 2000); Olwen Hufton, *The Poor of Eighteenth-Century France, 1750–1789* (Oxford, 1974), 245–283; and Hufton, "The Urban Criminal in Eighteenth-Century France," *Bulletin of the John Rylands University Library of Manchester*, LXVII (1984), 474–499. For two rare extant prosecutions of whites for the theft of livestock in Louisiana, see RSCL 1764/04/04/01 and 1764/04/07/02; 1766/10/04/01. See also Sophie White, "Slaves and Poor Whites' Informal Economies in an Atlantic Context," in Cécile Vidal, ed., *Louisiana: Crossroads of the Atlantic World* (Philadelphia, 2014), 89–102; and White, "Crime and Consumption in Early New Orleans," paper presented at the Annual Meeting of the Organization of American Historians, Apr. 6–9, 2017, New Orleans.

12. Louisiana's records far surpass those of all other French colonies, distantly followed by the records from Isle de France (present-day Mauritius) in the Indian Ocean, archived in the National Archives of Mauritius at Coromandel: for criminal cases, see group JB (1730–1851). On (African and Indian) slave testimony in New France, see, especially, the rich documentation pertaining to the trial of Angélique, convicted in 1734 of setting fire to Montreal, "Torture and Truth: Angélique and the Burning of Montréal," Great Unsolved Mysteries in Canadian History, https://www.canadianmysteries.ca/sites/ange

lique/proces/indexen.html (accessed Oct. 28, 2018). See also Brett Rushforth, *Bonds of Alliance: Indigenous and Atlantic Slaveries in New France* (Chapel Hill, N.C., 2012), 299–367. For transcriptions of select court testimony from French Atlantic archives, see Dominique Rogers, ed., *Voix d'esclaves: Antilles, Guyane, et Louisiane françaises, XVIIIe–XIXe siècles* (Paris, 2015); there are only a few extant trials dating from the first three quarters of the eighteenth century in the French Caribbean. See also John Garrigus, " 'Le secret qui règne parmi les nègres': Revisiting the Testimony of Makandal and His 'Accomplices,' 1757–1758," paper presented at the workshop on "Les résistances à l'esclavage dans le monde atlantique français à l'ère des Révolutions (1750–1850)," organized by the Groupe d'histoire de l'atlantique français in collaboration with the Haiti Lab (Duke University) and Le centre international de recherches sur les esclavages, held at McGill University, May 3–4, 2013, Montreal; and Rushforth, "Burning St. Pierre: Political Life and Political Economy in a Caribbean Slave Uprising," paper presented at the Rocky Mountain Seminar in Early American History, April 2017, Salt Lake City, Utah. On the policy of destroying slave judicial archives in the French Caribbean, see Marie Houllemare, "Vers la centralisation des archives coloniales françaises au XVIIIe siècle: Destruction et conservation des papiers judiciaires," in Marie-Pia Donato and Anne Saada, eds., *Autour d'archives: Créer, organiser, et utiliser des archives à l'époque moderne* (Paris, 2018).

13. Jon F. Sensbach, "Black Pearls: Writing Black Atlantic Women's Biography," in Lindsay and Sweet, eds., *Biography and the Black Atlantic,* 97; Julie Hardwick, "Family Matters: The Early Modern Atlantic from the European Side," *History Compass,* VIII (2010), 252; Marisa J. Fuentes, *Dispossessed Lives: Enslaved Women, Violence, and the Archive* (Philadelphia, 2016), 1. For examples of full-scale biographies of enslaved individuals, see Peabody, *Madeleine's Children;* Rebecca J. Scott and Jean M. Hébrard, *Freedom Papers: An Atlantic Odyssey in the Age of Emancipation* (Cambridge, Mass., 2012); Sensbach, *Rebecca's Revival: Creating Black Christianity in the Atlantic World* (Cambridge, Mass., 2005); James H. Sweet, *Domingos Álvares, African Healing, and the Intellectual History of the Atlantic World* (Chapel Hill, N.C., 2011); Annette Gordon-Reed, *The Hemingses of Monticello: An American Family* (New York, 2008); and Erica Armstrong Dunbar, *Never Caught: The Washingtons' Relentless Pursuit of Their Runaway Slave, Ona Judge* (New York, 2017). See also the section "Mobility" in Lindsay and Sweet, eds., *Biography and the Black Atlantic,* Part 2. Sensbach makes this point about the exceptionality of individuals who left behind larger footprints in the archives perfectly in an article on the challenges and payoffs of doing such work. See Sensbach, "Black Pearls: Writing Black Atlantic Women's Biography," ibid., 93–107. As David Nasaw frames it, "Historians are not interested in simply charting the course of individual lives, but in examining those lives in dialectical relationship to the multiple social, political, and cultural worlds they inhabit and give meaning to." See Nasaw, "Introduction," in "AHR Roundtable: Historians and Biography," *American Historical Review,* CXIV (2009), 573–661 (quotation, 574). Writing from her perspective as an historian of Europe, Hardwick also urges us to consider the role of gender and family in this mobility and fluidity. See Hardwick, "Family Matters: The Early Modern Atlantic from the European Side," *History Compass,* VIII (2010), 248–257, esp. 252–253.

14. It is only in 1764 that the Superior Council began to systematically resort to judi-

cial torture. See Thomas N. Ingersoll, "The Law and Order Campaign in New Orleans, 1763–1765: A Comparative View," in Sally E. Hadden and Patricia Hagler Minter, eds., *Signposts: New Directions in Southern Legal History* (Athens, Ga., 2013), 45–64.

15. Titre VI, Article 9, in Serpillon, *Code criminel ou commentaire sur l'ordonnance de 1670*, I, 478, and Titre XXIV, Article 3, III, 994. The rule about secrecy was reiterated in the 1712 edict establishing the Superior Council of Louisiana, which specified that "all judgments which [the judges] render must be pronounced orally" (Letters patent for the establishment of a Superior Council of Louisiana, Dec. 23, 1712, ANOM, Ser. A22, fol. 11v–12r).

16. Title VI, Article 9, in Serpillon, *Code criminel*, I, 478. On the plumitif, see Antoine Furetière, *Dictionnaire universel contenat generalement tous les mots François, tant vieux que modernes, et les termes des sciences et des arts: Divisés en trois tomes*, 2d ed., III (The Hague, 1727), s.v. "plumitif." On the process of turning a plumitif into a register, see also Frédéric-Antoine Raymond, "L'Ecriture au service de la communauté: Histoire des registres de délibérations de la communauté des procureurs au parlement de Toulouse (1693–1781)" (master's thesis, Université Laval, 2005), 48–53, 76–77. Plumitifs rarely survive; for one example from 1578–1605, see Yves Metman, ed., *Le registre ou plumitif de la construction du Pont Neuf (Archives nationales Z1f 1065)* (Paris, 1987). On the broader question of the importance of bureaucrats in Louisiana and how they were trained, see Alexandre Dubé, "Making a Career Out of the Atlantic: Louisiana's Plume," in Vidal, ed., *Louisiana*, 44–67.

17. RSCL 1748/01/06/01, 5. On the lack of punctuation in court records, see Arlette Farge, *The Allure of the Archives*, trans. Thomas Scott-Railton (New Haven, Conn., 2013), 3.

18. RSCL 1764/01/04/01; 1752/03/27/02, 3. On the ethnonym Bambara (shorthand for non-Muslim), see Peter Caron, "'Of a Nation Which the Others Do Not Understand': Bambara Slaves and African Ethnicity in Colonial Louisiana, 1718–60," *Slavery and Abolition*, XVIII, no. 1 (1997), 98–121.

19. RSCL 1767/06/10/02.

20. Interrogation of Estienne, July 1757, Natchitoches Parish Conveyance Record Book 1: 1738–1765, 1757/7, no. 186, NP; RSCL 1744/03/12/01, 10. On interpreting testimony in Caribbean colonies, see Natalie Zemon Davis, "Judges, Masters, Diviners: Slaves' Experience of Criminal Justice in Colonial Suriname," *Law and History Review*, XXIX (2011), 925–984; Zacek, "Voices and Silences," *Slavery and Abolition*, XXIV, no. 3 (December 2003), 24–39; Trevor Burnard, *Hearing Slaves Speak* ([Guyana], 2010), http://caribbeanpress.org/caribbean-press-downloads/ (accessed May 7, 2019); and Rushforth, "Burning St. Pierre." For a sampler of approaches to interpreting testimony in trials in medieval and early modern Europe, see, for example, Farge, *Allure of the Archives*, trans. Scott-Railton; Joanne Bailey, "Voices in Court: Lawyers' or Litigants'?" *Historical Research*, LXXIV (2001), 392–408; Gene Brucker, *Giovanni and Lusanna: Love and Marriage in Renaissance Florence* (Berkeley, Calif., 1986); Carlo Ginzburg, *The Cheese and the Worms*, trans. by John and Anne Tedeschi (Baltimore, 1980); Thomas Kuehn, "Reading Microhistory: The Example of *Giovanni and Lusanna*," *Journal of Modern History*, LXI (1989), 512–534; and Susan Alice McDonough, *Witnesses, Neighbors, and Community in Late Medieval Marseille* (New York, 2013).

21. John Gabriel Stedman, *Narrative of a Five Years Expedition against the Revolted*

Negroes of Surinam, ed. Richard and Sally Price (Baltimore, 1988), 480–482, quoted in Davis, "Judges, Masters, Diviners," *Law and History Review,* XXIX (2011), 926–927. For the original publication of the account, see Stedman, *Narrative, of a Five Years' Expedition against the Revolted Negroes of Surinam, in Guiana on the Wild Coast of South America; From the Year 1772 to 1777,* 2 vols. (London, 1796), II, 208–210. During interviews for her research, Zora Neale Hurston experienced a case of veering off script similar to that of the testimony of the runaway slave from Suriname. She described one African man Kossula's attempt to redirect her questions as follows:

> I was afraid that Cudjo might go off on a tangent, so I cut in with, "But Kossula, I want to hear about *you* and how *you* lived in Africa."
>
> He gave me a look full of scornful pity and asked, "Where is de house where de mouse is de leader? In de Affica soil I cain tellee you 'bout de son before I tellee you 'bout de father; and derefore, un unnerstand me, I cain talk about de main who is father *(et te)* till I tellee you bout de man who he father to him, *(et, te, te,* grandfather) now, dass right ain' it?"

See Hurston, *Barracoon,* ed. Plant, 20–21. For the unconnected but analogous example in the process whereby Parisian Jews responded to the French state's request that they document the household goods that had been seized from them during the Second World War, see Leora Auslander, "Beyond Words" *American Historical Review,* CX, no. 4 (2005), 1015–1045. The stated purpose of these inventories was to facilitate restitution, but, as Auslander has shown, the respondents instead produced "memory maps" that were of little use for identification purposes. "It did not really help authorities to know that a bed or a set of china had been a wedding gift from one's great-aunt forty years earlier. . . . These deviations from the mandate suggest that the motivation in filing these claims was only tangentially the possibility of recovery of their lost goods" (quotations, 1043).

22. Though there are no runaway advertisements for the French colonial period, there was a process for registering runaway slaves, and reports were occasionally filed with the Superior Council (see, for example, RSCL 1744/01/31/01 and 1748/05/21/01), but these contained few details and no references to appearance, suggesting that they existed to fulfill a legal requirement concerned with the accounting of property rather than as a tool to aid in the recapture of runaways. The requirement to file a report was used so seldomly that in 1763 the Superior Council passed a new edict ordering owners of runaway slaves to file a declaration within four days, requesting a census of all slaves, and imposing a fine of forty *sous* per slave on owners who did not comply. See Edict requiring owners of runaway slaves to file a declaration with the Superior Council within four days, Apr. 6, 1764, ANOM C13A 43, fol. 304. On runaway advertisements in Saint Domingue, which number 12,710 placed between 1760 and 1790, see the database Marronnage in Saint-Domingue (Haïti): History, Memory, Technology, http://www.marronnage.info/en/. Many nineteenth-century runaways from Louisiana are included in the database "Rediscovering the Stories of Self-Liberating People: A Database of Fugitives from American Slavery," Freedom on the Move, https://freedomonthemove.org/index.html. On runaway advertisements in colonial Anglo-America, see, for example, Jonathan Prude, "To Look upon the 'Lower Sort': Runaway Ads and the Appearance of Unfree Laborers in America, 1750–1800," *Journal of American History,* LXXVIII (1991), 124–159; and David Wald-

streicher, "Reading the Runaways: Self-Fashioning, Print Culture, and Confidence in Slavery in the Eighteenth-Century Mid-Atlantic," *William and Mary Quarterly,* 3d Ser., LVI (1999), 243–272.

23. Natalie Zemon Davis points out that, "on the whole among the African polities, structures of incarceration for criminals were not built until the nineteenth century. Persons accused of crimes were kept from running away by their families in their compounds" (Davis, "Judges, Masters, Diviners," *Law and History Review,* XXIX [2011], 937). On New Orleans's penal spaces, see Rashauna Johnson, *Slavery's Metropolis: Unfree Labor in New Orleans during the Age of Revolutions* (Cambridge, 2016), chap. 4. On the New Orleans prison building, see Samuel Wilson, Jr., "La Nouvelle Orléans: Le Vieux Carré," in Jean M. Farnsworth and Ann M. Masson, eds., *The Architecture of Colonial Louisiana: Collected Essays of Samuel Wilson, Jr., F.A.I.A.* (Lafayette, La., 1987), 331–332. The building stood until 1769, when it was replaced by the first Cabildo building. Its foundations still lie beneath the Cabildo. See Jill-Karen Yakubik and Herschel A. Franks et al., "Archaeology at the Cabildo," Louisiana State Museum, https://www.crt.state .la.us/Assets/Museum/publications/Archaeology_At_The_Cabildo.pdf (accessed Oct. 12, 2018).

24. Adrien de Pauger to Le Blond de La Tour, Apr. 14, 1721, ANF-AC, Cartes et Plans, LXVII, no. 5, fol. 135, pièce 13, quoted in Shannon Lee Dawdy, "La Ville Sauvage: 'Enlightened' Colonialism and Creole Improvisation in New Orleans, 1699–1769" (Ph.D. diss., University of Michigan, 2003), 70–71. Also quoted in Dawdy, "Ethnicity in the Urban Landscape: The Archaeology of Creole New Orleans," in Amy L. Young, ed., *Archaeology of Southern Urban Landscapes* (Tuscaloosa, Ala., 2000), 140. On the architecture of New Orleans, see Gilles-Antoine Langlois, "French Architect-Engineers of New Orleans, 1718–1730," in Greenwald, ed., *New Orleans,* 58–68; and Dawdy, "Madame John's Legacy (16OR51) Revisited: A Closer Look at the Archaeology of Colonial New Orleans," typescript, Greater New Orleans Archaeology Program, College of Urban and Public Affairs, University of New Orleans, 1998.

25. RSCL 1769/04/27/02, quoted in Dawdy, "Madame John's Legacy," 36. For eyewitness accounts professing to have observed the too-free movement of slaves, see Samuel Wilson, "Architecture of the Vieux Carré: French Colonial Period, 1718–1768," in Farnsworth and Masson, eds., *Architecture of Colonial Louisiana,* 326–329, Wilson, "La Nouvelle Orléans: Le Vieux Carré," 330–335; and Dawdy, "Ethnicity in the Urban Landscape," in Young, ed., *Archaeology of Southern Urban Landscapes,* 137–143.

26. On the Ursuline convent, see Clark, *Masterless Mistresses,* 128–129 (on Françoise Dufossat), 150–156; and Samuel Wilson, Jr., "An Architectural History of the Royal Hospital and the Ursuline Convent of New Orleans," in Farnsworth and Masson, eds., *Architecture of Colonial Louisiana,* 161–220. For an example of African-born slaves arriving in Louisiana via the islands, see the particularly well-documented case concerning the ship *La roue de fortune.* It docked in Martinique in 1765 with sixteen slaves (including two children) to be sold in Louisiana, many of whom were African-born, including four who identified as Congo or from Angola. The Superior Council interrogated the slaves but, predictably, given the demand for slaves in the colony, decided to permit the sale in spite of some clear irregularities. See RSCL 1765/11/12/03, 1765/11/13/01; 1765/11/16/04, 1765/12/04/01,

1765/12/06/02. On the challenges in interpreting the self-identification of African nations in Louisiana records, see, for example, Hall, *Africans in Colonial Louisiana;* Caron, "'Of a Nation Which the Others Do Not Understand,'" *Slavery and Abolition,* XVIII (1997), 98–121; and Jean-Pierre Le Glaunec, "'Un nègre nommè [sic] Lubin ne connaissant pas Sa Nation'": The Small World of Louisiana Slavery," in Vidal, ed., *Louisiana,* 103–122. On Catholicism in the kingdom of Kongo, see Fromont, *Art of Conversion.* See also Linda M. Heywood and John K. Thornton, *Central Africans, Atlantic Creoles, and the Foundation of the Americas, 1585–1660* (New York, 2007). On convents in the French Atlantic world, see Heidi Keller-Lapp, "Floating Cloisters and Heroic Women: French Ursuline Missionaries, 1639–1744," *World History Connected,* IV, no. 3 (2007) (accessed June 20, 2014). See also Sue Peabody, "'A Dangerous Zeal': Catholic Missions to Slaves in the French Antilles, 1635–1800," *French Historical Studies,* XXV (2002), 53–90.

27. For knowledge of West African judicial practices persisting in the colonies, see Emily Clark's book project "Noel Carriere's Liberty: From Slave to Soldier in Colonial New Orleans"; and Clark, "Noel Carriere, the Commander of the Free Black Militia, Deserves a Monument in New Orleans," *The Advocate* (New Orleans), July 8, 2015, https://www.theadvocate.com/baton_rouge/opinion/our_views/article_e3548cc4-6fb8 -5837-8e5f-fe3128de4643.html (accessed Aug. 23, 2018). See also Cécile Vidal, "The 1769 Oath of Fidelity and Allegiance to the Spanish Crown of the French 'Company of the Free Mulattoes and Negroes of This Colony of Louisiana': Dual Genealogy of a Social Event," paper presented at the 127th Annual Meeting of the American Historical Association, Jan. 3–6, 2013, New Orleans. On this subject, with reference to Martinique, see Rushforth, "Burning St. Pierre." With reference to Suriname, see Davis, "Judges, Masters, Diviners," *Law and History Review,* XXIX (2011), 925–984. With reference to the Kongo in Saint Domingue, see John K. Thornton, "'I Am the Subject of the King of Congo': African Political Ideology and the Haitian Revolution," *Journal of World History,* IV (1993), 181–214, esp. 199–201. For specific examples of judicial procedures, see Paul E. Lovejoy, *Transformations in Slavery: A History of Slavery in Africa,* 2d ed. (Cambridge, 2000), 3–4; Boubacar Barry, *The Kingdom of Waalo: Senegal before the Conquest* (New York, 2012), 48; and Robert M. Baum, *Shrines of the Slave Trade: Diola Religion and Society in Precolonial Senegambia* (New York, 1999), 53. Natalie Zacek points out how "a number of legal anthropologists have claimed that 'people who are relatively powerless in their relationships with others find courts to be powerful allies'" (Zacek, "Voices and Silences," *Slavery and Abolition,* XXIV, no. 3 [December 2003], 36). See also Mindie Lazarus-Black, "Slaves, Masters, and Magistrates. Law and the Politics of Resistance in the British Caribbean, 1736–1834," in Lazarus-Black and Susan F. Hirsch, eds., *Contested States: Law, Hegemony, and Resistance* (New York, 1994), 267.

28. Ibrahima Seck, *Bouki Fait Gombo: A History of the Slave Community of Habitation Haydel (Whitney Plantation) Louisiana, 1750–1860* (New Orleans, 2014), 129–139 (quotation, 129–130). See also Alcée Fortier, *Louisiana Folk-tales in French Dialect and English Translation* (Boston, 1895).

29. RSCL 1766/04[08]/02/02 (the correct date is August, not April, 1766).

30. RSCL 1766/07/29/04.

1. RSCL 1738/04/24/01, 2. On the prison building, which lies underneath the Cabildo, see Jill-Karen Yakubik and Herschel A. Franks, "Archaeology at the Cabildo," Louisiana State Museum, https://www.crt.state.la.us/Assets/Museum/publications/Archaeology _At_The_Cabildo.pdf (accessed 10/12/2018). See also Samuel Wilson, Jr., "La Nouvelle Orléans: Le Vieux Carré," in Jean M. Farnsworth and Ann M. Masson, eds., *The Architecture of Colonial Louisiana: Collected Essays of Samuel Wilson, Jr., F.A.I.A.* (Lafayette, La., 1987), 331–332.

2. On the 1670 Code criminel, see Richard Mowery Andrews, *Law, Magistracy, and Crime in Old Regime Paris, 1735–1789* (Cambridge, 1994). On the Coutume de Paris, see [François] Olivier-Martin, *Histoire de la coutume de la prévôté et vicomté de Paris*, 2 vols. (Paris, 1922–1930). For its application in Louisiana, see Jerah Johnson, *"La Coutume de Paris:* Louisiana's First Law," *Louisiana History,* XXX (1989), 145–155; and Hans W. Baade, "Marriage Contracts in French and Spanish Louisiana: A Study in 'Notarial' Jurisprudence," *Tulane Law Review,* LIII (1978), 1–92. On the Coutume de Paris in New France, see Yves F. Zoltvany, "Esquisse de la Coutume de Paris," *Revue d'histoire de l'Amérique française,* XXV (1971), 365–384.

3. For the original documents, see Code Noir, 1685; Code Noir, 1723, NAMC, A3/1 Z3A 1; and Code Noir, 1724. On the 1724 code noir, and comparisons of the 1685 and 1724 codes, see Guillaume Aubert, "'To Establish One Law and Definite Rules': Race, Religion, and the Transatlantic Origins of the Louisiana Code Noir," in Cécile Vidal, ed., *Louisiana: Crossroads of the Atlantic World* (Philadelphia, 2014), 21–43; Thomas N. Ingersoll, "Slave Codes and Judicial Practice in New Orleans, 1718–1807," *Law and History Review,* XIII (1995), 23–62; Vernon Valentine Palmer, "The Origins and Authors of the Code Noir," *Louisiana Law Review,* LVI (1996), 363–407; Palmer, *Through the Codes Darkly: Slave Law and Civil Law in Louisiana* (Clark, N.J., 2012); Mathé Allain, "Slave Policies in French Louisiana," *Louisiana History,* XXI (1980), 136–137; and Carl A. Brasseaux, "The Administration of Slave Regulations in French Louisiana, 1724–1766," *Louisiana History,* XXI (1980), 139–158. On the links between the 1723 and 1724 codes, see Marc Serge Rivière's study of the Mascarenes' code noir, in Rivière, *Codes Noirs et autres documents concernant l'esclavage* (Beau Bassin, Mauritius, 2009). See also Sophie White, "Les esclaves et le droit en Louisiane sous le régime français, carrefour entre la Nouvelle-France, les Antilles, et l'océan indien," in Éric Wenzel and Éric de Mari, eds., *Adapter le droit et rendre la justice aux colonies: Thémis Outre-Mer (XVIe–XIXe siècle)* (Dijon, France, 2015), 57–67. For examples of the invisibility of the 1723 code in important histories of Louisiana's slave codes, see Ingersoll, "Slave Codes," *Law and History Review,* XIII (1995), 23–62; and Palmer, "Origins and Authors of the Code Noir," *Louisiana Law Review,* LVI (1996), 363–407. Likewise, Louis Sala-Molins's comparison of France's codes noirs focuses exclusively on the 1685 and 1724 codes and makes no mention of the 1723 code. See Sala-Molin, *Le Code Noir ou le calvaire de Canaan* (1987; rpt. Paris, 2001). For a rare opposing view that the 1685 code was not based on local jurisprudence but almost exclusively derived from Roman law on slavery (and therefore free of racial underpinnings), see Alan Watson, "The Origins of the Code Noir Revisited," *Tulane Law Review,* LXXI (1997), 1041–1072. On the problem of historians' tenacious views of the 1685

and 1724 codes as largely devoid of racial ideology, see Aubert's discussion of the literature in Aubert, "To Establish One Law and Definite Rules," in Vidal, ed., *Louisiana,* 33–35. In contrast to the extant evidence about the composition of the 1685 code noir, little is known about the authors and origins of the 1723 and 1724 codes nor the underlying motivations for their creation. On the 1685 code as the first example of a European power codifying a judicial system for enslaved Africans, see Malick W. Ghachem, *The Old Regime and the Haitian Revolution* (Cambridge, 2012), 43–44.

4. "Règlement sur la police pour la province de la Louisiane," Feb. 28–Mar. 1, 1751, ANOM C13A 35, fol. 39. See also Minister of the navy to Pierre de Rigaud de Vaudreuil and Honoré Michel de Villebois de la Rouvillière, Sept. 26, 1750, Vaudreuil Papers, Loudoun Collection, LO 222, Huntington Library, San Marino, Calif., and Vaudreuil to unknown, [circa 1750], O/S LO 257. On the 1751 police code, see White, "Les esclaves et le droit en Louisiane sous le régime français," in Wenzel and Mari, eds., *Adapter le droit et rendre la justice aux colonies,* 63–64; and Ingersoll, "Slave Codes," *Law and History Review,* XIII (1995), esp. 40–41.

5. Code Noir, 1685; Code Noir, 1724.

6. Code Noir, 1685, Code Noir, 1724; RSCL 1764/06/16/02; Titre 6, Article 5, in François Serpillon, *Code criminel ou commentaire sur l'ordonnance de 1670 . . . ,* 4 vols. (Lyon, France, 1767), 468–470.

7. Code Noir, 1685; Code Noir, 1724. On free African women married to French men and how they were treated by the courts, see Jessica Johnson, "Wives, Soldiers, and Slaves: The Atlantic World of Marie Baude, la femme Pinet," in Emily Clark, Cécile Vidal, and Ibrahima Thioub, eds., *Saint-Louis, Senegal, and New Orleans: Mirror Cities in the Atlantic World* (Baton Rouge, La., forthcoming).

8. Code Noir, 1724; RSCL 1746/11/27/01.

9. RSCL 1751/06/15/02, 1751/06/24/02; Michel to the minister of the navy, July 15, 1751, ANOM C13A 35, fol. 286. On Ordonnateur Michel's increasingly erratic altercations with Governor and Madame de Vaudreuil over this and other events, see Nicole Deschamps, ed., *Lettres au cher fils: Correspondance d'Élisabeth Bégon avec son gendre (1748–1753),* 2d ed. (Montreal, Quebec, 1994), 31–32. See also Thomas N. Ingersoll, *Mammon and Manon in Early New Orleans: The First Slave Society in the Deep South, 1718–1819* (Knoxville, Tenn., 1999), 40; and Guy Fregault, *Le grand marquis: Pierre de Rigaud de Vaudreuil et la Louisiane* (Montreal, 1952), chap. 6. On Madame de Vaudreuil's business activities and political dealings in Louisiana and Michel's reactions to her, see Sophie White, "'A Baser Commerce': Retailing, Class, and Gender in French Colonial New Orleans," *William and Mary Quarterly,* 3d Ser., LXIII (2006), esp. 538–550.

10. Vaudreuil to the minister of the navy, Apr. 25, 1747, ANOM C13A 31, fol. 56. After 1724, there would be no repeat of the circumstances surrounding the first extant testimony by an enslaved African, which occurred in May 1723. Fifteen-year-old Jean-Pierre, "Catholic," was brought in to testify as a witness in a case against a colonist, Le Roux, accused of killing a cow with a gunshot, a day that Jean-Pierre identified as that of the *"fête de dieu"* (feast day of Corpus Christi). What is notable is that Jean-Pierre was not the only eyewitness; two white boys witnessed the incident and also testified. See RSCL 1723/05/29/01.

11. On the role of the Superior Council as the court for all civil and criminal cases, see Henry Plauché Dart, "The Legal Institutions of Louisiana," *Louisiana Historical Quarterly,* II, no. 1 (January 1919), 74. That slaves in Louisiana (as in the Mascarene Islands) were tried in the Superior Council stands in contrast with Saint Domingue, for example, where slaves were tried in the Sénéchaussée court, whose records were not preserved. On the policy of destroying slave judicial archives in the French Caribbean, see Marie Houllemare, "Vers la centralisation des archives coloniales françaises au XVIIIe siècle: Destruction et conservation des papiers judiciaires," in Marie-Pia Donato and Anne Saada, eds., *Autour d'archives: Créer, organiser, et utiliser des archives à l'époque moderne* (Paris, 2018). See also John Garrigus, " 'Le secret qui règne parmi les nègres': Revisiting the Testimony of Makandal and His 'Accomplices,' 1757-1758," paper presented at the workshop on "Les resistances à l'esclavage dans le monde atlantique français à l'ère des révolutions (1750–1850)," organized by the Groupe d'histoire de l'atlantique français in collaboration with the Haiti Lab (Duke University) and Le centre international de recherches sur les esclavages, held at McGill University, May 3-4, 2013, Montreal; and Malick Ghachem, "Prosecuting Torture: The Strategic Ethics of Slavery in Pre-Revolutionary Saint-Domingue (Haiti)," *Law and History Review,* XIX (2011), 985-1029.

12. Letters Patent for the Establishment of a Superior Council of Louisiana, Dec. 23, 1712, ANOM, Ser. A, Edits, Ordonnances, Declarations, et Arrêts, 22, fol. 10; Dart, "Legal Institutions of Louisiana," *Louisiana Historical Quarterly,* II, no. 1 (January 1919), 72-203, esp.74-75.

13. RSCL 1765/09/09/02, 1765/09/21/01; Interrogation of Estienne, July 1757, Natchitoches Parish Conveyance Record Book 1: 1738-1765, 1757/7, no. 186, NP. Estienne's court case is analyzed in Sophie White, "Geographies of Slave Consumption: French Colonial Louisiana and a World of Goods," *Winterthur Portfolio,* XLV (2011), 229-248; and White, "Marion, Eighteenth-Century Louisiana," in Erica L. Ball, Tatiana Seijas, and Terri L. Snyder, eds., *Women in the African Diaspora: A Collective Biography of Emancipation in the Americas* (Cambridge, forthcoming). On Fleuriau, see Carl A. Brasseaux, *France's Forgotten Legion: A CD-ROM Publication: Service Records of French Military and Administrative Personnel Stationed in the Mississippi Valley and Gulf Coast Region, 1699-1799* (Baton Rouge, La., 2000), Part I: Administrators, s.v. "François Fleuriau."

14. The sentences for the theft of handkerchiefs in France are cited in Olwen H. Hufton, *The Poor of Eighteenth-Century France, 1750-1789* (Oxford, 1974), 25n. On a death penalty sentence actually meaning service in the galleys, see Marie Houllemare, "Penal Circulations in the French Atlantic, 18th Century," paper presented at the "Emerging Histories of the Early Modern French Atlantic" conference held by the Omohundro Institute of Early American History and Culture, Oct. 16-18, 2015, Williamsburg, Va. On the judicial system in New France, see André Lachance, *Crimes et criminels en Nouvelle-France* (Montréal, 1984), 43-49; and Eric Wenzel, *La justice criminelle en Nouvelle-France (1670-1760): Le Grand Arrangement* (Dijon, France, 2012).

15. RSCL 1743/08/24/04; Andrews, *Law, Magistracy, and Crime,* 383.

16. RSCL 1753/04/23/01.

17. Title 6, Article 11, in Serpillon, *Code criminel,* I, 481. On the requirement in French law to record testimony with as much accuracy as possible and the exact procedure for doing so, see Introduction, above.

18. Éric Wenzel, "La sellette . . . sur la sellette, ou les vicissitudes d'un séculaire instrument de la justice criminelle au siècle des Lumières," in *Gens de robe et gibier de potence en France du Moyen Âge à nos jours* (Marseille, France, 2007), 247-259.

19. Code Noir, 1724; Ghachem, "Prosecuting Torture," *Law and History Review,* XIX (2011), 985-1029.

20. KM 25:8:27:1. On judicial torture in Europe, see John H. Langbein, *Torture and the Law of Proof: Europe and England in the Ancien Régime* (Chicago, 1977), 73-77. On judicial torture in Louisiana, see Thomas N. Ingersoll, "The Law and Order Campaign in New Orleans, 1763-1765: A Comparative View," in Sally E. Hadden and Patricia Hagler Minter, eds., *Signposts: New Directions in Southern Legal History* (Athens, Ga., 2013), 45-64. In terms of the timing of the increase in judicial torture in the years 1763-1765, Attorney General Nicholas Chauvin de La Frénière had just returned to Louisiana via Saint Domingue, where he had been exposed to a more systematic use of judicial torture than was practiced in New Orleans. See Ingersoll, *Mammon and Manon,* 89-92.

21. Andrews, *Law, Magistracy, and Crime,* 383, 449.

22. Ibid., 449.

23. RSCL 1764/04/07/03, 1764/04/07/02.

24. Pascal Bastien, "Le droit d'être cruel: L'exercice de la cruauté dans l'ancien droit français (l'exemple de Paris au xviie siècle)," in Charlotte Bouteille-Meister and Kjerstin Aukrust, eds., *Corps sanglants, souffrants, et macabres: Xvie-xviie siècle* (Paris, 2010), 181-183. On Louis Congo, see Chapter 5, below. See also Series of notices, Nov. 21, 1725, ANOM C13A 9, fol. 267v; Jacques de La Chaise to the Company of the Indies, Sept. 6, 1723, ANOM C13A 7, fol. 44v; Shannon Lee Dawdy, *Building the Devil's Empire: French Colonial New Orleans* (Chicago, 2008), 189-191; and Gwendolyn Midlo Hall, *Africans in Colonial Louisiana: The Development of Afro-Creole Culture in the Eighteenth Century* (Baton Rouge, La., 1992), 130-131. On the steps entailed in applying judicial torture, see Andrews, *Law, Magistracy, and Crime,* 447-450 (quotations, 448).

25. On the conventions for begging forgiveness in the French Antilles, see Gabriel Debien, "Le Marronage aux Antilles Françaises au XVIIIe Siecle," *Caribbean Studies,* VI (October 1966), 14-15.

26. RSCL 1765/09/09/02, 13, 15.

27. RSCL 1751/04/23/01; 1753/05/02/01, 4; 1755/04/27/01.

28. Code Noir, 1724, Articles 38 and 39. On a rare prosecution brought against a planter in Saint Domingue for illegal extrajudicial torture, see Ghachem, "Prosecuting Torture," *Law and History Review,* XIX (2011), 985-1029.

29. RSCL 1764/07/31/01, 1; 1764/08/04/01, 2-3.

30. RSCL 1744/03/03/01, 3.

31. Code Noir, 1724, Article 36. For Louis's trial, see RSCL 1764/09/10/02, 1764/09/10/01. This case is analyzed in White, "Slaves and Poor Whites' Informal Economies in an Atlantic Context," in Vidal, ed., *Louisiana,* 141-170. On Kongo belief systems, see Cécile Fromont, *The Art of Conversion: Christian Visual Culture in the Kingdom of Kongo* (Chapel Hill, N.C., 2014), chap. 2; and D. Ryan Gray, "Rediscovering the 'Antiguo Cementerio': Archeological Excavations at the St. Peter Street Cemetery (16oR92), Orleans Parish, Louisiana," Final Report, Louisiana Division of Archaeology, 2017, 231. On the principle of a retunta, see Andrews, *Law, Magistracy, and Crime,* 385. For law

and punishment in France, see the online exhibit "Les exécutions publiques dans la france d'ancien régime," Musée d'histoire de la justice, des crimes, et des peines, Jan. 13, 2014, https://criminocorpus.org/fr/expositions/peine-de-mort/justice-royale-execution -publique/le-rituel-de-lexecution/ (accessed Oct. 14, 2018).

32. RSCL 1764/09/10/02. For the torture, see RSCL 1764/09/10/01. On branding, see Andrews, *Law, Magistracy, and Crime,* 314, 316. For examples of sentences handed out to named slaves, including a couple of brandings with a "V" for *"voleur"* (thief), see, for example, RSCL 1764/07/24/01: Statement of slaves punished since March; and 1765/10/10/02: Statement of slaves punished from July 26, 1764, to Oct. 10, 1765.

33. Code Noir, 1724, Articles 27–32; Serpillon, *Code criminel,* I–IV; Andrews, *Law, Magistracy, and Crime,* Part II, 383, 436–493. For a discussion of the differences between those punishments meted out to colonists and those to the enslaved in Louisiana, see Allain, "Slave Policies in French Louisiana," *Louisiana History,* XXI (1980), 136–137. See also Ingersoll, "Slave Codes," *Law and History Review,* XIII (1995), 34–35, 40–41.

34. KM 30:12:20:1, 30:12:22:1, 30:12:22:2, 30:12:22:3; Code Noir, 1724, Articles 27 and 28. On Mamantouensa, see Sophie White, *Wild Frenchmen and Frenchified Indians: Material Culture and Race in Colonial Louisiana* (Philadelphia, Pa., 2012), 28, 110. On Amerindians' influence on prosecutorial practice in Montreal, see Jan Grabowski, "French Criminal Justice and Indians in Montreal, 1670–1760," *Ethnohistory,* XLIII (1996), 405–429.

35. [Antoine-Simon] Le Page du Pratz, *Histoire de la Louisiane . . . ,* 3 vols. (Paris, 1758), I, 348. On the 1733 sentence, see Edme-Gatien Salmon to the minister of the navy, July 18, 1733, ANOM C13A 17, fol. 152. On anxieties about slave criminality as resulting from a lack of food and clothing, see also Sophie White, "'Wearing Three or Four Handkerchiefs around His Collar, and Elsewhere about Him': Slaves' Constructions of Masculinity and Ethnicity in French Colonial New Orleans," *Gender and History,* XV (2003), 531–532.

36. RSCL 1765/10/09/01, 1765/10/10/01, 1765/10/11/01, 1765/10/11/02, 1765/10/12/07, 1765/10/12/10. The case against Babette is analyzed in White, "'Wearing Three or Four Handkerchiefs,'" *Gender and History,* XV (2003), 533–540.

37. On the duration of the "question," see Andrews, *Law, Magistracy, and Crime,* 448. Not all judicial systems omitted these sounds; for example, trials before the papal magistrates in Renaissance Rome noted the utterances that the accused made when tortured, though these primarily took the shape of swearing and comments about pain. See Thomas V. Cohen and Elizabeth S. Cohen, *Words and Deeds in Renaissance Rome: Trials before the Papal Magistrates* (Toronto, 1993), esp. 121–125. My thanks to Margaret Meserve for this reference.

CHAPTER 2

1. RSCL 1752/06/13/01, 2.

2. For the trial records, see RSCL 1752/06/08/01; 1752/06/08/02; 1752/06/12/01; 1752/06/12/02; 1752/06/12/03; 1752/06/13/01; 1752/06/13/02; 1752/06/17/02; 1752/06/19/01; 1752/06/20/01; 1752/06/21/01; 1752/06/21/02; 1752/06/26/02; 1752/06/28/01.

3. See Carl A. Brasseaux, *France's Forgotten Legion: A CD-Rom Publication: Service Records of French Military and Administrative Personnel Stationed in the Mississippi Val-*

ley and Gulf Coast Region, 1699–1769 (Baton Rouge, La., 2000), Part 5, "Enlisted Men 1699–1770," s.v. "Paul Pochenet." Pochenet's date of arrival in the colony is unknown. Pochenet should have been stationed at the English Turn in June 1752 with La Houssaye's company, but his illness prevented his deployment there. See ibid., Part 3, "Military Officers," s.v. "Paul Augustin Le Pelletier de la Houssaye." For a somewhat parallel case in Montreal, where a soldier was prosecuted in 1728 for killing an Indian slave, see Ollivier Hubert, "Entendre les mots d'une éthique vernaculaire de la violence: Justices et cultures de l'honneur à Montréal au XVIIIe siècle," paper presented at the symposium on "Voices in the Legal Archives in the French Atlantic," organized by Nancy Christie, Michael Gauvreau, and Clare Haru Crowston, May 28–30, 2018, North Hatley, Quebec.

4. On the garrison maintained by the French crown in Louisiana and the low status of soldiers as well as the disruptions that they were thought to cause to the social order, see Thomas N. Ingersoll, "A View from the Parish Jail: New Orleans," *Common-Place*, III, no. 4 (July 2003), http://www.common-place-archives.org/vol-03/no-04/new-orleans/ (accessed Dec. 15, 2016); Daniel H. Usner, Jr., *Indians, Settlers, and Slaves in a Frontier Exchange Economy: The Lower Mississippi Valley before 1783* (Chapel Hill, N.C., 1992); and Yevan Terrien "Forced European Migrants and Soldiers in French Colonial New Orleans / Les émigrants forcés européens et les soldats dans la colonie française de La Nouvelle-Orléans," in Erin Greenwald, ed., *New Orleans: The Founding Era / La Nouvelle-Orléans: Les années fondatrices,* trans. Henry Colomer (New Orleans, 2018), 80–93. Terrien has calculated that, of the 7,020 Europeans shipped across the Atlantic, 977 were soldiers (ibid., 80). Terrien is completing a dissertation on "Exiles and Fugitives: Labor, Mobility, and Power in French Colonial Louisiana, 1700–1769" (Ph.D. diss., University of Pittsburgh).

5. RSCL 1752/06/12/02, 1; Éric Wenzel, "La sellette . . . sur la sellette, ou les vicissitudes d'un séculaire instrument de la justice criminelle au siècle des Lumières," *Gens de robe et gibier de potence en France du Moyen Age à nos jours* (Marseille, France, 2007), 247–259.

6. Richard Mowery Andrews, *Law, Magistracy, and Crime in Old Regime Paris, 1735– 1789* (Cambridge, 1994), 548.

7. A list of the hospital's linens was produced in 1731. Those that would be laundered (excluding woolen blankets and other textiles that were not suited to being washed in water) included fifty-eight pairs of linen sheets, three pillow cases, twenty-nine chalis cloths, and thirty pounds of old linens for bandages. See Inventory of movables and utensils in the hospital, November 1731, ANOM C13A 13, fol. 23. The Ursulines are documented as running a commercial laundry that deployed slave labor from the 1820s until the Civil War, but it is possible that they had begun charging for laundry before this, since it was a common practice for convents, including the Ursuline convent of Quebec, to offer such services. See Emily Clark, "Peculiar Professionals: The Financial Strategies of the New Orleans Ursulines," in Susanna Delfino and Michele Gillespie, eds., *Neither Lady nor Slave: Working Women of the Old South* (Chapel Hill, N.C., 2002), 206. On charges for laundering in the Quebec Ursuline convent, see Recette and depense de 1715 à 1746, 1742, Livres de Contes, SA-2-3-34, fol. 126v, Archives of the Ursulines of Quebec, Quebec.

8. RSCL 1752/06/19/01, 5; 1752/06/13/02, 8–9. For one inn that served a mixed cli-

entele, see Shannon Lee Dawdy, "Madame John's Legacy (16OR51) Revisited: A Closer Look at the Archaeology of Colonial New Orleans," typescript, Greater New Orleans Archaeology Program, College of Urban and Public Affairs, University of New Orleans, 1998. On alcohol, see ibid., 33. The term "Creole" denoted anyone of foreign extraction born in the colony, whether of African or European descent. On the location of the market, see Dumont de Montigny, *Regards sur le monde atlantique: 1715–1747* (Sillery, Quebec, 2008), 170.

9. RSCL 1752/06/13/02, 10. Her formal name was Marianne, but she was known by the diminutive form "Manon" ("Marianne dite [known as] Manon"). For the reference to Manon and her children in the probate records pertaining to the estate of Joseph Le Kintrek dit Dupont and his wife Marguerite Anne Marie Dos, see RSCL 1747/01/04/01, esp. 7. There were two other slaves listed, a fifty-year-old man named Janvier and a twelve-year-old Creole boy named Alain. How Le Kintrek acquired Manon is not known; he had purchased two slaves from the Company of the Indies in 1736, but they were both male. See RSCL 1736/09/22/01.

10. RSCL 1752/06/13/02, 10.

11. RSCL 1752/06/13/02, 4.

12. RSCL 1752/06/13/01, 2; 1752/06/13/02; 1752/06/19/01.

13. Samuel Wilson, "An Architectural History of the Royal Hospital and the Ursuline Convent of New Orleans," in Jean M. Farnsworth and Ann M. Masson, eds., *The Architecture of Colonial Louisiana: Collected Essays of Samuel Wilson, Jr., F.A.I.A.* (Lafayette, La., 1987), 161–220, Wilson, "La Nouvelle Orléans: Le Vieux Carré," 332.

14. On the Ursuline order in France, see Philippe Annaert, *Les Collèges au féminin: Les Ursulines: Enseignement et vie consacrée aux XVIIe et XVIIIe siècles* (Namur, Belgium, 1992); Elizabeth Rapley, *The Dévotes: Women and Church in Seventeenth-Century France* (Montreal, 1990); and Rapley, *A Social History of the Cloister: Daily Life in the Teaching Monasteries of the Old Regime* (Montreal, 2001). The key source on the Ursulines in New Orleans is Emily Clark, *Masterless Mistresses: The New Orleans Ursulines and the Development of a New World Society, 1727–1834* (Chapel Hill, N.C., 2007). See also Tracy Ebbs, "Subjected and Productive Bodies: The Educational Vision of the Ursulines in Early Colonial New Orleans" (Ph.D. diss., University of Pennsylvania, 1996), which focuses primarily on their pedagogy; and Jane Frances Heaney, *A Century of Pioneering: A History of the Ursuline Nuns in New Orleans,* ed. Mary Ethel Booker Siefken (New Orleans, 1993). The land for the Ursulines' plantation was granted to them as a subsidy. See Contract between the Ursulines and the Company of the Indies, Sept. 13, 1726, ANOM C13A 10, fol. 87–88, esp. fol. 87 (Clause 24). This estimate of 2,282 slaves held by French orders and congregations can be compared to the approximately 30,000 slaves held worldwide by religious corporations in the eighteenth century. These figures were extrapolated by Nathan Marvin, who stresses that they are not necessarily complete. See Marvin, " 'Biens curiaux, biens nationaux': The French Revolution and the Sale of Church Slaves on Réunion Island," paper presented at the 46th Annual Conference of the Western Society for French History, Nov. 1–3, 2018, Portland, Maine.

15. [Marie Madeleine] Hachard to her father, Feb. 22, 1727, in Hachard, *Relation du voyage des religieuses Ursulines de Rouen a la Nouvelle-Orléans en 1727, et précédée d'une*

notice par Paul Baudry (Rouen, France, 1865), 17, translation taken from Emily Clark, ed., *Voices from an Early American Convent: Marie Madeleine Hachard and the New Orleans Ursulines, 1727–1760* (Baton Rouge, La., 2007), 33. See also Clark *Masterless Mistresses,* 72–73, 161.

16. On servants, see Clark, *Masterless Mistresses,* 68–74; and Bulle de Bordeaux, 24–26, cited in Annaert, *Les Collèges au féminin,* 93–95 ("will only be"). On Anne Galbrun, see Sophie White, "'A Baser Commerce': Retailing, Class, and Gender in French Colonial New Orleans," *William and Mary Quarterly,* 3d Ser., LXIII (2006), 536. On Renée Yviguel, see Lettres circulaires, 228, UCANO, discussed in and translation taken from Clark, *Masterless Mistresses,* 100 ("what our most lowly," "most humiliating").

17. For the convent population, see Table A2 in Clark, *Masterless Mistresses,* 271. The nuns took in slaves as boarders (some perhaps the illegitimate daughters of their masters) for instruction preceding baptism and first communion. For a mixed-race female slave whose master owed the Ursulines for unpaid boarding fees, see Hachard to her father, Apr. 24, 1728, in Clark, ed., *Voices from an Early American Convent,* 82n. For the convent layout and architecture, see Wilson, "Architectural History of the Royal Hospital and the Ursuline Convent," in Farnsworth and Masson, eds., *Architecture of Colonial Louisiana,* 161–220; and Clark, *Masterless Mistresses,* 150–156.

18. Agreement between Ordonnateur Sébastien François Ange Le Normant de Mezy, stipulating for the king, and the superior of the Ursulines, Dec. 31, 1744, ANOM, C13A 28, fol. 343; General inventory of the king's hospital in New Orleans, Dec. 31, 1744, ANOM C13A 28, fol. 350. See also Contract between the Ursulines and the Company of the Indies, Sept. 13, 1726, ANOM C13A 10, fol. 88.

19. Agreement between Ordonnateur Le Normant, stipulating for the king, and the superior of the Ursulines, Dec. 31, 1744, ANOM C13A 28, fol. 343–344; General inventory of the furniture and utensils of the King's Hospital in New Orleans, Dec. 31, 1744, ANOM C13A 28, fol. 346 (see fol. 351v); Statement of the *nègres, negresses,* and *negrillons* belonging to the king, with their occupation, Jan. 1, 1760, ANOM C13A 42, fol. 67; RSCL 1748/02/10/01, 2.

20. Samuel Wilson, Jr., "The Plantation of the Company of the Indies," *Louisiana History,* XXXI (1990), 174; [Antoine-Simon] Le Page du Pratz, *Histoire de la Louisiane . . . ,* 3 vols. (Paris, 1758), III, 227–228. The plantation was owned by the Company of the Indies until 1731, when it was handed over to the crown.

21. RSCL 1748/02/10/01, 2. The young apprentice also bled the enslaved Angelique (on Dubreuil's plantation) on the foot and arm. See RSCL 1748/06/10/06. For the reference to François making tisanes in the pharmacy, see RSCL 1752/06/13/02, 8.

22. For the 1770 Natchitoches trial, see Athanaze de Mézières, Mar. 20–24, 1770, Natchitoches, Papeles Procedentes de Cuba, Archivo General de Indias, Seville, Legajo 188-A (microfilm available at the Historic New Orleans Collection, New Orleans, Louisiana); translation of testimony adapted from Gerald L. St. Martin, trans., "A Slave Trial in Colonial Natchitoches," *Louisiana History,* XXVIII (1987), 78, 83. On enslaved Africans' medical and healing knowledge, see also James H. Sweet, *Domingos Álvares, African Healing, and the Intellectual History of the Atlantic World* (Chapel Hill, N.C., 2011); and Natalie Zemon Davis, "Decentering History: Local Stories and Cultural Crossings in a

Global World," *History and Theory*, L (2011), 197-202. For the case involving Baron, see RSCL 1753/08/30/01, 4. As explored in more depth in the Epilogue, the cure involved in the latter case might have been for something other than a medical problem.

23. Wilson "Architectural History of the Royal Hospital and the Ursuline Convent," in Farnsworth and Masson, eds., *Architecture of Colonial Louisiana*, 161-220; Clark, *Masterless Mistresses*, 151-158; General inventory of the furniture and utensils of the King's Hospital in New Orleans, Dec. 31, 1744, ANOM C13A 28, fol. 346-351v, esp. fol. 349.

24. On slave marriage and family units, see Cécile Vidal and Emily Clark, "Famille et esclavage à La Nouvelle-Orléans sous le Régime français (1699-1769)," *Annales de démographie historique*, no. 122 (2011), 99-126; and Chapter 5, below.

25. On the retention of pay, see Agreement between Ordonnateur Le Normant, stipulating for the king, and the superior of the Ursulines, Dec. 31, 1744, ANOM C13A 28, fol. 344.

26. RSCL 1752/06/13/02, 11. For a similar example of a soldier demanding that an enslaved woman help him gather wood (in exchange for money) and hitting her when she refused, saying she did not have the time, see Le Page du Pratz, *Histoire de la Louisiane*, III, 304-305. On cultural notions of cleanliness and the centrality of women in body work, see Kathleen M. Brown, *Foul Bodies: Cleanliness in Early America* (New Haven, Conn., 2009); and Douglas Biow, *The Culture of Cleanliness in Renaissance Italy* (Ithaca, N.Y., 2006), 95-143. On laundry as women's work in Louisiana, see Sophie White, "'To Ensure That He Not Give Himself Over to the Indians': Cleanliness, Frenchification, and Whiteness," *Journal of Early American History*, II (2012), esp. 135-136; and White, *Wild Frenchmen and Frenchified Indians: Material Culture and Race in Colonial Louisiana* (Philadelphia, Pa., 2012), 195-196. On payment for laundry services, see, for example, the invoice in the Azemar succession for three livres, fifteen sous, the cost of two days' laundry work by African women slaves *("deux journées de negresse qui ont blanchy le linge")* in RSCL 1768/11/14/02. See also the list of slaves on the De Noyan plantation, which included two specialist washerwomen, Calamboüe and Catherine, both in their twenties and appraised respectively at eighteen hundred and fifteen hundred livres, more than a female domestic slave and the same as two enslaved seamstresses on the plantation; RSCL 1763/10/22/01. For an example of a male slave commissioning a female slave to launder his garb, see RSCL 1765/09/09/02.

27. KM 39:3:7:1; Antoine Laumet de La Mothe Cadillac to the minister of the navy, Oct. 26, 1713, ANOM C13A 3, 1, 17; RSCL 1752/06/12/02 (quotation, 2); 1752/06/19/01 (quotation, 6). For a reference to a colonist implicitly acknowledging an offer to be supplied with the sexual services of an enslaved women, see Epilogue, below.

28. Wilson, "Architectural History of the Royal Hospital and the Ursuline Convent of New Orleans," in Farnsworth and Masson, eds., *Architecture of Colonial Louisiana*, 59.

29. "Règlement sur la police pour la province de la Louisiane," Feb. 28-Mar. 1, 1751, ANOM C13A 35, fol. 39.

30. Ibid.

31. RSCL 1744/04/24/01; 1748/01/06/01, 4; 1744/03/13/01, 7. In another highly unusual instance, a scribe in the Illinois Country provided what seems a verbatim quote of the interrogator, slipping from the usual third person into the familiar "tu" in addressing the enslaved defendant accused of infanticide (the mole refers to a molar pregnancy): "In-

terrogated why she had hidden from Dame Beauvois that she had given birth to a child before the mole, the said Dame Beauvais told you that you could well have delivered a child before the mole" *(Interrogé pourquoi elle a caché à la Dame Beauvois quelle avoit mis un enfant au monde avant la molle Laquelle dame Beauvois t'a dit que tu pouvoit bien bien avoir accouché d'un enfant avant la molle)*. See KM 48:7:16:2, 1. This court case is discussed in Chapter 3, below.

32. RSCL 1752/06/19/01, 4; 1752/06/12/02, 3.

33. RSCL 1766/06/04/03, 1766/06/07/06.

34. Interrogation of Michel known as Michau, Sept. 21, 1711, Extract of the minutes of the civil and criminal court of the island of Martinique, ANOM F3 (Collection Moreau de Saint-Méry), 250, fol. 414v (quotation), Interrogation of Jeannot, Sept. 21, 1717, fol. 408v (quotation); RSCL 1748/04/15/01, 3; 1764/08/10/01, 2. On the case against Michaut, see also Dominique Rogers, ed., *Voix d'esclaves: Antilles, Guyane, et Louisiane françaises, XVIIIe–XIXe siècle* (Paris, 2015), 15–59; and Brett Rushforth, "Burning St. Pierre: Political Life and Political Economy in a Caribbean Slave Uprising," paper presented at the Rocky Mountain Seminar in Early American History, April 2017, Salt Lake City, Utah. On La Réunion, see Prosper Eve, *Les esclaves de Bourbon: La mer et la montagne* (Paris, 2003), 278–279.

35. On missionaries' accounts of slaves' professions of faith, see the examples analyzed by Sue Peabody, "'A Dangerous Zeal': Catholic Missions to Slaves in the French Antilles, 1635–1800," *French Historical Studies*, XXV (2002), 54–90. For counterexamples of European reports of Barbary pirates, who, on gaining their freedom, narrated stories of having resisted conversion to Islam (or converted simply as a means of avoiding death), see Lauren Benton, *Law and Colonial Cultures: Legal Regimes in World History, 1400–1900* (New York, 2002), 75.

36. RSCL 1743/09/10/03, 3.

37. Code noir, 1724, Articles 2–5, 7–8, and 11; RSCL 1764/10/23/01. Marguerite's case is discussed in more detail in the Introduction, above.

38. Clark notes that the Jesuits must have performed these sacraments prior to their expulsion in 1763. See Clark, *Masterless Mistresses*, 168n.

39. Corinne Thépaut-Cabasset, *L'esprit des modes au Grand Siècle* (Paris, 2010), 213; Hachard to her father, Apr. 24, 1728, quoted in Clark, ed., *Voices from an Early American Convent*, 83, Hachard to her father, Jan. 1, 1728, 78; Clark, *Masterless Mistresses*, chap. 5. The word *"sauvage"* is kept in preference to the English translation "savage" in order to retain the original French definition of the word as meaning "wild" or "untamed."

40. Emily Clark, "'By All the Conduct of Their Lives': A Laywomen's Confraternity in New Orleans, 1730–1744," *William and Mary Quarterly*, LIV (1997), 769–794; Clark, "Peculiar Professionals," in Delfino and Gillespie, eds., *Neither Lady nor Slave*, 198–220.

41. Clark, ed., *Voices from an Early American Convent*, 114–116.

42. NAMC KA3: June 4–Dec. 31, 1737; NAMC JB4 Boite B2 no. 2, cotté 36, contenant 7 pieces: see pièce no. 3, Aug. 18, 1745, 1; NAMC JB5 Boite B2 no. 12, cotté no. 26, 15 pieces, 1749: pièce no. 13, 1. On the presence of missionaries and nuns in French colonies, see Peabody, "'A Dangerous Zeal,'" *French Historical Studies*, XXV (2002), 53–90; Heidi Keller-Lapp, "Floating Cloisters and Heroic Women: French Ursuline Missionaries, 1639–1744," *World History Connected*, IV, no. 3 (2007), http://worldhistoryconnected

.press.uillinois.edu/4.3/lapp.html (accessed June 20, 2014); and Keller-Lapp, "Floating Cloisters and Femmes Fortes: Ursuline Missionaries in Ancien Régime France and Its Colonies" (Ph.D. diss., University of California, San Diego, 2005), chaps. 4–6. See also Marvin, "'Biens curiaux, biens nationaux.'"

43. Shannon Lee Dawdy et al., "Archaeological Investigations at Ursuline Convent (16OR49), New Orleans, Louisiana: 2011 Field Season," typescript, University of Chicago, Department of Anthropology prepared for the Office of Archives of the Archdiocese of New Orleans, the National Science Foundation, and the National Endowment for the Humanities, 2015. On the St. Peter Street Cemetery excavations, see D. Ryan Gray, "Rediscovering the 'Antiguo Cementerio': Archaeological Excavations and Recovery of Human Remains from the St. Peter Street Cemetery (16OR92), Orleans Parish, Louisiana: Final Report," typescript, University of New Orleans, Department of Anthropology, 2017. For Burial no. 11, see ibid., esp. 228–239 (quotation, 229). The site was excavated once in 1984 and a second time in 2011. On the shells, see ibid., 226. My special thanks to Dr. Gray for discussing his findings with me. On the popularity of Saint Anthony in the kingdom of Kongo, see Cécile Fromont, *The Art of Conversion: Christian Visual Culture in the Kingdom of Kongo* (Chapel Hill, N.C., 2014), 207–212. See also Dawdy et al., "Archaeological Investigations at St. Anthony's Garden (16OR433), New Orleans, Louisiana," 3 vols., typescript, University of Chicago, Department of Anthropology, prepared for Cathedral of St. Louis King of France and the Getty Foundation, 2008–2014. On the Capuchin order in Louisiana, see Claude L. Vogel, "The Capuchins in French Louisiana (1722–1766)" (Ph.D. diss., Catholic University of America, 1928). On Kongo and Catholic cosmologies, see Gray, "Rediscovering the 'Antiguo Cementerio,'" 238. On the Kongo cross, see Fromont, *Art of Conversion,* esp. chap. 2.

44. On the Ursulines' emphasis on confession and communion, see Clark, *Masterless Mistresses,* 105–107. On the likely timing of the confession before Easter, my thanks to Clark (personal communication, Nov. 8, 2013).

45. RSCL 1752/06/08/02, 1752/06/19/01 (quotation, 3); 1752/06/08/01, 1752/06/08/02. Medical information was also included in Raguet's report. See RSCL 1752/06/13/01. My thanks to Dr. Bryon Thomas for help with interpreting the medical descriptions.

46. On the importance of teachings about covering the head as seen in missionary activities among Amerindians in Louisiana, see White, *Wild Frenchmen and Frenchified Indians,* 56–58. On jumps and stays, see Valerie Steele, *The Corset: A Cultural History* (New Haven, Conn., 2001), chap. 1. On the definition of "corset" in the early eighteenth century, see Thépaut-Cabasset, *L'esprit des modes au grand siècle,* 170n. My thanks to Dr. Susan North, Senior Curator, Victoria and Albert Museum, and Linda Baumgarten, Curator, Colonial Williamsburg Foundation, for allowing me to examine rare surviving stays and corsets in their collection. On the construction of jumps ("corset" in French) as opposed to stays, see Steele, *Corset.*

47. Code Noir, 1685; Code Noir, 1724, Articles 18, 20, and 24; RSCL 1736/02/24/02: Lease between George Auguste de Vanderech, lieutenant in the colonial troops, and a German settler, Christian Grevert, for the latter to manage Vanderech's plantation; see clause 5. Vandereck was singled out for his sadism the following year. See Edmé-Gatien Salmon to the minister of the navy, Dec. 16, 1737, ANOM C13A 22, fol. 212. On the 1744 agreement, see Agreement between Le Normant, stipulating for the king, and the superior

of the Ursulines, Dec. 31, 1744, ANOM C13A 28, fol. 343. See also Le Normant to the minister of the navy, Oct. 17, 1745, C13A, 29, fols. 116v–117. Prior to the new 1744 agreement, the king paid for food and clothing for these slaves. For an example of a slave justifying his running away on the basis that his master did not adequately feed or clothe him, see RSCL 1748/06/11/02.

48. RSCL 1746/11/27/01 (corset); 1744/03/13/01, 7–8 (Alexandre). On ways that the enslaved supplemented their wardrobes, see Sophie White, "Slaves and Poor Whites' Informal Economies in an Atlantic Context," in Cécile Vidal, ed., *Louisiana: Crossroads of the Atlantic World* (Philadelphia, 2014), 89–102. On courtship and gift giving, see Chapter 4, below.

49. Sophie White, "'Wearing Three or Four Handkerchiefs around His Collar, and Elsewhere about Him': Slaves' Constructions of Masculinity and Ethnicity in French Colonial New Orleans," *Gender and History*, XV (2003), 528–549; White "Geographies of Slave Consumption: French Colonial Louisiana and a World of Goods," *Winterthur Portfolio*, XLIV (2011), 229–248; and White, "Slaves and Poor Whites' Informal Economies," in Vidal, ed., *Louisiana*, 89–102.

50. Code noir, 1724; "Règlement sur la police pour la province de la Louisiane," Feb. 28–Mar. 1, 1751, ANOM C13A 35, fol. 39.

51. Code noir, 1724, Article 25; RSCL 1752/06/13/01; Agreement between Ordonnateur Le Normant, stipulating for the king, and the superior of the Ursulines, Dec. 31, 1744, ANOM, C13A 28, fol. 343; General inventory of the king's hospital in New Orleans, Dec. 31, 1744, ANOM C13A 28, fol. 350. For the identification of the nuns, I consulted Clark, *Masterless Mistresses*, Appendix 1, 265–274.

52. For an example of a master filing suit on behalf of his slave, see RSCL 1744/12/26/04: Jean Pugeol's declaration of a theft from his slaves' cabins in Cannes Bruslées. For the denunciation, see RSCL 1752/06/28/01.

53. KM 38:8:20:1; Agreement between Ordonnateur Le Normant, stipulating for the king, and the superior of the Ursulines, Dec. 31, 1744, ANOM, C13A 28, fol. 343; General inventory of the king's hospital in New Orleans, Dec. 31, 1744, ANOM C13A 28, fol. 350. See also Contract between the Ursulines and the Company of the Indies, Sept. 13, 1726, ANOM C13A 10, fol. 88.

54. Clark, *Masterless Mistresses*. My thanks to Emily Clark for information regarding the Ursulines' register of deliberations and discussions; personal communication, Feb. 18, 2014. My thanks to her also for pointing me toward this interpretation of the nun's political position within the colony at the time of the trial. See respectively, Abbé de Lisle-Dieu, excerpts from letters sent from Louisiana, December 1752, ANOM C13A 36, fol. 331; Jean-Baptiste Le Moyne de Bienville and Edmé Gatien Salmon to the minister of the navy, May 12, 1733, C13A 16, fols. 89v–91; Louis Billouart de Kerlerc and Guillame Le Sénéchal d'Auberville to the minister of the navy, Apr. 20, 1753, ANOM C13A 37, fols. 42–43v; Kerlerec to the minister of the navy, Apr. 28, 1753, ANOM C13A 37, fols.48–48v; d'Auberville to the minister of the navy, July 5, 1754, ANOM C13A 38, fol. 151v; d'Auberville to the minister of the navy, July 6, 1754, ANOM C13A 38, fols. 155–158, all cited in Heaney, *Century of Pioneering*, ed. Siefken, chap. 6, esp. 127–132.

55. Abbé de Lisle-Dieu, excerpts from letters sent from Louisiana, December 1752, ANOM C13A 36, fols. 330–333v (quotation, fols. 332v–333). On the governor and ordon-

nateur's positions, see respectively Kerlérec and d'Auberville to the minister of the navy, Apr. 20, 1753, ANOM C13A 37, fol. 41; and d'Auberville to the minister of the navy, July 5, 1754, ANOM C13A 38, fol. 151.

56. On the nuns' enthusiastic work with the enslaved, see Clark, *Masterless Mistresses;* and Clark and Virginia Meacham Gould, "The Feminine Face of Afro-Catholicism in New Orleans, 1727-1852," *William and Mary Quarterly*, LIX (2002), 409-448. On Marie Turpin and how the Ursulines simultaneously accepted and racialized her by imposing limitations on her vocation and her place within the convent, see White, *Wild Frenchmen and Frenchified Indians* 168-170; White, "'À la française': Amérindiennes et Africaines dans un couvent de la Nouvelle-Orléans," in Jean-Pierre Le Glaunec and Nathalie Dessens, eds., *Interculturalité: La Louisiane au carrefour des cultures* (Quebec, 2015); and Clark, *Masterless Mistresses,* 71-73. For Mathieu Mulquet's testimony, see RSCL 1752/06/13/02.

57. Statement of the *negres, negresses,* and *negrillons* belonging to the king, Jan. 1, 1760, ANOM C13A 42, fol. 66-67, esp. fol. 67; RSCL 1752/06/17/02; 1752/06/26/02. On Pochenet's punishment as meeting the sentencing guidelines for the military, see De Briquet, "Ordonnance du roi . . . ," (Louis XIV), July 25, 1707, Article 25, in *Code militaire ou compilation des ordonnances des rois de France, concernant les gens de guerres,* new ed. (Paris, 1741), II, 87. For the commuting of Pochenet's sentence, see Honoré Michel de Villebois de la Rouvillière to the minister of the navy, Sept. 20, 1752, ANOM C13A 36, fol. 267. Michel included a copy of the criminal trial with his letter, but it is now missing, and no further information has been located pertaining to the commuting of Pochenet's sentence. Michel enclosed the documents in his correspondence as part of an effort to draw the minister's attention to drunkenness in the canteens. On the galleys as civil death (including the confiscation of the convict's property), see Richard Mowery Andrews, *Law, Magistracy, and Crime in Old Regime Paris, 1735-1789* (Cambridge, 1994), 86.

58. Michel to the minister of the navy, Sept. 20, 1752, ANOM C13A 36, fol. 267.

CHAPTER 3

1. KM 48:7:16:2, 1-2.

2. RSCL 1748/07/15/01, 3-4. This document is a clearer copy of the original produced in the Illinois Country, KM 48:07:15:01.

3. KM 48:7:15:1; 48:7:16:2; 48:7:16:3; 48:7:17:1, 3; 48:7:17:2; RSCL 1748/07/15/01; 1749/07/01/02, 5 (emphasis mine). The term "Creole" denoted anyone of foreign extraction born in the colony, whether of African or European descent. Neither Lisette nor any of the other witnesses were transported to New Orleans, but a near-identical copy of the trial proceedings in the Illinois Country was sent down, forming the basis for the Superior Council's investigation and interrogation of Marie-Jeanne. See RSCL 1748/07/15/01; 1748/07/16/01; 1749/06/17/01; 1749/06/21/01; 1749/06/21/02; 1749/06/27/01; 1749/07/01/01; 1749/07/01/02.

4. KM 48:07:15:01; 48:7:17:01, 3; RSCL 1748/07/15/01; 1749/07/01/02, 5. On other examples of Indian slaves testifying, see, especially, the rich documentation pertaining to the trial of Angélique, convicted in 1734 of setting fire to Montreal: "Torture and Truth: Angélique and the Burning of Montréal," Great Unsolved Mysteries in Canadian History, https://www.canadianmysteries.ca/sites/angelique/proces/indexen.html (accessed Oct.

28, 2018). See also Brett Rushforth, *Bonds of Alliance: Indigenous and Atlantic Slaveries in New France* (Chapel Hill, N.C., 2012), chap. 6; and papers on Indian slavery presented by Linford Fisher, Margaret Newell, and Rushforth at the conference on "Slave Narratives in British and French America, 1700–1848," held at the University of Notre Dame Global Gateway, July 14–15, 2017, London, which will be published in Sophie White and Trevor Burnard, eds., *Slave Narratives in French and British America 1700–1848* (Abingdon, U.K., forthcoming).

5. KM 48:7:16:2, 1; 48:07:15:01, 1. On the Braseau property, see Natalie Maree Belting, *Kaskaskia under the French Regime* [Urbana, Ill., 1948], 35.

6. KM 30:1:23:1; Marthe Faribault-Beauregard, ed., *La population des forts français d'Amérique (XVIIIe siècle): Répertoire des baptêmes, mariages, et sépultures célèbres dans les forts et les établissements français en Amérique du Nord au XVIIIe siècle*, 2 vols. (Montreal, 1982–1984), II, 15–16. Vincenne's widow was described as deceased in a document from 1747. See KM 47:12:3:1. For Dame Lasource's leasing out of Marie-Jeanne, see KM 48:7:15:1. It is unclear why Dame Lasource became acting agent, replacing Charles Huet Dulude. For the purposes of this book, the phoneme "8" or "8" is represented by the number "8," which has become the conventional way to represent the word in typescript, although Brett Rushforth has persuasively argued that the symbol is in fact "8," the Greek ligature commonly used to render the Latin "ou" (personal communication, January 2012). See also Michael McCafferty, *Native American Place-Names of Indiana* (Urbana, Ill., 2008), 21, 24–26, 32. On intermarriage and French-Indian relations in the Illinois Country, see Sophie White, *Wild Frenchmen and Frenchified Indians: Material Culture and Race in Colonial Louisiana* (Philadelphia, 2012), Part 1; Susan Sleeper-Smith, *Indian Women and French Men: Rethinking Cultural Encounter in the Western Great Lakes* (Amherst, Mass., 2001); Tracy Neal Leavelle, *The Catholic Calumet: Colonial Conversions in French and Indian North America* (Philadelphia, 2012); Robert Michael Morrissey, *Empire by Collaboration: Indians, Colonists, and Governments in Colonial Illinois Country* (Philadelphia, 2015); Robert Englebert and Guillaume Teasdale, eds., *French and Indians in the Heart of North America, 1630–1815* (East Lansing, Mich., 2013); Karen L. Marrero, "Women at the Crossroads: Trade, Mobility, and Power in Early French America and Detroit," in Thomas A. Foster, ed., *Women in Early America* (New York, 2015), 159–185; Carl J. Ekberg, with Anton J. Pregaldin, "Marie Rouensa-8cate8a and the Foundations of French Illinois," *Illinois Historical Journal*, LXXXIV (1991), 146–160; and Belting *Kaskaskia*, 80–83. Among those prominent men who married half-Indian women was the royal storekeeper, Nicolas Chassin; he married Agnes Philippe (the daughter of Marie Rouensa-8cate8a, herself the daughter of the chief of the Kaskaskia and the woman responsible for initiating French-Indian Catholic intermarriage in the Illinois Country). See White, *Wild Frenchmen*, chap. 2. Some widowers actively sought women of Indian or mixed parentage as spouses. When Suzanne Baron's Indian mother, Marie Catherine Illinoise, passed away, her father, Jean-Baptiste Baron, contracted a second marriage with Domitille Rolet, the daughter of a settler and Domitille Apanis8 of the Peoria nation (KM 48:8:18:1). Louis Turpin married Dorothée Mechip8e8a, the widow of another Frenchman, Charles Danis, going from being the widower of a French-Canadian woman to being the husband of an Indian woman (KM 24:7:25:1; Faribault-Beauregard, *Populations*, II, 232). Daniel Legras married the Indian Suzanne Keramy, widow of Leonard (Belting,

Kaskaskia, 81). Nicolas Boyer, widower of the half-Indian Marie Rose Texier, married the half-Indian Dorothée La Boissiere (KM 47:12:13:1, 49:4:21:1). On slaves as wet nurses, see the petition of Baptiste Charras concerning the slave he leased to Madame Daunois as a wet nurse for sixteen months in New Orleans; RSCL 1748/02/12/02. See also Sue Peabody, *Madeleine's Children: Family, Freedom, Secrets, and Lies in France's Indian Ocean Colonies* (Oxford, 2017), chap. 6.

7. KM 30:2:11:1 and 35: — : —; KM 36: — : — :59 and 36:—: — :60. Since the only date on the sales contract is 1736, it is unknown if this agreement was entered into before or after Vincennes's death, though the fact that his wife was the one named on the document suggests that it was after. For other transactions in which Vincennes's wife leased out her enslaved Africans, see KM 36:—: — :106 (a male); 37:2:25:1 (a male and female). On the Coutume de Paris, see [François] Olivier-Martin, *Histoire de la coutume de la prévôté et vicomté de Paris,* 2 vols. (Paris, 1922–1930). For the law's application in Louisiana, see Hans W. Baade, "Marriage Contracts in French and Spanish Louisiana: A Study in 'Notarial' Jurisprudence," *Tulane Law Review,* LIII (197[8]–1979), 3–92; and Jerah Johnson, *"La Coutume de Paris:* Louisiana's First Law," *Louisiana History,* XXX (1989), 145–155.

8. *Le dictionnaire de l'académie françoise,* 1st ed. (Paris, 1694), s.v. "mole."

9. RSCL 1749/06/21/01, 2.

10. KM 48:7:15:1, 6–7. The version of this document kept by the Superior Council reads Marie-Jeanne was "extraordinarily open" and that she kept fainting *("s'evanouissant à tous moment").* See RSCL 1748/07/15/01, 5.

11. RSCL 1748/07/15/01, 3; Belting, *Kaskaskia,* 35n.

12. RSCL 1748/07/15/01, 3.

13. KM 48:07:15:01; RSCL 1748/07/15/01. On children testifying in French courts, see Titre VI, Article II, in François Serpillon, *Code criminel, ou commentaire sur l'ordonnance de 1670 . . . ,* 4 vols. (Lyon, France, 1767), I, 445. On the use of interpreters, see Titre XIV, Article XI, ibid., 668–670.

14. RSCL 1748/07/15/01, 3. See also KM 48:07:15:01.

15. KM 48:7:17:1, 2–3; 48:07:15:01; RSCL 1748/07/15/01; 1749/07/01/02, 4, 1749/06/17/01, 2.

16. Éric Wenzel, "La sellette . . . sur la sellette, ou les vicissitudes d'un séculaire instrument de la justice criminelle au siècle des Lumières," in *Gens de robe et gibier de potence en France du Moyen Âge à nos jours* (Marseille, France, 2007), 247–259.

17. Kenneth J. Banks, *Chasing Empire across the Sea: Communications and the State in the French Atlantic, 1713–1763* (Montreal, 2002), 92; N. M. Miller Surrey, *The Commerce of Louisiana during the French Régime, 1699–1763* (New York, 1916), 45–49; Daniel H. Usner, *American Indians in Early New Orleans: From Calumet to Raquette* (Baton Rouge, La., 2018), 10 ("patchwork"). Convoys were regularly manned by slaves and free blacks. See Carl J. Ekberg, "Black Slavery in Illinois, 1720–1765," *Western Illinois Regional Studies,* XII, no. 1 (Spring 1989), 5–19; Gwendolyn Midlo Hall, *Africans in Colonial Louisiana: The Development of Afro-Creole Culture in the Eighteenth Century* (Baton Rouge, La., 1992), 174–175; and Usner, *Indians, Settlers, and Slaves in a Frontier Exchange Economy: The Lower Mississippi Valley before 1783* (Chapel Hill, N.C., 1992), 227–230. On Marie Turpin, who became Sister St. Marthe, a converse nun in the New

Orleans convent, see White, *Wild Frenchmen*, chap. 4; and Emily Clark, *Masterless Mistresses: The New Orleans Ursulines and the Development of a New World Society, 1727–1834* (Chapel Hill, N.C., 2007), 71–73, 211. The quotation "sainted girl" is from her obituary in the convent register. See "Registre pour écrire les réceptions des religieuses de France et postulantes [Mar. 4, 1726–Sept. 20, 1893] et les lettres circulaires [July 6, 1728–Jan. 31, 1894]," UCANO, Reel 2.

18. On dress, see White, *Wild Frenchmen*, chap. 1. On Indians in New Orleans, see Usner, *American Indians in Early New Orleans*.

19. Samuel Wilson, "Architecture of the Vieux Carré: French Colonial Period, 1718–1768," in Jean M. Farnsworth and Ann M. Masson, eds., *The Architecture of Colonial Louisiana: Collected Essays of Samuel Wilson, Jr., F.A.I.A.* (Lafayette, La., 1987), 326–329, Wilson, "La Nouvelle Orléans: Le Vieux Carré," 330–335; Shannon Lee Dawdy, "Ethnicity in the Urban Landscape: The Archaeology of Creole New Orleans," in Amy L. Young, ed., *Archaeology of Southern Urban Landscapes* (Tuscaloosa, Ala., 2000), esp. 137–143.

20. Sometimes described as a "confederacy," the Illinois as a composite group actually had few features of a confederacy beyond similar origin traditions and geographic, linguistic, and cultural ties. See Margaret Kimball Brown, *Cultural Transformations among the Illinois: An Application of a Systems Model*, Publications of the Museum, Anthropological Ser. I, no. 3 (East Lansing, Mich., 1979); J. Joseph Bauxar, "History of the Illinois Area," in William C. Sturtevant, ed., *Handbook of North American Indians*, XV, *Northeast*, ed. Bruce G. Trigger (Washington, D.C., 1978), 594–601, Charles Callender, "Illinois," 673–680; Christopher Bilodeau, "'They Honor Our Lord among Themselves in Their Own Way': Colonial Christianity and the Illinois Indians," *American Indian Quarterly*, XXV (2001), 352–377; and Jacob Fielding Lee, "Rivers of Power: Indians and Colonists in the North American Midcontinent" (Ph.D. diss., University of California Davis, 2014). French settlement patterns in the Illinois Country are discussed by Carl J. Ekberg, *French Roots in the Illinois Country: The Mississippi Frontier in Colonial Times* (Urbana, Ill., 1998); and Renald Lessard, Jacques Mathieu, and Lina Gouger, "Peuplement colonisateur au pays des Illinois," *Proceedings of the Twelfth Meeting of the French Colonial Historical Society, Ste. Geneviève, May 1986*, ed. Philip P. Boucher and Serge Courville (Lanham, Md., 1988), 577–568. On the legacies of the French in the area, see, for example, Robert Englebert, "The Legacy of New France: Law and Social Cohesion between Quebec and the Illinois Country, 1763–1790," *French Colonial History*, XVII (2017), 35–65; M. Scott Heerman, "'That "A'cursed Illinois Venture'": Slavery and Revolution in Atlantic Illinois," *Journal of Illinois History*, XIII (2010), 107–128; and Jay Gitlin, *The Bourgeois Frontier: French Towns, French Traders, and American Expansion* (New Haven, Conn., 2010).

21. Joseph Zitomersky, "The Form and Function of French-Native American Relations in Early Eighteenth-Century French Colonial Louisiana," in Patricia Galloway and Philip P. Boucher, eds., *Proceedings of the Fifteenth Meeting of the French Colonial Historical Society: Martinique and Guadeloupe, May 1989* (Lanham, Md., 1992), 154–177. See also Zitomersky, *French Americans-Native Americans in Eighteenth-Century French Colonial Louisiana: The Population Geography of the Illinois Indians, 1670s–1760s: The Form and Function of French-Native Settlement Relations in Eighteenth-Century Louisi-*

ana (Lund, Sweden, 1994); and Christian Ayne Crouch, *Nobility Lost: French and Canadian Martial Cultures, Indians, and the End of New France* (Cornell, N.Y., 2014).

22. Ekberg, *French Roots*. On household furnishings, see White, *Wild Frenchmen*, chap. 1; Cécile Vidal, "Les implantations françaises au Pays des Illinois au XVIIIe siècle (1699–1765)," 2 vols. (Ph.D. diss., École des Hautes Études en Sciences Sociales, 1995), 594.

23. Census, January 1726, ANOM G1, 464; Census of villages in the Illinois Country, [1752], Vaudreuil Papers, O/S LO 426, Huntington Library, San Marino, Calif. (there are inconsistencies within the document; calculations are taken from the recapitulation); see also Cécile Vidal, "Africains et Européens au pays des Illinois durant la période française (1699–1765)," *French Colonial History*, III (2003), 51–68; Ekberg, "Black Slavery in Illinois," *Western Illinois Regional Studies*, XII, no. 1 (Spring 1989), 5–19; Christian Ayne Crouch, "The Black City: African and Indian Exchanges in Pontiac's Upper Country," *Early American Studies*, XIV (2016), 284–318; and M. Scott Heerman, "Beyond Plantations: Indian and African Slavery in the Illinois Country, 1720–1780," *Slavery and Abolition*, XXXVIII (2017), 489–509; M. Scott Heerman, *The Alchemy of Slavery: Human Bondage and Emancipation in the Illinois Country, 1730–1865* (Philadelphia, 2018), chap. 1.

24. KM 47:4:29:1; 47:5:7:1. On conditions for enslaved Africans in the Illinois Country, see Vidal, "Africains et Européens," *French Colonial History*, III (2003), 53; and Ekberg, "Black Slavery in Illinois," *Western Illinois Regional Studies*, XII, no. 1 (Spring 1989), 9. On the cultivation of wheat and the trade in flour and hogs, see Carl J. Ekberg, "The Flour Trade in French Colonial Louisiana," *Louisiana History*, XXVII (1996), 261–282; and Ekberg, *French Roots*, 115–123, 206–210. For the edict, see ibid., 119–120. On the 1748 harvest, see Belting, *Kaskaskia*, 56.

25. The 1752 census of the Illinois Country counted 1,682 pigs. See Table 5, in Ekberg, *French Roots*, 207.

26. Archives of the Ministry of Marine, Oct. 25, 1720, transcribed by Pierre Margry, ed., *Découvertes et établissements des français dans l'ouest et dans le sud de l'Amérique Septentrionale (1614–1754)* . . . , 6 vols. (Paris, 1876–1886), VI, 316. On the legality of Indian slavery in New France, see David Gilles, "La norme esclavagiste, entre pratique coutumière et norme étatique: Les esclaves panis et leur statut juridique au Canada (XVIIe-XVIIIe s.)," *Ottawa Law Review / Revue de droit d'Ottawa*, XL (2008–2009), 73–114, esp. 82n. Gilles argues that no Indians from allied nations were enslaved in New France, especially after the Great Peace of Montreal (1701); see ibid., 79. On France's involvement in the Indian slave trade in North America, see Rushforth, "'A Little Flesh We Offer You': The Origins of Indian Slavery in New France," *William and Mary Quarterly*, 3d Ser., LX (2003), 777–803; and Rushforth, *Bonds of Alliance*. On Indian slavery in Louisiana, see ANOM C13A 1, fol. 514–519; C13A 2, fol. 57–69; C13 2, fol. 359–362, and C13A 3, fol. 110, discussed in Surrey, *Commerce of Louisiana*, 228–229; A. P. Nasatir, ed., *Before Lewis and Clark: Documents Illustrating the History of the Missouri, 1785–1804* (Norman, Okla., 1952), 19n; and Rushforth, "'A Little Flesh We Offer You,'" *William and Mary Quarterly*, LX (2003), 779. For the 1739 ordinance, see Ordinance, Mar. 9, 1739, ANOM B68, fol. 5–5v. On Indian slavery in broader context, see Andrés Reséndez, *The Other Slavery: The Uncovered Story of Indian Enslavement in America* (Boston, [2016]).

27. For voyageur expeditions around the date of Lisette's arrival, see, for example, KM 48:1:11:1: Acknowledgement by Joseph Philippe, voyageur who has just arrived from Detroit, of receipt of funds from Jacques Michel Dufrene; KM 48:3:26:1: Agreement by Charles Boisvert, voyageur in the Illinois, to enter the service of Jean Baptiste La Chapelle and Company, to travel to the post of Michilimackinac; KM 48:5:19:1: Agreement by Jean Baptiste Amiot, voyageur in the Illinois, to enter the service of Joseph Desruissaux travel with him to the Missouri; and KM 47:9:10:1: Partnership agreement between Michel Durivage voyageur in the Illinois, and Marin Urtubise, voyageur-trader in the Illinois, to travel to the Fox tribe.

28. Ordinance of Governor Vaudreuil, May 1, 1747, ANOM F3 243, fol. 13. See also Vidal, "Africains et Européens," *French Colonial History*, III (2003), 60.

29. For references to legal intermarriage in the Illinois Country, see note 6, above. On the land survey, see White, *Wild Frenchmen*, Part I; KM 30:10:23:1, 37:7:6:1, 33:5:18:1, discussed in White, *Wild Frenchmen*, 110–111; Ekberg, *French Roots*, 76–77; and Belting, *Kaskaskia*, 77n.

30. Code Noir, 1724. On the 1670 Code criminel, see Chapter 1, above.

31. KM 48:07:15:01; RSCL 1748/07/15/01.

32. KM 48:7:17:1, 3, 48:7:16:2, 3; RSCL 1749/07/01/02, 6. For the report of the surgeons, see RSCL 1749/07/01/01.

33. RSCL 1748/07/15/01, 3; KM 48:07:15:01; RSCL 1748/07/15/01. For the distinction between "nubile" girls and those girls under twelve years of age, see Jean Jacques de Macarty Mactigue to Pierre de Rigaud de Vaudreuil, Census of the Illinois Country, 1752, Vaudreuil Papers, O/S LO 426, Huntington Library. On gestures, see Céline Carayon, "'The Gesture Speech of Mankind': Old and New Entanglements in the Histories of American Indian and European Sign Languages," *American Historical Review*, CXXI (2016), 461–491.

34. Rushforth, "'A Little Flesh We Offer You,'" *William and Mary Quarterly*, LX (2003), 799. See also Sophie White, "Mardi Gras, Massacre, and Torture in Early New Orleans," *William and Mary Quarterly*, LXX (2013), 497–538, 526–528. There are some parallels with European judicial practices. On the disfigurement, evisceration, pulling apart, and parading of the head and genitals of the executed in seventeenth-century France, see Pascal Bastien, "Le droit d'être cruel: L'exercice de la cruauté dans l'ancien droit français (l'exemple de Paris au xviie siècle)," in Kjerstin Aukrust and Charlotte Bouteille-Meister, eds., *Corps sanglants, souffrants, et macabres: XVIe–XVIIe siècle* (Paris, 2010), 177–188, esp. 178.

35. RSCL 1749/06/21/02; 1749/07/01/01, 4.

36. On infanticide accusations in early modern France, see Leslie Tuttle, *Conceiving the Old Regime: Pronatalism and the Politics of Reproduction in Early Modern France* (Oxford, 2010); Soman, "Anatomy of an Infanticide Trial," Wolfe, ed., *Changing Identities in Early Modern France*, 248–272; Christophe Regina and Stéphane Minvielle, "Crimes familiaux: Tuer, voler, frapper les siens en Europe du xve au xixe siècle," *Annales de démographie historique*, CXXX (2015), 5–23; Antoine Follain and Rosine Hochuli, "Un procès pour infanticide dans la juridiction de Boulay-Moselle en 1606," in Christophe Regina and Lucien Faggion, eds., *La violence: Regards croisés sur une réalité plurielle* (Paris,

2010), 261–284; Mark Jackson, ed., *Infanticide: Historical Perspectives on Child Murder and Concealment, 1550–2000* (Aldershot, U.K., 2002); Stéphane Minvielle, "Marie Bonfils, une veuve accusée d'infanticide dans le Bordelais de la fin du xviie siècle," *Dix-septième siècle*, no. 249 (2010), 623–643; and Daniela Tinková, "Protéger ou punir? Les voies de la décriminalisation de l'infanticide en France et dans le domaine des Habsbourg (xviiie–xixe siècles)," *Crime, histoire, et sociétés / Crime, History, and Societies*, IX, no. 2 (2005), 43–72. On infanticide accusations against the enslaved in French colonies, see Bernard Moitt, *Women and Slavery in the French Antilles, 1635–1848* (Bloomington, Ind., 2001), 93–94; Megan Vaughan, *Creating the Creole Island: Slavery in Eighteenth-Century Mauritius* (Durham, N.C., 2005), chap. 5; and Karol K. Weaver, "'She Crushed the Child's Fragile Skull': Disease, Infanticide, and Enslaved Women in Eighteenth-Century Saint-Domingue," *French Colonial History*, V (2004), 93–109. My thanks to Christina Mobley for sharing a draft of her article "The Mystery of the 'Mondongue': Cannibalism, Witchcraft, and Terror from the Loango Coast to Saint Domingue," which offers rich interpretation of a 1786 infanticide case against an enslaved woman in Saint Domingue, elucidating one important aspect of myth-making surrounding infanticide. See also, on accusations of infanticide against the enslaved beyond French colonies, Jennifer L. Morgan, *Laboring Women: Reproduction and Gender in New World Slavery* (Philadelphia, 2004), chap. 4, esp. 230–231n; Marcela Echeverri, "'Enraged to the Limit of Despair': Infanticide and Slave Judicial Strategies in Barbacoas, 1788–98," *Slavery and Abolition*, XXX (September 2009), 403–426; Wendy Warren, *New England Bound: Slavery and Colonization in Early America* (New York, [2016]), 167–171; and Margaret Newell, "In the Borderlands of Race and Freedom (and Genre): Embedded Indian and African Slave Testimony in Eighteenth-Century New England," in White and Burnard, eds., *Slave Narratives in French and British America*. Beyond issues of malnutrition and other physical implications of slave labor, Barbara Bush also argues that control over reproduction through abortion and infanticide served as a form of resistance. See Bush, *Slave Women in Caribbean Society, 1650–1838* (Bloomington, Ind., 1990), 137, 147–149.

37. On the shift in approach toward fallen women and infanticide, see Tinková, "Protéger ou punir?" *Crime, histoire, et sociétés / Crime, History, and Societies*, IX, no. 2 (2005), 43–72; and Soman, "Anatomy of an Infanticide Trial," in Wolfe, ed., *Changing Identities in Early Modern France*, 265–266. There was a parallel drop in the rate of prosecutions and executions of white women for infanticide in Anglo-America. See Kirsten Fischer, *Suspect Relations: Sex, Race, and Resistance in Colonial North Carolina* (Cornell, N.Y., 2002), 106. On forced and voluntary emigration of women to Louisiana, see Jennifer M. Spear, *Race, Sex, and Social Order in Early New Orleans* (Baltimore, 2009), 42–45; and Thomas N. Ingersoll, *Mammon and Manon in Early New Orleans: The First Slave Society in the Deep South, 1718–1819* (Knoxville, Tenn., 1999), chap. 1. On policies and debates about intermarriage between French men and Indian women, see White, *Wild Frenchmen and Frenchified Women*, Part 1; Spear, *Race, Sex, and Social Order*, 42–50; Spear, "'They Need Wives': Métissage and the Regulation of Sexuality in French Louisiana, 1699–1730," in Martha Hodes, ed., *Sex, Love, Race: Crossing Boundaries in North American History* (New York, 1999), 35–59; and Guillaume Aubert, "'The Blood of France': Race and Purity of Blood in the French Atlantic World," *William and Mary Quarterly*, LXI (2004),

439–478. See also Sleeper-Smith, *Indian Women and French Men*. In French, the word *fille* has a dual meaning, as "girl" and "daughter."

38. Arrêt du Conseil Supérieur de la louisianne du 29 Juillet 1727 sur la grossesse des filles et femmes non mariées, ANOM Series A, 23, fol. 86v.

39. RSCL 1749/07/01/02, 5 (emphasis mine); KM 48:07:17:1. For the definition, see *Le dictionnaire de l'académie françoise*, s.v. "denaturé, denaturée."

40. On accusations of infanticide against the enslaved, see note 36, above. On negative conceptualizations of enslaved Africans as mothers in the British Atlantic, see also Sasha Turner, *Contested Bodies: Pregnancy, Childrearing, and Slavery in Jamaica* (Philadelphia, 2017); and Susan E. Klepp and Roderick A. McDonald, "Inscribing Experience: An American Working Woman and an English Gentlewoman Encounter Jamaica's Slave Society," *William and Mary Quarterly*, LVIII (2001), 637–660.

41. On infanticide in French colonies, see note 36, above.

42. NAMC, JB1 Boite B1 cotté no. 74: Mar. 24–26, 1734.

43. RSCL 1748/04/15/01, 2–3.

44. RSLC 1746/01/15/03.

45. All references to this court case are from Ste. Genevieve Civil Records, Slaves, no. 196, n.p., quotation from deposition taken Apr. 24, 1773. See also Carl J. Ekberg, *Stealing Indian Women: Native Slavery in the Illinois Country* (Urbanna, Ill., 2007), Part II, esp. 162–163, 172, 181; and White, *Wild Frenchmen*, 105–107. Céladon would be accused of murdering another Indian slave, which generated a large body of documents about his actions and those of Marianne.

46. Vaughan, *Creating the Creole Island*, 139–140 (quotation, 139).

47. Megan Vaughan introduced two such court cases, dating to 1746 and 1751–1752, but I have identified another two cases of alleged abduction, from 1745 and 1749. Such cases might have carried on beyond 1752, but we are here confronted with a lacuna in the archival records, since archivists destroyed portions of the records of the Superior Council of Mauritius from 1754–1766 (Ser. JB7, JB8, JB9) after the records were damaged in 1961 as a result of Tropical Cyclone Beryl. See Vaughan, *Creating the Creole Island*, chap. 5. On marronnage in Mauritius, see especially Richard B. Allen, *Slaves, Freedmen, and Indentured Laborers in Colonial Mauritius* (Cambridge, 1999), Part I; and Amédée Nagapen, *Le maronnage à l'Isle de France—Ile Maurice: Rêve ou riposte de l'esclave?* (Port Louis, Mauritius, 1999).

48. Interrogation of Laurence, Sept. 21, 1711, Collection Moreau de Saint-Méry, ANOM, F3, 26, 400–405 (quotation, fol. 402v).

49. Affaires Criminelles, Oct. 28, 1739, NAMC JB3 Boite B no. 1; Against Thereze, Fanchon, Anne, Margot, Zaza her child, and Hector, March 1745, NAMC JB4 Boite B2 no. 2, cotté 36. On the Martinique court case, see Brett Rushforth, "Burning St. Pierre: Political Life and Political Economy in a Caribbean Slave Uprising," paper presented at the Rocky Mountain Seminar in Early American History, April 2017, Salt Lake City, Utah.

50. Code noir, 1685, Articles 12 and 13; Code noir, 1724, Articles 9 and 10; Guillaume Aubert, "'To Establish One Law and Definite Rules': Race, Religion, and the Transatlantic Origins of the Louisiana Code Noir," in Cécile Vidal, ed., *Louisiana: Crossroads of the Atlantic World* (Philadelphia, 2014), 54–60.

51. Antoine-Simon Le Page du Pratz, *Histoire de la Louisiane . . . , 3* vols. (Paris, 1758), I, 335. On pregnancy and slavery, see Turner, *Contested Bodies;* and Morgan, *Laboring Women.*

52. Code Noir, 1724, Articles 7, 8, 43, and 46.

53. RSCL 1748/06/10/06, 1; 1748/01/05/04, 1; 1748/05/18/03, 1 (emphasis mine). In at least one case where the child identified his or her parents in court, it was the court that asked the child to name his parents, perhaps signaling a temporary shift in how interrogations were conducted. See also Cécile Vidal and Emily Clark, "Famille et esclavage à La Nouvelle-Orléans sous le Régime français (1699-1769)," *Annales de démographie historique,* no. 122 (2011), 106-107.

54. In contrast to there being no mention of skin, only bones, with regard to the fetal matter found in the Illinois Country, see the way the surgeon in Mauritius in 1778 carefully sought to identify the skin color of a baby whose body was found drowned, when, after examining the body under a lamp he pronounced it to be a white baby; discussed in Vaughan, *Creating the Creole Island,* 128. For a chilling analysis of coercion, see Wendy Anne Warren, " 'The Cause of Her Grief': The Rape of a Slave in Early New England," *Journal of American History,* XCIII (2007), 1031-1049. See also Daina Ramey Berry and Leslie M. Harris, *Sexuality and Slavery: Reclaiming Intimate Histories in the Americas* (Athens, Ga., 2018).

55. RSCL 1730/04/29/01; 1730/08/30/01.

56. RSCL 1730/09/05/02, 3; 1730/04/29/01, 1-2.

57. RSCL 1730/04/29/01, 1.

58. Code Noir, 1724, Articles 20 and 24; RSCL 1730/09/05/02.

59. Code Noir, 1724, Article 6.

60. RSCL 1749/06/21/01, 1; 1749/06/21/02; 1749/06/21/02; 1749/07/01/01, 2.

61. See Title XXV, Article XIII, Clause 24, in Serpillon, *Code criminel ou commentaire sur l'ordonnance de 1670,* III, 1090-1091, 1134.

CHAPTER 4

1. RSCL 1766/07/29/04. The "b." was a polite abbreviation of "bougre" ("bugger" in English). For another instance of its use, see the testimony of Pluton, where he quotes a woman using that word in addressing him: RSCL 1748/01/06/01, 5.

2. RSCL 1766/04[08]/02/02, 1 (the correct date is August, not April, 1766). The records of this investigation are found in RSCL 1766/04/02/02, 1766/07/04/01, 1766/07/04/02, 1766/07/04/03, 1766/07/23/02, 1766/07/25/02, 1766/07/29/04, 1766/07/29/05, 1766/07/31 /06, and 1766/08/02/04. For an analysis of this court case focusing primarily on dress, see Sophie White, " 'Wearing Three or Four Handkerchiefs around His Collar, and Elsewhere About Him': Slaves' Constructions of Masculinity and Ethnicity in French Colonial New Orleans," *Gender and History,* XV, (2003), 528-549. As Meïssa Niang reminds us, what constitutes criminality in any given society and period depends on cultural values. See Niang, "La criminalité au Sénégal" (Ph.D. thesis, Université de droit, d'économie, et des sciences d'Aix-Marseille, 1995), 3-4.

3. RSCL 1766/07/29/04, 1; Code noir, 1724, Article 30.

4. RSCL 1766/07/01/01, 1766/07/04/01, 1766/07/04/03 (two appearances, on July 4,

5, 1766), 1766/07/29/05, 1766/04[08]/02/02, 1766/08/02/04 (when his sentence was pronounced, though he did not speak in court); 1766/07/29/04, 1766/07/29/05.

5. RSCL 1766/07/31/06; 1766/06/30/01; 1766/07/04/02, 1766/07/04/01, 1766/07/04/03.

6. RSCL 1766/07/04/01, 1766/04[08]/02/02, 3; 1765/03/02/01 (François); Code Noir, 1724, Article 24. For further references to thefts committed by slaves from other slaves, which gives an idea of the frequency of such occurrences, see RSCL 1744/12/26/04, 1746/11/27/01, 1748/04/06/01, 1758/07/10/01, 1760/09/03/01, 1764/09/03/01, 1766/06/30/01, 1766/07/29/04. In addition to details of the sundry items and clothing taken, one of the richest descriptions of items stolen from slaves also specifies that they were taken from a locked chest and provides a layout of the slave's quarters; see RSCL 1765/08/02/04.

7. Interrogation of Marion, July 1757, Natchitoches Parish Conveyance Record Book 1: 1738-1765, 1757/7, no. 186, NP; RSCL 1748/02/10/01, 4, 7.

8. On slave dress in French colonial Louisiana, see White, "'Wearing Three or Four Handkerchiefs around His Collar,'" *Gender and History,* XV (2003), 528-549; White, "Geographies of Slave Consumption: French Colonial Louisiana and a World of Goods," *Winterthur Portfolio,* XLIV (2011), 229-248; White, "Slaves' and Poor Whites' Informal Economies in an Atlantic Context," in Cécile Vidal, ed., *Louisiana: Crossroads of the Atlantic World* (Philadelphia, 2014), 89-102; and White, "Dressing Enslaved Africans in Colonial Louisiana," in Beverly Lemire and Giorgio Riello, eds., *Dressing Global Bodies: The Politics of Fashion in World History, 1600-2000* (Abingdon, U.K., forthcoming). On slave dress in colonial America, see, for example, Linda Baumgarten, "'Clothes for the People': Slave Clothing in Early Virginia," *Journal of Early Southern Decorative Arts,* XIV (1988), 26-70; Steeve O. Buckridge, *The Language of Dress: Resistance and Accommodation in Jamaica, 1760-1890* (Kingston, Jamaica, 2004); Robert S. DuPlessis, *The Material Atlantic: Clothing, Commerce, and Colonization in the Atlantic World, 1650-1800* (Cambridge, 2016), esp. chap. 4; Chaela Pastore, "Consumer Choices and Colonial Identity in Saint-Domingue," *French Colonial History,* II (2002), 77-92; Shane White and Graham White, *Stylin': African American Expressive Culture from Its Beginnings to the Zoot Suit* (Ithaca, N.Y., 2008); Jonathan Prude, "'To Look upon the "Lower Sort"': Runaway Ads and the Appearance of Unfree Laborers in America, 1750-1800," *Journal of American History,* LXXVIII (1991), 124-159; and David Waldstreicher, "Reading the Runaways: Self-Fashioning, Print Culture, and Confidence in Slavery in the Eighteenth-Century Mid-Atlantic," *William and Mary Quarterly,* 3d Ser., LVI (1999), 243-272. See also Tamara J. Walker, *Exquisite Slaves: Race, Clothing, and Status in Colonial Lima* (Cambridge, 2017).

9. RSCL 1766/07/29/04. For restrictions on slaves bearing arms, see Code Noir, 1724, Article 12.

10. RSCL 1766/07/29/04, 2-3.

11. RSCL 1766/07/04/01, 2 (testimony dated July 25, 1766); 1766/07/29/04.

12. RSCL 1766/07/01/01; 1766/04[08]/02/02.

13. RSCL 1766/07/01/01. Though not necessarily conclusive, a search of runaway slave advertisements in the *Pennsylvania Gazette* pulled up no record of any enslaved runaway named Francis. On the malleability of identity, see, for example, James H. Sweet, "Mistaken Identities? Olaudah Equiano, Domingos Álvares, and the Methodological Chal-

lenges of Studying the African Diaspora," *American Historical Review,* CXIV (2009), 279–306.

14. RSCL 1766/08/02/02, 2.

15. On Vilemont, see Fontaine Martin, *A History of the Bouligny Family and Allied Families* (Lafayette, La., 1990), 81–96; and Marc de Villiers du Terrage, *The Last Years of French Louisiana,* trans. Hosea Phillips (Lafayette, La., 1982), 259–260.

16. RSCL 1766/07/01/01, 1. On English and Spanish smuggling into Louisiana, see Shannon Lee Dawdy, *Building the Devil's Empire: French Colonial New Orleans* (Chicago, 2008), esp. chap. 3; and Abraham P. Nasatir and James R. Mills, *Commerce and Contraband in New Orleans during the French and Indian War: A Documentary Study of the Texel and Three Brothers Affairs* (Cincinnati, Oh., 1968). For the revolutionary period, see Cathy Matson, "Crossing Empires: Philadelphia's Trade with New Orleans, Havana, and Cap François in [a] Generation of War," paper presented at the Forum on European Expansion and Global Interaction (FEEGI) Bi-Annual Conference, Tulane University, Feb. 21–22, 2014, New Orleans. On (free and enslaved) black sailors in the Atlantic world, see W. Jeffrey Bolster, "An Inner Diaspora: Black Sailors Making Selves," in Ronald Hoffman, Michel Sobel, and Fredrika J. Teute, eds., *Through a Glass Darkly: Reflections on Personal Identity in Early America* (Chapel Hill, N.C., 1997), 419–448; and Peter Linebaugh and Marcus Rediker, *The Many-Headed Hydra: Sailors, Slaves, Commoners, and the Hidden History of the Revolutionary Atlantic* (Boston, 2000), 143–173.

17. Journal of d'Abbadie, director general of New Orleans, June 21, 1763, to Dec. 20, 1764, ANOM C13A 43, fol. 249, reproduced in Carl A. Brasseaux, trans. and ed., *A Comparative View of French Colonial Louisiana, 1699 and 1762: The Journals of Pierre Le Moyne d'Iberville and Jean-Jacques-Blaise d'Abbadie* (Lafayette, La., 1979). See also Carl Brasseaux, "Jean Jacques Blaise d'Abbadie," 64 Parishes, ed. David Johnson, Louisiana Endowment for the Humanities (2010), article published July 11, 2011, https://64parishes .org/entry/jean-jacques-blaise-dabbadie (accessed Mar. 26, 2019). For d'Abbadie's postmortem auction sale inventory and the reference to Marie and her children, see RSCL 1765/02/26/02, 34.

18. RSCL 1766/07/01/01, 1. No sale contract survives. Convoys were regularly manned by slaves. See Carl J. Ekberg, "Black Slavery in Illinois, 1720–1765," *Western Illinois Regional Studies,* XII, no. 1 (Spring 1989), 5–19. See also RSCL 1738/04/09/01. For three slave leases contracted in August 1737 for voyages to the Illinois Country where each slave earned his master fifteen hundred pounds of Illinois flour for his work on the trip, see RSCL 1737/08/15/03 (lease of two slaves by Louis Tixerand to René Boucher de Monbrun); and 1737/08/16/02 (lease of slave by Henry de Louboey to François Rivard). Other similar contracts can be found in RSCL 1738/04/09/01, 1739/07/06/02. See also Gwendolyn Midlo Hall, *Africans in Colonial Louisiana: The Development of Afro-Creole Culture in the Eighteenth Century* (Baton Rouge, La., 1992), 174–175; and Daniel H. Usner, Jr., *Indians, Settlers, and Slaves in a Frontier Exchange Economy: The Lower Mississippi Valley before 1783* (Chapel Hill, N.C., 1992), 227–230. There are a number of extant contracts where free blacks engaged themselves for the trip between New Orleans and the Illinois Country, and slaveowners also leased out their slaves to other masters for the trip. See, for example, the contracts entered into by "Scipion Negre Libre" from New Orleans. In 1736, he contracted to travel up and down the river as a rower for two hundred livres

(RSCL 1736/08/21/01). Three years later, he engaged himself to another voyageur for the same wage in currency but with enhanced terms, including the right to trade (alcohol) on his own account, the right of portage for his clothing, and the right to hire himself out while in the Illinois Country. See RSCL 1739/03/10/03. The case of Jacques Duverger, a free black identified as a voyageur and master surgeon, is discussed in Margaret Kimball Brown, *The Voyageur in the Illinois Country: The Fur Trade's Professional Boatmen in Mid America* (St. Louis, Mo., 2002), 7. One of the wealthiest residents of the Illinois Country was appointed as administrator of Duverger's estate, a sign of Duverger's importance in the community. On Senegambians' navigation skills, see Ibrahima Seck, "The Relationships between St. Louis of Senegal, Its Hinterlands, and Colonial Louisiana," in Bradley G. Bond, ed., *French Colonial Louisiana and the Atlantic World* (Baton Rouge, La., 2005), 265–290. On the hierarchy of the canoe and convoy, see Carolyn Podruchny, *Making the Voyageur World: Travelers and Traders in the North American Fur Trade* (Lincoln, Neb., 2006), 65–71, 121–123. The convoy that Francisque was likely meant to be on was referenced in RSCL 1766/04/29/01: declaration by Nicolas Pertuis. Pertuis stated that Jacques Tarascon had assaulted him with a stick such that he was unable to go to Illinois as per his agreement with Maxent, whose boat was already loaded with merchandise and ready to depart.

19. RSCL 1766/07/01/01.

20. RSCL 1766/04[08]/02/02 (quotations, 2 and 3). On fears of poisoning, see, for example, John Garrigus, "'Le secret qui règne parmi les nègres': Revisiting the Testimony of Makandal and His 'Accomplices,' 1757–1758," paper presented at the workshop on "Les résistances à l'esclavage dans le monde atlantique français à l'ère des révolutions (1750–1850)," May 3–4, 2013, Montreal; John Savage, "Between Colonial Fact and French Law: Slave Poisoners and the Provostial Court in Restoration-Era Martinique," *French Historical Studies,* XXIX (2006), 565–594; and Savage, "'Black Magic' and White Terror: Slave Poisoning and Colonial Society in Early 19th Century Martinique," *Journal of Social History,* XL (2007), 635–662. French anxieties about slave poisoning stretched beyond the Atlantic; see, for example, Megan Vaughan, *Creating the Creole Island: Slavery in Eighteenth-Century Mauritius* (Durham, N.C., 2005), chap. 4.

21. Rebecca J. Scott and Jean M. Hébrard, *Freedom Papers: An Atlantic Odyssey in the Age of Emancipation* (Cambridge, Mass., 2012); Jon F. Sensbach, *Rebecca's Revival: Creating Black Christianity in the Atlantic World* (Cambridge, Mass., 2005); and James H. Sweet, *Domingos Álvares, African Healing, and the Intellectual History of the Atlantic World* (Chapel Hill, N.C., 2011). On the movement of slaves across the Atlantic and Indian Oceans, see also Sue Peabody, *Madeleine's Children: Family, Freedom, Secrets, and Lies in France's Indian Ocean Colonies, 1750–1850* (Oxford, 2017).

22. RSCL 1766/07/23/02; 1766/07/25/02. See also Carl A. Brasseaux, *France's Forgotten Legion: A CD-ROM Publication: Service Records of French Military and Administrative Personnel Stationed in the Mississippi Valley and Gulf Coast Region, 1699–1799* (Baton Rouge, La., 2000), Part 2: Officers, s.v. "Declouet de Piette, Alexandre François Joseph"; and Ancestors of John Allan DeClouet, http://www.declouet.net/ancestorjohn /a1.html (accessed Mar. 26, 2019).

23. On Livaudais, who was among the first (and would become the most important) pilot helping direct ocean vessels upriver and downriver from New Orleans, see

Kenneth J. Banks, *Chasing Empire across the Sea: Communications and the State in the French Atlantic, 1713–1763* (Montreal, 2003), 86.

24. RSCL 1773/05/06/01, 21; 1738/10/13/01, 13. See also "Hector," Afro-Louisiana History and Genealogy, 1718–1820, http://www.ibiblio.org/laslave/individ.php?sid=9399 (accessed Oct. 28, 2018). Jacques Esnoul de Livaudais married Marie Genevieve Babin de La Source (daughter of deceased Pierre de La Source and Françoise Jallot) on January 3, 1733, in New Orleans. See Earl C. Woods and Charles E. Nolan, eds., *Sacramental Records of the Roman Catholic Church of the Archdiocese of New Orleans*, I (New Orleans, La., 1987), 8. Her widowed mother, Françoise Jallot, married François Carrière on April 29, 1718. See Sidney L. Villere, "The French-Canadian Carriere's (sic) in the Louisiana Province and Some of Their Descendants," *New Orleans Genesis*, VIII [1969], 70–80, 72. It is probable that François Carriere had their slaves baptized at the Ursuline convent by the Jesuit chaplains; personal communication, Emily Clark, Oct. 24, 2018. My thanks to Clark for this lead on Hector.

25. RSCL 1773/05/06/01, 29.

26. Livauday's plantation was given as a reference point in a 1752 deed of sale for an adjoining plantation. See RSCL 1752/10/04/02. For references to the Company of the Indies's plantation, see Antoine-Simon Le Page du Pratz, *Histoire de la Louisiane . . .* , 3 vols. (Paris, 1758), III, 226–227. On slaves using plantation horses to attend slave gatherings, see RSCL 1753/04/25/01, 3.

27. Le Page du Pratz, *Histoire de la Louisiane*, I, 341–342. On slave housing in Louisiana, see Samuel Wilson, Jr., "The Plantation of the Company of the Indies," *Louisiana History*, XXXI (1990), 161–191; and Marcel Giraud, *A History of French Louisiana*, V, *The Company of the Indies, 1723–1731*, trans. Brian Pearce (Baton Rouge, La., 1991), 188–189. On Dumont de Montigny, see Gordon M. Sayre and Carla Zecher, eds., *The Memoir of Lieutenant Dumont, 1715–1747: A Sojourner in the French Atlantic; Jean-François-Benjamin Dumont de Montigny*, trans. Sayre (Chapel Hill, N.C., 2012), 225–226.

28. Code Noir, 1724, Articles 22 and 23. See also Thomas N. Ingersoll, "Slave Codes and Judicial Practice in New Orleans, 1718–1807," *Law and History Review*, XIII (1995), 37–38. For an explicit reference to a slave owning goods see, for example, NONA, vol. 5, 7965–8156: Succession of Charles François de Cremons, 1736–1737; RSCL 1723/07/13/01, 1724/07/27/01, 1736/09/09/03, 1744/03/21/03, 1765/08/02/04. See also Amy L. Young, "Risk Management Strategies among African-American Slaves at Locust Grove Plantation," *International Journal of Historical Archaeology*, I (1997), 5–37; Patricia M. Samford, *Subfloor Pits and the Archaeology of Slavery in Colonial Virginia* (Tuscaloosa, Ala., 2007); and Ann Smart Martin, "Complex Commodities: The Enslaved as Petty Entrepreneurs and Consumers," paper presented at the Omohundro Institute of Early American History and Culture Annual Conference, June 1997, Winston-Salem, N.C. For Raguet's report, see RSCL 1746/11/27/01.

29. RSCL 1766/07/29/04. On "final passages," see Gregory E. O'Malley, *Final Passages: The Intercolonial Slave Trade of British America, 1619–1807* (Chapel Hill, N.C., 2014).

30. On the Igbo, see Gwendolyn Midlo Hall, *Slavery and African Ethnicities in the Americas: Restoring the Links* (Chapel Hill, N.C., 2005), 126–127; Hall, *Africans in Colonial Louisiana*, 255 (suicide link); Carolyn A. Brown and Paul E. Lovejoy, eds., *Reper-*

cussions of the Atlantic Slave Trade: The Interior of the Bight of Biafra and the African Diaspora (Trenton, N.J., 2011); Toyin Falola, ed., *Igbo Art and Culture and Other Essays by Simon Ottenberg* (Trenton, N.J., 2006); Michael A. Gomez, *Exchanging Our Country Marks: The Transformation of African Identities in the Colonial and Antebellum South* (Chapel Hill, N.C., 1998), chap. 6; and Obiora F. Ike and Ndidi Nnoli Edozien, *Understanding Africa: Traditional Legal Reasoning Jurisprudence and Justice in Igboland* (Uwani, Enugu State, Nigeria, 2001). Hall argues that "Igbo" was not simply an ethnonym but that the enslaved who identified as Igbo did so with intent. Sarcastically rebutting the idea that "all Africans were so isolated and immobilized that they were unaware that there were other Africans who were different from themselves" and responding to assertions that "terms for African Ethnicities appearing in American documents arose not in Africa but rather in the Americas after slaves were first exposed to Africans unlike themselves," she argues forcefully that "a word is an imperfect representation of reality. Regardless of which word they did or did not use to identify themselves in the past, it did not prevent them from considering themselves an internally related group different from others." See Hall, *Slavery and African Ethnicities*, 131, 134–135 (quotations, 134). See also James Sidbury and Jorge Cañizares-Esguerra, "Mapping Ethnogenesis in the Early Modern Atlantic," *William and Mary Quarterly*, LXVIII (2011), 181–208.

31. Hall, *Africans in Colonial Louisiana*, 35.

32. Ibid., chap. 8.

33. Ibid., 135. On Igbo society, see Marcellinus Chukwudebclu Onyejekwe, *Rites of Initiation in Africa: The Igbo Experience: A Clue to Our African Understanding of Religious Consecration* (Rome, 2000); Paul E. Lovejoy, "Autobiography and Memory: Gustavus Vassa, alias Olaudah Equiano, the African," in Brown and Lovejoy, eds., *Repercussions of the Atlantic Slave Trade*, 180–181; Lovejoy, "Scarification and the Loss of History in the African Diaspora," in Andrew Apter and Lauren Derby, eds., *Activating the Past: History and Memory in the Black Atlantic World* (Newcastle upon Tyne, U.K., 2010), 99–138; and Gomez, *Exchanging Our Country Marks*, 123–124. Gomez points out that some types of Igbo facial scarification were not simply a mark of initiation but corresponded to social titles or "marks of grandeur" (ibid., 131).

34. Personal communication, Emily Clark, who is working on a book project on Noel Carriere, an important commander of Louisiana's free black militia. See also Clark, "Noel Carriere, the Commander of the Free Black Militia, Deserves a Monument in New Orleans," *Advocate* (July 8, 2018), https://www.theadvocate.com/baton_rouge/opinion/our_views/article_e3548cc4-6fb8-5837-8e5f-fe3128de4643.html (accessed Aug. 23, 2018); and Cécile Vidal, "The 1769 Oath of Fidelity and Allegiance to the Spanish Crown of the French 'Company of the Free Mulattoes and Negroes of This Colony of Louisiana': Dual Genealogy of a Social Event," paper presented at the 127th Annual Conference of the American Historical Association, Jan. 2–6, 2013, New Orleans. On storytelling traditions among the Komo secret male society of the Bambara, see Ibrahim Seck, *Bouki Fait Gombo: A History of the Slave Community of Habitation Haydel (Whitney Plantation) Louisiana, 1750–1860* (New Orleans, 2014), 137–138. On the existence of a secret society in Martinique, see Brett Rushforth, "Burning St. Pierre: Political Life and Political Economy in a Caribbean Slave Uprising," paper presented at the Rocky Mountain Seminar in Early American History, April 2017, Salt Lake City, Utah.

35. On the presence of West African judicial practices with reference to Martinique, see Rushforth, "Burning St. Pierre." On Suriname, see Natalie Zemon Davis, "Judges, Masters, Diviners: Slaves' Experience of Criminal Justice in Colonial Suriname," *Law and History Review*, XXIX (2011), 925–984. With specific reference to the Kongo in Saint Domingue, see John K. Thornton, "'I Am the Subject of the King of Congo': African Political Ideology and the Haitian Revolution," *Journal of World History*, IV (1993), 181–214, esp. 199–201.

36. RSCL 1766/07/04/02, 3.

37. On the significance of hair and hair styling (including the sociability of grooming), see White and White, *Stylin'*, 37–62. Derived from sailor's dress and introduced into Louisiana by the Canadian founders and early inhabitants of the new colony and either imported ready-made into the colony or sewn up locally, the capot featured among the articles of clothing traded or gifted to Indians and was frequently issued to soldiers as a component of their uniforms. See Francis Back, "Le capot canadien: Ses origines et son évolution aux XVIIe et XVIIIe siècles," *Canadian Folklore*, X (1988), 99–127; Jacqueline Beaudoin-Ross, "A la Canadienne: Some Aspects of 19th Century Habitant Dress," *Dress*, VI (1980), 71–82; and René Chartrand, "The Winter Costume of Soldiers in Canada," *Canadian Folklore*, X (1988), 155–180. It also became a staple of slave dress in the colony, so much so that in the early nineteenth century a visitor to Louisiana would comment that "all the inhabitants as well as their slaves . . . have capots for wintertime." See C. C. Robin, *Voyages dans l'interieur de la Louisiane, de la Floride occidentatle et dans les Iles de la Martinique et de Saint-Dominigue pendant les années 1802, 1803, 1804, 1805 et 1806,* II (Paris, 1807), 104. See also White, "Dressing Enslaved Africans in Colonial Louisiana," in Lemire and Riello, eds., *Dressing Global Bodies*. In a 1737 extant account of a gentleman cadet's expenditure, trade shirts were purchased for him at just over four livres each; his plain shirts cost six livres apiece. These modest values contrast markedly with the twenty-five to thirty livres paid for each fine ruffled shirt *(chemise garnie)* purchased for him to wear when in New Orleans. The account is analyzed in Sophie White, "'To Ensure That He Not Give Himself Over to the Indians': Cleanliness, Frenchification, and Whiteness," *Journal of Early American History*, II (2012), 111–149. See also White, *Wild Frenchmen and Frenchified Indians: Material Culture and Race in Colonial Louisiana* (Philadelphia, 2012), 216–217.

38. RSCL 1765/02/26/02. For d'Abbadie's post-mortem auction sale inventory, see RSCL 1765/02/26/02, 10–11.

39. RSCL 1766/07/25/02, 1; 1764/09/04/02, 10; 1764/07/31/01, 5. On trousers in the eighteenth century, see Beverly Lemire, "A Question of Trousers: Seafarers, Masculinity, and Empire in the Shaping of British Male Dress, c. 1600–1800," *Cultural and Social History*, XIII (2016), 1–23. On Louis dit Foÿ, see White, "Slaves' and Poor Whites' Informal Economies," in Vidal, ed., *Louisiana*, 89–102.

40. No sumptuary legislation existed in French colonial Louisiana, but a 1720 statute in the French West Indies restricted the wearing of white cloth to freedmen alone. See Gabriel Debien, *Les esclaves aux Antilles françaises, XVII–XVIIIe siècles* (Basse-Terre, Guadeloupe, 1974), 240; and Pastore, "Consumer Choices and Colonial Identity in Saint-Domingue," *French Colonial History*, II (2002), 77–92. On sartorial laws in the English

colonies and the effect of their adoption on elite items of clothing in particular, see Shane White and Graham White, "Slave Clothing and African-American Culture in the Eighteenth and Nineteenth Centuries," *Past and Present*, no. 148 (August 1995), 156–158, and 162. See also DuPlessis, *Material Atlantic*, esp. chap. 1.

41. RSCL 1766/07/29/04; White, "Wearing Three or Four Handkerchiefs," *Gender and History*, XV (2003), esp. 541–543.

42. For a rare surviving example of an uncut length of red patterned cotton printed with four chintz handkerchiefs, see "Handkerchiefs Manufactured in India for Export to Europe," reproduced in René d'Allemagne, *80 Toiles imprimées et indiennes de traite* (Paris, 1948). The Victoria and Albert Museum in London also has plainer uncut lengths of fabric intended for handkerchiefs: see, for example, a length of Bengali silk bandana (acc. no. IS 678-1883) and another length of eight uncut Madras checks. My thanks to Rosemary Crill, Senior Curator, Asian Department, Victoria and Albert Museum, London, for sharing this information with me. On the 1738 purchase at auction of uncut handkerchiefs, see Succession of Georges Amelot, Feb. 25, 1738, NONA, F4-02. On the hemming of handkerchiefs in Louisiana, see also White, "Geographies of Slave Consumption," *Winterthur Portfolio*, XLIV (2011), 239–242. On the involvement of enslaved individuals in the making and supplying of clothing goods, see White, "Slaves' and Poor Whites' Informal Economies," in Vidal, ed., *Louisiana*, 89–102. On textiles and the slave trade, see Gaston Martin, *Nantes au xviiie siècle: L'ère des négriers, 1714–1774* (Paris, 1931), 46–53; Jean Meyer, *L'armement nantais dans la deuxième moitié du xviiie siècle* (Paris, 1969); Joseph E. Inikori, "Slavery and Atlantic Commerce, 1650–1800," *American Economic Review*, LXXXII (1992), 151–157; Inikori "Slavery and the Revolution in Cotton Textile Production in England," *Social Science History*, XIII (1989), 343–379; Colleen E. Kriger, *Cloth in West African History* (Lanham, Md., 2006); Giorgio Riello, "The Globalization of Cotton Textiles: Indian Cottons, Europe, and the Atlantic World, 1600–1850," in Riello and Prasannan Parthasarathi, eds., *The Spinning World: A Global History of Cotton Textiles, 1200–1850* (Oxford, 2009), 230–247, 261–287, Beverly Lemire, "Revising the Historical Narrative: India, Europe, and the Cotton Trade, c. 1300–1800," 205–226; and White, "Geographies of Slave Consumption," *Winterthur Portfolio*, XLIV (2011), 240–247.

43. The best account of West African sources on the head and head wraps is provided by Helen Bradley Foster, *"New Raiments of Self": African American Clothing in the Antebellum South* (New York, 1997). See also White and White, *Stylin'*, esp, 37–62; and White, "Geographies of Slave Consumption," *Winterthur Portfolio*, XLIV (2011), 240–242. Examples from New Orleans of such features are documented in RSCL 1741/01/10/01, 1752/03/27/02; and Succession of Georges Amelot, Feb. 25, 1738, NONA, F4-02. On de Batz, see David I. Bushnell, Jr., *Drawings by A. DeBatz in Louisiana, 1732–1735, with Six Plates* (Washington, D.C., 1927). The originals are at the Peabody Museum of Archaeology and Ethnology, Harvard. On these various artists, see Mia L. Bagneris, *Agostino Brunias: Capturing the Carribean [sic], c. 1770–1800* (London, 2010); Bagneris, *Colouring the Caribbean: Race and the Art of Agostino Brunias* (Manchester, U.K., 2017); Séverine Laborie, "Joseph Savart (1735–1801), 'maître-peintre' à Basse-Terre," *Bulletin de la Société d'histoire de la Guadeloupe*, CLXIII (September–December 2012), 1–16; Laborie,

"La représentation d'une société coloniale complexe," L'histoire par l'image, http://www
.histoire-image.org/etudes/representation-societe-coloniale-complexe?language=de (accessed Feb. 13, 2018); Jacques Foucart, "Note sur le peintre Le Masurier: A propos d'un
récent achat du Musée d'Aquitaine," La tribune de l'art (2013), http://www.latribune
delart.com/note-sur-le-peintre-le-masurier-a-propos-d-un-recent-achat-du-musee-d
-aquitaine (accessed Feb. 13, 2018); Anne Lafont, "Fabric, Skin, Color: Picturing Antilles' Markets as an Inventory of Human Diversity," *Anuario Colombiano de historia social
y de la cultura,* XLIII, no. 2 (July–December 2016), 121–154 (quotation, 129); Susan P.
Shames, *The Old Plantation: The Artist Revealed* (Williamsburg, Va., 2010); Beth Fowkes
Tobin, *Picturing Imperial Power: Colonial Subjects in Eighteenth-Century British Painting* (Durham, N.C., 1999), 151–173; and Hugh Honour, *The Image of the Black in Western
Art,* IV, *From the American Revolution to World War I* (Cambridge, Mass., 1976), 32–33.

44. In an engraving made from another Brunias painting, again showing a group of
slaves or free blacks gathered together for a dance, the same male dancer sports a handkerchief on his head with another asymetrically draped across one shoulder. See Agostino Brunias, *Dancing Scene in the West Indies,* circa 1764–1796, Acc. no. T13869, Tate
Museum, London. For the variant, see Brunias, *The Handkerchief Dance,* circa 1770–1780,
CTB.1996.27, Carmen Thyssen-Bornemisza Collection, Malaga and Madrid, Spain.

45. RSCL 1746/09/03/05.

46. RSCL 1764/08/10/01, 1–2.

47. Code Noir, 1724, Articles 3, 14; "Règlement sur la police pour la province de Louisane," Feb. 28–Mar. 1, 1751, ANOM C13A 35, fol. 39.

48. A. Baillardel and A. Prioult, eds., *Le chevalier de Pradel: Vie d'un colon français
en Louisiane au XVIIIe siècle d'après sa correspondance et celle de sa famille* (Paris, 1928),
260. On St. Louis, see also Sylvia Frey, "New Orleans: Cultural Blender of the Atlantic
World," paper presented to the McGill French Atlantic History Group, Apr. 13, 2011,
Montreal.

49. On music and dancing in African American culture, see, for example, Philip D.
Morgan, *Slave Counterpoint: Black Culture in the Eighteenth-Century Chesapeake and
Lowcountry* (Chapel Hill, N.C., 1998), 580–594; Shane White, "'It Was a Proud Day':
African Americans, Festivals, and Parades in the North, 1741–1834," *Journal of American
History,* LXXXI (1994), 13–50; and Laurent Dubois, *The Banjo: America's African In-
strument* (Cambridge, Mass., 2016). For a rich reading of the ubiquity of gestures across
diasporan communities, see W. T. Lhamon, Jr., *Raising Cain: Blackface Performance from
Jim Crow to Hip Hop* (Cambridge, Mass., 1998).

50. RSCL 1764/09/04/02, 14–15; 1764/07/14/04, 1. This case is discussed in White,
"Slaves' and Poor Whites' Informal Economies," Vidal, ed., *Louisiana,* 89–102. On the
Mandinga, see Charlotte A. Quinn, *Mandingo Kingdoms of the Senegambia: Traditional-
ism, Islam, and European Expansion* (Evanston, Ill., 1972).

51. RSCL 1764/07/14/04, 7; 1764/07/14/04, 6–7; 1764/07/10/03, 2.

52. RSCL 1744/03/21/03, 1, 10; 1744/03/21/02. On gift giving in courtship, see Ann
Smart Martin, "Ribbons of Desire: Gendered Stories in the World of Goods," in John
Styles and Amanda Vickery, eds., *Gender, Taste, and Material Culture in Britain and
North America (1700–1830)* (New Haven, Conn., 2006), 179–200. On male suitors giving

busks, see Sarah Anne Bendall, "To Write a Distick upon It: Busks and the Language of Courtship and Sexual Desire in Sixteenth- and Seventeenth-Century England," *Gender and History*, XXVI (2014), 199–222.

53. RSCL 1744/03/12/01, 9; 1744/03/12/01, 8.

54. RSCL 1744/03/12/01, 10–12.

55. RSCL 1740/08/25/02.

56. RSCL 1766/07/04/01, 2.

57. RSCL 1764/04/12/01, 1–2.

58. Code Noir, 1724, Articles 20, 21, and 32; RSCL 1764/04/12/01, and 1764/04/14/02. Community support was clearly perceived as a form of community service. See also RSCL 1741/01/10/01, and 1741/01/11/01.

59. RSCL 1766/07/01/01, 4.

60. RSCL 1748/01/11/01; 1748/01/10/01, 1748/01/05/04, 2. As used in Louisiana, the identifier "Bambara" seems to have been shorthand for non-Muslim. See Peter Caron, "'Of a Nation Which the Others Do Not Understand': Bambara Slaves and African Ethnicity in Colonial Louisiana, 1718–60," *Slavery and Abolition*, XVIII, no. 1 (April 1997), 98–121.

61. On these parallel justice systems, see, for example, Davis, "Judges, Masters, Diviners," *Law and History Review*, XXIX (2011), 925–984. On Jean-Baptiste, see White, "Slaves' and Poor Whites' Informal Economies," in Vidal, ed., *Louisiana*, 89–94.

62. RSCL 1741/01/10/01. See also Hall, *Africans in Colonial Louisiana*, 207–212. On the topic of maroons being illicitly employed in the French West Indies, see Rushforth, "Burning St. Pierre."

63. RSCL 1766/04[08]/02/02, 3. On Hector, see the entry for "Hector," Afro-Louisiana History and Genealogy, 1718–1820, http://www.ibiblio.org/laslave/individ.php?sid=84172 (accessed Oct. 24, 2018). He was sold with sixty-eight other slaves on the plantation La Réunion in Plaquemines.

64. RSCL 1766/08/02/04. It was the exact sentence pronounced against another slave, Paul, condemned for four thefts and sentenced at the same time as Francisque.

65. *Affiches américaines*, Feb. 25, 1767, 64, Le marronnage dans le monde atlantique: Sources et trajectoires de vie, http://marronnage.info/fr/index.html (accessed May 25, 2019), *Affiches américaines*, May 5, 1770, 216. There are other advertisements in Saint Domingue for runaways known as Francisque, but these are the only two that mention a judicial branding on the cheek.

CHAPTER 5

1. RSCL 1767/06/10/02.

2. RSCL 1767/07/04/01, 2; 1767/07/04/01. Jean Baptiste's owner stated that his slave's pronouncement on being caught was told to him in a letter written by those who had captured the runaway in Mobile. On tar production, see N. M. Miller Surrey, *The Commerce of Louisiana during the French Regime, 1699–1763* (New York, 1916), chap. 20. Tar and pitch, a product of pine forests, was used in the export trade with France and especially the French West Indies; according to Marcel Giraud, pine trees were particularly abundant in the Mobile sector, and it was a Basque colonist named Belsaqui (or Belsagui) who

initiated tar and pitch production there. See Giraud, *A History of French Louisiana*, V, *The Company of the Indies, 1723–1731,* trans. Brian Pearce (Baton Rouge, La., 1993), 143–144, 344–347. See also Gordon M. Sayre and Carla Zecher, eds., *The Memoir of Lieutenant Dumont, 1715–1747: A Sojourner in the French Atlantic; Jean-François-Benjamin Dumont de Montigny,* trans. Sayre (Chapel Hill, N.C. 2012), 287. Dumont de Montigny referenced leasing out five of his slaves "to some men who were making bricks and tar over on the far side of Lac Saint-Louis" (ibid., 275).

3. RSCL 1767/07/04/01, 4. On the presence of Indians in the area, see Daniel H. Usner, *American Indians in Early New Orleans: From Calumet to Raquette* (Baton Rouge, La., 2018), esp. chaps. 1 and 2; and Elizabeth Ellis, "Petite Nation with Powerful Networks: The Tunicas in the Eighteenth Century," *Louisiana History,* LVIII (2017), 133–178.

4. RSCL 1767/06/10/02, 3; 1767/08/13/03, 2; 1767/06/10/01, 2–3. The term "bert" seems to be a local adaptation of the French term for a baby's cot. Possibly derived from sailor's terminology, in Louisiana it described a bed, perhaps, given that both Kenet and Jean-Baptiste spoke of being under their "bert," one with some kind of mosquito netting or other cover. For another example of the usage of the word with this meaning, see the estate papers of Claude Joseph Villars Dubreuil in Henry P. Dart, "The Career of Dubreuil in French Louisiana," *Louisiana Historical Quarterly,* XVIII (1935), 306. The information on Jean-Baptiste's age is contradictory: he is intermittently recorded as giving his age as twenty-five (RSCL 1767/06/10/01), thirty (RSCL 1767/08/13/01), and thirty-five (RSCL 1767/07/04/01). Kenet initially described herself as aged "thirty-five or thereabouts" (RSCL 1767/06/10/02) and later as forty-five (RSCL 1767/08/13/03). On the invisibility and silencing of enslaved women, see Jon Sensbach, "Black Pearls: Writing Black Atlantic Women's Biography," in Lisa A. Lindsay and John Wood Sweet, eds., *Biography and the Black Atlantic* (Philadelphia, 2014), 98–99. See also Marisa J. Fuentes, *Dispossessed Lives: Enslaved Women, Violence, and the Archive* (Philadelphia, 2016).

5. Code Noir 1724, Articles 8 and 63. Most legal scholars and historians attribute the prohibitions on slave marriage in English colonies (or, in the absence of prohibitions, the lack of any legal rights accorded to married couples) to views of slaves as chattel and therefore as lacking legal capacity to make contracts. See, for example, Nancy F. Cott, *Public Vows: A History of Marriage and the Nation* (Cambridge, Mass., 2000), 32–34; and Darlene C. Goring, "The History of Slave Marriage in the United States," *John Marshall Law Review,* XXXIX (2006), 299–347. But the case of the French colonies shows that slaves could be considered as lacking these rights while also being allowed to enter into sanctioned Catholic marriages. See also, on New England, where marriage was legal, Gloria McCahon Whiting, "Power, Patriarchy, and Provision: African Families Negotiate Gender and Slavery in New England," *Journal of American History,* CIII (2016), 583–605; and Wendy Warren, *New England Bound: Slavery and Colonization in Early America* (New York, 2016), 159–167. The expression "amanceués à la maniere Des negres" is used in RSCL 1747/01/02/02, discussed below.

6. Though it deals primarily with the nineteenth century, the most thorough and nuanced treatment of the question of slaves and marriage is Tera W. Hunter, *Bound in Wedlock: Slave and Free Black Marriage in the Nineteenth Century* (Cambridge, Mass., 2017).

7. RSCL 1767/07/04/01. The 1670 Code criminel permitted civil trials to be converted

to criminal trials provided that judges anticipated a crime that carried a sentence of corporal punishment. See François Serpillon, *Code criminel, ou commentaire sur l'ordonnance de 1670 . . .*, 4 vols. (Lyon, France, 1767), III, 937-951. On the interrogation on the sellette, see Éric Wenzel, "La sellette . . . sur la sellette, ou les vicissitudes d'un séculaire instrument de la justice criminelle au siècle des Lumières," *Gens de robe et gibier de potence en France du Moyen Âge à nos jours* (Marseille, France, 2007), 247-259.

8. RSCL 1767/06/10/01, 2.

9. RSCL 1752/07/28/01; Edna B. Freiberg, *Bayou St. John in Colonial Louisiana, 1699-1803* (New Orleans, 1980), 69-70, 356-357. The suit filed by Graveline's wife took two years to be settled (RSCL 1754/10/30/01), and it is not inconceivable that Graveline acquired further slaves after the separation. Graveline was the paternal uncle of Marie Catherine Baudreau, Widow Gervais, whose own commercial activities are discussed in Sophie White, "'A Baser Commerce': Retailing, Class, and Gender in French Colonial New Orleans," *William and Mary Quarterly*, 3d Ser., LIII (2006), 517-550. See also Jay Higginbotham, *Old Mobile: Fort Louis de la Louisiane, 1702-1711* (Tuscaloosa, Ala., 1977), 389-391, 394-395. The standard reference on the Coutume de Paris is [François] Olivier-Martin, *Histoire de la coutume de la prévôté et vicomté de Paris*, 2 vols. (Paris, 1922-1930). For the law's application in Louisiana, see Hans W. Baade, "Marriage Contracts in French and Spanish Louisiana: A Study in 'Notarial' Jurisprudence," *Tulane Law Review*, LIII (197[8]-1979), 3-92; and Jerah Johnson, "*La Coutume de Paris:* Louisiana's First Law," *Louisiana History*, XXX (1989), 145-155. On marital community property law in Louisiana, including women's property rights, see Vaughan Baker, Amos Simpson, and Mathé Allain, "*Le Mari Est Seigneur:* Marital Laws Governing Women in French Louisiana," in Edward F. Haas, ed., *Louisiana's Legal Heritage* (Pensacola, Fla., 1983), 7-17; and Susan C. Boyle, "Did She Generally Decide? Women in Ste. Genevieve, 1750-1805," *William and Mary Quarterly*, XLIV (1987), 775-789. See also France Parent and Geneviève Postolec, "Quand Thémis rencontre Clio: Les femmes et le droit en Nouvelle-France," *Les cahiers de droit*, XXXVI (1995), 293-318; Yves F. Zoltvany, "Esquisse de la Coutume de Paris," *Revue d'histoire de l'Amérique française*, XXV (1971), 365-384; and Allan Greer, *Peasant, Lord, and Merchant: Rural Society in Three Quebec Parishes, 1740-1840* (Toronto, 1985), 48-55.

10. RSCL 1767/06/10/01, 1. On Jean-Baptiste's age, see Note 4, above.

11. On Kenet's age, see Note 4, above. I have not identified the source or meaning of her name. On Desruisseaux, see Freiberg, *Bayou St. John*, 359, 361-362. On the Coutume de Paris and inheritance, see Olivier-Martin, *Histoire de la coutume de la prévôté et vicomté de Paris;* Baker, Simpson, and Allain, "*Le Mari Est Seigneur,*" in Haas, ed., *Louisiana's Legal Heritage*, 7-17; Boyle, "Did She Generally Decide?" *William and Mary Quarterly*, XLIV (1987), 775-789; and Johnson, "*La Coutume de Paris,*" *Louisiana History*, XXX (1989), 145-155.

12. RSCL 1767/01/28/01 [will of Desruisseaux]; 1767/06/15/01; 1767/07/11/01. Kenet provided a timeline when she stated that she left her master's one year earlier, when La Ronde established his tar works (RSCL 1767/06/10/02).

13. Code Noir, 1724, Article 9. On the requirement that proprietors of runaway slaves make a declaration within four days, see "Ruling of the Superior Council of Louisiana

ordering that owners of runaway slaves make a declaration within four days following their marronnage and ordering a census of all slaves and imposing a prime of 40 *sous* per slave," Apr. 6, 1763, ANOM C13A 43, fol. 304.

14. Daniel H. Usner, Jr., *Indians, Settlers, and Slaves in a Frontier Exchange Economy: The Lower Mississippi Valley before 1783* (Chapel Hill, N.C.), 233–234.

15. RSCL 1767/08/06/04.

16. RSCL 1767/08/13/03, 1; 1767/06/10/02, 1767/08/06/04, 1767/07/04/01. The records do not make clear the precise timeframe of the incident with La Ronde's women.

17. For approaches to household and family formation in Louisiana and the Atlantic world, see Cécile Vidal and Emily Clark, "Famille et esclavage à La Nouvelle-Orléans sous le Régime français (1699–1769)," *Annales de démographie historique,* no. 122 (2011), 99–126; Arlette Gautier, "Les familles esclaves aux Antilles françaises, 1635–1848," *Population,* LV (2000), 975–1001; James H. Sweet, "Defying Social Death: The Multiple Configurations of African Slave Family in the Atlantic World," *William and Mary Quarterly,* LXX (2013), 251–272; Julie Hardwick, Sarah M. S. Pearsall, and Karin Wulf, "Introduction: Centering Families in Atlantic Histories," *William and Mary Quarterly,* LXX (2013), 205–224; and Bianca Premo, Wulf, and Hardwick, in the cluster "Rethinking Gender, Family, and Sexuality in the Early Modern Atlantic World," *History Compass,* VIII (2010), 223–257.

18. RSCL 1730/11/25/01. For a reverse case of a free Senegalese woman married to a French man in Louisiana, see Jessica Johnson, "Wives, Soldiers, and Slaves: The Atlantic World of Marie Baude, la femme Pinet," in Clark, Vidal, and Ibrahima Thioub, eds., *Saint-Louis, Senegal, and New Orleans: Mirror Cities in the Atlantic World* (Baton Rouge, La., forthcoming).

19. RSCL 1764/07/04/01.

20. As a result of the laws in British North American colonies, there is understandably sparse scholarship on (legally sanctioned) slave marriages in the colonial period in Anglo-America. For an important exception, which deals with New England, see Whiting, "Power, Patriarchy, and Provision," *Journal of American History,* CIII (2016), 603–604.

21. RSCL 1767/08/13/01, 1; 1767/06/10/01, 2 (mentioned twice); 1767/06/10/02, 2. For other witnesses corroborating this information, see RSCL 1767/06/15/01, 2; 1767/06/27/01, 2; 1767/06/10/01, 1; 1767/06/10/02, 1.

22. RSCL 1767/08/13/03, 1–2; 1767/08/13/01; and 1767/08/13/03.

23. RSCL 1767/06/15/01, 1–2; 1767/06/27/01, 2.

24. RSCL 1767/07/04/01, 2.

25. Code Noir, 1724, Article 8.

26. RSCL 1741/01/16/02, 1. Aside from the ambiguity of the word *femme,* it is also notable that the word *épouse* ("spouse") is not used in connection with the enslaved in these archives. If I can determine the meaning from the context or the syntax, I will do so; if not, I will translate "femme" as "woman / wife" to maintain the ambiguity of the original rather than interpret it for the reader. For the law concerning children, see Code Noir, 1724, Article 9. Children also followed the condition of the mother when born to a marriage between a free black and an enslaved African; see ibid., Article 10.

27. RSCL 1765/02/16/01, no. 1859. On the ethnic identifier "Nago," see "The Nago,"

Haitian Marronnage: Voyages and Resistance, http://sites.duke.edu/marronnagevoyages/nations/nago/.

28. RSCL 1748/05/26/01, 2.

29. Code Noir, 1724, Article 8; Arlette Gautier, "Les esclaves femmes aux Antilles françaises, 1635-1848," *Historical Reflections/Réflexions historiques,* X (1983), 403-433; and Gautier, "Les familles esclaves aux Antilles françaises, 1635-1848," *Population,* XXV, no. 6 (2000), 975-1001. On men's expectations that they be given access to women, see also Trevor Burnard, *Hearing Slaves Speak* ([Guyana], 2010), http://caribbeanpress.org/caribbean-press-downloads/ (accessed May 7, 2019). On masters coercing enslaved women (and men) to procreate, see Wendy Anne Warren, "'The Cause of Her Grief': The Rape of a Slave in Early New England," *Journal of American History,* XCIII (2007), 1031-1049.

30. RSCL 1764/10/23/01, 1-2. For more on Marguerite, see Introduction, above. On Catherine, see RSCL 1767/07/12/02 (her interrogation is not extant, but her words were recorded in the official confrontation with Louis); 1767/08/08/04 (claim against Jourdan); 1767/08/29/01 (sentence); 1767/08/11/01 (sale). Her master filed a claim to have Jourdan reimburse him for the loss of six months' labor, incurred when she ran away to be with the man, and he demanded further compensation should she be convicted and branded, which he claimed would result in a diminution of her value. She was convicted and branded with the fleur-de-lis on the shoulder (and Jourdan was ordered to pay three hundred livres damages plus costs), but her owner still achieved a respectable price of three thousand livres for her when he sold her shortly after.

31. RSCL 1748/02/10/01, 1, 4, 7.

32. See Tera Hunter's discussion of the range of domestic arrangements and the varieties of intimacy that could be defined as marriage in Hunter, *Bound in Wedlock,* 7-8. For more on courtship practices among enslaved Africans, see Chapter 4, above, especially.

33. Code Noir, 1724, Articles 2, 7, 9. On priests' actions, see Vidal and Clark, "Familles et esclavage à La Nouvelle-Orléans," *Annales de démographie historique,* no. 122 (2011), 99-126, esp. 104.

34. For the analysis of marriage rates using both baptismal and marriage records, see Vidal and Clark, "Familles et esclavage à La Nouvelle-Orléans," *Annales de démographie historique,* no. 122 (2011), 104-105. For some possible exceptions to the finding about spouses belonging to the same master, see ibid., 120n.

35. Emily Clark, "Peculiar Professionals: The Financial Strategies of the New Orleans Ursulines," in Susanna Delfino and Michele Gillespie, eds., *Neither Lady nor Slave: Working Women of the Old South* (Chapel Hill, N.C., 2002), 198-220. On similar marriage strategies practiced by Lazarist priests toward their bondspeople in eighteenth-century La Réunion (Isle de Bourbon), see Nathan Marvin, "'Biens curiaux, biens nationaux': The French Revolution and the Sale of Church Slaves on Réunion Island," paper presented at the 46th Annual Conference of the Western Society for French History, Nov. 1-3, 2018, Portland, Maine.

36. Placing of seals on property of Jesuits in New Orleans, [1763], ANOM C13A 43, fol. 315, 328 (emphasis mine); RSCL 1763/10/22/01; Dart, "The Career of Dubreuil," *Louisiana Historical Quarterly,* XVIII (1935), 309.

37. Vidal and Clark, "Familles et esclavage à La Nouvelle-Orléans," *Annales de démographie historique,* no. 122 (2011), 104; [Antoine-Simon] Le Page du Pratz, *Histoire de la Louisiane . . . ,* 3 vols. (Paris, 1758), I, 350–351 (English translation taken from Le Page du Pratz, *The History of Louisiana . . .* [London, 1774], 386).

38. RSCL 1744/12/30/01; Code Noir 1724, Article 43.

39. Code Noir, 1724, Article 3.

40. RSCL 1747/01/02/02.

41. The current title of the painting was assigned between 1980 and 1999. When previously exhibited in 1980, it was entitled *Antillaise au plateau de fruits (Caribbean woman with platter of fruit).* On the painting, see *Regards sur les Antilles: Collection Marcel Chatillon* (Bordeaux, France, 1999), 192; and François Hubert et al., *Bordeaux au xviiie siècle: Le commerce atlantique et l'esclavage / Bordeaux in the 18th century: Trans-Atlantic trading and slavery,* trans. Lucy Edwards ([Bordeaux, France], 2010), 182. On the anonymity of black female models in European art, see Denise Murrell, *Posing Modernity: The Black Model from Manet and Matisse to Today* (New Haven, Conn., 2018)

42. RSCL 1764/06/22/01, 1.

43. On the preponderance of enslaved Africans from Senegambia, see Gwendolyn Midlo Hall, *Africans in Colonial Louisiana: The Development of Afro-Creole Culture in the Eighteenth Century* (Baton Rouge, La., 1992), esp. chap. 2. On Baraca, see RSCL 1748/02/10/01. On Mamourou and Fatima (or Fatteman), see, for example, Dart, "The Career of Dubreuil," *Louisiana Historical Quarterly,* XVIII (1935), 301, 302. On circumcision, see Jennifer L. Morgan, *Laboring Women: Reproduction and Gender in New World Slavery* (Philadelphia, 2004), 64–67. On Muslim slaves in colonial North America, see, for example, Sylviane A. Diouf, *Slavery's Exiles: The Story of the American Maroons* (New York, 2014); Diouf, *Servants of Allah: African Muslims Enslaved in the Americas* (New York, 1998); and Michael A. Gomez, "Muslims in Early America," *Journal of Southern History,* LX (1994), 671–710.

44. The best discussion of polygyny in colonial Louisiana is Vidal and Clark, "Familles et esclavage à La Nouvelle-Orléans," *Annales de démographie historique,* no. 122 (2011), 115–156. On Joseph Léveillé, Victoire, and Marie-Thérèse Carrière, see ibid., 115–116.

45. RSCL 1748/02/10/01, 4, and 1748/04/15/01, 4. In Louisiana, "Bambara" served as shorthand for non-Muslim. See Peter Caron, " 'Of a Nation Which the Others Do Not Understand': Bambara Slaves and African Ethnicity in Colonial Louisiana, 1718–60," *Slavery and Abolition,* XVIII, no. 1 (April 1997), 98–121.

46. RSCL 1767/06/10/01; 1767/06/10/02.

47. RSCL 1767/06/10/01.

48. Morgan, *Laboring Women.* On gendered definitions of skilled and specialized work, see Daina Ramey Berry, " 'In Pressing Need of Cash': Gender, Skill, and Family Persistence in the Domestic Slave Trade," *Journal of African American History,* XCII (2007), 22–36.

49. G[abriel] Debien, "Le marronage aux Antilles françaises au XVIIIe siècle," *Caribbean Studies,* VI, no. 3 (October 1966), 3–43; David Geggus, "Marronage, Voodoo, and the Saint Domingue Slave Revolt of 1791," *Proceedings of the Meeting of the French Colonial Historical Society,* XV (1992), 22–35; Sylviane A. Diouf, *Slavery's Exiles: The Story of the American Maroons* (New York, 2014); and Le marronnage dans le monde atlantique:

Sources et trajectoires de vie, http://marronnage.info/fr/index.html (accessed Apr. 28, 2019).

50. Interrogation of Laurence, Sept. 21, 1711, Collection Moreau de Saint-Méry, ANOM F3 26, fols. 400–405 (quotation, fol. 402v). The word "adjoupa / ajoupa" referred to a dwelling with a thatched roof. See Lise Winer, ed., *Dictionary of the English / Creole of Trinidad and Tobago: On Historical Principles* (Montreal, 2008), s.v. "ajoupa, adjoupa, ajupa, joupa, jupa." I thank Brett Rushforth for sharing a copy of the manuscript of this trial. Rushforth discusses this court case in "Burning St. Pierre: Political Life and Political Economy in a Caribbean Slave Uprising," paper presented at the Rocky Mountain Seminar in Early American History, April 2017, Salt Lake City, Utah. An edited transcription of the court case has been published in Dominique Rogers, ed., *Voix d'esclaves: Antilles, Guyane, et Louisane françaises, XVIIIe–XIXe siècles* (Paris, 2015), 15–59.

51. NAMC JB6 Boite B3 no. 2 cotté no. 46, 15 pièces, Nov. 15, 1752, pièce 3, against Cupidon; NAMC JB5 Boite B2 no. 5 cotté no. 45, 8 pieces, Aug. 5, 1747, against Barbe, Silvie, La Roze, et Pierrot. On the testimony of the enslaved in Mauritius, see Megan Vaughan, *Creating the Creole Island: Slavery in Eighteenth-Century Mauritius* (Durham, N.C., 2005), 140; and Sophie White, "Les esclaves et le droit en Louisiane sous le régime français, carrefour entre la Nouvelle-France, les Antilles, et l'océan indien," in Eric Wenzel and Éric de Mari, eds., *Adapter le droit et rendre la justice aux colonies: Thémis outre-mer (XVIe–XIXe siècle)* (Dijon, France, 2016).

52. Michael A. Gomez, *Exchanging Our Country Marks: The Transformation of African Identities in the Colonial and Antebellum South* (Chapel Hill, N.C., 1998), 126.

53. RSCL 1748/02/10/01. For domestic violence among white colonists, see RSCL 1743/08/30/01; and Sophie White, *Wild Frenchmen and Frenchified Indians: Material Culture and Race in Colonial Louisiana* (Philadelphia, 2012), 89–90. See also White, "A Certain Article of Furniture: Women and Marriage in the Illinois Country," paper presented at the Western Michigan University / Fort St. Joseph symposium, Aug. 4, 2010, Niles, Mich.

54. RSCL 1748/02/10/01; 1748/04/15/01, 1. On the Fulbe, see Boubacar Barry, *Senegambia and the Atlantic Slave Trade* (Cambridge, 1998); Martin A. Klein, *Slavery and Colonial Rule in French West Africa* (Cambridge, 1998); and Rebecca J. Scott and Jean M. Hébrard, *Freedom Papers: An Atlantic Odyssey in the Age of Emancipation* (Cambridge, Mass., 2012), 8–9. On the Fulbe in French colonies, see David Geggus, "Sex Ratio, Age and Ethnicity in the Atlantic Slave Trade: Data from French Shipping and Plantation Records," *Journal of African History*, XXX (1989), 23–44. On the Islamic suffix "Baraca," used for both men and women in Louisiana, see Hall, *Africans in Colonial Louisiana*, 166, 408. On practices surrounding food preparation, see Vidal and Clark, "Familles et esclavage à La Nouvelle-Orléans," *Annales de démographie historique*, no. 122 (2011), 113; and Arlette Gautier, *Les sœurs de solitude: Femmes et esclavage aux Antilles du XVIIe au XIXe siècle* (Rennes, France, 2010), II, 39, 81–82.

55. Jean-Baptiste Labat, *Nouvelle relation de l'Afrique occidentale contenant une description exacte du Senegal et des païs situés entre le Cap-Blanc et la riviere de Serrelionne . . . : L'histoire naturelle de ces païs, les differentes nations qui y sont répanduës, leurs religions, et leurs mœurs: Avec l'etat ancien et present des compagnies qui y font le commerce . . .*, II (Paris, 1728), 299–302. See also Hall, *Africans*, 39.

56. Interrogation of Estienne, July 1757, Natchitoches Parish Conveyance Record Book 1: 1738–1765, 1757/7, no. 186, NP; RSCL 1764/09/04/02, 14–15; 1741/01/16/02. The case involving Marion and Etienne is discussed in Sophie White, "Geographies of Slave Consumption: French Colonial Louisiana and a World of Goods," *Winterthur Portfolio,* XLIV (2011), 229–247; and White, "Marion, Eighteenth-Century Louisiana," in Erica L. Ball, Tatiana Seijas, and Terri L. Snyder, eds., *Women in the African Diaspora: A Collective Biography of Emancipation in the Americas* (Cambridge, forthcoming). The case involving Louis and Comba is discussed in White, "Slaves and Poor Whites' Informal Economies in an Atlantic Context," in Cécile Vidal, ed., *Louisiana: Crossroads of the Atlantic World* (Philadelphia, 2014), 89–102.

57. Vidal and Clark, "Familles et esclavage à La Nouvelle-Orléans," *Annales de démographie historique,* no. 122 (2011), 112. For an article that discusses Africans' and Indians' contributions to food preparation, see Shannon Lee Dawdy, "'A Wild Taste': Food and Colonialism in Eighteenth-Century Louisiana," *Ethnohistory,* LVII (2010), 389–414.

58. RSCL 1765/02/16/01; 1748/02/10/01, 6 (emphasis mine).

59. RSCL 1767/06/10/01, 2. On enslaved female laborers, see Morgan, *Laboring Women.*

60. The term "committed conjugal relationship" is taken from Tera Hunter, *Bound in Wedlock,* 6.

61. Copy of deliberations of Superior Council of Louisiana, Oct. 24, 1725, New Orleans, ANOM C13A 9, fol. 259, Nov. 21, 1725, fol. 267v. On Louis Congo, see Shannon Lee Dawdy, *Building the Devil's Empire: French Colonial New Orleans* (Chicago, 2008), 189–191; and Hall, *Africans in Colonial Louisiana,* 130–131. On judicial sentences including judicial torture and executions in Louisiana, see Chapter 1, above.

62. Report by La Chaise, Sept. 6, 1723, ANOM 7, fol 7.

63. RSCL 1727/11/28/01, 1727/11/28/02, 1729/10/21/02.

64. RSCL 1744/03/06/03; 1745/11/09/03. On the free black militia, see Emily Clark's forthcoming book on Noel Carrière, who would become the commander of Louisiana's free black militia, "Noel Carriere's Liberty: From Slave to Soldier in Colonial New Orleans." See also Clark, "Noel Carriere, the Commander of the Free Black Militia, Deserves a Monument in New Orleans," *Advocate* (July 8, 2015), https://www.theadvocate .com/baton_rouge/opinion/our_views/article_e3548cc4-6fb8-5837-8e5f-fe3128de4643 .html (accessed Aug. 23, 2018); and Cécile Vidal, "The 1769 Oath of Fidelity and Allegiance to the Spanish Crown of the French 'Company of the Free Mulattoes and Negroes of This Colony of Louisiana': Dual Genealogy of a Social Event," paper presented at the 127th Annual Conference of the American Historical Association, Jan. 3–6, 2013, New Orleans.

65. Code Noir 1724, Article 34; RSCL 1743/08/24/04.

66. RSCL 1767/08/13/04, 2–3. For another example of this sentence in Louisiana see RSCL 1765/09/21/05. The case is discussed in White, "Slaves and Poor Whites' Informal Economies in an Atlantic Context," in Vidal, *Louisiana.* A similar sentence was rendered in the Martinique court case. See Sentencing, Oct. 30, 1711, Collection Moreau de Saint-Méry, ANOM, F3 26, fol. 451.

67. RSCL 1767/08/13/04, 1–2. Banishment to the galleys (whether permanent or term)

was always preceded by branding, which marked the body in case of recidivism. See François Serpillon, *Code criminel ou commentaire sur l'ordonnance de 1670 . . .*, 4 vols. (Lyon, France, 1767), III, 1078. After 1752, being banished to the galleys actually meant being condemned to a forced labor camp *(le bagne)*. See Marie Houllemare, "Penal Circulations in the French Atlantic, 18th Century," paper presented at the "Emerging Histories of the Early Modern French Atlantic" conference held by the Omohundro Institute of Early American History and Culture, Oct. 16-18, 2015, Williamsburg, Va. My thanks to Alexandre Dubé for pointing me to the role of La Balise as a forced labor camp in Louisiana and for sharing his archival finds. See his unpublished manuscript, "The Baroque Necessity." See also "Mémoire sur l'état de la Louisiane en 1746," Archives des Affaires Étrangères, La Courneuve, Mémoires et documents, Amérique, 2, 205; and RSCL 1747/04/22/02.

EPILOGUE

1. RSCL 1753/08/14/01, 3-4

2. RSCL 1753/08/30/01, 6.

3. RSCL 1753/08/18/01 (quotation, 1); 1753/08/30/01, 4. On Africans' medical knowledge in Louisiana, see Chapter 2, above.

4. RSCL 1753/08/30/02, 5; 1753/08/30/01.

5. RSCL 1753/09/10/03; 1753/08/29/11; 1753/08/30/02.

6. For the summation of the complete trial record that the Superior Council assembled, see RSCL 1753/08/30/02. For the sentence, see 1753/10/05/01 and 1753/10/06/08. On the verdict of "more amply informed," which was pronounced when there was not enough proof to absolve or condemn the accused, see Title XXV, Article XIII, Clause 24, in François Serpillon, *Code criminel, ou commentaire sur l'ordonnance de 1670 . . .*, 4 vols. (Lyon, France, 1767), III, 1090-1091. See also Chapter 3, above.

7. RSCL 1753/08/14/01, 1-2; 1753/08/16/01; 1753/08/16/01 (Boccart's testimony); 1753/08/29/09 and 1753/08/29/09 (the horse).

8. RSCL 1753/09/10/03, 7.

9. RSCL 1753/08/14/01, 1-2; 1753/08/16/01; 1753/08/30/01, 4. Soldiers were among the most marginalized segments of the European population in Louisiana. See Yevan Terrien, "Forced European Migrants and Soldiers in French Colonial New Orleans / Les émigrants forcés européens et les soldats dans la colonie française de La Nouvelle-Orléans," in Erin Greenwald, ed., *New Orleans: The Founding Era / La Nouvelle-Orléans: Les années fondatrices,* trans. Henry Colomer (New Orleans, 2018), esp. 89-93. On the presumption that colonists sought out paid sexual services from enslaved women, see RSCL 1752/06/12/02 (quotation, 2), and Chapter 2, above.

10. RSCL 1753/08/30/02.

11. Code Noir, 1724, Article 3: "With respect to outrages and acts of violence committed by slaves against free persons, it is our will that they be severely punished, even with death, should the case require it." See also "Règlement sur la police pour la province de Louisiane," Feb. 28-Mar. 1, 1751, ANOM C13A 35, fol. 39, Article 23: "Any *negre* who shall be found in the streets and public ways, carrying a cane, rod, or stick, will be punished by the first white who will find him. And if the *negre* was bold enough to put up

a defense or try to run away, the white will be held responsible for denouncing him and having him punished according to the severity of the case."

12. Leslie M. Harris, "Imperfect Archives and the Historical Imagination," *Public Historian,* XXXVI, no. 1 (February 2014), 77–80 (quotation, 79); Sophie White, "Notes from the Field: Lured in by the Archives," in *Collections: A Journal for Museum and Archives Professionals,* XI (2015), 167–170.

INDEX

Darby, Sieur, 184–185, 212
Dauphine Island, 217, *218,* 220
Death penalty, 37, 45–46, 118, 130–131, 169
Debt, 132, 139
Degouté dit Fleury, Pierre, 37
Deloré, Sr., 76
Démocrite (enslaved), 132–140, 145–152, 160, 168–169, 225
Denatured persons, definition of, 120
De Noyan plantation, 195
Desruisseaux, Joseph, 172–173, 181–182, 188
Desvaux, Sr., 205
Digueny (also known as Marie) (enslaved), 126
Dizier, Françoise (Dame Braseau), 96, 99, 101–104, 115
Dorimanie (enslaved), 128
Douville, Madame, 163
Dreux, Françoise Claudine (Madame Dufossat), 1–2, 19
Drunkenness, 53–54
Dubet (enslaved), 162
Dubic, Barthelemy, 60
Dublanc, Sieur, 137, 165
Dubois, Mr., 166
Dubreuil, Joseph Villars, 2, 34, 40, 126
Dufossat, Guy, 1–2
Dufossat, Madame. *See* Dreux, Françoise Claudine (Madame Dufossat)
Du Longpré, Marie, 99
Dumont de Montigny, Jean-François-Benjamin, 148, *149, 180*
Dupont dit Le Kintrek, Joseph, 57
Durse, M., 170
Duval, Widow, 159
Duvergé, Bernard de, 197, 199
Duvernay, Louis, 188

Edict of the Superior Council of Louisiana (1727), 118–119
Emé (enslaved), 195
Emigration, forced French, 118, 119
Enslaved, the: vulnerability of, 4, 5; voices

of, 5–6; literacy of, 5–6, 159; subjugation of, 7, 30, 43, 90, 144; behavioral expectations for, 22; access of, to testimony, 28; prosecution of, 30–32; in civil suits, 31; criminal complaints by, 31; ill-treatment of, 32; perceived criminality of, 46; convent labor and regime, 61–62; housing of, *65, 66,* 67, 142–143, 148, *149;* 153; kin relations of, 68; professions of Catholic faith by, 77–78; and religion as means of resistance, 89–90; and property ownership, 94, 148–149; in Louisiana, 108, 110, *111;* sold as family units, 117, 125; and parenting, 121–127, 129–130, 194; informal economy of, 133, 169, 172–175; informal justice of, 134–136; testimony of, 137; gender imbalance of, in New Orleans, 209. *See also* Catholicism; Code noir (1685); Code noir (1723); Code noir (1724); Intimacy; Labor; Violence
—masters of: and financial compensation, 43, 91; Ursulines as, 60, 67, 78, 83, 90; and benefits from slave pregnancy, 124, 127, 181–182, 196; and promotion of reproduction among slaves, 127, 181–182, 190, 196; slave testimony against, 129
—relations of, with masters: control, power, and authority in, 8, 30, 184–187, 201, 203; deference in, 74–75; extrajudicial negotiations in, 76; submissiveness within, 76, 83; Ursulines and, 90–95; power dynamics in, 117; and food preparation and poisoning, 144; and attending assemblies, 158–159; and marriage, 177, 194–195, 201; and interference in slave relationships, 189–192. *See also* Mercy, begging for; Punishment
Erneville, Pierre Henri d', 32
Essom (enslaved), 190–191, 209
Estates, settling of, 181
Estienne (enslaved), 34, 208
Executioners, 38, 211–212. *See also* Louis Congo (free person of color)
Extrajudicial investigations and punish-

ments, 8, 32, 40, 43; as negotiations between slaves and masters, 38–43, 76. *See also* Code noir (1724): on prohibition of torture by masters

Fabou (enslaved), 164

Family formation, 68, 79, 99, 178, 195–196

Fanelon (enslaved), 195

Fathers. *See* Men, enslaved

Favrot, Sr., 27

Femme: wife vs. woman, xvii–xviii

Feticide, 127, 128. *See also* Abortion

Flatagué, Antoine (enslaved overseer), 191–192, 201, 207

Fleuriau, François (Attorney General), 27–28, 33

Food: theft of, from slaves, 133; gendered preparation of, 144, 161–162, 206–210; in courtship, 161–162; in West African culture, 206–210; and sociability, 209

Fort de Chartres, 108

Fox Indians. *See* Meskwaki Indians

Foÿ. *See* Louis dit Foÿ (enslaved)

Francis. *See* Francisque (enslaved)

Francisco. *See* Francisque (enslaved)

Francisque (enslaved), 132–145, 151–158, 160, 165–171, *170*, 225

François. *See* Francisque (enslaved)

François (enslaved baby and possible progeny of Francisque), 143

François (enslaved butcher), 195

François (enslaved child), 126, 143

François (enslaved husband of Boguio and son of Emé), 195

François (enslaved man attacked by soldier), 52–54, 57, 63, 68–69, 72, 73–74, 90, 95, 159

François (enslaved man at Ursuline convent), 53, 58, 63; and medical knowledge, 64

François (enslaved man punished for staying at dance), 77, 158–159

François (enslaved recidivist runaway), and theft from another slave, 137

François dit Baraca (enslaved), 76–77, 122, 138, 191–192, 201, 206–210

François Sarra noir de Guinée (enslaved), 121, 123, 130

François Tiocou. *See* Tiocou, François (free person of color)

François-Xavier (enslaved), 24, 25, 67, 216–225, 226

Freedom: degrees of, for runaways, 24, 178; legal, 34, 184–189, 210–213. *See also* Manumission

Fulbe (nation). *See* Poulard (nation)

Galbrun, Anne (widow Dubic), 60

Gamelle, Louis dit Jupiter (enslaved), 43, 74, 88, 162–164

Gammenon (enslaved), 138

Geneviève (enslaved), 197–199

Gift giving, 88, 155, 160–163, 165, 192; reciprocated with meals, 209

Girardy, Marie Françoise, 181

Graveline. *See* Baudreau dit Graveline, Jean Baptiste

Great Peace of Montreal, 112–113

Guenet. *See* Kenet (enslaved)

Guinée (nation), 121, 162

Gumbo, 161

Hachard, Marie Madeline. *See* St. Stanislas, Sister

Handkerchiefs: laundering of, 24, 57, 69–70, 72–73; theft of, 34, 40–42, 152; purchase of, 46, 156; uses of, 72, 155–156; as headcoverings, 72, 156; as gifts, 88, 163; wearing of, for sartorial uses, 133, 152–153, 155–157; and parallels with West African dress, 156; envy of, 157; in *Handkerchief Dance*, 157; in *Deux Antillaises*, 194. *See also* Head wraps

Hats: and respectability, 86, 88

Head wraps, 156–157, *157*, *176*, 194. *See also* Handkerchiefs

Hebert, Charlotte, 90

Hector (enslaved), 132, 135–136, 138–139, 145–151, 160, 225

Karacou *See* Charlot dit Kakaracou (enslaved child)

Kaskaskia (French village), 98, 106, 113; separation of, from Kaskaskia Indian village, 107–108, 109

Kaskaskia Illinois Indians, 45, 107, as legal wives and daughters of Frenchmen, 93, 98, 100, 113–114

Kenet (enslaved), 24, 172–184, 192–193, 196–197, 199, 201–204, 206, 210, 212, 214–215, 225

Kerlérec, Louis Billouart de, 92

Kongo, kingdom of, 2; and spread of Catholicism, 19, 81; and belief systems, 43, 81. *See also* Congo (nation)

Labarre, M., 167

Labat, Jean Baptiste, 208

Labor: domestic work, in convent, 60–61; field work, 67, 111, 127, 142, 160, 203–204, 110; compensation for, done on the side, 69–70, 72; field work, as punishment, 160; gendered division of, 111–112, 202–211; division of, mapped onto European conceptions of gender 111–112, 203–204; hierarchy of, among enslaved, 112; of enslaved on Illinois convoys, 143–144; norms of, within slavery, 178; control over, of women, 178, 203; negotiations over, in manumission contracts, 184, 210–214; division of, mapped onto West African conceptions of gender, 203–214

La Chaise, Jacques de, 37, 212

La Chenay, Madame, 70

La Croix, Marie Louise (Dame Beauvois), 91, 96, 98, 101

Ladies' Congregation of the Children of Mary, 79

Laferme, Pierre Ignace Bardet, 216, 223

Lafleur (enslaved), 122, 128

La Frénière, Nicholas Chauvin de, 37–38, 126

La Houssaye, Mr., 132

Lake Pontchartrain, 25, *147*, 175–176, 182–183, 210

Lange, Jean-Guillaume, 162, 189–190

La Néréide (slave ship), 19

La Nuit. *See* St. Louis dit La Nuit (enslaved)

Laoursot. *See* Joseph dit Laoursot (enslaved overseer)

La Petite Jeanneton (enslaved), 61, 130, 146

La Réunion. *See also* Isle de Bourbon; Mascarene Islands

La Rochelle (soldier), 46

Lasource, Dame, 100

Laundering, 48, 54, 57, 69–70

Laurence (enslaved), 124, 204–206

Laval, Sr., 77

Laville, M., 170

Lawyers. *See* Court procedures

Le Boullenger, Antoine Robert, 91

Le Breton, Mr., 132

Leideck, Conrad, 216, 220, 222–223

Le Kintrek dit Dupont, Joseph, 57

Le Masurier, 156

Le Page du Pratz, Antoine-Simon, 46, 64, 125, *147*, 196

Le Roy. *See* Charpentier dit Le Roy, Jacques

Léveillé, Joseph. *See* Joseph Léveillé (enslaved overseer)

Lisette (enslaved Indian child), 24, 96–99, 103, 104, 105, 108, 112–118, 120, 131

Lisle-Dieu, Abbé de, 92

Literacy, 5–6, 159. *See also* Enslaved, the: literacy of

Livaudais, Jacques Esnould de, 145 *147*, 168

Longuet, M., 170

Lorier, Mistress de, 46

Louis (enslaved), *33–34*, 39–40

Louis Congo (free person of color), 38, 210, 211–213

Louis dit Foÿ (enslaved), 43–45, 47, 154–155, 161–162, 168, 209

83, 122, 160; in deposition of Louison (enslaved), 48–50, 51–53, 74, 77. *See also* Extrajudicial investigations and punishments

Meskwaki Indians (Fox), 113, *176*, 190–191

Michaut (enslaved), 76

Militia, free black, 151, 213. *See also* African traditions, survival of

Millet, René, 62

Millon, Etienne Maurice, 173, 181

Mingo, John (free person of color), 184–186, 212–213

Mobile, 163, 173, 175, 179, 181–183, 186, 216, 217, *218*, 219, 220, *221*

Monique (enslaved), 130

Montegut, 183

Mulquet, Mathieu, 93

Murder, 32, 54, 89, 206–207, 209

Music, 136, 138, 155, *158*, 160; drum, 139, 152, 157, 158; violin, 160. *See also* Dancing

Muslim: 151, 197, 200–201, 208, 210; ceddo warlord states, 151; religious titles, 200, 208; and gender, 200, 208–209. *See also* Polygyny

Nago (nation), 41, 154, 190

Narratives, autobiographical. *See* Autobiography, testimony as; Slave narratives

Natchitoches, 8, 34, 64, 113, 138, 208, 209

New France, 7, 28, 34, 80, 107–108, 112; absence of code noir for, 28; Louisiana as province of, 28; Illinois Country as part of, until 1717, 112; Indian slavery in, 112–113

New Orleans: design of, 15, 18, *56*, 106–107; courtyards in, 18–19, 107

Nianga (enslaved), 167

Nicolas (enslaved), 62

Nicolet, Sr., 46

Nuns, 2. *See also* Convents; Ursulines

Odawa. *See* Ottawa Indians

Ottawa Indians, 97–98, 113, 115

Pain, Mr., 64

Pantalon, Joseph (free person of color), 78

Parens, Dame, 216, 222

Patissier, Jean. *See* Jean Patissier (enslaved)

Pauger, Adrien de, 15

Pecherit, Mistress Olivier, 46

Perico (enslaved), 35

Petit, Joseph, 97, 104, 114, 165

Petit de Coulange, Françoise, 142

Petites nations, 175

Philadelphia, 24, 134, 141, 169

Philippe, Agnès, 114

Pierot (enslaved), 27–28

Pierre (enslaved), 162

Pierrot (Charlot dit Karacou) (enslaved). *See* Charlot dit Kakaracou (enslaved child)

Pierrot (enslaved accomplice in theft), 138

Pierrot (enslaved man belonging to Joseph Roy de Villeré), 12

Pierrot (enslaved man from Ursuline Convent), 61

Plains Indians, 123

Plaisance (enslaved), 128

Plantations, 41, 42, 60, 62, 64, 126, 135, 146–148, *149*

Pluton (enslaved), 75

Pochenet, Pierre Antoine, 52, 54, 57–59, 62–63, 69–74, 75, 77, 80, 83, 86, 89–91, 93–95, 220

Police code (1751), 30, 72–73, 89, 159

Polygyny, 197, 200, 208

Poulard (nation), 208

Poupart, Madame, 173

Pradel, Jean-Charles de, 74, 159–160, 162, 189

Pregnancy: miscarriages / molar, 96–100, 114; 1727 edict concerning, 118–119; as benefit to slaveowners, 124, 127, 181–182, 190, 196. *See also* Infanticide; Reproduction

Prevost, Mr., 74–75

Prison, 15, *16–17*, 28, 35–36, 37, 107, 137, 220, 221

Prostitution, enslaved women and, 70, 89, 223; French women and, 118, *119*

Punishment: confinement as, 1, 15, 78; justifications for, 36; whipping as, 36–37, 40, 41, 45–46, 124; attempts by enslaved to mitigate, 39–40; as motive for running away, 40, 45, 76, 197; pardon from, 41; beating as, 46, 169, 214; of slaves by slaves, 134–135; relocation as, 137, 183; and curfew violations, 159; demotion to field laborer as, 160. *See also* Code noir (1724): on branding; Code Noir (1724): on whipping; Extrajudicial investigations and punishments; Sentences

Quenet / Quenel. *See* Kenet (enslaved)

Raguet, Jean-Baptiste, 31, 70, 88, 90, 149

Rape, 127–129. *See also* Sexual abuse; Violence

Real, Elizabeth (Widow Marin), 18–19

Recidivism. *See* Punishment: branding as

Relationships: loving, 175–178, 183–185, 192, 214; and cohabitation, 175–179. *See also* Marriage; Sex

Reproduction, 99, 118, 124, 127, 196; increase of slave population due to, 7, 189–190; of French, 124. *See also* Abortion; Code noir (1724): and status of enslaved children as determined by the mother; Edict of the Superior Council of Louisiana (1727); Feticide; Pregnancy

Rieux, Vincent, 173, 186, 188

Rivière, Sieur, 76

Ronde, de la, Mr., 172, 181, 183

Rose (enslaved), 124, 138

Rose, André, 214

Rose, John, 156

Rosine (enslaved), 185

Rousset, Jean, 137, 153

Roy de Villeré, Joseph, 12

Roze Rosalie (enslaved), 195

Runaways: and branding for recidivism, 45; negotiating return of, 76–77, *84;* and accusations of infanticide, 121; and children left behind, 122–123; dressing above station, 133, 151–158; policing of, through informal justice, 134–136, 140; court cases concerning, 134–143, 152–157, 178–183, 186–187, 190–191, 214; survival tactics of, 134, 144; testimony describing, 136–139; prosecution of, 140–145; backgrounds of, 145–151; depictions of, 156–157, *157, 176;* community support for, 165–171; named in court, 166; risks to, 167–168; capture of, 172–175, 181, 187, 190, 203; in relationships, 175–178, 183–185, 192, 197–198, 214; destinations of, 181–182

Running away: interrogations for, 1; sentences for, 1–2; motives for, 45, 88, 97, 164–165, 166, 187–190, 197, 224; prosecutions for, 137; types of, 203, 204, 224. *See also* Maroon communities

Saint Domingue, 141, 144–145, 150, 169, 171

Sans Quartier (enslaved), 61

Sans-Soucy (enslaved), 189–190, 192, 196, 200, 209

Saroux, Sieur, 137, 143–144

Sarra. *See* François Sarra noir de Guinée (enslaved)

Savart, Marie Joseph Hyacinthe, 156

Senegal (nation), 88

Senegambia, 7, 150–151, 200, 208; Islam in, 200; gendered practices in, 207–208

Sentences: for running away, 1–2; secret instructions for, 44–45; as consistent with the law, 45; reactions to, 46–47; commuted, 46, 94–95; as civil death, 94; differences of, for white and black persons, 215. *See also* Punishment

—afflictive (corporal), 36, 38, 43–46

—branding, 2, 41, 45, 72, 124, 137, 166, 169, 214–215, 169